Language teacher education

Language teacher education

Jon Roberts
Centre for Applied Language Studies, University of Reading

A member of the Hodder Headline Group
LONDON • NEW YORK • SYDNEY • AUCKLAND

In memory of:
John Haycraft

and Don McGovern
Ben Warren
David Woolger

First published in Great Britain in 1998 by
Arnold, a member of the Hodder Headline Group
338 Euston Road, London NW1 3BH
175 Fifth Avenue, New York, NY 10010

Distributed exclusively in the USA by
St Martin's Press, Inc.
175 Fifth Avenue, New York, NY 10010

British Library Cataloguing in Publication Data
A catalogue entry for this book is available from the British Library

Library of Congress Cataloguing-in-Publication Data
Roberts, Jon.
    Language teacher education   Jon Roberts.
        p.   cm.
    Includes bibliographical references and index.
    ISBN 0-340-64626-8 (hb).—ISBN 0-340-64625-X (pb)
    1. Language teachers—Training of.   I. Title.
    P53.85.R63   1998
    418'.0071'1—dc21   97-25919
                                                        CIP
ISBN 0 340 64625 X (pb)
ISBN 0 340 64626 8 (hb)

Composition by Phoenix Photosetting, Lordswood, Chatham, Kent
Printed and bound in Great Britain by JW Arrowsmith, Bristol

Table of contents

Acknowledgements   vii
List of abbreviations   ix

Introduction   1
From teacher to trainer   1
Sociality   3
Summary   4
Using the book   6
Point of view   6

Part 1: foundations of language teacher education   9

1. Theories of learning and implications for teacher education   11
  1.1 Models of the person and teacher education   13
  1.2 Reflection and teacher development   47
      Appendix 1.1   61

**2. Research on learning to teach: from pupil to established
teacher**   62
  2.1 Introduction   63
  2.2 Classroom culture: some examples   64
  2.3 The pupil   66
  2.4 The student–teacher   67
  2.5 The new language teacher   83
  2.6 Learning as an established teacher   88

3. Approaches to the teacher education curriculum   101
  3.1 Introduction   102
  3.2 Assumptions about teaching and teacher education   103
  3.3 Knowledge-centred and person-centred paradigms   109

Part 2: initial teacher education   125

4. Two aspects of ITE design   127
4.1 Introduction   127
4.2 Preconditions and design   128
4.3 Coherent design   134
    Appendices 4.1–4.3   138

5. Provider roles in ITE   152
5.1 Input and self-awareness   152
5.2 Supervision and feedback   154
5.3 The assessment of teaching   161
    Appendices 5.1–5.2   173

6. Case studies of ITE   180
6.1 Introduction   180
6.2 University of Reading/Schools Partnership: the 1995-96
    PGCE secondary course   181
6.3 The Cambridge/RSA Certificate in English Language
    Teaching to Adults   198
    Appendices 6.1–6.2   213

Part 3: inservice education and training   219

7. INSET: focus on design   221
7.1 Diversity   221
7.2 The importance of social context   225
7.3 The INSET cycle   230
    Appendices 7.1–7.6   241

8. Case studies of INSET   257
8.1 Introduction   257
8.2 Professional development for primary-school teachers of
    English in the Basque Country   258
8.3 Self-directed curriculum inquiry in a secondary school   275
8.4 Exploring a new curriculum: 'Teachers' Voices'   281
8.5 Professional development in the Baltic States: the
    Professional Development Programme (PDP)   288
8.6 Preventive approaches to disruption (PAD): a training
    resource pack   297
8.7 How teachers learn: a summary   308
    Personal note   310
    Appendices 8.1–8.5   310

Bibliography   325
Index   341

Acknowledgements

The author would like to thank the following.

For their generous help in providing information and feedback for the case studies:

Anne Burns, NCELTR, Macquarie University, Sydney
Karen Giblin, British Council, Latvia
Sue Hood, Linguistics Department, University of New South Wales
Peter James, formerly British Council D.T.E. Bilbao
Pnina Linder, University of Haifa-Oranim School of Education of the
  Kibbutz Movement
Ernesto Macaro, Faculty of Education and Community Studies, University
  of Reading
Martin Parsons, Faculty of Education and Community Studies, University
  of Reading
Monica Poulter, UCLES
Michèle le Roux, The British Institute in Paris
Chris Tribble, British Council, Baltic States
Michael Weller, Faculty of Education and Community Studies, University
  of Reading
Rosemary Wilson, UCLES

For their kind feedback on an early draft:

Peter Brandt, British Council, Athens
Elizabeth Colclough
Kevin Germaine, St Mary's University College
Michèle Le Roux

Elsevier Science Ltd, for Appendix 1.1 (Janice's practical theory) reprinted
from *The development of student teachers' practical theories of teaching* by B.
Kettle and N. Stellars (1992).

Sage Publications Inc., for Table 7.3, Figure 7.3 and Figure 7.4 from J. R.

Sanders, *Evaluating school programmes: an educator's guide* (Corwin Press, 1992).

Sydney University Press for Figure 5.1 (supervision cycle) from C. Turney, L. G. Cairns, K. J. Eltis, D. M. Thew, J. Towler and R. Wright, *Supervisor development programmes: role handbook* (Sydney University Press, 1982).

University College London, for activity planning checklist (Appendix 7.3), and Delphi technique (in Appendix 7.1) from T. Cline, A. Frederickson and A. Wright, *Effective in-service training: a learning resource pack* (1990).

List of abbreviations

AMEP	Adult Migrant English Program (Australia)
ARELS	Association of Recognised English Language Schools
BC	British Council
BSE	British Standard English
CBTE	competency-based teacher education
CELTA	Certificate in English Language Teaching to Adults (Cambridge)
CIEFL	Central Institute of English and Foreign Languages
CILTS	Cambridge Integrated Language Teaching Schemes
COTE	Certificate for Overseas Teachers of English (Cambridge)
CS	complementary studies
CST	complementary studies tutor
CTEFLA	Certificate in the Teaching of English as a Foreign Language to Adults (Cambridge)
DIEA	Department of Immigration and Ethnic Affairs (Australia)
DIMA	Department of Immigration and Multicultural Affairs (Australia)
DOTE	Diploma for Overseas Teachers of English (Cambridge)
DTEFLA	Diploma in the Teaching of English as a Foreign Language to Adults (Cambridge)
EFL	English as a foreign language
ELT	English language teaching
ELTE	English language teacher education
ESP	English for special purposes
FELCO	Federation of English Language Course Organisers
GRIDS	Guidelines for Review and Internal Development in Schools
HEI	higher education institution
IATEFL	International Association of Teachers of English as a Foreign Language
IH	International House
INSET	inservice teacher education
ITE	initial teacher education
L1	first language

L2	second language
LMS	local management of schools
LT	learner-teacher
LTE	language teacher education
MT	method tutor
NCELTR	National Centre for English Language Teaching and Research
NNS	non-native speaker
NS	native speaker
OD	organisational development
OHP	overhead projector
PAD	Preventive Approaches to Disruption
PCK	pedagogic content knowledge
PD	professional development
PDP	professional development programme
PGCE	Post Graduate Certificate in Education
PPP	Presentation, practice, production (the traditional lesson sequence in a structuralist approach; e.g. Alexander, 1978)
PT	professional tutor
QTS	qualified teacher status
RSA	Royal Society of Arts
SBTE	school-based teacher education
ST	supervising teacher
TCD	teacher/curriculum development
TD	teacher development
TE	teacher education
TEFL	teaching English as a foreign language
TL	target language
TP	teaching practice
TR	technical rationality
UCLES	University of Cambridge Local Examinations Syndicate

Introduction

A note on style

The writer has opted to use 'we' to express his views. This simply is a device to avoid overuse of the first person or the passive voice. We have also chosen to use 's/he', and at times 'she' rather than 'he', to reflect equal status between teachers of each gender.

From teacher to trainer

This book is intended for language teachers who will make, or have made, the step from teaching to training. As language teachers, we develop special knowledge of language systems. We learn to present information and convey new concepts. We know how to manage learning activities and can draw on our classroom experience to give demonstrations and discuss practical issues. We develop skills in monitoring learners and fine-tuning instruction. We deepen our understanding of cultural and individual differences.

By becoming trainers, providers of language teacher education (LTE), we become agents of change in others, in ways they would not necessarily change themselves. We affect their future lives. We need to relate to learners in unfamiliar ways, fill new roles. Of these (see Table I.1), the role of 'instructor' is perhaps the most familiar. Others are likely to be new, for example those of assessor, feedback, counsellor, and process leader.

In assessing teaching, there are few certainties on which to base our judgement. The nature of good teaching is essentially a matter of opinion rather than certainty. 'Good teaching is a direct function of the judge's value systems. And judges do not always agree' (Brown, 1975: 10). However, as providers we are required to make these judgements. Issues of uncertainty and assessment are discussed in section 5.3.

Then, offering feedback to learner-teachers requires us, at times, to contradict their perceptions of their practice and challenge their beliefs about themselves. Learner-teachers need feedback, but feedback which they can take on board and which does not damage their self-esteem and confidence (see section

Table I.1 Provider roles (after Turney *et al.*, 1982b: 5)

Role	Duties
Instructor	Presenting, questioning, problem-solving, guiding discussion
Manager	Planning, liaising, organising
Counsellor	Relating, responding, helping, handling difficulties
Observer	Establishing frames of reference, focusing, observing and recording interaction, analysis of observations
Feedback	Stimulating recall of the lesson/incidents, analysing performance, sharing interpretations, forward planning
Assessor	Communicating with learner-teachers, obtaining and assessing evidence, reaching summative assessments
Process leader	Guiding the processes by which a group operates

5.2). For this reason it is often a sensitive and difficult role, one for which well-developed people skills are needed.

This is particularly so when we work with established teachers. Their years of professional experience confirm a view of themselves which can be disrupted by proposed changes in practice. For anyone, change in working routines can produce a stage of confusion and emotional turbulence, a temporary period of disorganisation before we reorganise our practice and our view of self (Eraut, 1994). Providers need to be able to recognise this stage and offer appropriate emotional and practical support.

Another role required by work with experienced teachers is that of process leader: to guide the process by which a group works. It is crucially important for providers to support groups of teachers engaged in self-directed, collaborative work (see sections 7.1, 7.3.3, 8.3, 8.6). To do this with fellow teachers without imposing on matters of content is none too easy.

Of course, a further challenge for providers is that learner teachers, novice or experienced, are not a mere row of empty vessels to be filled with our knowledge of theory and good practice. How easy the job would be if they were! Their personal theories constantly filter and mediate the attempts of others to change them (section 1.1.3; Appendix 1.1; also Mitchell and Martin, 1997). This suggests that providers need to understand learner-teachers' perceptions before providing input or trying to lead them to change (Richards and Lockhart, 1994; Lamb, 1995; Salmon, 1995; Bailey *et al.*, 1996). It is for this reason that: 'The importance of taking teachers' attitudes as a starting point in any teacher training course is gradually being recognized by teacher educators' (Karavas-Doukas, 1996: 194).

Sociality

When we change role from teacher to provider we need to develop our knowledge, skills, and self-awareness. We need content knowledge of classroom skills, language systems, and learning theories. We need process skills: to attend respectfully to learner-teachers, to elicit their views, and to see what can most effectively be done in any given context. However, to realise our knowledge and skills as good practice, we also need self-awareness: the ability to monitor our actions and reassess the assumptions that underpin them. Without this, we may make false assumptions about learner-teachers, their culture and their work situations, and fail to understand how they perceive us and react to us.

In LTE we often work at cultural boundaries: to communicate we need to establish common ground with learner-teachers. To do this requires a critical awareness not only of their culture and work situation but also of our own. As an example, reflecting on her own values and their usefulness in other contexts, Jarvis (1991: 4) observed:

> In primary ELT, do we cope with the anomaly of offering change experiences based on British primary ideology – with its one class teacher, who believes in teaching the 'whole child', and who teaches a teacher-devised 'whole curriculum' by an experiential learning approach? Do we use this ideology with a Tanzanian teacher who has 35 minutes of English, based on one textbook, with 85 ten-plus year olds in a small chair-less, paper-less room next to the Headteacher's office?

Similarly, McLaughlin (1996), in his work in Papua New Guinea, argued that providers need to do some 'cultural homework' to understand how learner-teachers see them (Appendix 7.6). A provider lacking such insight into self risks being ineffective or even destructive: s/he may fail to establish common ground with teachers; s/he might even inadvertently deny their beliefs, experience and social reality.

There will always be a limit to the common ground of experience and perception that providers and learner-teachers share, whatever their backgrounds. Therefore, our goal as providers should be to establish with all learner-teachers 'shared interest, agreed perspectives and meanings held in common' (Salmon, 1995: 36). To attain this we need to attain *sociality*, 'a broad and sensitive attention to how another construes the world. It represents the willingness and capacity to step into another person's shoes; to begin to see the world as the person sees it, to adopt, for the moment, the terms and dimensions of meaning through which that person makes sense of things' (Salmon, 1995: 36).

To attain sociality, we need to be conscious of our own ways of seeing to understand those of others. Critical self-awareness has been widely claimed as a means for teacher development (section 1.2). It applies equally to provider development. As Calderhead (1990: 154) commented:

Making our assumptions about teaching and professional learning explicit both helps to remove ambiguities and inconsistencies within our thinking about teacher training, and enables questions about the appropriateness and effects of current practices to be raised.

Summary

Part 1 – foundations of language teacher education (LTE)

In Part 1 of this book we consider the questions which underpin a teacher education curriculum: how do teachers learn to teach, and how do models of teaching influence LTE design? We approach these questions in terms of general models of learning (Chapter 1), some evidence on teacher learning (Chapter 2) and more general issues of approach in LTE (Chapter 3).

Chapter 1 considers human learning in terms of four 'views of the person' and their implications for LTE:

- learning as determined by external influences, as in behaviourist learning theory: *person as input-output system*;
- learning as the realisation of one's unique self, as in humanistic theory: *person with self-agency*;
- learning as a cognitive process, where each of us constructs inner representations of the world which then determine our perceptions and subsequent learning: *person as constructivist;*
- a social perspective on learning, where the individual adapts to and enacts socially constructed roles, and learns by means of social exchange: *person as social being.*

Each perspective throws light on a particular dimension of the complex process of learning to teach, respectively the behavioural, the personal, the cognitive and the social. We argue that each dimension needs to be integrated for LTE to be effective, and that a broadly *social constructivist* view offers the best overall framework with which to think about teacher learning (section 1.1.5). We then relate notions of reflective teacher education to these views of human learning and suggest different types of reflection distinguished by approach and purpose (section 1.2). The purpose of Chapter 1 is to argue for the approach to LTE which is upheld throughout this book.

In Chapter 2 we outline some research findings on learning to teach, following the life history of a teacher: from pupil at school; to student-teacher on an initial teacher education (ITE) programme; to new teacher; to established teacher with a secure personal expertise in language teaching. This division into four stages does not imply that each is independent of the others, as if teacher development were like walking though the compartments of a train. On the contrary, the personal knowledge of teaching we develop at each stage grows out of all our prior experiences, and serves as the base for subsequent growth in our thinking and behaviour. We therefore prefer to view teacher development as essentially cumulative, evolutionary and individually variable (sections 1.1.3, 2.4.6, 3.3.4 and 7.1).

While research gives us valuable guidelines for LTE design, we must bear in mind that it is never value-free. It takes place in a political and ethical context which determines the questions which are asked and those which are not. We therefore invite readers to interpret research in terms of its context. The overall purpose of Chapter 2 is to outline some evidence on learning to teach, for readers to select from as they think relevant and useful.

In Chapter 3 we present some general perspectives on LTE design, and issues of approach. We relate models of teaching to LTE objectives, and suggest features of language teaching that should inform an LTE design. Then in section 3.3 we consider the two intellectual traditions that underlie differing views of teaching and teacher expertise, traditions which respectively focus on *external* and *internal* dimensions of knowledge. We end with some 'health warnings' on the use of paradigms (section 3.3.5). The purpose of Chapter 3 is to argue for a critical approach to models and paradigms in LTE.

Part 2 – initial teacher education (ITE)

In Part 2 we consider aspects of ITE design and implementation. In Chapter 4 we comment on two fundamental issues: preconditions in design, and the need for coherence in programme structure and learning activities. In Chapter 5 we discuss three challenging provider roles: input, supervision and feedback, and assessment.

In Chapter 6 we present two ITE case studies. The first is a school-based programme for state system teachers which attempts to resolve the theory-practice divide common to many tertiary-level courses. The other concerns the UCLES CELTA course, an initial training which is offered to state and private sector ELT teachers in a wide variety of contexts. We hope the descriptions do justice to the real-world complexities of providers' work, and also help to illustrate the more abstract content of other chapters.

Part 3 – inservice education and training (INSET)

In Chapter 7 our purpose is to offer a general framework for INSET design. We consider the rich variety of ways teachers learn, the importance of context and social relationships, and argue for a view of INSET as a process, not as a collection of isolated events. We outline policy and resource issues and emphasise the diversity of teachers' needs. We then suggest an INSET planning framework.

In Chapter 8 we present four case studies of INSET for ELT. These are: an award-bearing course for primary-school teachers in the Basque country;

self-directed action research in an Israeli secondary school; larger-scale, centrally co-ordinated action research in Australia; and the development of support structures for Latvian secondary-school teachers. We then analyse a set of training materials which illustrates a coherent approach to LTE design: the integration of skill training, theory, direct experience, social interaction and private reflection (see also section 1.1.5, Box 4.3 and Table 8.4). As in Chapter 6, our purpose is to illustrate the abstract principles presented in other chapters, in particular teachers' need for dialogue and support when taking responsibility for their own learning.

Using the book

The chapters have different purposes and can be read in different ways:

- to argue a point of view on LTE: Chapter 1, section 1.1;
- to raise providers' awareness of some general issues in approaches to LTE: Chapter 1, section 2, and Chapter 3;
- to offer a convenient summary of research into learning to teach, to be read for reference rather than in sequence: Chapter 2;
- to suggest frameworks for LTE design: Chapters 4 (ITE) and 7 (INSET);
- to explore particularly challenging ITE provider roles (input, feedback and assessment) and suggest principles with which to approach them: Chapter 5;
- to provide case studies which illustrate abstract principles and show the interdependence of design and context: Chapters 6 (ITE) and 8 (INSET);
- to provide appendices which illustrate general principles and could be of practical help to providers (Chapters 4, 5 and 7); and which flesh out the case studies (Chapters 6 and 8).

You can therefore take different routes through the book. Section 1.1 argues our general position and should be read in close conjunction with the case studies. It may suit you to read Chapters 1, 6 and 8 first, and then read selectively from others according to your interests. However, each reader will have personal ways of approaching a text like this, so, to help independent and selective reading, along with the main table of contents we provide contents lists at the beginning of Chapters 1 to 3, and a detailed index.

Point of view

Learning to teach involves multidimensional personal change, interdependent developments in thinking, perception, classroom behaviour and ways of relating to others. We argue that, while this change is located within each of us, it cannot be understood in terms of the individual abstracted from his or her social context.

Teaching is a very public job: it affects the life chances of children and working adults; it is powerfully affected by the norms and expectations of society at large; it is a legitimate concern of a whole community of learners, parents, employers, administrators, religious leaders and others. We cannot exclude the social dimension from teacher education, because teaching is socially defined. Learning to teach involves adaptation to a socially constructed role.

Furthermore, our personal development cannot be isolated from our social experience. While each learner-teacher constructs his or her own understandings in personal terms, this takes place in a social context, where our development is inseparable from our personal and working relationships, such that 'social exchanges are continuous and essential bases for advances in individuals' ways of thinking and acting' (Hennessy in Bell and Gilbert, 1996: 13). Furthermore, in developing our own identity as teachers we inevitably refer to and select from models of teaching which exist as traditions and which are available to us by our social experience (e.g. section 2.3.1).

Therefore, throughout this book we adopt a broadly *social constructivist* approach to teacher learning, which recognises the personal and social dimensions of learning to teach. It is a view explored in sections 1.1, 1.1.3 and 1.1.4, and summarised in sections 1.1.5 and 8.7. It is also implicit in our discussions of design (Chapters 4, 5 and 7) and in the case studies.

By adopting a social constructivist view of teacher learning, we recognise that all personal knowledge is to some extent idiosyncratic and 'skewed': we all have different experiences, different relationships and differing access to public knowledge which we then interpret in personal ways. This applies equally to the knowledge of the author and so he makes no claims that this book is comprehensive or 'state of the art'. It is based on personal selection and interpretation, a personal point of view. However, it is a view of LTE which tries to be as inclusive as possible: by considering the whole lifespan of the learning teacher; by considering teachers for whom English was their mother tongue and those for whom it was not; and considering state and private system language teachers in the UK and elsewhere. It is offered to readers in the hope that it will help them develop their own approach to learner-teachers, to their practice, and to LTE design.

Part 1: foundations of language teacher education

1

Theories of learning and implications for teacher education

1.1 Models of the person and teacher education
1.1.1 Person as input-output system: model-based learning
Behaviourism
Model-based learning and teacher education
Criticisms of model-based teacher education
1.1.2 Humanistic psychology: person with self-agency
Nondirective intervention
Humanistic theory and language teacher education
Critique
1.1.3 Person as constructivist
Constructivism and ELT
Constructivism and teacher education
General criticisms
Kelly and Kolb: constructivist theories of learning
1.1.4 Person as social being
Occupational culture and professionalism
Teacher development and the school
Lewin and action science
1.1.5 Conclusion: a social constructivist approach
Implications for LTE

1.2 Reflection and teacher development
1.2.1 Dewey and reflective thinking
Reflection
Progressive education and personal experience
1.2.2 Schön's view of expertise: the reflective practitioner
Implications for LTE
Criticisms
1.2.3 Reflection in teacher education
Types of reflection
Issues in reflective activities

This chapter is in two sections. In section 1 we outline four perspectives on learning and relate them to LTE (Table 1.1 and Box 3.2).[1] First we consider the view of the person as an externally driven *input–output system*, the basis for behaviourist learning theory and 'model-based' approaches to LTE. Then we consider the view of the *self-actualising person* central to humanistic theory (Rogers, 1961; 1982). After this, we outline theories based on the view of *person as constructivist*, of learning as the development of each person's mental representations of the world. We outline mainstream constructivism and the theories of Kelly and Kolb. Then we consider aspects of the *person as social being*: occupational culture, teacher development in the context of school, Lewin and action science. Then in section 1.1.5 we try to bring these strands together: we suggest that behavioural and humanistic perspectives throw useful but only partial light on teacher learning, and that a synthesis of constructivist and social perspectives, a broadly *social constructivist* view, provides the most helpful and appropriate general framework for teacher education design.

In section 1.2 we discuss some aspects of reflection, commenting on the work of Dewey and Schön (sections 1.2.1 and 1.2.2), and suggesting a typology of activities (section 1.2.3).

Table 1.1   Views of the person and approaches to language teacher education

View of person	Behaviour and development determined by:	Parent theory	Consistent with LTE as:
'input–output' system	external conditions	empirical science, behaviourism	model-based, e.g. micro-teaching
with self agency	self-actualisation	humanistic psychology	person-focused, e.g. counselling models of supervision
constructivist	personal constructions of the outside world	cognitive psychology	reflective, e.g. self-awareness activities
		experiential learning	experiential e.g. loop input methods
social being	group identity	social psychology	social constructivist e.g. related activity cycles

[1] An authoritative review of perspectives on human learning related to language teaching appears in Williams and Burden (1997: Chapters 1 and 2).

1.1 Models of the person and teacher education

The four *models of the person*[2] which underpin different descriptions of human learning have consequences for the objectives, content and process of teacher education because they suggest different models of the *teacher:* what a teacher is, what s/he knows and how s/he learns. After Roth (1990) we summarise these models as follows.

- *Person as input-output system*: all behaviour can be explained in terms of general laws which explain connections between input (via the senses) and output (behaviour); human behaviour can be predicted under certain well defined external conditions.
- *Person with self-agency*: the person is an autonomous and self-determining agent; individual experience motivates action.
- *Person as constructivist*: the person functions as an intelligent system, developing increasingly differentiated representations of the world which frame our perceptions and actions; learning involves ongoing reconstruction of these representations.
- *Person as social being*: our behaviour is determined by social rules in our relationships with others and in the norms we follow to achieve acceptance by others. However, our actions are not wholly socially determined: we can choose the groups we wish to associate with, and can impose a personal style on our roles.

1.1.1   Person as input-output system: model-based learning

Behaviourism

Behaviourist psychology views the description of mental events as merely speculative, and observable behaviour as the only reliable basis for theory building (Roth, 1990). It proposes that precise laws can associate observed behaviours with external stimuli. Learning (lasting behaviour change) takes place when external stimuli beneficial to the person reinforce behaviours. Thus a behaviour is learnt by operant conditioning (positive and negative external reinforcements in the form of rewards and denial of rewards). Complex behaviours are learnt by shaping: an individual's behaviour is brought progressively closer to a target behaviour by operant conditioning. From this perspective, all social behaviour is seen as externally 'shaped and maintained by its consequences' (Roth, 1990: 272), when the consequences are positive for the person.

Skinner argued that operant conditioning could be used to cure socially unacceptable behaviour such as crime and deviance, not by changing minds but by shaping behaviour (Skinner, 1971). His view was widely criticised on ethical

---

[2] We omit the biological view of human learning and behaviour as irrelevant to teacher education, as it focuses on the relationships between behaviour, physiological structures and heredity.

grounds as a denial of individual rights and as a gross oversimplification of change in personal behaviour. Currently, other than in cases of extreme disability, education in which a person is trained to produce a finite set of acceptable behaviours on cue is widely seen both as irrelevant to human functioning and as ethically questionable.

Behaviourist theory offers an approach to curriculum design in which a model of a target behaviour is broken into discrete sub-behaviours. Its lasting contribution to education appears to lie in this approach to the learning of complex tasks. It provides a means to break down global learning targets into clearly defined and graded subcompetencies, which can then be learnt step by step. While open to criticisms of reductionism, this approach has supported much effective curriculum design. However, its approach to the learning process, based on the imitation of models, has been superseded by constructivist models (see section 1.1.3) and so processes of imitation and shaping would not necessarily be used when following a curriculum of graded skills or tasks.

In language teaching, audio-lingualism gives us a clear demonstration of behaviourist principles. Learning is seen as determined by external stimuli. Correct 'speech habits' are established by means of pattern drilling, repetition, and reinforcement by immediate correction of error and praise of success.

Criticisms of behaviourism can be summarised as follows:

- behaviourist theory excludes mental states from the explanation of behaviour; however, observation of complex animal and human action shows it to be determined by mental states (such as intention) and to be proactive rather than simply reactive;
- complex social behaviour such as teaching, and complex learning such as language acquisition, cannot be explained without reference to thinking and self-direction;
- shaped behaviour rarely transfers to conditions different from those of the original training;
- the concept of learning as shaping to a social norm violates the human right to self-determination and self-expression.

Model-based learning and teacher education

A teacher-education course based on behaviourist principles will define content as an inventory of discrete behavioural skills presented in the form of visual or written models. In process, it will try to shape learner-teachers to conform to a model. We consider two aspects of teacher education directly based on this view: classical micro-teaching and competency-based teacher education (CBTE). We also consider the traditional apprenticeship approach to teacher education, which pre-dates behaviourism but which also bases professional education on imitation of models.

Classical micro-teaching

Micro-teaching was introduced at Stanford University in 1963 as a preparation for school-based teaching practice. In a micro-teaching programme a single model of a target behaviour is presented and student-teachers' behaviour is then shaped to match it by means of observation, imitation and reinforcement by feedback. To enable step-by-step learning, teaching skills are defined in lists of precise behavioural *competencies* to specify learning objectives and serve as assessment criteria.

Competencies are practised in scaled-down 'micro' settings (a small number of learners, a short period, a limited teaching objective, a focused skill) and are assumed then to transfer to the more complex conditions of the classroom (Brown, 1975; Turney, 1977; Perrott, 1977; Wallace, 1979; Carver and Wallace, 1981; Wallace, 1991). A helpful resume of micro-teaching issues can be found in Dunkin (1987: section 6) and a very detailed treatment in McIntyre *et al.* (1977). For English language teaching (ELT) Wallace's account of micro-teaching has yet to be bettered (Wallace, 1991: Chapter 6).

The test of micro-teaching is that skills transfer to the active repertoire of teachers in classrooms. Experience of transfer problems, and a general shift in psychology toward a cognitive perspective (section 1.1.3), led to its modification to incorporate the contextual and cognitive dimensions necessary for transfer to real conditions (see section 2.4.4). Micro-teaching in this modified form is a widely used and undoubtedly valuable pre-service training strategy, which can be modified to incorporate reflective processes (Mace, 1996), particularly when linked to a structured programme of observation (Sharkova, 1996).

Competency-based teacher education (CBTE)

The notion of teacher competencies originated in the definition of behavioural skills but has since been broadened to include aspects of knowledge and more complex pedagogic actions (see, for example, Appendix 6.1).

A dominant trend in teacher education in the USA through the 1970s, CBTE was an essentially objectives-driven approach to LTE, characterised by its 'reliance on objectives specified in advance and known to the learner' (Houston, 1987: 89). This was seen to provide clear expectations for student teachers; to link theoretical principles to practice; and to allow a degree of individualisation (Turney, 1977; Houston, 1987; Furlong and Maynard, 1995: 26–36).

A weaknesss of the movement is that 'almost no basic definitive research was conducted to prove or disprove its effectiveness' Houston: 187: 89. However, it has been widely adopted in the USA and more recently in UK state systems, in part because it meets bureaucratic and political demands for objective, testable standards of training and institutional accountability (section 6.2). As Houston (1987: 91) observes:

> . . . as with many issues, the ultimate positions of individuals and institutions were taken on political rather than educational grounds . . .

There is a close similarity between CBTE and practically orientated LTE in which objectives are defined in terms of learning activities (such as types of controlled oral practice) and observable teaching skills (such as eye contact).

The craft approach to professional education

Craft/apprenticeship-based teacher education shares the view of teacher learning as essentially *imitative* in process and *model-based* in content. The craft model of professional education prevailed in traditionalist initial teacher education (ITE) design in the UK until the 1950s. The student-teacher worked alongside a master teacher in school and followed her/his instructions, advice and personal example as does an apprentice a master craftsman. S/he learned to teach from the model of the experienced master teacher.

As in CBTE, objectives were model-based but they were not framed as precise competencies: they were implicit, represented by the craft knowledge of the supervising teacher. In fact, in most cases, practical LTE objectives were not defined at all (Stones and Morris, 1972).

A craft model may be appropriate where resources are limited or where there is an undersupply of teachers: school-leavers can be trained cheaply by apprenticeship in school rather than by entry to higher education institutions. It is also consistent with a conservative culture: if a stable society values seniority and tradition, then it might well promote apprenticeship as a valid form of ITE.

Criticisms of model-based teacher education

Objections to behaviourist learning theory in general, to ITE based on behaviourist theory (classical micro-teaching and behavioural CBTE) and to traditionalist ITE (craft/apprenticeship) tend to be mutually consistent. They criticise their reliance on imitation as a learning process and the behavioural-prescriptive definition of teaching (Stones and Morris, 1972; Alexander *et al.*, 1984; McIntyre, 1990). Criticisms of prescription are summarised in section 5.3.2, in essence arguing that it is impossible to prescribe a single set of 'good teaching' practices that can be used effectively in uncertain and diverse teaching contexts.

Criticisms of imitation as a learning *process* in LTE are as follows:

- training to enact behaviours fails to address the appropriate use of these behaviours: skill lies in knowing when and with which students to use a 'behaviour' such as peer correction or mime; training should therefore complement skill practice with the analysis of classroom situations and choices teachers make (see section 6.2);
- exposure to a single model of teaching perpetuates the fiction that there is one best way to teach, prevents exposure to alternative

teaching strategies and the exploration of the conditions under which these alternatives might be appropriate (see section 8.6);
- behavioral imitation fails to develop planning and self-evaluation skills (see sections 6.2, 6.3);
- model-based training ignores individual differences in student-teachers' beliefs, values and experiences;
- the craft knowledge of the master teacher is built from his past experience and it may become obsolete if the goals of language instruction change (see section 8.5);
- model-based training is inflexible: it only equips teachers for the conditions assumed by the initial training; if circumstances or curriculum objectives change and the ITE routines cease to be appropriate, teachers may lack the tools to cope with new teaching demands;
- modelled teaching behaviours may not transfer to culturally different settings because their meaning is not the same (e.g. strong eye-contact between teacher and pupil may signal attention in one culture but defiance in another).

For example, after a short course in 'structural-situational teaching' (it was the late 1960s) and a few months teaching in a London school, a young teacher went to work in Libya, to be utterly thrown by the fact that the learners responded to structural drills and repeated doses of Alexander with a) bafflement and b) no evidence at all of language learning. The techniques did not suit the context or the learners. The young teacher had no tools with which to deal with the situation: the prescription was not working, the toolkit of methods he carried into class turned out not to suit the job. Model-based training may send a teacher away with some initial confidence, but s/he is liable to run into situations where the techniques do not work, so that s/he is left 'naked in the classroom'. Learner-teachers are all different, and ultimately they will all have to work in uncertain situations in ways that suit them as a person, with no master trainer there to pull the strings.

Clearly there is a need for skill training, but it need not depend on single models and learning by imitation (see sections 6.2, 8.6). It should be complemented by activities to develop self-awareness; awareness of learners' perspectives; and monitoring and evaluation skills (Pennington, 1990; Wright, 1990; also sections 2.4.7, 4.3; Appendices 5.1 and 5.2, and case study sections 6.2 and 6.3).

There is no necessary conflict between personal development and the provision of classroom skill practice so long as it is accompanied by the development of observational and analytic skills, and is presented through multiple exemplars, not single models. To respect individual differences in perceptions and in rates of development, these activities are best accompanied by broadly based and flexible assessment (see section 5.3 and the approach to assessment in section 6.2). Issues relevant to the role of skills-based LTE appear in Chapter 4 and in sections 6.2, 6.3, and 8.6.

We should note that model-based LTE imposes a directive role on supervisors: 'to direct and inform the teacher, model teaching behaviours, and evaluate the teacher's mastery of defined behaviours' (Gebherd, 1990: 156). Further discussion of supervision in LTE approaches appears in section 5.2.

Having outlined features of model-based teacher education, we consider the other end of the spectrum, theories where learning and teacher education are based on the notion of self-determination.

1.1.2   Humanistic psychology: person with self-agency

Humanistic theory is represented in the work of Rogers (e.g. 1961), Maslow (e.g. 1968) and Kelly (see section 1.1.3). A core feature is its emphasis on self-agency and personal change that is enabled but not directed by others. It arose as a reaction against prevailing positivist approaches in psychology and psychoanalysis (see section 3.3.2 for an outline of the positivist view). Indeed its development cannot be separated from emancipatory and mould-breaking social movements in the USA and Europe in the late 1950s and the early 1960s. It viewed behaviourism and experimental psychology as deterministic[3] and one-dimensional. It also reacted against the strongly deterministic view of psychoanalysis 'that people are driven by sexual and aggressive impulses and unconscious ideas that they cannot consciously control' (Slife and Williams, 1995: 32). Here, the reader is offered no more than a thumbnail sketch of humanistic theory, and is referred to authoritative sources (e.g. Rogers, 1961; Heron, 1986; Roth, 1990; Williams and Burden, 1997).

Humanistic psychology emerged in the 1950s with the formation of the American Association for Humanistic Psychology (whose founders included Rogers, Maslow and Kelly). It stood for a 'an orientation to the whole of psychology' (AAHP, 1962: 2) with an interest in:

> topics having little place in existing theories and systems e.g. love, creativity, self, growth . . . self actualization, higher values, being, becoming, spontaneity, play, humour, affection, naturalness, warmth . . . autonomy, responsibility . . .
>
> (AAHP from Roth, 1990: 419)

Essential humanistic concepts are:

- each person is unique and is a whole;
- we each have an innate potential for a fully developed self;
- that self is essentially good;
- we know intuitively what we need for our own growth;
- we have *self-agency*, that is we can exercise individual choice to determine our own personal growth;

---

[3] Deterministic view: that forces beyond our control determine our actions.

- healthy development is enabled by 'mankind's tendency to actualize himself, to become his potentialities . . . to express and activate all the capacities of the . . . self' which 'awaits only the proper conditions to be released' (Rogers, 1961: 351);
- the psychologist should work from a person's perceptions of self and of the world, not from the outsider's point of view;
- three conditions support the self-actualizing person:
  - the freedom to pursue our development and to make our own choices;
  - to meet the most basic of our needs, such as safety, before higher needs such as self-actualisation can be fulfilled;
  - to connect with and act on our true needs and feelings, rather than be pushed by others into behaving in ways that deny them.

Nondirective intervention

Rogers developed his theories in the context of psychotherapist–client relationships. The essence of his approach is to offer the client unconditional regard, to value the client's inner world so that s/he can become open to her/his true feelings, the inhibition or distortion of which have caused illness. Nondirective intervention assumes that, with support, the client is capable of growth by means of inner resources and that attempts to impose change will not work:

> no approach which relies on knowledge, upon training, upon the acceptance of something which is taught, is of any use in changing a person.
>
> (Rogers, 1961: 32)

Thus, Rogers provides a rationale for nondirective intervention in a wide range of settings (e.g. counselling, staff development, teacher education and teaching). His influence has been far-reaching (see also Kelly and Kolb in section 1.1.3; Schön in section 1.2.2). One example in commerce and education would be the development of 'action learning' techniques in which peer groups serve as a positive environment for self-directed development (McGill and Beaty, 1992). In teacher education, his approach has provided a basis for nondirective approaches to supervision (Gebherd, 1990; Heron, 1993; sections 5.2 and 7.1).

A common metaphor in humanistic thinking is that of growth and fruition. An absence of regard, of a sense of value, stunts the growth of a person, which is best promoted by offering the emotional climate and nutrition needed for personal development.

Humanistic theory and language teacher education

Humanistic theory recognises the autonomy and individual needs of the person (Rogers, 1982). It argues that learning must be internally determined, rather than externally controlled as in model-based approaches to education.

Therefore it views positive teacher-learner relationships as necessarily co-operative, with the teacher serving to facilitate development and not to control it as if s/he were a master puppeteer.

A comparable view has emerged in teacher education (TE), including the following features:

- recognition of the need to respect teachers' personal autonomy when system-wide change is introduced in the curriculum (e.g. Day *et al.*, 1987; Cline *et al.*, 1990; Elliott, 1991; sections 8.2–8.6);
- adaptation of counselling models to intervention with experienced teachers (e.g. Day *et al.*, 1987);
- partnership relationships between supervisors and student teachers in ITE (e.g. Turney *et al.*, 1982a; section 6.2);
- the notion of ITE as process of self-realisation (Smyth, 1987; Diamond, 1988);
- a recognition of the emotional dimension to personal change and therefore of teachers' needs for support (e.g. Easen, 1985; Rudduck, 1988; sections 8.3–8.6).

The humanistic perspective has also complemented conventional TE syllabuses by highlighting the need for skills which enable self-directed development. These would include, for example, self-assessment and working effectively in groups (see Appendix 6.2). It is now widely recognised that LTE should provide teachers with the tools for further independent development both in award-bearing courses (e.g. sections 6.2, 6.3 and 8.2) and in other forms of LTE (e.g. sections 8.3–8.6).

Humanistic theory has stimulated considerable innovation in ELT. Perhaps its influence can be explained by the shift in language acquisition theory in the 1970s from behaviourist to broadly constructivist views of language learning in which the concept of a natural sequence of language acquisition suggested that a teacher could not determine its course by means of formal plans and structured teaching of form. This was because of the learners' tendency to 'interpret the teacher's version of the original plan to make it their own' (Breen, 1989: 166). As a result, the teacher's role should be to support the self-determining learner, in a process of joint implementation and review. This view of a teacher as collaborating with learners who determine the course of their own learning is consistent with humanistic values and constructivist theory (section 1.1.3).

It also seems that some language teachers have been particularly receptive to humanistic notions of warmth, openness and wholeness (e.g. Moskowitz, 1978; Rinvolucri, 1985; Stevick, 1990). Perhaps this was a reaction against the mechanical and impersonal nature of audio-lingual methods, based as they were on the logic of behaviourist learning theory. Furthermore, as language teaching is a skill subject, many teachers have come to recognise that feelings, relationships and language use are inseparable, or as Cogan (1995: 3) puts it: 'language teaching is essentially concerned with the mediation of interpersonal communication through language. It is about relating to people and helping learners to relate effectively with other people in another language.'

Humanistic values have influenced teacher education in ELT. Apart from the influence of humanistic models of teaching, it is possible that a widespread lack of inservice teacher education (INSET) provision by employers, in the private and state systems, has promoted teacher self-help groups and the expectation of self-directed learning for which humanistic theory offers a good framework. Thus, there are many instances of ELT teacher education influenced by humanistic perspectives, including Gebherd (1990), Freeman (1990; 1992), Woodward (1991; 1992), Underhill (1992) and Edge (1992). Humanistic perspectives are also relevant to section 5.2 on supervision and sections 8.3–8.6 where we describe INSET structures designed to support teacher development with the exercise of personal autonomy.

Critique

We suggest that, in the context of LTE, five features of humanistic theory should be questioned: the ethics of self-agency; the reliance on one's inner feelings as a guide for action; the relevance of therapeutic models to nontherapeutic situations; a focus on the individual abstracted from society; and appropriacy to cross-cultural settings.

The first issue is related to a more general questioning of an individualist social philosophy. Critics argue that the lack of any construct within humanistic theory to prevent out-and-out selfishness suggests that 'there seems to be a clear warrant for seeking our own satisfaction' (Slife and Williams, 1995: 36); and that morality or any other common standards become entirely relative and individualist. This criticism is apparently supported by Maslow's comment that in healthy, self-actualised people 'the dichotomy between selfishness and unselfishness disappears altogether' (Maslow, 1987: 149). However, both Maslow and Rogers would reject the criticism on the grounds that people are fundamentally good and will show a concern for the autonomy of others as for themselves.

The second criticism questions tacit personal knowing as a sound basis for personal choice. Inner resources alone may not be enough: there may be gaps in a person's knowledge and experience, or blind spots about themselves. In such a case, others are needed to make the person aware of these gaps and help them to find the knowledge they need. We need feedback to learn, whether it is formal and from a supervisor, or informal and from peers (e.g. sections 6.3 and 8.3).

Then, one can question whether a theory developed to account for client–therapist relationships transfers wholesale to other kinds of social relationship, in particular where the client is well and does not have the same needs as one who is unwell. For example, Lansley (1994) and Cogan (1995) have pointed out that in many cases (such as in ITE courses) learner-teachers require constructive feedback and a clear indication of the criteria by which performance is being judged: critical challenge, a framework of expectations and feedback are needed, as well as support. However, it is clear that in certain provider roles, such as process leader, humanistic theory provides a relevant and helpful framework (see McGill and Beaty, 1992; Heron, 1993; also section 7.1).

Humanistic theory proposes 'self-agency' (Curran, 1976) as the means to personal development. We would argue that this inherently individualist model of the person does not take sufficient account of the social aspects of teacher work. School culture imposes norms of behaviour and ways of relating to others which teachers cannot ignore, and so a teacher's development cannot be abstracted from her social setting (Somekh, 1993; Richards and Lockhart, 1994; Bell and Gilbert, 1996; also sections 1.1.4 and 1.1.5).

LTE typically takes place in cross-cultural settings. Therefore, providers need to be sensitive to possible mismatches between an ethic of self-realisation and the beliefs of learner-teachers who might find individualism inconsistent with their view of themselves as members of schools and the community. Learner self-determination is consistent with a pluralist and individualistic culture, and would therefore be in head-on conflict with group-orientated school culture, where good teachers and good learners are expected to maintain group cohesion rather than to assert personal needs or idiosyncratic styles of work (e.g. Richards and Lockhart, 1994: 98–100; Kramsch and Sullivan, 1996).

However, the humanistic perspective offers us vital insights into teacher learning. Above all, it reminds us that in all situations, and especially in formal learning (attended by change and risk as it is), it is essential for learners to feel valued. It also tells us that change interventions in LTE need to start from a sympathetic understanding of the identity and perceptions of the teacher as s/he is. When we consider teacher development at any stage, it is essential to take into account the whole person: their personal history and emotional and interpersonal world as well as the technical and public aspects of their role.

To conclude, we suggest that teacher learning cannot be understood only in terms of self-agency, important as it is to value the individuality and autonomy of teachers and to recognise the emotional aspects of personal change. One has to take into account the public face of teaching, the social imperatives that act on us all. As Bell and Gilbert (1996: 68) put it, rather than absolute self-determination, 'learners as developing people have partial agency'. Thus a teaching identity develops through exchange between our personal theories and self-concept on one hand, and the demands of our social and occupational context on the other (sections 1.1.4, 1.1.5, 2.6.1 and 7.2). Every seedling carries a predetermined inner make-up, and a drive to develop. However, the shape and size of the adult plant derives from its context: the rain, sun, wind and space it needs to grow.

1.1.3   Person as constructivist

In this section we discuss constructivism as a general approach before considering Kelly and Kolb and the relevance of their work to LTE.

The core principle of constructivism is that people 'will make their own sense of the ideas and theories with which they are presented in ways that are personal to them ... (and that) ... each individual constructs his or her own reality' (Williams and Burden, 1997: 2).

Piaget's work on child development originated constructivist models of human thinking, in that: 'central to Piaget's theory is the development of mental representations of behaviour, and of the world and its objects' (Light and Oates in Roth, 1990: 93). In Piaget's theory, mental representation or construction is the means by which we internalise knowledge and perceive the world.

Chomsky's demolition of behaviourist language acquisition theory marked a decisive shift from behavioural to cognitive perspectives on learning (Skinner, 1957; Chomsky, 1957; 1959). The adequacy of a cognitive model of language acquisition encouraged researchers in other fields and contributed to the 'cognitive revolution' of the 1960s and the predominance of constructivist models of learning in contemporary educational thinking (Roth, 1990; Richards and Lockhart, 1994; Salmon, 1995; Bell and Gilbert, 1996; Williams and Burden, 1997).

Constructivism consists of a family of theories based on the notion that we operate with mental representations of the world which are our knowledge, and which change as we learn: 'all learning takes place when an individual constructs a mental representation of an object, event or idea' (Bell and Gilbert, 1995: 44). This view indicates that all learning involves relearning, reorganisation in one's prior representations of the world: 'there is no intellectual growth without some reconstruction, some reworking' (Dewey, 1938: 64).

A constructivist view suggests the following learning cycle:

- the person filters new information according to his or her expectations and existing knowledge of the world;
- s/he constructs the meaning of the input;
- this meaning is matched with her prior internal representations relevant to the input;
- matching confirms or disconfirms existing representations;
- if there is a match, then s/he maintains the meaning as presently constructed (assimilation);
- if there is a mismatch she revises her representation of the world to incorporate the new information (accommodation).

Thus learners actively construct and test their own representations of the world and then fit them into a personal framework. New inputs and experiences may affect the person's construction of the world in two different ways. If they interpret the input to fit with their existing knowledge, then they are engaged in assimilation. If they revise their knowledge to take the input into account, then they are involved in accommodation. Therefore, when teachers 'misinterpret' training inputs, often they are assimilating them into their prior ways of thinking.

Our constructions of reality determine our expectations, mediate our experience and set parameters to our subsequent learning. Therefore, a constructivist view of LTE will see an intervention (such as a classroom experience, a lecture on learning theory, or a peer observation) not as a model or as a 'bolt-on' additional bit of content, but as an experience which we select from and then construe in our own way. Change occurs as we accommodate new information, as confirmed or challenged by our interactions with other people.

A Japanese family who rented a house in the UK for a year were baffled by a small flap in the back door. Bringing their knowledge of the world to bear, which excluded culture-specific knowledge of milkmen and pets, they construed it as the place for the milkman to pass bottles into the house, and collect the empties. No milk came. Empties left there stayed where they were. Given this denial of the original construction, they were required to reconstrue the flap. On learning that it was a catflap, to let a cat come and go, they had to accommodate this new information and reconstrue English domestic culture. English families in Japan have no doubt had similar constructivist learning experiences.

Constructivism and ELT

A constructivist model of language acquisition has strongly influenced language curriculum design. It is widely accepted that learners use their own strategies and mental processes 'to sort out the system that operates in the language with which they are presented' (Williams and Burden, 1997: 13). For example, comprehension is now conventionally seen as the mental representation of a text according to the person's purpose, knowledge of the world, expectations of discourse and linguistic knowledge. Comprehension-skill teaching now emphasises the exploration of learner expectations and prior knowledge, and reasonable interpretations of text (e.g. Grellet, 1981; Barr *et al.*, 1981; Brown and Yule, 1983; Ur, 1984; Underwood, 1989; Williams and Moran, 1989).

Similarly, constructivism views the learners' inner representations of the language system, their 'internal syllabus', as mediating input and structuring the course of language acquisition. Breen (1987a: 159) explicitly adopts a constructivist position to justify process-orientated syllabuses:

> mainstream second language acquisition studies assert the primacy of the learner's inherent psychological capacity to acquire linguistic competence when this capacity acts upon comprehensible language input . . . (they will) . . . superimpose their own learning strategies and preferred ways of working upon classroom methodology (i.e. the tasks the teacher sets, and the teacher's own interventions).

Thus ELT has widely adopted constructivist views of language learning (see Williams and Burden, 1997).

Constructivism and teacher education

The shift from model-based to constructivist frameworks in LTE is nicely exemplified in Griffiths' (1977) reinterpretation of classical micro-teaching. He recognised that learning by means of micro-teaching could be explained in terms of conceptual development arising from input, skill practice and personal experience, rather than behaviourial change resulting from efficient 'shaping'. He adopted an explicitly constructivist model to account for learning by micro-teaching:

1. Before entering micro-teaching programmes, each student has distinctive, complex conceptual schemata relating to teaching.
2. There are large individual differences in these conceptual schemata, but large areas of commonality may also exist through the embedding of these schemata within the ideologies of teaching subjects.
3. The conceptual schemata show a high degree of stability, but gradual change can occur through the acquisition of new constructs and principles from instruction and experience.
4. Students' conceptual schemata to a large extent control their teaching behaviour, and changes in teaching behaviour result from changes in schemata.

Griffiths (1977: 194)

In other words, beneath the visible behavioural tip of student-teacher learning, there lies the reality of the constructivist iceberg.

This view suggests certain changed emphases in micro-teaching, and by implication in TE in general:

- it recognises the personal differences between each learner-teacher (LT), located in their *ways of seeing*;
- learning lies in the conceptual development which determines behaviour change, not only in the behaviour itself;
- feedback should focus on the thinking and the perceptions of the LT, as well as their actions;
- LTs can learn by developing their perceptions (e.g. by structured observation) as well as skill training;
- models can be used for exemplification and analysis and not merely for imitation;
- the LTs' ability to recognise and analyse effective teaching becomes part of the micro-teaching syllabus.

These principles can be applied to specific activities (Appendices 5.1, 5.2 and 8.1) and also to the structure of whole programmes as exemplified in section

6.2, where course structure enables student-teachers to develop their own thinking by integrating experience and skill practice with observation, analysis of context, self-awareness and the analysis of links between theory and classroom events.

The implications of the 'person as constructivist' view in ITE can be summarised as follows:

- it anticipates LTs' diverse expectations of and responses to the ITE course itself (Haggerty, 1995a);
- it accepts that one has to work from the personal theories which each student brings to a course;
- it justifies space in the curriculum to develop self-awareness and also to explore each student's interpretations of input and their own classroom experiences;
- student-teachers' thinking is likely to be influenced by knowledge of learners' perspectives (Kagan, 1992);
- it suggests that novices may benefit from sharing the thinking of effective teachers to enrich their own thinking (as in mentoring schemes; McIntyre et al., 1993; also section 6.2).

In the case of experienced teachers' learning, a constructivist view suggests that their perceptions and beliefs are progressively reinforced by teaching experience, becoming increasingly central to their view of themselves as they become confident in meeting role demands. The power of these ways of looking is reflected by the ability of established teachers to 'skew' (i.e. assimilate) training inputs to conform to their prior beliefs. For some providers, this can be a little exasperating: 'courses designed to train teachers . . . focus on transmitting information about the new approach and persuading teachers of its effectiveness. When the teachers return to their classrooms they misinterpret the new ideas and translate them to conform to their existing classroom routines – at the same time believing they are doing exactly what the new approach calls for' (Karavas-Doukas, 1996: 194).

A constructivist view makes sense of the way in which teachers can filter out training interventions, or interpret input so that it fits in with their framework of thinking about teaching. It would not view them as 'misinterpreting' inputs, but as assimilating them, fitting them into their existing personal theories and prior experience. Take the example of an experienced Egyptian teacher who watched a demonstration of a communication game where only one child can see a picture and the others ask questions about it, but then led the game himself as a frontal question-and-answer exercise, using the picture as a cue card. He had assimilated the demonstration into a view of classroom discourse where the teacher mediates all talk. He could not see the changes he made to the activity as significant for the way learners processed language.

This tendency to assimilate inputs indicates the need to uncover teachers' implicit theories and beliefs in order to make them available for conscious review: 'While tacit knowledge may be characteristic of many things that teachers do, our obligation as teacher educators must be to make the tacit explicit' (Shulman, 1988: 33).

The constructivist view indicates the need to supplement conventional knowledge bases (section 3.2.2) with that of self and of learners: 'since every teacher and learner is different, teaching is most effective when it is based on two kinds of knowledge: knowledge of the students and knowledge of oneself' (Pennington, 1990: 135).

This view is a key feature of 'reflective' teacher education – Shulman (1988), Pennington (1990), Wright (1990), Denicolo and Pope (1990), Griffiths and Tann (1992), Valli (1992), Richards and Lockhart (1994). It is also illustrated in several other sections: discussion in section 6.2; awareness activities in Appendices 5.1 and 5.2; the CELTA syllabus in Appendix 6.2; and reflective activities in Appendices 8.1 and 8.5.

General criticisms

The two main criticisms of constructivism focus on the vagueness of key terms and its incomplete view of the person (see also sections 1.1.4 and 1.1.5).

Terms

Constructivism offers a general view of human learning and there is a great diversity of subtheories which are consistent with it. As a result, there has tended to be a confusing proliferation of terms. As Sendan (1995b: 39) pointed out, different authors coming from different frames of reference have used a wide range of terms to describe teacher thinking. These include: teacher constructs; decision strategies; metaphors/beliefs/implicit theories; personal constructs; teachers' conceptions; image; teacher perspectives; scripts and schema; subjective theories; intuitive theories; teacher perspectives; teachers' theories; and personal theories. As a result, it is hard to pin down how these terms relate to each other.

Sometimes, writers use terms in overlapping ways. For example, Kagan (1992) refers to cognitive structures in a number of apparently synonymous ways such as: 'pre-existing beliefs/images and prior experience'; 'image of self as teacher'; 'personal beliefs about teaching: images of good teachers, images of self as teacher and memories of themselves as pupils ...'; 'expectations or images' (Kagan, 1992: 140).

Such looseness in the use of key terms is bound to create difficulties in relating one piece of research to another and also in defining LTE objectives. In this book we use the term 'image' for mental representations of persons, such as good teachers and 'personal theory' when we refer to the beliefs and constructs teachers apply to teaching (e.g. Table 1.2 and Appendix 1.1).

Individualism

Constructivism provides a helpful framework for us to understand personal change. It explains why 'each individual . . . learns different things in very different ways even when provided with what seem to be very similar learning experiences' (Williams and Burden, 1997: 2). It highlights the need for providers to 'start where teachers are' before any attempt to bring about personal change.

However, constructivism tends to exclude some significant aspects of human learning which are of great importance in LTE: 'it has little to say about the affective aspects of learning, non-rational thinking and skill learning, or about culture and power in the classroom' (Bell and Gilbert, 1996: 54).

An adequate approach to LTE should consider cognitive, affective, and behavioural dimensions, and, given the social nature of teaching, LTE must also address the social dimensions of experience and learning: 'all human experience is ultimately social: . . . it involves contact and communication' (Dewey, 1938: 38).

A view of a learner-teacher as an individual constructivist is too limited because it focuses on inner processes and thereby abstracts the person from the sociocultural landscape in which they live and work (Bell and Gilbert, 1996; Williams and Burden, 1997). No LTE approach can treat an individual as independent of society: 'Teacher development as learning needs to take into account the existing socially constructed knowledge of what it means to be a teacher' (Bell and Gilbert, 1996: 58).

Thus, in developing a sense of self as teacher, we all draw on existing constructions of teaching available in our society, 'traditional ways in which other language teachers throughout history have made sense of what it means to be a language teacher' (Williams and Burden, 1997: 52). We would not suggest rejecting a constructivist perspective for these reasons, but would argue for a broader *social* constructivist framework as it admits the social aspects of teacher work and learning, and recognises the dynamic interaction between personal change and social circumstances (sections 1.1.4 and 1.1.5). This recognises that the observation of behavioural models, access to explanatory theory, skill practice, feedback, and the interpretations of others of shared experiences all contribute to development in thinking. The Egyptian teacher did shift in his perceptions and practice, but only after a period of personal experience of communicative activities as a learner, theoretical inputs on communicative objectives and methods, and discussion. The case for designs based on such 'multilevel' related activities is developed in section 1.1.5 (also see sections 4.3, 5.2 and 8.6, Box 4.3, and Table 8.4).

Kelly and Kolb: constructivist theories of learning

In this section we outline the theories of Kelly and Kolb. Both theories are consistent with constructivism and both offer valuable insights for LTE design.

Kelly: constructive alternativism

Constructivism and humanistic theory are mutually consistent, in that they value the perceptions of the individual and see learning in terms of personal change. A unique synthesis of the two views is found in Kelly's personal construct psychology (PCP).

Constructs

Kelly uses the term *construct* to refer to bipolar concepts we use to *construe* the world, that is to interpret our reality and to predict future events. He suggests that persons use their construct systems 'to observe, classify, explain, predict and control the events they are interested in' (Sendan, 1995b: 24). In other words, their construct systems serve as a kind of template (sometimes referred to as our personal 'goggles') with which we make sense of persons, events, information and even catflaps!

Constructive alternativism

'It is we who create our "prisons" and we can also, critically, demolish them' (Lakatos, 1970: 104). Kelly's work placed special emphasis on the self-determining characteristics of man. He developed constructivist theory by proposing that each person has the potential to be endlessly creative in reinterpreting and, in a sense, recreating the world in which s/he lives:

> The constructs we erect as our navigational model of the world have a dual function, that of theory testing and theory building. Our construct system is that with which we *anticipate* future events. Persons are not reactive to their environment but have the potential for constructing new horizons.
>
> Pope (1993: 20)

Kelly proposes that each person develops a *unique* repertoire of constructs based on his/her experience of the world and assumes that 'the events we face today are subject to as great a variety of constructions as our wits will enable us to contrive. This is not to say that one construction is as good as any other ... but it does remind us that all our present perceptions are open to question and reconsideration, and ... that even the most obvious occurrences of everyday life might appear utterly transformed if we were inventive enough to construe them differently' (Kelly, 1970: 1). For this reason, his approach to learning theory is referred to as *constructive alternativism* (Salmon, 1995: 23), which integrates change in perception with learning and personal change (Kelly, 1955; Bannister and Fransella, 1980; Myers, 1993; Fransella, 1995).

Pope (1993: 20–21) has suggested that the implications of Kelly's theories for teacher learning include:

- the world is real but individuals vary in their perception of it;
- an individual's conception of the real world has integrity for that individual;
- teachers use personally pre-existing theories to explain and plan their teaching;
- teachers test these theories for fruitfulness and modify them in the light of such testing.

This suggests that teachers learn when they are able to reflect on and test out their personal theories by means of direct personal experience (section 1.1.5, Box 4.3 and Table 8.4). Pope's notion of 'fruitfulness' is that it is the teacher, not an outsider, who should be helped to assess how useful or relevant his/her current theories are for her personal or teaching goals. For example, a teacher with a strong sense of self as a kindly and protective knower who guides and supports her learners might come to see that such values affirm teacher-centred methods and so inhibit learner independence in communication skill development. Such self-assessment is extremely hard to do alone, and needs support and dialogue over time (Newell, 1996; Bailey, 1996). For example, our case study in section 8.3 describes teachers who are testing out their beliefs in equality of opportunity and mixed-ability teaching: the reader will note the structure, timescale, dialogue and personal support such testing needed.

We only summarise the features of PCP here, and refer readers to Fransella (1995) as an excellent introduction, and Salmon (1995) for a discussion of its implications for teachers.

PCP and teacher thinking

Repertory grid methodology enables us to represent the way in which individuals construe significant elements of their experience (Sendan, 1995a; 1995b; Sendan and Roberts, forthcoming). In essence, repertory grid consists of a structured interview to elicit the constructs the person uses to discriminate a set of elements (for details of the method, see Pope and Keen, 1981). For example, Sendan (1995b) and Sendan and Roberts (forthcoming) report that one student-teacher ('Saadet') applied the ten constructs in Table 1.2 to discriminate nine elements: effective and less effective teachers known to him personally. Once these constructs were elicited, Saadet rated each teacher on their relative closeness to one pole or the other. He could also rate 'the teacher I am now' and 'the teacher I want to be' on the same constructs. In this way, repertory grid technique revealed his personal theories on effective teaching at that time (see also Appendix 1.1 for an example of a teacher's personal theories elicited by other methods; also Mitchell and Martin, 1997, on language teachers' beliefs on effective teaching).

The bipolar constructs in Table 1.2 are not independent of each other in Saadet's thinking. They are organised as a system in which each construct is

Table 1.2   Saadet's constructs on effective teachers

Effective	Ineffective
1 Tolerates lack of seriousness	Very strict
2 Relates teaching to real life	Teaching limited to plan and syllabus
3 Adequate in involving students	Inadequate in involving students
4 Good at transferring what he knows	Has difficulty in transferring what he knows
5 Supplements textbook with different materials	Very dependent on textbook
6 Has close relationship with students	Distant teacher–student relationship
7 Takes account of students' general knowledge	Does not take account of students' general knowledge
8 Motivates students	Starts teaching without motivating students
9 Leads students to think	Directs students to memorisation
10 Increases students' level of attention with jokes	Does not take into account students' attention

associated more or less closely with the others. Some attributes may be very tightly associated, in clusters. A consequence of this clustering is that once one attribute is perceived (in self or in others) then there is an expectation that the other attributes also will be or should be present. Another person, with similar constructs but a different system of associations between them, may form quite different expectations in the face of the same observed characteristic (Myers, 1993). For example, in Saadet's case, a consequence of these associations will be an expectation that any teacher who relates teaching to real life will supplement the textbook and be successful in maintaining learner attention, while one who does not is likely to depend on rote learning.

A construct system can therefore be described in terms of *content* and *structure*. The content is the nature of the constructs, the structure the way they are related to each other as a system. This distinction suggests that development can occur even if the content does not change. This is because the same content, the same constructs, can be reassociated with resulting changes in a learner-teacher's perception of situations, other teachers or self. It is as if s/he can play with basically the same deck of cards, but arrange them into different groups and patterns, with very different consequences for his/her perceptions and judgements.

This view is supported by Sendan's research into student teachers' conceptual development over a 15-month period which suggested relative stability in the content of their personal theories about effective teachers but notable structural changes as they changed the links between ideas, and organised isolated attributes as coherent themes (Sendan, 1995b; Sendan and Roberts, forthcoming; also section 2.4.6).

This view challenges previous research which has adopted Piaget's notion of discrete successive stages in student-teacher learning (see 'stage theories', section 2.4.3; and Berliner, 1987). Instead it proposes a more complex process in which change in student-teachers' thinking is evolutionary and cyclic. Each tests his or her personal theories against new information and personal experience in classrooms, and thereby elaborates, restructures and clarifies them. In this way our social experience of the world contradicts or validates the way we construe it.

The process is essentially evolutionary because new ideas are incorporated gradually into an existing system. The student-teachers in Sendan's study seemed to retain certain stable sets of ideas against or upon which to test out the association of new ideas. 'Old' ideas were not jettisoned in favour of new, but were used as a base for experimentation and development over time. Thus, new ideas did not simply replace old ones nor were they merely bolted on to the existing set of constructs. Their incorporation required the whole system of associations to be changed. This view is paralleled by research on the way teachers incorporate innovations into their classrooms. Typically it is done as progressive trial and error, testing the water with a toe rather than going in at the deep end with wholesale changes (Olson and Eaton, 1987).

PCP has been adopted in some approaches to teacher education (Ben-Peretz, 1984; Diamond, 1985; Yaxley, 1991) but its influence in ELT has been somewhat limited up to the time of writing (but see Belleli, 1993; Myers, 1993; Sendan, 1995a; Saka, 1995; Roberts *et al.*, 1996; Sendan and Roberts, forthcoming). It promises to reveal the personal theories of ELT learners and teachers, and to provide a helpful explanatory framework for individual teacher learning. It challenges simplistic model-based approaches to training and emphasises learner-teachers' needs to test their personal theories against classroom experience, and to reflect on their own experience through writing and dialogue. It also helps explain the drawbacks inherent in certain LTE activities such as 'cascade' training models (see sections 7.2 and 8.5) and the notion of mentoring as a simple process of a novice 'downloading' the knowledge of an experienced teacher (see section 6.2).

Kelly's approach to human learning is framed in terms of individual perception, meaning making and action. He has relatively little to say about the social dimension of personal experience, other than the useful concept of sociality (see Introduction). We see his work as throwing an intensely bright, but narrow, light on the nature of teacher thinking and development. As we argue throughout this book, teaching is a socially constructed role, and in learning to teach, the expectations of others and relationships with others play a profoundly important part. Individualist theory remains incapable of addressing these dimensions of becoming a language teacher. We therefore recognise that, while each teacher develops his/her thinking by personal construction and reconstruction, social validation plays a critical part in the process (section 1.1.5).

Kolb: experiential learning

Kolb's work is based on constructivist assumptions. He acknowledges Lewin, Dewey and Piaget as the 'foremost intellectual ancestors of experiential learning theory' (1984: 15). He endorses the progressive and democratic values of Lewin (see section 1.1.4) and Dewey (section 1.2.1) and draws on Piaget to develop his model of experiential learning and its implications for instruction. Thatcher (1990) provides an excellent summary of his thinking.

Kolb defines concrete experience as direct contact with an object of study rather than its anticipation or recall. He sees experiential learning as a cycle of experience, reflective observation, abstract conceptualisation and active experimentation. He argues that in *concrete experience* we should be involved as fully as possible in new experiences; in *reflective observation* we observe and reflect on these experiences from diverse perspectives; in *abstract conceptualisation* we store abstract concepts to integrate our observations into 'logically sound theories' and then in *active experimentation* we use these theories to make decisions and solve problems.

For example, as a language learner, we might be taught 'mind-mapping' to associate and recall new vocabulary. The direct experience of using it may lead us to contrast it with former methods we used, such as listing. We may generalise from this a conceptualisation of how words relate to each other, and how we learn best. As active experimentation, we may use mapping with new words and even in other areas such as grammar, and from this confirm or develop our new understandings both of language and of self as a learner.

Thus Kolb adopts a constructivist view of learning as the development of personal schema or theories which are progressively confirmed and disconfirmed by experience, a view that: 'learning is the process whereby knowledge is created through the transformation of experience' (Kolb, 1984: 38). We should note that, in Kolb's use of the term, reflection is conceived as the rational analysis of an action or experience (see section 1.2).

Experiential learning theory and teacher education

Kolb's theory of experiential learning offers a flexible and helpful framework for formal (i.e. course-based) and informal teacher learning. It suggests a structure for the design of teacher learning activities: cycles that integrate experience, reflection and discussion, access to public knowledge and opportunities for experiment (see section 8.6). It suggests the following principles:

- direct personal experience is essential for conceptual development;

- reflection on this experience is essential to conceptual development;
- there is value in access to abstract theory (by reading and formal instruction) to explain cases and to provide terms with which to analyse experience;
- there is no need to see either experience or abstraction as prior, so long as they are both available to the learner;
- the experiential learning cycle can be entered *at any point* so long as it is ongoing.

These principles have been observed in much effective LTE work (also activities in Appendices 5.1 and 5.2). They can be recognised in our case studies, especially in the course structures described in sections 6.2, 6.3 and 8.2, and in the design of materials in section 8.6 and Table 8.4.

Dialogue

Kolb's view of experiential learning stresses the function of dialogue in clarifying our ideas and our use of words. Talk is the essential bridge between privately constructed meaning and social activity. It helps us to negotiate between our private meanings and those of others. As Thatcher argues, 'in promoting learning we are about the business of trying to increase the area of shared meaning we have for words and thus for ideas expressed in words' (Thatcher, 1990: 290). It is through reflection and discussion of shared concrete experiences (such as being taught a foreign language or watching a video) that we can best arrive at a shared understanding of terms and concepts. This is because we can match our use of words with that of others within the framework of shared experiences (see Knezevic and Scholl, 1996 on collaborative projects; Brown and Palinscar, 1989, Newell, 1996).

In ELT it has been recognised for some time that teacher learning is very much about acquiring a professional vocabulary that is both publicly shared and personally meaningful (e.g. Brown, 1990). Novices need to develop such a vocabulary through observation, analysis, discussion and reading in order to engage constructively with teaching practice and feedback. With experienced teachers, a key task for the provider is to develop a 'shared language' for the discussion of teaching. The development of a shared language is evidence of sociality: mutual comprehension of our personal constructions of reality (Salmon, 1995).

Integrated activities

A feature of Kolb's treatment of the components of the learning cycle is that they are interdependent, whereas other models tend to suggest the primacy of one or other of these elements. Indeed, it may be that some approaches even to experiential learning itself have been ineffective because teachers wrongly assumed that experience alone was sufficient for learning to take place. Jarvis (1991: 8) observed:

> There is a growing body of research into the limitations of the ways in which experiential learning has been implemented, and a reassessment of alternatives. Mercer and Edwards (1987) have ... shown that children can happily perform learning tasks without drawing the learning conclusions we hope they will. They need overt support to see the purposes and principles behind the activity. Perhaps adults are in the same position when it comes to teaching techniques. Not all learning takes place through the route of direct experience, it seems to me there is a place for telling, sharing, showing and modelling ... a place for overt discussion of the learning principles behind these activities.

As Jarvis argues, experience alone is not enough: it needs to be complemented by interpretation of the experience (see Box 4.3, Table 8.4 and section 1.1.5).

Individualism

While recognising the interaction between private and public knowledge, Kolb tends to discuss learning in individualistic terms. For example, he sees personal experience and experimentation as freeing the person from unthinking reliance on received knowledge. He sees the proper attitude for the creation of knowledge as neither what he calls apprehension (subjective experience) nor comprehension (public, generalised knowledge) but 'an attitude of partial scepticism' by which our appeal to our own experiential knowledge frees us to choose what we believe and to 'chart the course of our own destiny' (Kolb, 1984: 109).

We conclude that while experiential learning theory offers a fruitful framework for LTE, we should complement Kolb's view in three ways. One is to emphasise the social dimension of learning: that our theories and beliefs are tested and confirmed in social contexts, validated by the responses of others: learning is located within us, but its validation depends on social exchange.

A second notion is that reflection should not only be seen in terms of rational analysis and generalisation. It is also an emotional process, because it involves a degree of self-confrontation and self-questioning which entails risk and turbulence, especially for the experienced teacher (Rudduck, 1988). For this reason, learner-teachers are likely only to engage 'open-heartedly' in reflective activities if they are in the right interpersonal and emotional climate (see section 1.2.3; also the positive climate described in sections 8.3 and 8.4; and the 'ground rules' in section 8.6.1).

Finally, we need to recognise the tacit nature of much of our knowledge: people do not know what they know (Eraut, 1994). Therefore, reflective learning requires a degree of self-awareness to uncover our beliefs and make them available for reassessment. In this way we can be capable of developed views of ourself and broader interpretations of our experience (Argyris and Schön, 1974; Shulman, 1988; Griffiths and Tann, 1992; Eraut, 1994; Appendices 5.2, 7.4 and 8.1).

1.1.4   Person as social being

In this section we consider LTE from the standpoint of social learning, where we 'incorporate mental representations of other people and one's own roles in life' (which helps) 'to explain the far from straightforward relationships between what happens and a person's . . . response. The rules imposed by society define the limits within which role behaviour can develop' (Roth, 1990: 845). In other words, learning to teach is not a private journey, but it involves the adoption of a social role, a process of defining oneself as a teacher informed by our images of others and the traditional views of teaching available to us. For this reason, our social landscape intimately affects the nature of our development as teacher.

We have already suggested in sections 1.1.2 and 1.1.3 that teacher learning cannot be explained simply in terms of personal cognitive processes. A major limitation of humanistic theory and of constructivism is that they tend to focus exclusively on individuals, whereas in learning to teach, each individual is developing a social identity, so as to fulfil a significant public role.

In the state sector, schools influence the life chances of the young, spend public money, serve as a focus for political conflict, and provide a means for one generation to shape the next. In the ELT private sector, schools constitute a major service industry, and in many societies play a crucial role in helping students on to career 'escalators'. The teacher in either sector is an agent in key social processes. Therefore in LTE we have to consider a social perspective on teachers' work. It helps us understand how teaching, as all other occupations, is powerfully affected by society at large; what the particular attributes of the occupation are; how people enter it; how the occupational culture affects people who are part of it; and how social rules may affect socialisation into teaching and the development of personal craft knowledge. To suggest this exchange between the person and context, Fig. 1.1 represents individual growth as an exchange between social forces within and beyond the school and the individual, his/her prior knowledge, expectations and values. An adequate view of teacher learning should recognise the interaction between internal development and the person's social landscape.

A social perspective helps us see that there is far more to learning to teach than picking up a toolkit of techniques and some specialist knowledge. It is a process of socialization, defined by Merton (in Lacey, 1977: 13) as: 'the process by which people selectively acquire the values and attitudes, the interests, skills and knowledge – in short the culture – current in groups to which they are, or seek to become, a member'.

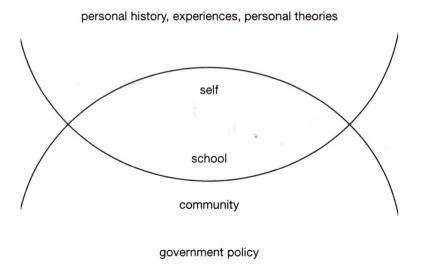

personal history, experiences, personal theories

self

school

community

government policy

wider economic/cultural/political forces

Fig. 1.1   Influences on teacher behaviour and learning

Just as child socialisation instils beliefs about self and social relationships in general, so socialisation into teaching instils beliefs about the nature of the occupation and the knowledge needed for it: 'teaching cultures are embodied in work-related beliefs and knowledge teachers share – beliefs about appropriate ways of acting on the job and rewarding aspects of teaching' (Feiman-Nemser and Floden, 1986: 508). Similarly, in the ELT field, Richards and Lockhart (1994) have argued that language teachers' beliefs emerge from a complex of social and individual influences: experience as a pupil, development of craft knowledge through teaching experience, personality preferences, public educational theories acquired from training courses or from reading. They also provide illuminating examples of language teachers' personal theories.

A social perspective helps us to understand crucial influences on teacher learning:

- the structural aspects of the occupation which determine its social status (see 'professionalism' below and Lortie, 1975; Schön, 1983);
- the knowledge and attitudes which affect the receptiveness of student-teachers to ITE: the 'pattern of orientations and sentiments' (Lortie, 75: viii) which mediate teacher development (section 2.3.1);
- the norms enacted by school culture (e.g. section 2.2 and Lortie, 1975; Schön, 1985; Somekh, 1993; Richards and Lockhart, 1994);
- norms of classroom interaction which affect teachers' practice and development (section 2.2 and Zeichner *et al.*, 1987; Calderhead, 1990; Kramsch and Sullivan, 1996).

The social dimension is significant in our case studies: the exchange between school climate and teacher development is illustrated in section 8.3; the impact of large-scale social change on teacher development is exemplified in sections 8.4 and 8.5; the link between occupational status and course incentives is illustrated in section 8.2; and the effect of socially framed role expectations on mentor-student discourse is discussed in section 6.2.

In the rest of this section, we look into three aspects of the social dimension in teacher development. These are: the relationship between self-concept and the social status of teaching ('Occupational culture and professionalism'); the impact of school culture on individual development ('Teacher development and the school'); and an approach to change that relies on collective action and group process ('Lewin and action science'). These three rather disparate topics are related by a common theme: the social preconditions and processes which affect teacher learning.

Occupational culture and professionalism

In normal usage a 'professional' is someone in a nonmanual occupation who is highly trained, skilled and self-disciplined. In this sense, there are many professional language teachers. However, a more rigorous definition applies stricter criteria: self-regulation, 'the legal right to govern their daily work affairs' (Lortie, 75: 22), high social status, restricted entry, and a homogeneous consensual knowledge base.

By these criteria, the law, medicine and architecture are 'major professions' but in many social contexts, teaching is not (Lortie, 1975; Schön, 1983; Eraut, 1994). For example, Lortie concluded, in the context of his study and according to strict criteria, that teaching was not a profession, for the following reasons:

- 'teachers continue to be employed subordinates' (Lortie, 1975: 22) who are 'employed in organizations where those who govern do not belong to the occupation' (Lortie, 1975: 56);
- there was no consensual base of professional knowledge;
- membership was not carefully screened by the occupational group itself;
- entry to teaching was eased by society, as compared with the professions: entry requirements were relatively lacking in rigour and length and the decision to enter could be made at almost any age.

Lortie notes the effect on self-concept of entry to major professions. Members of such restricted groups tend to see entry as a true personal turning-point, in that 'the selves of the participants tend to merge with the values and norms built into the occupation' (Lortie, 1975: 56). In contrast, he argued that the relatively short period of professional education, the absence of a 'shared ordeal' of rigorous screening, the absence of a common body of highly complex knowledge, and the absence of self-regulation according to occupational norms all meant that: 'in that case the attitudes, values, and orientations people bring with them continue to influence the conduct of work' (p. 56) and that 'the diversity so permitted has important consequences for the inner life of the occupation' (p. 39). This theme of diversity is developed in section 2.4 and 7.1.

We do not suggest that all language teachers are the same as those in Lortie's study. We do suggest that social influences on an occupation will affect the self-concept of its members, and that this is profoundly important for a theory of LTE. This is because it explains the way in which learner-teachers' personal theories on teaching are affected by their social experience, and that they then affect their expectations of and reactions to LTE.

Teacher development and the school

Each teacher's practice and beliefs develop in complex interaction with experiences in school. Zeichner *et al.* (1987) describe this exchange between the person and the group in terms of new teachers who use: 'active and creative responses to the constraints, opportunities and dilemmas posed by the immediate contexts of the classroom and the school', noting that it is through the culture of the school 'that the wider structure of society and the state have their impact' (Zeichner *et al.*, 1987: 28).

Their study of four novice teachers illustrates this interaction between personal theories and school culture, which influences at three interdependent levels. In the classroom, teachers learn through *interaction* with pupils who effectively affirm certain teaching strategies and veto others, implicitly confirming certain values and denying others. At an *institutional* level, development is affected through the enactment of social norms, implicit rules of teacher behaviour (Somekh, 1993). There is room for teachers to assert their personal style, however, because schools often contain subcultures which the new teacher can opt into. Finally there are social influences from *outside the school*, such as the impact of material resources on teachers' practical classroom options. Thus the nature of the practical experience from which each teacher constructs her knowledge is intimately affected by external conditions and social policy (see section 7.2 for examples of these connections).

Zeichner *et al.*, argued that teachers develop their beliefs and practice in terms of the relative match between a school's ethos and their own personal theories. A close match is likely to confirm and strengthen their personal theories. In the case of a mismatch, there are at least three possible responses which will determine how their personal theories then evolve: a teacher may maintain his/her beliefs covertly and 'play along' with the school system; or s/he may fit in with the system and begin to rethink her/his values in line with the school's. Then, s/he might persist in her/his practice, which would have an impact on the school as much as the school on the teacher.

In the early 1970s, Mexican secondary-school teachers we trained in 'oral-aural' methods worked in some schools in which principals saw undue noise and movement as a threat to order. One student-teacher even found that all her visual aids had been taken and burnt because they made the place untidy. She could have kept to her beliefs, but compromised by quietening her classes down and using more seat work and reading. Alternatively, she could have fitted back into a translation and book-based style, perhaps thinking that it best suited schools of this type. In fact she brought a lockable chest into school to store her materials and carried on just as before! Her development and her view of self would have taken a different course had she acted otherwise.

In terms of the effect of school on the person, research shows a link between school climate and teacher development: some schools provide positive conditions for teacher learning, others do not. At its simplest, as Fullan (1982) points out, a school where teachers talk to each other about teaching and have some sense of collegiality provides positive conditions for teacher learning (Easen, 1985). A school with a privatist culture offers less favourable conditions for development. Thus we cannot consider a teacher's development without considering her interaction with school culture.

Lewin and action science

In this section we touch on the work of Lewin because of the social perspective he brings to teacher learning. Lewin made unique contributions to social psychology and professional education. He originated the notions of action science, leadership training, team-building, participation and ownership, action planning, force-field theory, group dynamics and sensitivity training (Kemmis, 1982).

As a German Jewish refugee working though the period of the Second World War, his work reflects urgent concerns in human social behaviour: prejudice and tolerance, the rights of ethnic minorities, authoritarianism, participation in decision-making and individual autonomy. After the war there was widespread concern in the USA regarding intergroup relations. As Lewin said, 'we know today better than ever before that they are potentially dynamite' (Lewin, 1946, in Kemmis, 1982: 35). At the time, this concern expressed itself in the commitment of funding bodies and community groups such as Jews and Afro-Caribbeans to improve minority rights and intergroup relationships. The imperative for social research was that it should contribute to a better society as well as to theory-building on group behaviour and social change.

In response to these concerns, Lewin proposed an alternative to the two traditional approaches to these concerns: positivism and phenomenology (section 3.3). He proposed a third paradigm, action science, where social scientists would work with interested parties to bring about change, and through this would also construct theories of social change. It is important to appreciate the social perspective of his practical work and theorising. He conceives of action science applying to groups of all kinds. A focus on isolated individuals would have been irrelevant to promoting effective social action and adequate theory.

Action research

Action research is the methodology of action science. Current models applied to curriculum inquiry and teacher development derive from Lewin's original formulation (e.g. Kemmis, 1982; McNiff, 1988; Nunan, 1989; Elliott, 1991; also sections 8.2–8.4).

To Lewin, the following elements would constitute an action research project:

- a problem of real meaning to all participants;
- their commitment to its resolution;
- involvement of participants at each stage as a prerequisite for change;
- participants taking responsibility for change and for the monitoring of the change;
- an emphasis on group processes and group decision-making at each stage in order to clarify problems and to commit participants to action;
- a role for a scientist trained as a group facilitator and as a theorist, working in dialogue with participants.

These general principles are reflected in our accounts of collaborative curriculum inquiry as a means to teacher development (see sections 8.2, 8.3 and 8.4).

To Lewin, participants learn from action research *by means of concrete evidence as to the effect of their actions*: 'If we cannot judge whether an action has led forward or backward, if we have no criteria for evaluating the relation between effort and achievement, there is nothing to prevent us from coming to the wrong conclusions and encouraging the wrong work habits. Realistic fact-finding and evaluation is a prerequisite for any learning' (in Kemmis, 1982: 40). Fig. 1.2 presents Lewin's own visualisation of action-research processes: reconnaissance of results, i.e. fact-finding, informs decisions so that inquiry is guided by objective evidence and not by hunch, prejudice or wishful thinking.

Lewin's view indicates that teachers engaged in curriculum inquiry should not rely on general impressions and selective incidents which merely confirm what they had hoped to see. To Lewin, systematic collection of classroom data

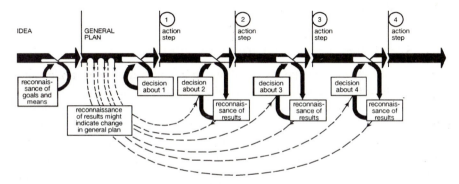

Fig. 1.2 Planning, fact-finding and execution, adapted from Kemmis (1982)

is a key feature of curriculum inquiry. In the case of a language classroom, this could take the form of test data (Fukuda, 1996), quantified classroom interaction data (Philpott, 1993), learner feedback and evaluation data (Nunan, 1989; Pennington, 1996) or structured self-monitoring (Appendix 8.3).

Practical and personal change

To Lewin, social and personal change were interdependent. For example, he recognised that discrimination arises not only from the prejudice of majority groups but also from the guilt and low self-esteem of individuals in minority groups. He saw change in self-concept as inseparable from effective action. This implies that problems have to be tackled in terms of practicalities and also the beliefs of participants about themselves and others: effective action is not merely a matter of adopting better teaching practices, it also involves change in our perspectives (see Appendices 5.2, 7.4, 8.1 and 8.5).

Action research is now widely used in formal courses as a means to integrate curriculum development and teacher development. In general education, action research has been integrated into award-bearing programmes (Vulliamy and Webb, 1991; Diamond, 1991; Yaxley, 1991) and curriculum projects (Day, 1990). In ELT, there have been comparable developments in courses (Halden, 1995; James, 1996; Lennon and James, 1995; Thorne and Wang, 1996; also section 8.2) and in curriculum development projects, for example in India (CIEFL, 1994; 1995; Mathew, 1996; Mathew and Eapen, 1996), in Australia (Burton and Mickan, 1993; Burns and Hood, 1995), in Hong Kong (Richards and Lockhart, 1994; Pennington, 1996), and in Japan (Fukuda, 1996; Sano, 1996). A related form of inquiry, 'exploratory practice', has been developed in Brazil (Lenzuen and Bannell, 1994; Allwright and Lenzuen, 1997). Guides to methodology are readily available (Elliott, 1981; Kemmis and McTaggart, 1982; McNiff, 1988; Nunan, 1989; 1990; Allwright and Bailey, 1991; Hopkins, 1993; Richards and Lockhart, 1994). The theoretical case is argued in Carr and Kemmis (1986), Whitehead and Lomax (1987) and Elliott (1991). We explore issues in action research in our case studies (sections 8.2–8.4) and also discuss its role as a means of teacher development in section 2.6.3.

1.1.5   Conclusion: a social constructivist approach

We have outlined four perspectives on human learning and their implications for LTE. Of course, LTE design and implementation are strongly determined by here-and-now considerations as well as approach: what we do is as much affected by the size of a room or the number of teachers as by our general approach! However, awareness of these perspectives can help an LTE provider place particular strategies in a wider framework and anticipate their inherent strengths and limitations. Furthermore, it can help each person to define his/her own approach to LTE.

Our view is that each perspective throws light on one facet of teacher learning. A behavioural perspective provides insights into skill learning (section 1.1.1). However, the use of practical models and structured skill training does not commit us to a view that teachers learn by imitation. The mediating power of each trainee's prior knowledge and personal theories tells us that simplistic models of behavioural training should be revised in order to address personal, conceptual and contextual dimensions of skill acquisition (section 2.4.4). To do this involves such strategies as: the use of multiple, realistic exemplars rather than a single idealised model (e.g. section 8.6); structured observation of real teaching to engage with real rather than 'laboratory' conditions (e.g. sections 6.2 and 6.3); use of 'uncovering' activities to raise teachers' awareness of their own teacher images and personal theories about 'the teacher I am' and 'the teacher I want to be' (sections 1.1.3, 5.1 and 8.2; Appendix 1.1); and adequate opportunities to experiment and self-evaluate in real teaching conditions (sections 6.2, 6.3 and 8.2–8.6).

We have argued that the humanistic theory of personal change, with its emphasis on self-determination, cannot be transferred wholesale to LTE design. This is because learner-teachers are bound by public requirements, whether to meet external accreditation criteria, or to fulfil the role that schools and society at large have constructed for them: they have only partial agency in their own development.

However, the humanistic perspective is essential to our understanding of personal change. It recognises the whole person and emotional aspects of development, particularly when work is central to a teacher's view of self. This suggests that one function of the provider is to address these emotional dimensions, and to recognise that teachers engaged in deep personal change need consistent support in secure social situations. This is particularly the case with experienced teachers, whose established patterns of thinking and action can be challenged by major role changes (section 8.2, 8.4 and 8.5).

Constructivism provides a fruitful framework for us to understand individual conceptual change. It explains personal differences in perception and behaviour and indicates the need for providers to relate all new learning to teachers' prior practices and beliefs. In LTE this indicates the need to 'start from where teachers are', an apparently self-evident principle which has in fact been ignored in many system-wide training programmes in the past (e.g. see Clark, 1987, on the Hong Kong primary schools project).

As Bell and Gilbert (1996: 58) observe:

> Teacher development as learning by teachers needs to take into account the existing knowledge, experiences, opinions and values of the teachers. This will include their prior knowledge of teaching and learning, and the nature and status of knowledge. It will also include taking into account their ways of learning. In doing this, teacher development convenors or facilitators need to expect and plan for unintended learning outcomes.

The second principle implied by a constructivist view is that reflection on experience can lead to personal change (Bell and Gilbert, 1996: 58):

> Learners can reconstruct their knowledge through reflection. Meta-cognition is an important part of learning and can involve reflection on the degree of understanding or the nature of the thoughts . . .

Constructivist theory is framed essentially in terms of individuals. However, as argued in section 1.1.4, each person's development occurs in constant exchange with their social circumstances: their immediate working relationships, the climate of the school and the wider social forces that affect it: 'learners make their own sense of the world, but they do so within a *social context*, and through *social interactions*' (Williams and Burden, 1997: 28).

We therefore suggest that a broadly *social constructivist* approach offers the most adequate framework for LTE design. This is because it recognises the interdependence of the personal and social dimensions of teacher development: 'Learners as developing people have partial agency. They are partially determining and partially determined . . .' (Bell and Gilbert, 1996: 57).

Each teacher's work-life and development are set in a social landscape. Its main constituents are: the structure of the education system, and the extent to which classrooms and schools are isolated units; the quality and approach of school management; the relative flexibility of the curriculum, and the values inherent in it; prevalent teaching styles and assumptions about the nature of knowledge; the manner and focus of assessments; the availability and style of inspection and appraisal; and the availability of opportunities for development (Bell and Gilbert, 1996). Teachers therefore have to 'navigate' their professional and personal lives within such a landscape, and, as their landscapes differ, so will the course and nature of their development.

Apart from the practical environment of an education system, we also live within a personal environment of relationships and social exchange. Our sense of ourselves, privately and at work, is defined by our relationships. As teachers, the relationships we have with learners, colleagues and superiors all help define our sense of self as teacher. Therefore, our development will be framed by the relationships and dialogue that are available to us. For example, every teacher can recall the first few months of teaching, the uncertainty, successes and failures; and each of us will be able to recall the personal environment in which this took place. Readers may well remember an informal 'mentor', a colleague in the teachers' room who took the time to listen and to discuss what they were doing, and the effect it had on their confidence and ability to go on learning.

Implications for LTE

What does a social constructivist perspective actually mean for LTE? First, it implies that providers and teachers alike need to assess the relationships between their work and wider social conditions: 'Learning by teachers in teacher development situations is occurring within wider social and political contexts. They need to be assessed, not ignored.' (Bell and Gilbert, 1996: 57–58).

Such an assessment should not view the teacher's culture and conditions as 'constraints' or problems, barriers to the intervention we wish to introduce. Much LTE in the past has paid lip-service to cultural awareness, while planning how to impose its own ways of seeing and doing (e.g. Clark, 1987). The teacher's social world *is* the reality, the base from which each teacher will develop. Our case studies reflect this view. Section 6.2 reports an ITE structure which engages student-teachers in the realities of school work; section 8.2 describes a course which culminated in the teacher's self-directed inquiry into their own classrooms; section 8.5 reports a design rooted in the realities of the situation.

Next, the social constructivist perspective recognises dialogue, talk, to be central to teacher learning. This is nothing new, as talk has long been seen as part of the experiential learning cycle, and humanistic perspectives stress the social and interpersonal climate which promotes learning. However, the emphasis on dialogue in a social constructivist view is that collaborative, and task-focused talk is of special value, in that it offers opportunities to clarify one's own meanings and offers social relationships that support changing views of self as teacher. In the context of teacher collaboration, Knezevic and Scholl (1997: 79) observe:

> The process of having to explain oneself and one's ideas, so that another teacher can understand them and interact with them, forces team teachers to find words for thoughts which, had one been teaching alone, might have been realized solely through action. For these reasons, collaboration provides teachers with rich opportunities to recognise and understand their tacit knowledge.

This position is strongly supported by clear evidence of teachers' need for the right social relationships during professional change (see section 2.6.2; also Fullan, 1982: 67; Day *et al.*, 1987; Brown and Palinscar, 1989; Newell, 1996).

A consistent theme in our case studies is that of the need for structures which offer teachers opportunities for collaborative talk as they learn: see section 6.2 on the grouping of student teachers into teams and the role of mentors; section 8.2 on collaborative awareness raising; section 8.3 on the role of the colleagues and of school climate; section 8.4 on participants' need for practical and peer support; section 8.5 on local tutors' need for ongoing support and discussion as their role developed; and section 8.6 on a design which promotes the formation of a collaborating, task-focused teacher group. These cases are consistent with the view of Bell and Gilbert (1996: 57) that: 'Social interaction, for example in dialogues, accounting and narratives – promotes learning of socially constructed knowledge, personal construction of meaning, and the reconstruction of social knowledge.'

However, productive dialogue depends on the right preconditions. It cannot be imposed. To talk openly, on issues of concern, it is critically important for teachers to have a sense of control and participation in processes of change. It is for this reason for example, that groups function best when conventions are observed to protect the rights of each member (see Appendix 8.5).

Finally, a social-constructivist framework suggests that teacher learning is best promoted by cycles of related activities which integrate the dimensions of teacher learning discussed in sections 1.1.1–1.1.4. This suggests the need for LTE to offer combinations of the following activity types:

- access to new information (by reading, lectures and models, e.g. Pennington, 1996; section 8.6);
- activities to raise the learner-teachers' self-awareness of past experiences, and current beliefs, practice and knowledge (e.g. Pennington, 1990; also Appendices 1.1, 5.2 and 8.5);
- direct personal experience, in language learning, micro-teaching and teaching practice (Wallace, 1991; Woodward, 1992);
- indirect experience of teaching, for example by structured observation (Wajnryb, 1993; also section 6.2);
- opportunities to reflect privately on these inputs and experiences, for example by means of reflective writing (sections 6.2 and 8.2);
- opportunities for dialogue with fellow teachers and others, addressing one's practice, beliefs and the social pressures affecting one's work (e.g. sections 7.2, 8.3, 8.4 and 8.6);
- development of skills and attitudes which enable teachers to get the most from the above activities: study skills, observation skills, and team skills (e.g. Appendices 5.1 and 8.1; sections 6.3, 8.4 and 8.6).

The need to integrate these aspects of teacher learning leads us to the metaphor of 'concerted' cycles (section 4.3 and case study section 8.6; also Box 4.3 and Table 8.4). Borrowing Karen Giblin's metaphor, we can consider teacher learning not as cascade, nor as drip feed, nor immersion, but as a jacuzzi! Each activity type works in concert with the others in the context of social activity between and with teachers. By building on individual constructivist views of learning, on social dimensions to teacher work and on the notion of individual reflection as a means to learning, we argue that a social constructivist position is the most adequate framework for LTE design.

Many LTE providers have been constructivists for years: 'I've been a constructivist and didn't know it'. This is suggested by the participatory and teacher-focused activities used in many ELTE programmes (e.g. Richards and Nunan, 1990; Wright, 1990; Woodward, 1992; Richards and Lockhart, 1994; Freeman and Richards, 1996). The social dimension of language teaching is similarly gaining more and more recognition (e.g. Richards and Lockhart, 1994; Kramsch and Sullivan, 1996). The notion of social constructivism is not 'an organ transplant' that might be rejected by the body of LTE practice: it is already implicit in much effective LTE work. Therefore in this section we make no claims to have 'discovered' an approach novel to LTE. However, we do attempt to offer a framework within which providers can locate and crystallise their own personal theories of LTE, and perhaps can also reflect on their own working 'landscapes'.

1.2   Reflection and teacher development

In this section we discuss notions of reflective teacher education in the light of section 1.1. In section 1.2.1, we outline Dewey's ideas on progressive education and reflective thought which have influenced thinking in education throughout this century. His notion of reflective thinking (problem framing, identifying alternative solutions and choosing from options according to the outcome we want and the situation at hand) provides one version of reflection that is still appropriate to LTE.

Then in section 1.2.2 we consider Schön's influential work in professional education. We suggest that his criticisms of a 'technical rationality' model of professional education are appropriate. However, we suggest that his account of the reflective practitioner is idealised and in some ways inappropriate to teaching. We also suggest that Dewey's notion of reframing (developed by Argyris and Schön, 1974, and Argyris et al., 1985) continues to be appropriate in LTE design, particularly in work with experienced teachers. We define it as the ability to interpret a task or problem from a number of standpoints rather than a single view determined by a person's assumptions and tacit personal theories. It has much in common with Eraut's (1994) notion of meta-processing: 'the evaluation of what one is doing and thinking, the continuing redefinition of priorities, and the critical adjustment of cognitive frameworks and assumptions' (Eraut, 1994: 117).

Finally, in section 1.2.3 we try to summarise different conceptions of reflection according to their purpose, focus and theoretical 'parentage'.

1.2.1   Dewey and reflective thinking

Dewey's ideas have influenced schooling and professional education throughout the twentieth century. They assert the values of self-determination, individual responsibility and citizenship in a democracy. His views on reflection, progressive education and personal experience have influenced teacher education to this day.

Reflection

In *How We Think* (1910) Dewey lays the ground for later progressive and person-centred models of learning by characterising reflection as disciplined, conscious, explicit and critical thought which contributes to the intellectual and moral development of the person. He defines it as: 'active, persistent, and careful consideration of any belief or supposed form of knowledge in the light of the grounds that support it, and the further conclusions to which it tends' (Dewey, 1910: 6).

Dewey argued that reflective thought occurs when the smooth progress of our normal activity is interrupted by perplexity or surprise. He refers to this as a 'forked road' situation, in which we are presented with a dilemma which proposes alternative solutions (1910: 11). Once reflection is triggered by surprise, a complete cycle can follow (1910: 68–78). His description integrates personal experience, feeling and thinking, as follows.

(i)   There is a 'feeling of discrepancy or difficulty' likely to be experienced as an emotional disturbance as much as explicit thought. It could result from a mismatch between the ends we want and the means we have at our disposal; or between our expectations and what actually takes place; or between our beliefs and incidents we cannot explain.

(ii) We 'observe' to define the difficulty. The more deliberately and critically this is done, the better the eventual resolution will be. Dewey stresses the need to suspend judgement in order to 'determine the nature of the problem before proceeding to attempts at its solution' (1910: 74).

(iii) We cultivate a variety of alternative 'suggestions' to solve the problem.

(iv) We think through the implications of each suggestion as a solution. We then select the best idea to resolve the original difficulty.

(v)   We observe again to confirm our 'theory' and if we can, adopt it as personal knowledge.

We can set Dewey's reflective cycle in a classroom as follows.

(i)   A teacher sets up a group-based language task she has used effectively before, expecting students to get 'on task' in the TL. This time, half the class goes into mother tongue quite soon, and a few even start to do something else altogether.

(ii–iii) She runs through some explanations, during or after the lesson: 'the problem was they went off-task almost at once; perhaps I set it up badly; maybe it was too hard; or maybe they didn't see the point; perhaps they were messing me about; or perhaps they are easing off because we are near the holidays.'

(iv)   She thinks, 'I have done it before and it worked OK; generally this class works quite well; they should have the TL to do this; perhaps they thought it was waste of time. Was it too hard? No, too easy if anything. Perhaps they finished it quickly and had nothing else to do. Better raise the challenge; and give them a series of tasks not just one.'

(v)   She sets a series of tasks, with later ones more challenging than last week's 'failed' task; she also thinks more carefully about a good topic. She monitors the students more closely than usual: they get down to business, in English. The teacher has adapted the level and structure of tasks for this class, and by implication has elaborated her general strategy for other classes too.

To Dewey, reflection contributes to personal growth because it frees us from a single view of a situation which would restrict how we define problems and so the resulting solutions. Reflection enables us to reframe problems in a variety of ways which therefore allows a wider range of possible solutions, and contributes to change in our perspectives.

Thus, Dewey suggested the notion of reframing as later developed by Argyris and Schön (1974), Schön (1983) and Argyris *et al.*, (1985): that our ability to conceptualise alternative perspectives on a problem lies at the very heart of professional development and also of creative, appropriate problem-solving. Thus in our example, the quality of the teacher's solution depended on her ability to define the problem in a number of appropriate ways, and also contributed to her future approach to task setting.

As another example of the importance of reframing, imagine that you are explaining a grammar point and see a student writing in her notebook and apparently not listening. You might feel frustrated because she is not paying attention, and so might fire a question to catch her out. You have framed the situation as 'student is not attending to me, she is being difficult; the others might follow suit'. You therefore take a punitive line.

The same situation could be reframed as 'she is ahead of the rest and is being a good student, because she is using the time well'; or as 'she is lost and resorting to something she can do, better keep an eye on her'; or as 'she is listening and making notes'. In each case, your perception will determine quite different actions.

How we frame a situation depends on our learnt expectations of students. If we assume that off-task behaviour means 'bad student' then we will respond to it in one set of ways. If we reframe it as either 'good student doing what she needs' or 'what have I done to cause it?', then we will respond in very different ways. It is in this way that our effectiveness depends on our ability to frame and reframe situations to come up with appropriate interpretations and actions. On the other hand, it is clear that we have to learn smooth routines to cope with the demands of the job. Indeed, routinisation is a crucial means by which teachers become skilled enough to focus away from self and on learners. Much of our practice will be led by our established frames and routines unless and until there is good reason to reconsider them.

Reframing is a critical element in professional/personal change, particularly in the case of experienced teachers. Its development is a long-term goal of LTE designed to foster teacher autonomy and self-determination. However, we should recognise the demanding emotional aspects of reframing. It not just an intellectual process but can involve shifts in self-concept. If fixed perspectives are to be 'unfrozen', then it is likely to be associated with a period of uncertainty which can be emotionally turbulent (Day *et al.*, 1987; Rudduck, 1988; Eraut, 1994; Booker, 1996).

Dewey's view of reflective thinking has been qualified by more recent research into teachers' practical thinking which suggests that it is not as rational and systematic as his characterisation suggests. Teachers seem to work from their recall of typical cases and episodes against which present incidents are matched. Given the uncertainty of situations in teaching, it is not surprising that correspondingly fuzzy but flexible notions are often used by teachers to represent them in the language of metaphor rather than abstract propositions (Cortazzi, 1993; Williams and Burden, 1997: 201). This suggests a place for 'nonrational' exploration of practical thinking, such as visualisation and metaphor (Denicolo and Pope, 1990; James, forthcoming; Appendix 8.1).

Progressive education and personal experience

Dewey characterises progressive education as follows: 'To imposition from above is opposed expression and cultivation of individuality; to external discipline is opposed free activity; to learning from texts and teachers, learning through experience' (Dewey, 1938: 19). The rest of this passage is specially relevant to ELT, particularly the distinction between Type A and Type B syllabuses we discuss in section 3.3: 'to acquisition of isolated skills and techniques by drill is opposed acquisition of them as means of attaining ends which make direct vital appeal; to preparation for a more or less remote future is opposed making the most of opportunities of present life.'

The power of inner experience, a private realm of purely personal events, underpins progressive approaches to education because direct experience is seen as the means to develop personal systems of knowing. In the progressive view the quality of learning, the *process*, is an essential variable in the way *content* is acquired. With his emphasis on personal responsibility, the personalisation of knowledge by experience and the creativity of mental processes, we can see that Dewey prefigures humanistic and constructivist views of learning (sections 1.1.2 and 1.1.3) and Kolb's view of experiential learning theory (section 1.1.3).

1.2.2   Schön's view of expertise: the reflective practitioner

Schön's theory of professional expertise has been highly influential in many areas of professional education. He rejects a positivist view of professional expertise, that objective knowledge about the world is an adequate guide for action (see section 3.3) and instead views the essence of professional expertise as a capacity for rapid and creative problem-solving appropriate to context.

In outline, his view of professional expertise is as follows.

- We normally work by using smooth and familiar routines of action ('knowing-in-action').
- On occasions we encounter a surprise or a sense of unease about a situation, where it fails to meet our expectations.
- We may ignore it; or reinterpret it in a way that confirms preconceptions; or, we may we attend to it and try to make sense of it.
- Reflection is triggered by our attempt to make sense of this puzzling 'doesn't fit' experience.
- We may reflect **on** action, that is after the event;
- The hallmark of expertise is the ability to *reflect in action*: thinking which 'can still make a difference to the situation at hand' and which is simultaneous with action. Schön suggests that reflection *in* action has the following characteristics:
  - it is to some extent conscious;
  - we consider the surprise ('what is this?') and the assumptions in the 'knowing in action' that got you there ('how have I been thinking about it?') so that 'our thought turns back on the surprising phenomenon, and at the same time, back on itself' (Schön, 1987).
- To Schön reflection **in** action questions the assumptions underlying the routine that has been disrupted: 'we think critically about the thinking that got us into this fix or this opportunity; and we may, in the process, restructure strategies of action, understandings of phenomena or ways of framing problems' (1987: 28).
- Reflection in action leads to on-the-spot experiment; 'we think up and try out new actions intended to explore the newly observed phenomena, test our tentative understandings of them, or affirm the moves we have invented to change things for the better' (1987: 28).

This view is consistent with Dewey's description of reflection except that Schön identifies 'reflection-*in*-action' as the essence of expertise, and therefore as the desirable goal of professional education. He seems to see this key element in expertise as a kind of real-time reframing.

In summary, we suggest that there are considerable limitations in this view, as follows:

- it is narrow: it applies to only one aspect of professional expertise, creativity, not to expertise as a whole (as characterised in section 3.2.2);
- it is idealised: he offers no empirical evidence that these processes exist;
- it is ambiguous: it is by no means clear how reflection **in** action is different from the commonplace idea of reflection **on** action.

Apart from these objections, we argue that while reflection on action is no different from Dewey's notion of reflective thinking, the notion of reflection in action is of dubious relevance to teaching. We think it fanciful that busy teachers could, on their feet and in full gaze of 30 learners, 'think critically about the thinking that got us into this fix' rather than what best action to take next to get through the lesson as planned. When you are treading water you do not normally have time to reflect on your technique. Experience suggests that questioning our assumptions takes time, and that we benefit from some 'time out' away from the classroom to do it (see sections 8.2, 8.4 and 8.5).

Implications for LTE

There seem to be two general implications of Schön's view of expertise. One is that reflection in action is inherently educative and enables further self-development. The other is that, like Rogers, he sees professional learning as self-discovery in the context of practical activity. For him, professional expertise should be acquired by a deep-end strategy in which 'novices' conduct reflective dialogues with themselves and with master coaches (sic), their own ideas being confronted by the alternative perspectives and observations of the 'master'.

It is not easy to pin down what Schön has in mind as the critical features of these novice-master dialogues. They are exemplified in idealised 'vignettes' of interactions between professionals (such as musicians and architects; e.g. 1987: 101–18). Eraut summarises this interaction, using one of Schön's major examples, as follows: 'The master looks at her drawings, listens to her accounts of her problems, then quickly reframes the problems in his own terms and begins to demonstrate the working out of a design solution' (Eraut, 1994: 145). The master sketches his own solutions and explains his thinking at the same time. He also explains more general principles and praises her work. (The reader will note the respective genders of master and student!)

It therefore seems that to Schön a key learning process is for the novice progressively to frame and reframe situations and problems, informed by the perspectives of more experienced and knowledgeable others.

Criticisms

We suggest three criticisms of Schön's view of professional learning. First, it is only relevant to those already equipped with basic professional knowledge and competence: it assumes that the person has the resources for self-agency in learning. The imaginary design student is already equipped with basic design skills. On how these should be provided, Schön has nothing to say.

Second, learning through dialogue with a master is not a simple matter of downloading that person's perspectives. Evidence on student-teacher learning suggests that there has to be a close value match between novice and master for productive dialogue to take place, otherwise the views of the 'master' are likely to be misconstrued or ignored. We may assume such a match as this in counselling relationships, for example, but have no reason to assume it in student-supervisor interactions (Turney *et al.*, 1982a; Tillema, 1994; Haggerty, 1995a). Indeed teaching tends to be characterised by value diversity (Lortie, 1975; section 1.1.4).

Finally, Schön himself explicitly excluded teaching from his characterisation of professional expertise, on the grounds that it does not enjoy the consensual knowledge base to guide action as enjoyed by the 'major professions'; a fact which has not deterred extensive reference to his work in the literature of teacher development. He also argued that conventional school culture, orientated to maintaining stability and order, militates against reflective practice (1983: 329). His account of the characteristics of conventional school culture makes it entirely clear that in his view reflective thinking is most unlikely to occur while a teacher is engaged in day-to-day work.

We believe therefore that Schön's distinction between technical rationality and reflective models, while marking a shift towards 'internal' perspectives of teacher learning, offers an oversimplified and only partially relevant view of teachers' professional learning. For this reason we suggest it does not in itself provide an adequate basis for LTE design (see also sections 1.2.2 and 3.3.5).

Subsequent work in reflective teacher education has recognised the need for self-awareness as a departure point for development (Shulman, 1988; Griffiths and Tann, 1992). However, rethinking assumptions does not necessarily happen spontaneously. It requires dialogue and structure (e.g. Pennington, 1990; Wright, 1990; Woodward, 1992; Denicolo and Pope, 1993; James, forthcoming; Appendices 4.2, 7.4 and 8.1; also Table 8.4).

The perspectives of Dewey and Schön suggest that the term *reflection* can be used in different ways, which may embrace three very different strands of meaning:

- rational deliberative thought; a closely related meaning would be the ability to draw critically on diverse knowledge bases when addressing pedagogic issues, as in decision-maker models of teaching (Strasser, 1972; Clark, 1986);
- reframing, where the teacher recasts problems in order to arrive at original and apt solutions;
- self-awareness, whether of one's own images of teachers, one's personal theories, or any current knowledge relevant to a new learning task; a closely related meaning would also be the capacity for critical self-management – as 'meta-processing' (Eraut, 1994) and 'meta-cognition' (Bell and Gilbert, 1996; section 1.1.5).

We explore these distinctions in our typology below (section 1.2.3).

1.2.3   Reflection in teacher education

It is generally recognised that the term *reflection* is vague. As a result there may be great variation in the nature of 'reflective activities' in LTE programmes because providers conceptualise it differently (Munby and Russell, 1993). Reflection may be seen as conscious self-assessment according to the formal criteria of one's ITE course at one end of the scale (e.g. section 6.3), to the exploration of tacit personal metaphors of teaching at the other (e.g. section 8.2).

In this section we try to tease out the main purposes and forms of reflection in teacher learning. We distinguish them by considering reflection in terms of function: *'on what; and for what purpose'*, and draw on certain 'parent theories' as framing different notions of reflection. They are as follows:

- Dewey: his view of reflective thinking underpins notions of delibera-tive thought; he sees disciplined deliberative thinking as a basis for personal development and citizenship.
- Schön: 'the idea that professionals engage in reflective conversations with practical situations, where they constantly frame and reframe a problem as they work on it, testing out their interpretations and solu-tions' (Calderhead and Gates, 1993: 1).
- Kolb: the notion that individuals personalise public knowledge through experience and reflection.
- Constructivism: public knowledge is reconstructed as each individual represents it internally; new learning requires the reconstruction of current knowledge: all learning is relearning.
- Lortie: teachers' responses to LTE will be affected by idiosyncratic images of teaching, which though powerful are also not readily acces-sible to critical analysis (section 2.2.1).

Given the diversity of meanings, background theories and contexts of LTE design, it is not surprising that 'reflection' and 'reflective teacher education' mean so many different things to different people. Context particularly affects the way 'reflection' is construed. For example, in the case of a centralised cur-riculum innovation the purposes of reflection might be seen as: a) to uncover current practices and beliefs, as they may support or block the adoption of practices as planned; and b) to promote self-monitoring to ensure the delivery of a new curriculum as intended. In contrast, in the context of an open-ended developmental approach, the purpose of reflection might instead be to uncover current routines and modes of thinking, but for the teacher herself to assess the need for change in terms of their utility to her and to her teaching objectives.

Types of reflection

We summarise different concepts of reflection in terms of purpose, context, sample activities and 'parent theory'. We do not try to organise these into a framework, because we have no wish to suggest a hierarchy of importance or a necessary sequence in which they should take place.

Purpose: raise awareness of personal images of teaching

To uncover the influence of personal experience of instruction, tacit influences on one's ways of thinking and behaving in class from past school experience.
Context: Particularly suitable in initial LTE.
Activity: Reflective autobiography e.g. snakes; autobiographical letters; role play.
Theory: It is necessary to become aware of one's own socialisation into teaching to be released from it (Lortie, Griffiths and Tann; social constructivist view).

Purpose: raise awareness of one's personal theories, values and beliefs

To uncover beliefs beneath routine actions; to enable critical awareness of one's own established practice and assess its appropriateness to teaching goals.
Context: Work with experienced teachers, particularly in dialogue with fellow teachers and a trained facilitator; either for individual development or to cope with imposed changes.
Activity: A range of 'uncovering' activities: repertory grid; mind maps, structured conversations with supervisors; exploration of metaphors and images (Pennington, 1990; Wright, 1990; Denicolo and Pope, 1993; section 8.2).
Theory: the constructivist view that awareness of implicit beliefs is a prerequisite for personal change (Argyris and Schön, 1974; Griffiths and Tann, 1992).

Purpose: reflect on one's own language learning style

To identify one's own style as a language learner and uncover one's assumptions about language; to explore connections between oneself as a learner and one's practice as a teacher; to contrast one's learning style with those of one's students.
Context: In either ITE or INSET situations; particularly suitable for non-native speakers to explore their own experience of learning the second language (L2).
Activity: Recall incidents from your own L2 learning and contrast them with those of fellow teachers; contrast one's learning style with those of students.
Theory: Constructivist view that we need awareness of our assumptions about L2 learning; the view that teachers assume that pupils share their approach to L2 learning (Kagan, 1992); Kolb's view that we develop our personal theories by analysing our experiences.

Purpose: raise awareness of one's current performance as a learner (e.g. study skills)

To improve effectiveness of modes of study by becoming more aware of one's habits in formal learning and one's personal strengths and weaknesses.

Context: Any course of study.

Activity: Make a detailed record of one's conduct of a recent learning activity (e.g. reading a text, making notes, using references); identification of patterns of behaviour and contrast with peers; assessment of patterns that may be dysfunctional.

Theory: Constructivist view that awareness of unconscious patterns enables development (Thomas and Hari-Augstein, 1985).

Purpose: develop ability to analyse teaching situations

To become aware of classroom interactions/learner experiences which are normally not attended to while teaching. To bring further variables to attention in deliberative thinking about teaching.

Context: ITE: necessary to develop novice teachers' conceptual systems and vocabulary to discuss teaching.

Activity: Structured observation and description (Wajnryb, 1993).

Theory: Constructivism and observational learning.

Purpose: recall and analyse new and recent learning experiences

To provide teachers with direct experience of learning processes and task types new to them.

Context: Either ITE or INSET where new activities are to be presented; as a complement to observed models; particularly suited to direct language learning experience.

Activity: Direct language instruction: analysis and discussion of rationales and contrasts between different teaching strategies; 'loop-input': analysis and discussion of modes of instruction that illustrate general principles in language teaching (Woodward, 1990).

Theory: Direct personal experience is necessary to comprehend theoretical input and to develop one's own representation of a theory (constructivism and experiential learning theory).

Purpose: review and assess your own actions in class

To become more aware of variables that affect planning, problem-solving, analysis of situations, evaluation and conscious decision-making.

Context: ITE: clinical supervision procedures (5.2); student teacher self-assessment (6.2); INSET: collaborative curriculum inquiry (case studies 8.2–8.5); formal coaching (section 2.4.5).

Activity: recall incidents e.g. by using on-the-spot data collection such as note-taking or from simple recall; assess one's teaching according to course criteria; discussion with supervisors and peers (ITE). In INSET, self-assessment according to one's goals and personal theories; discussion with peers or facilitator (e.g. sections 8.3 and 8.4).

Theory: The view that effective teachers are capable of self-evaluation; that this is developed by improving awareness of one's practice and of criteria for self-evaluation (Dewey, 1910; Day *et al.*, 1987); Kolb's view that we develop our theories by analysing direct personal experiences.

Purpose: raise awareness of one's routines and their rationale

To become aware of one's habitual actions in class; to contrast these with new training inputs or a centrally imposed curriculum change; or to assess the effectiveness of these actions in getting learners to where you want them to be.

Context: Suited to established teachers who have developed classroom routines.

Activity: Structured recall and discussion activities; feedback from others on one's current practice (e.g. section 8.6).

Theory: Dewey's view of reflection as leading to personal development; Schön's identification of 'theory in action' inherent in patterns of professional practice; the notion that people 'do not know what they know' (Argyris and Schön, 1974; Eraut, 1994).

Purpose: test the consistency between classroom events and educational theories

To try to interpret theoretical frameworks and concepts in terms of classroom incidents; to understand and personalise the meaning of theoretical propositions; to test the relevance of theories to the classroom.

Context: Formal courses where theory (readings, lectures etc) is presented to teachers (ITE or INSET).

Activity: Structured presentations (e.g. seminars) or formal writing (assignments) in which a theory is applied to classroom events to assess the relevance and truthfulness of the theory (e.g. section 6.3; Wallace, 1996).

Theory: Experiential learning theory; social constructivism.

Purpose: become able to reframe interpretations of one's practice

To become increasingly disposed to view professional problems from more than one standpoint, to see problem-solving as involving reframing as well as reaching good technical solutions

Context: Professional development with the help of skilled facilitator.

Activity: Reflective conversations and reflective writing; collaborative curriculum inquiry with skilled facilitator; action research with rigorous use of feedback and evaluative data to support critical discussion (section 8.3).

Theory: Constructivist models of professional development in terms of a developing ability to reframe situations (Dewey, 1910; Argyris and Schön, 1974; Argyris *et al.*, 1985).

Purpose: become aware of the social and political significance of one's work

To become aware of the political, social and institutional conditions that affect our teaching; to assess the social and political meaning of one's work.
Context: Developing professional and social awareness of experienced teachers.
Activity: Structured discussions and writing (e.g. Bartlett, 1990).
Theory: Critical theory: a teacher's development should include an awareness of the impact of social forces and interests on one's work (Carr and Kemmis, 1986).

Issues in reflective activities

Experience in using reflective activities suggest the following issues and conditions for effective learning (e.g. Calderhead, 1987a; Valli, 1992; Griffiths and Tann, 1992; Calderhead and Gates, 1993).

(i)   Salient and recent experiences are likely to be better remembered. They are therefore a better basis for reflective thinking than distant experiences, unless the person identifies these as particularly significant.

(ii) Personal dispositions to be reflective seem to vary, with some student-teachers and experienced teachers naturally more ready to deliberate on their own actions and beliefs. This may be due to such factors as personality differences or levels of commitment to the occupation, or the value they give to their own knowledge as compared to general theory and expert opinion.

(iii) As reflection implies imminent self-disclosure and change, the person has to be in a good shape to address ideas central to the self. Some individuals might be at a point in their personal lives such that they just cannot face potential destabilisation in their work. Similarly, many ITE students are so concerned with self-presentation that they will resist reflection on difficult areas. In the same way, experienced teachers may be unwilling to risk unsettling routines that cope with the work.

(iv) Some forms of reflection require an adequate base of experience and knowledge. For example, ITE students may lack the specialised concepts and vocabulary to link personal and public knowledge (Tann, 1993). Similarly, reflection on personal theories presupposes that the person has already crystallised systematic beliefs about teaching. There are good reasons to question whether novice teachers, at the early stages, have yet built up personal ways of working and personal theories of teaching to engage in such activities with any profit.

(v) It seems that growth through reflection is very difficult to achieve unless there is a social or collective element to it. A trusted and interested listener and critic provide best conditions for rethinking and self-assessment. A collective process gives individuals the impetus to work through critical reflection (Lewin, 1946, in Kemmis, 1982; Easen, 1985; Cline et al., 1990). Therefore facilitators should try to establish positive preconditions before introducing reflective activities, for example by team-building, and the design of structures enabling long-term contact and support (sections 6.2, 8.2, 8.5 and 8.6).

(vi) Assessment seems to be inimical to any form of reflection that requires the disclosure of weaknesses. Assessment demands the meeting of external requirements and the disguise of personal weaknesses; neither condition is productive of reflection on aspects of self in need of change. There is also an associated danger that learner-teachers will interpret reflective developmental tasks as imposed course requirements, with no real meaning for themselves.

(vii) It is still unclear how student-teachers and experienced teachers can be best prepared to reflect (for any of the purposes outlined above). However, it seems clear that a focus on genuine teaching concerns, and genuine control over process, are two important conditions (Day et al., 1987): 'most of the texts on action research and reflective practice contain implicit (sometimes explicit) messages about suitable topics for reflection. It is probable that such topics would only coincide with any particular teacher's own personal theories by good luck. Yet reflection on one's *own* ... theories is precisely what distinguishes the reflective practitioner model' (Griffiths and Tann, 1992: 73).

(viii)The ITE or INSET programme cannot operate independently of the teachers' school context. Some school cultures (those with a hierarchical power structure and a privatist climate) may be inherently inimical to reflective thinking, because there are no opportunities for discussion, and because there are powerful sanctions against destabilising an institution committed to maintaining stability and continuity (Schön, 1983: 329). Teachers may therefore need to take time out away from school if they are to rethink their practice (sections 8.2, 8.4 and 8.5).

(ix) Reflective activity is difficult: 'the difficulties attendant on discovering personal theories are rarely given more than scant attention' (Griffiths and Tann, 1992: 72). Encouraging another person to recall and assess their practice and then uncover tacit beliefs requires considerable interpersonal skills: they include emotional empathy, attending skills and tactful probing skills. The process needs to be carefully structured, with step-by-step focus and analysis (e.g. Appendices 7.4 and 8.5; Denicolo and Pope, 1990). In a study on portfolios as a tool for reflective thinking, Wade and Yarbrough (1996) concluded that the process stimulated reflective thinking in some students, and that a number of strategies would best prompt it: attending to student-teachers' understanding of the process; encouraging ownership and individual expression; some structuring, and evaluating process.

(x)   It would be wrong to assume that any piece of classroom practice can be explored to uncover personal theories. Many routines are carried through without the teacher attending to them or are done as 'borrowed' routines with no investment by the person, what Maingay (1980) referred to a rituals (section 3.2.2). This would be particularly true in the case of language teaching routines taken from ITE or the textbook, or activities that are school conventions (e.g. reading aloud in turn). This would also be the case for teachers who, for whatever reason, base their practice rigidly on available materials or school conventions: they represent their personal theories only to the extent that the teacher has accepted external norms and routines.

(xi) It is possible that some reflective activities in LTE have been less than effective because they have been attempted in isolation rather than within concerted cycles of related activities integrating input, private critical reflection, awareness of personal theories and practices, critical discussion, and experimentation (sections 1.1.5 and 4.3). Our case studies illustrate this integration, either as implicit in programme structure (6.2 and 8.2) or in specific activity cycles (sections 8.3 and 8.6).

Appendix 1.1   A teacher's personal theories: an example (Kettle and Sellars, 1996: 16)

Janice's practical theory, 1992

Janice's overriding principles:

Teachers 'act as co-ordinator of resources (*and show students how to access these resources*) to me that is the ultimte aim with teaching'

Within this framework – utilise a hands-on approach – *modify the strategies to suit the situation.*

Encourage enquiry	Exchange ideas	Make kids feel they're important	Work from children's own knowledge base
• adopt a hands-on approach • involve students physically with what they are doing • encourage students to work it out for themselves • set out resources with directions on how to do it and let students try and 'break through' the problem • encourage students to ask the questions – 'Why is that happening?' 'What happens if you do it this way?' • instil in children an enthusiasm for what they are doing • have students complete projects on particular topics • students should tell the other children what they have done • sometimes you can't use an inquiry approach you just have to show them what to do • *use open questions to get children to think about things*	• be approachable • interact with children • assist children in their interactions with each other • exchange ideas at different levels – between teacher and students – between student and student • utilise group as well as whole class work • show children how to access resources	• use their experiences and ideas • use resources they are interested in • take time with them • be approachable • be warm and open to their ideas • be fair and make exceptions for how children are • use praise • try and find the positive side of things • use peer tutoring	• understand where the children are at • help them realise that the knowledge they bring to class is important • help them build on that knowledge base • provide experiences and resources to take them that little bit further

Note: Italicised components are additions made by Janice in the second semester, 1992.

2

Research on learning to teach: from pupil to established teacher

2.1 Introduction
2.1.1 Using research

2.2 Classroom culture: some examples

2.3 The pupil
2.3.1 What do pupils learn about teaching?
The apprenticeship of observation: images of effective teachers
Implications

2.4 The student-teacher
2.4.1 What do student-teachers *not* know?
2.4.2 Who enters teaching?
Recruitment and diversity
2.4.3 How do student-teachers react to input?
Filtering
Perception of self as competent
Stability and ITE interventions
Dependence on personal experience
What are student-teachers' concerns?
Stages of concern
Role transition
How do student-teachers react to reflective tasks?
2.4.4 Effective skills training
2.4.5 Conventional ITE courses: a fractured curriculum
Supervision: the 'triad'
2.4.6 How does student-teacher thinking develop?
2.4.7 What are the implications for ITE design?
Implications for activities
ITE structures: Partnership schemes
Providers' expectations

2.5 The new language teacher
2.5.1 How does a new teacher's thinking develop?

Self and the school
A tendency to privatism
2.5.2   What do new teachers learn about their subject?
2.5.3   What are the concerns of a new teacher?
2.5.4   What does ITE contribute?
'Marginal teachers'
2.5.5   What are the implications for a new teacher?

2.6   **Learning as an established teacher**
2.6.1   How do adults learn?
2.6.2   What is effective INSET?
General principles
Successful planned change
2.6.3   Three INSET strategies
Courses
Coaching
Curriculum development projects
2.6.4   Non-native speaker language teachers
2.6.5   What are the implications for INSET design?
INSET as process
Summary

2.1   Introduction

This chapter offers a selective summary of research on teacher learning and its implications for LTE design, drawing on research from general education and language teaching.

In section 2.2 we provide some examples of the relationship between culture, classroom norms and LTE. The rest of the chapter follows the working life of a teacher as s/he moves from one social context to another: pupil, student-teacher, new teacher, established teacher.

This division into stages does not suggest that they should be segregated. The teacher stays the same person. S/he brings her accumulated experience, skills, knowledge and expectations to each new situation. For that reason, what is relevant to one stage continues to be relevant for the rest of a teacher's career. A language teacher moves from one situation to another with an accumulated personal history just as does a child on its first day at school. For example, the apprenticeship of observation (section 2.3.1), or the interaction with school culture (2.5.1) will influence a teacher's development in the long term, not only at one stage. We therefore stress the evolutionary nature of teacher learning. As Denicolo and Pope (1990: 164) commented on teacher thinking:

> William James likened the mind and consciousness to a rope made up of
> many threads which if cut across would give a false impression of its

construction. One needs to follow the threads over time to gain insight into the structure of the rope.

Two important aspects of LTE which could have appeared here are discussed in Chapter 5 as they are of special relevance to ITE providers' roles: supervision (section 5.2) and assessment (section 5.3).

2.1.1   Using research

There is much we do not know about learning to teach. Incomplete as it is, it is better to work from knowledge that is well grounded rather than from paradigms that oversimplify (see section 3.3.5). As Calderhead (1990: 154) observes:

> The paradigms, slogans and beliefs that we use to justify particular approaches to teacher education contrast sharply with the complex picture of learning to teach that is currently emerging from research on student teachers and on comparisons of experienced and inexperienced teachers.

However, when using research it is essential to keep in mind the social and political context in which it has been done. In the case of research in the USA, UK and Europe we should be very cautious in generalising it to other contexts.

2.2   Classroom culture: some examples

Classroom culture studies have illuminated relationships between culture and classroom norms (e.g. Philips, 1972; Phillips and Owens, 1986; Malvankar, 1988; Omokhodion, 1989; Rowell and Prophet, 1990; Kramsch and Sullivan, 1996). In her classic study, Philips was able to explain the nonparticipation of Native American children by identifying culture-specific modes of learning which relied on observation of elders and practice in secret rather than questioning and skill rehearsal in public. As another example, Malvankar (1988) reports strategies teachers used to cope with difficult conditions such as loose school organisation, limited time for exposure to the language by formal instruction, and frequent absenteeism. They coped by using class time to ensure the delivery of information for examinations: dictation, rote learning, dependence on written assignments and the required acquiescence of students. Students coped by private tuition, rote learning, and, it is hinted, what an outsider would condemn as cheating but students saw as necessary in a system stacked against them. He concludes (1988: 253):

> teachers' ... strategies in the classroom have to be seen in response to societal constraints, mediated through the institution, namely the school,

and not just a matter of situational adjustment by individual teachers for their personal survival.

ELT teachers have long been aware of cultural diversity (e.g. West, 1960). As an issue, cultural identity has come to be of special importance as economic globalisation in the medium of English has led to a reassertion of national, regional and ethnic identities. The resulting debate on the ownership of English, English varieties and the respective status of the LI and English has led to arguments for culturally appropriate pedagogy (Widdowson, 1994; Lamb, 1995; Hyde, 1995; Bisong, 1995; Ellis, 1996) embodied in the notion of local solutions for local problems (e.g. Bose, 1996, on positive strategies to use 'bazaar notes'). This awareness has also stimulated research into ELT classroom culture. Recent small-scale studies have illuminated such areas as teacher and pupil expectations (Richards and Lockhart, 1994: 52–56, 108) while Kramsch and Sullivan (1996) provide interesting insights into classrooms in Vietnam, characterised by such notions as learning group as family, the supportive and collective orientation of pupils, teacher as moral mentor, and language learning as play.

Not only do we need to understand the effects of cultural background on classrooms, but also its impact on perceptions of training. For example, Phillips and Owens (1986) found that in spite of apparent acceptance of practical training, a group of Indonesian teachers did not implement it. They ascribed this in part to cultural taboos that prevented teachers from giving feedback to the expatriate 'experts' about their inputs, because it would affront 'face' and authority.

Saka (1995) shows that the secondary-school teachers in her study construed teacherless tasks quite differently from outsider-consultants. While the received view of teacherless tasks is that they enable greater pupil practice time and a degree of creativity, the teachers perceived them as a management problem. They characterised pair work in such terms as 'difficult to give feedback; noisy; less control; difficult to manage; out of order; discipline is a problem; I can't use the blackboard' while also noting that the 'administration asks us to use it very often'. They perceived these activities as problematic and imposed on them by central authorities.

These examples suggest that as providers we need to understand teachers and students *in their own terms* before we make any attempt to introduce change. Classroom studies greatly benefit LTE design and provider awareness, because they show the discrepancies in 'ways of looking' that can exist between teachers and those responsible for the introduction of change, which if ignored can vitiate LTE schemes (see Lamb, 1995, and section 2.6.2). They suggest the need for both providers and learner-teachers to be aware of the culturally determined aspects of their role perceptions and behaviour, so that they can be explored openly, not merely set aside as 'constraints' (Hyde, 1995; Salmon, 1995).

2.3   The pupil

2.3.1   What do pupils learn about teaching?

The apprenticeship of observation: images of effective teachers

We all have personal theories about the characteristics of teachers, classrooms and schools. Initially, these are built from incidents we experience during our 'apprenticeship of observation', the thousands of hours we have spent in classrooms (Lortie, 1975). Lortie observed that pupils are exposed to teaching as no other occupation: they may spend some 15,000 hours in 'protracted face to face consequential interactions with established teachers' (1975: 61) which they never do with other occupations. He notes the power of this experience. It is close up: pupils and teachers are physically very close and confined. It is also charged with affect: interaction with a teacher has important consequences for pupils. They rely on the teacher for approval and good grades, and this encourages them to get in the teacher's shoes to the extent that can get what they want, 'to engage in at least enough empathy to anticipate the teacher's probable reaction to his behaviour' (1975: 62).

However, Lortie comments that pupils' images of teaching are incomplete because they do not experience their teachers' private thoughts, only their public face:

> They assess teachers on a wide variety of personal and student oriented bases, but only partially in terms of criteria shared with their teacher and with teachers in general. It is improbable that many students learn to see teaching in an ends-means frame or that they normally take an analytic stance toward it. Students are undoubtedly impressed by some teacher actions and not by others, but one would not expect them to view the differences in a pedagogical explanatory way. *What students learn about teaching, then, is intuitive and imitative rather than explicit and analytical; it is based on individual personalities rather than pedagogical principles.*
>
> (Lortie, 1975: 62; our italics)

This suggests that we come to ITE with personal theories built from images of teachers but that owing to 'the unreflective nature of prior socialisation' (Lortie, 1975: 71), these images may act as an obstacle to ITE interventions:

> The student's learning about teaching ... is more a matter of imitation, which, being generalised across individuals becomes tradition. It is a potentially powerful influence which transcends generations but the conditions of transfer do not favour informed criticism, attention to specifics, or explicit rules of assessment. (1975: 63)

Implications

An ITE programme should not leave the 'apprenticeship of observation' unexamined. Student-teachers need to recall and explore their personal images of teaching, not because they are inherently wrong but because they are tacit, and 'not likely to instil a sense of the problematics of teaching' (Lortie, 1975: 65). Similarly, many teachers engaged in INSET may have gone through ITE programmes where their personal models of teaching have not been uncovered or questioned.

Working from tacit images imprisons the teacher in a single frame of reference, which may be inappropriate to the curriculum with which s/he has to work now or in future. Therefore it would seem important to raise teachers' awareness of the power of their own experiences as learners. Awareness of one's own apprenticeship of observation is therefore one form of reflective ITE activity, by such means as biographical writing or visualisation and discussion (e.g. Denicolo and Pope, 1990; James, forthcoming; case studies in sections 6.2 and 8.2; Appendices 7.4 and 8.1). This process would seem to be essential to escape from potentially limiting images of teaching.

The test of these personal images is not whether they are inherently 'right or wrong' according to an outsider's perceptions, but the extent to which they are useful for the teacher. For example, teachers required to work in a communicative curriculum may be hindered by personal images of good directive teachers. On the other hand, should the same teacher be asked to present information to peers in a formal setting, these same images of effective transmission teaching could be helpful, because they are appropriate to the task at hand.

2.4   The student-teacher

2.4.1   What do student-teachers *not* know?

By exploring differences between novices and more experienced teachers (Calderhead, 1987a; Berliner, 1987; Bromme, 1987; Carter and Doyle, 1987; Olson and Eaton, 1987; Wilson *et al.*, 1987), the deficits in novice teachers' knowledge appear to include:

- novice teachers' perceptions of classroom events are relatively undiscriminating and simpler than those of experienced teachers;
- they are less able to select which information is salient when planning a lesson;
- they lack 'typificatory knowledge' (Calderhead, 1987a: 7) i.e. what to expect of pupils, what challenges to set and what difficulties to anticipate;
- they tend to work from the textbook rather than in terms of pupil attainment levels;

- they lack practical classroom management routines to keep pupils on task;
- their concern with control makes it difficult for them to focus on pupil learning;
- they lack an established teacher's 'pedagogic content knowledge' (section 2.5.2);
- they lack the practical experience from which to construct personal meanings for theoretical or specialised terms;
- they lack a coherent system of concepts with which to think about teaching;
- they lack a specialised vocabulary with which to analyse and discuss teaching.

Information on student language teachers is limited but we can assume that they share the characteristics of teachers in general. We speculate that discipline-specific deficits may be related to language, in such areas as:

- their performance levels in the target language (TL), as matched against the level required for accreditation;
- analytic knowledge of TL systems;
- assumptions about the nature of language and about the TL as a school subject (perceptions which could be skewed towards function, form or content).

These deficits suggest the need for ITE programmes to provide, along with conventional skill practice, planning in real contexts, activities focused on the learner, and the interpretation of personal experience (see sections 2.4.7, 6.2 and 6.3).

2.4.2   Who enters teaching?

Recruitment and diversity

Conditions of entry to teaching are certain to affect the occupational culture of any group of teachers, with effects on their expectations of and reactions to LTE (see section 1.1.4). While Lortie's (1975) study is specific to its time and place, it does suggest variables which may also apply to language teachers. These include differing attractions to teaching (e.g. material or service orientated); social influences on entry (such as parental pressure on daughters; people entering from a first career they have found uncongenial; those who have taken a teachers' course as second best after failing professional entrance); and the tendency for any particular group to be skewed in terms of gender, class, age range, or education.

We are unaware of comparable research specific to language teaching, and so can only speculate on the effects on LTE of teachers' entry. For example, we can speculate that the choice to go into teaching in private language schools may be made because the person does not want to identify with conventional school norms. If so, s/he may be more disposed to innovation than those in Lortie's study, who tended to display conservative attitudes. Similarly, s/he may be less orientated to a 'cellular' and hierarchical view of teacher work than in conventional schools, and more orientated to experimental and collaborative forms of teacher development activity. On the other hand, if teachers enter the private sector as a means to travel or live abroad for a relatively short period, then they may see personal development as lying in areas other than teaching. Thus we expect that the motivations and conditions affecting entry to language teaching will affect teachers' orientations to ITE and INSET.

2.4.3   How do student-teachers react to input?

Filtering

The 'apprenticeship of observation' leads to the mediation of ITE inputs by our personal theories of teaching (Lortie, 1975; Zeichner and Grant, 1981; Tabachnik and Zeichner, 1984; Zeichner et al., 1987; Calderhead and Robson, 1991; Kagan, 1992). Student-teachers enter ITE with beliefs about teaching based on images of good teachers they know, experiences as pupils and images of self as language teacher. These personal theories inevitably 'provoke questions about their receptiveness to instruction in pedagogy' (Lortie, 1975: 66), and it is widely suggested that learner-teachers *filter* ITE inputs. In a major research review, Kagan (1992) concludes that 'each study documented the central role played by pre-existing beliefs/images and prior experience in filtering the content of education course work. . . . These studies introduce a theme that echoes throughout the remaining sections of this review: the important role played by a novice's image of self as teacher' (Kagan, 1992: 140).

Kagan (1992: 145) also suggested that student-teachers will assume that pupils share their approach to learning:

> In constructing images of teachers, novices may extrapolate (albeit unconsciously) from their own experience as learners, in essence, assuming that their pupils will possess learning styles, aptitudes, interests, and problems similar to their own. This may partially explain why novice's images of pupils are usually inaccurate.

Therefore Kagan argues for the need to develop student-teachers' insight into pupils' perceptions by such means as classroom studies and learner feedback (e.g. Appendix 7.4).

Stability and ITE interventions

The notion of filtering has led to a view that ITE programmes have a comparatively limited impact on student-teachers. In her survey of ITE research, Kagan concluded that: 'Each study . . . testified to the stability and inflexibility of prior beliefs and images' (Kagan, 1992: 140). Implicit beliefs, values and practices, it is believed, tend to prevail over programme interventions, 'regardless of the underlying conception of teaching or philosophy of the training course' (Tann, 1993: 55). This has led to a widely held view that, as Zeichner *et al.*, suggest, 'preservice programs are not very powerful interventions' (1987: 28). Similarly McIntyre comments that, 'whether we like it or not, interns [students] will make their own judgements about what matters in teaching and about how best they can teach' (1988: 106).

This strong view implies that input and classroom experience alone are necessary but not sufficient to influence student-teacher thinking. Other interventions are needed to free them from tacit images of teaching:

- the uncovering and analysis of these images;
- access to others' perspectives on concrete and shared teaching incidents (as in analysing videos of teaching);
- direct experience as an L2 learner (see also section 5.1; case studies in sections 8.2 and 8.5).

Dependence on personal experience

A few recent studies suggest that some student-teachers only perceive ITE inputs as learnt once they have been experienced personally. This does not devalue input but suggests that direct experience is needed to personalise abstract knowledge:

> students from the beginning expected to learn by trying things out ... the reason for this emphasis on learning from their own teaching seemed to be that however much they had read or observed things on a conceptual level ... they did not say they had learnt until learning became personal through their own teaching.
>
> (Haggerty, 1995b: 43)

This is supported by Sendan (1995b) who showed that students' personal theories tended to converge when following courses but then to diverge after teaching practice, probably because experience caused them to develop their personal theories in individually different ways. Both studies seem to confirm the relevance of activities derived from experiential constructivist principles and justify the integration of abstract and practical course components (sections 1.1.5, 2.4.7, 4.3, 6.2, 6.3).

What are student-teachers' concerns?

It is widely believed that student-teachers enter training with priorities which need to be resolved before they can address other aspects of their course (McIntyre, 1988). In other words, they attend to course input seriously only when it fits their own agenda or when they are alerted by a need to know (Haggerty, 1995a).

Their concerns typically focus on threats to their self-esteem in meeting new role demands, such as failing to manage a class and being seen to lose control. Also, they may fear poor grades and the low esteem of staff and peers. These priorities often produce coping strategies designed to minimise risk and loss of face. As a result student-teachers may use failsafe activities to keep control (e.g. dictation, revision, structured writing) and standard 'display' lessons to satisfy supervisors (Turney *et al.*, 1982; Wragg, 1982). Interestingly, self-defence strategies are used both by successful student-teachers, who will not want to play about with a successful formula, and the weaker ones, who will use control and display techniques to mask their difficulties.

McIntyre (1988: 110) argues that these concerns must be addressed to free up the student-teacher for further development:

> in their new professional contexts many interns will need to be convinced that they are competent as teachers and are recognised as being competent before they will have the sense of security necessary to examine their teaching objectively and openly in relation to their own aspirations as educators.

It is commonly suggested that coping strategies obstruct attention to pupil learning: 'their inadequate knowledge of classroom procedures also appears to prevent novice teachers from focusing on what pupils are learning from academic tasks. Instead, working memory is devoted to monitoring their own behaviour as they attempt to imitate or invent workable procedures' (Kagan, 1992: 145; also McIntyre, 1988).

Perception of self as competent

Many student-teachers are concerned with threats to their self-esteem. However, in a context such as an elite and strictly screened course, the general standard of student-teachers can be much better than average teachers in school. For example, Sendan (1995b) found that some students rated themselves as close to their personal image of 'most effective teacher' and by implication as much more competent than run-of-the-mill secondary-school teachers. Such a self-concept could act as an obstacle to development, because it offers little motivation to change.

Stages of concern

In the past, novice teachers' coping strategies have been used to justify stage theories of teacher learning, deriving from Piaget's model of discrete sequential stages in children's conceptual development. They argued that teacher learning is essentially sequential in nature, passing through a series of stages of concern: from a concern with survival; to a focus on teaching situations; to a focus on the learner, and learner differences (Fuller and Brown, 1975; Berliner, 1988; Kagan, 1992). It was argued that it was necessary to resolve needs at one stage to be able to progress to the next, as in Piaget's model of child development (Roth, 1990).

Student-teachers' concerns should be addressed to help them survive in class but this does not commit us to a 'stage' model of student-teacher development. Stage theories are too inflexible to account for such a complex process as learning to teach, which we suggest is not linear or compartmentalised but essentially cumulative and multidimensional. It seems more likely that at any time a student-teacher will have high-priority concerns but these will vary according to the task at hand (classroom-based or course-based), nor will lower-priority concerns necessarily be excluded from their thinking altogether (Sendan, 1995b). Also, there is no need to abandon attention to future concerns: the ITE student needs wider perspectives than exclusive attention to immediate, often highly practical issues.

Additionally, stage theories are too simplistic to serve as a guide to design because each student's concerns will vary; they will tend to address their own priorities and so at any one time they may be out of step with each other and the 'official' syllabus sequence.

This view suggests that initial survival skill courses should be complemented with broader perspectives, such as the analysis of different teaching styles. It also suggests that ITE programmes need to be capable of some individualisation (see year structure and assessment in section 6.2).

Role transition

Student-teachers are engaged in a dramatic role change from pupil to teacher, from dependant to adult. Given their recent experience as pupils in school, it is not surprising that they sometimes exhibit tensions and difficulties of identification. This is suggested by the tendency of some student-teachers to identify more closely with pupils than experienced staff. Because they are closer in age, some student-teachers may find positional authority relationships difficult to carry out (Wragg, 1982). This may also explain their sometimes uneasy relationships with mentors, which may be because they cannot as yet relate to them as peers (Turney et al., 1982a; Wragg, 1982; Haggerty, 1995).

Also, Wragg (1982) reports that student-teachers exhibit high stress levels and emotional ups and downs. This is common among HEI students in general but can also be related to the nature of student-teachers' change in role, and their concerns with classroom survival.

How do student-teachers react to reflective tasks?

Many ITE courses now include reflective tasks, such as autobiographical writing and self-assessment. Empirical evidence on student-teachers' responses to reflective activities is still limited, not least because of the ambiguity over what a reflective task is (see section 1.2.3; Calderhead, 1987a; Valli, 1992; Griffiths and Tann, 1993). However, there is practical experience that student-teachers vary considerably in their readiness to reflect on their personal theories. Also, there is some evidence that survival concerns may militate against risk-taking and the admission of difficulties: novices are unlikely to question their assumptions while they are still establishing routines, the more so in dialogue with assessors (Calderhead, 1987a). This suggests that reflection on practices and beliefs requires the person to have established some secure routines to reflect on in the first place.

It has also been observed that reflective conversations are sometimes hampered by experienced teachers' difficulty in talking about their own teaching (Griffiths and Tann, 1992; Haggerty, 1995b; also section 6.2).

2.4.4 Effective skills training

We define training as a TE activity led by convergent objectives for the development of skills, behaviours and strategies defined by an external norm or standard. The key issue in training is not whether it is ideologically desirable. Teachers, as in any other occupation, may need training at any point in their career. The test of training is whether it is seen to be used in the active repertoire of teachers in school and whether this contributes to improved language education.

Research has identified conditions for effective skill training which can be generalised to ITE or INSET. Joyce and Showers (1980; 1984) suggest them to be:

- a close match between conditions of training and those of actual use;
- unambiguous description of skill;
- demonstration or modelling of skill;
- establish the basic skills before going on to finer tuning;
- optimal practice time;
- individual skill-focused feedback on task performance;
- multiple contexts of demonstration and use.

Apart from these essentially behaviourist principles, Joyce and Showers also argue for positive cognitive and contextual conditions for training to be effective:

- understanding of principles underlying behavioural skills (by means of reading or lectures);
- the availability of coaching after training: 'hands-on, in-classroom assistance with the transfer of skills and strategies to the classroom' (Joyce and Showers in Hopkins, 1984: 292).

The attention given to teacher thinking and conceptual change in the past decade should not lead us to ignore basic principles of effective skills training, which incorporate behavioural, cognitive and contextual dimensions (sections 1.1.5, 2.4.4 and 8.6).

2.4.5   Conventional ITE courses: a fractured curriculum

Conventional state system ITE design has often been based on a two–part structure: relatively abstract courses in the higher education institution (HEI) and short blocks of teaching practice in schools. This structure contributed to a serious lack of integration between abstract and practical course components (Stones and Morris, 1972; Lortie, 1975; Department of Education and Science, 1982; 1983; Turney, 1986; Chisholm *et al.*, 1986; McIntyre, 1988; Sendan, 1995b). We summarise the major problems as follows.

At the HEI	*At school*
Vague objectives	
Statements of objectives and criteria of teaching competence were ambiguous or absent	
A fractured curriculum	
Student finds educational theory provided in the HEI irrelevant to school tasks	Student has no opportunity try out proposals from HEI courses
	Student does not know what to look for when observing experienced teachers
	Student meets conflicting values and practices but cannot analyse or synthesise them: HEI proposals may be denigrated by school staff as impractical
	Student is a transient presence in school with no standing or responsibility
Role relationships	
HEI supervisors	*Co-operating teachers*
They design and control the course without input from effective teachers	No participation in course design
Lack of credibility: no recent teaching experience so cannot offer credible assistance with practical concerns	High credibility challenges the standing of HEI staff with student-teachers

HEI supervisors (cont.)

Tutor as 'passing cloud': cannot visit often enough to have influence over students in school

Infrequency of visits limits function to assessment only

Dependence on schools for practical curriculum

Co-operating teachers (cont.)

A free hand in students' practical curriculum

As supervisors, they offer variable quality and quantity of observation, diagnostic feedback and curricular support

Not selected or trained according to an ability to explain their practice and so unable to make it available to student-teachers

Staff development needs

Denied the opportunity to relate theoretical concerns to practical cases

Denied development opportunities by access to up-to-date theory/ information on good practice

Student-teachers' learning opportunities

Reflection is theoretically orientated and not tied to a context

Too much time elapses between HEI input and school experiences

Courses offer no practical guidance on classroom management

Reflection is short-term and survival-orientated

Student has too few settings in which to reflect critically on own trial-and-error experiences

These failings provided guidelines for the design of partnership schemes (see sections 2.4.7 and 6.2).

Supervision: the 'triad'

Research on supervisor/student-teacher relationships suggests that in a *fractured curriculum* the student-teacher becomes part of a difficult triadic relationship: student-teacher/supervisor/cooperating teacher (Turney *et al.*, 1982a). Poor communication between HEI and school produces role confusion and inconsistent supervision criteria, leading student-teachers to cope by giving display lessons, withholding their difficulties, or siding with one party against another (see also section 5.2).

In more recent *school-based* designs (e.g. section 6.2) research suggests better integration between school and college curricula, and coherent linkage between theory and practice. However, there are continuing areas of difficulty in

student-teacher/supervisor relationships. In part these arise from organisational slippage which reduces time for exploratory discussion. Also, there is
some evidence of difficulty in attaining a key objective of partnership designs,
which is that experienced teachers share their pedagogic reasoning with student-teachers. There are some doubts about teachers' readiness to reveal their
thinking and also suggestions that there is a need for a match in personal theories between teacher-supervisors and students for them to have the necessary
common ground for discussions to be productive (Haggerty, 1995; Tillema,
1994; section 6.2).

2.4.6   How does student-teacher thinking develop?

There is still much ignorance about how people learn to teach, although it is
recognised as complex and individually variable (Calderhead, 1990).

Sendan (1995b) describes cognitive change in Turkish student teachers of
English. Their constructs on effective teachers, 'the teacher I want to be' and
'the teacher I am now', were elicited and change in their content and structure
measured over a period of 15 months. The findings are reported in detail elsewhere (Sendan, 1995a; 1995b; Sendan and Roberts, forthcoming; and section
1.1.3) but suggest the following:

- the content of student-teacher thinking changed gradually (i.e. relatively few new 'good teacher' attributes were added to their thinking);
- the structure of their thinking did change, i.e. there were changes in
  the way that particular constructs were associated with each other, so
  reflecting personal theory development;
- conceptual change seemed to be essentially evolutionary in nature,
  with pre-existing ideas undergoing reorganisation and discrimination;
- conceptual change was not simply linear; data suggested alternating
  cycles of stability and reorganisation as new ideas were incorporated or
  certain attributes changed in relative priority;
- however, there was evidence that their thinking became more organised thematically, suggesting more coherent construction of teaching;
- positive images ('most effective teacher I know') remained unchanged;
- 'the teacher I want to be' remained closely associated with this most
  effective teacher;
- teaching practice may cause dramatic changes in self-concept. For
  example, as a result of a difficult practicum one student re-rated himself negatively on the following attributes:
  - adequate in involving students;
  - good at transferring what he knows;
  - supplements textbooks with different materials;
  - motivates students;
  - directs students to thinking;

     – increases students' attention with jokes,

     – develops a desire for learning;

     however, while this student's view of himself had changed markedly, the attributes with which he construed effective teaching remained stable;

- direct personal experience tended to lead to less consensual thinking between students, whereas theoretical courses led groups towards consensus.

Thus a general picture emerged in which conceptual change was not a simple additive process but one in which existing ideas were progressively reorganised as a system. Changes were orientated by the 'compass points' of the perceived attributes of teachers known to the person.

2.4.7   What are the implications for ITE design?

We discuss the implications of sections 2.4.1–2.4.6 in terms of specific activities, the structure of courses; and supervisors' expectations. We would argue that a general insight from the research is that ITE should not be seen as merely a process of stocking up student teachers with a 'kit bag' of performance skills, but of developing a personal identity as teacher:

> the process of becoming a teacher ... must be viewed in relationship to biography and conceptions of self-as-teacher and to the teacher's entire life situation. ... The problem of finding oneself as a teacher, of establishing a professional identity, is conspicuously missing from most lists of beginning teachers' problems.
>
> (Bullough, 1990: 357)

Such a view recognises that learning to teach encompasses changes in thought, feeling, skills and in social identity.

Implications for activities

Awareness

Specialised language

Student-teachers lack a framework of specialised concepts and terms with which to analyse and discuss teaching, which suggests the following activities (see also sections 6.2 and 8.6):

- directed discrimination training or open-ended description and analysis activities (Fanselow, 1987; Maingay, 1988; Brown, 1990; Wajnryb, 1993; Sharkova, 1996; sections 6.3, 8.6);
- exploration of incidents and cases (e.g. Harington *et al.*, 1996).

Uncovering images

Personal images of teaching exert a powerful effect on student-teachers' beliefs (Lortie, 1975; Zeichner *et al.*, 1987; Kagan, 1992). Students and TE staff may 'talk past each other' because their conceptions of teaching may be framed in different ways. This suggests the following activities:

- uncovering personal theories and images by the use of metaphor (Appendix 8.1 and James, forthcoming); role analysis (Wright, 1990);
- comparison of actual and ideal circumstances (Pennington 1990);
- narratives (Cortazzi, 1993);
- concept mapping (Morine-Dershimer, 1993);
- biography (Denicolo and Pope, 1990; Appendix 7.4);
- rating scales (Karavas-Doukas, 1996);
- reflection linked to input (sections 5.2 and 8.6.2);
- repertory grid (Diamond, 1991; Belleli, 1993; Sendan, 1995b; Sendan and Roberts, forthcoming);
- classroom inquiry (e.g. Richards and Lockhart, 1994).

Need to change

All professional development depends upon a self-concept of being in need of change. This suggests:

- the need for early classroom experience to challenge assumptions and expectations;
- the availability of support when certainties are upset;
- the need to review and develop personal learning objectives throughout an ITE programme.

These features require a course structure which offers sufficient teaching practice and regular supervision (see section 6.2).

Privatism

Privatist occupational culture can inhibit development and professional effectiveness: 'Unless students in training can experience at least some sense of genuine collegiality – some sharing of technical problems and alternative solutions – they will be ill-prepared for such efforts when they work alongside one another' (Lortie, 1975: 66).

This prescient observation suggests that, unless ITE offers students opportunities for collegial, team-based teaching and explicit discussion of pedagogic alternatives, the cycle of privatism and unreflective teaching might be perpetuated: see the team/group organisation of student-teachers in section 6.2 (also Ashton *et al.*, 1989; Bailey, 1996; Newell, 1996).

Feelings

Priority concerns

Student-teachers are concerned with survival and maintaining self-esteem, which suggests:

- provision of support systems (regular tutor meetings, peer study groups etc.);
- a need for safe learning environments in the early stages, (e.g. graded teaching practice);
- anticipate *resistance* to reflective activities and to self-evaluation (Calderhead, 1987a);
- work with student-teachers on their own orientation to the course: 'the agendas of the learner-teachers are the major determinants of what they learn; *it is only through influencing these agendas and through responding to them that teacher educators can achieve their goals*' (McIntyre, 1988: 103; our italics).

The possibility of working with learner-teachers on their own sense of priorities depends very much on a course structure which offers ongoing cycles of experience, input and dialogue (sections 5.2, 6.2 and 8.6).

Skills

Graded tasks

Student-teachers have to simplify early teaching encounters in order to cope with the complexity of classroom interactions (Doyle, 1986). This suggests that providers should:

- interpret some novices' practical mistakes as simplifications of complex interactions (e.g. teaching only the front row);
- provide graded experience in practical teaching (e.g. observation/micro-teaching/small group teaching in school/team teaching/full class teaching).

Classroom competence: survival skills

Their lack of practical routines suggests that early teaching experiences will be anxiety-producing because student-teachers are unable to anticipate learners' reactions. Therefore it is essential to learn specific survival strategies early on, for example how to conduct one's first-ever teaching-practice lesson in school.

These principles are met in ITE 'survival' courses (section 6.3) and in skill development in INSET programmes (see sections 8.2, 8.6 and option 1 courses in section 8.5).

The role of models

Models of teaching (video or live) enable skill recognition and the development of a personal technical vocabulary. However, the presentation of single models perpetuates the notion of learning by imitation, and of there being only one way to teach (see section 5.3.2). Preferable strategies are to present multiple exemplars where each teacher displays a personal mix of strengths and weaknesses (e.g. 8.6); and to engage in observation of different teaching styles early in a course (sections 6.2 and 6.3).

Just as in communicative language teaching the analysis of language samples is now preferred to the imitation of paradigms, so the student-teacher needs experience of multiple models from which to select attributes that are personally and contextually appropriate.

Learning from experienced teachers

A developmental approach to ITE suggests the need for discussion with an experienced teacher who can offer examples of practical reasoning under the unique conditions of their particular classroom. For such 'cognitive apprenticeship' to work, it is necessary for the established teacher to be able to explain her reasoning and for the student to be able to question and probe the teacher. However, this form of discourse is not necessarily easy to achieve, an important issue discussed in more detail in sections 5.2 and 6.2, and by Haggerty (1995a).

It has even been suggested that learner-teachers may be helped to develop their own teaching identity not by the particular content of a mentor's thinking but by the attitude they display towards their own practice. Contact with established teachers who question and reflect on their teaching beliefs may be the best way to facilitate learner-teacher reflection (Kagan, 1992).

Learning about learners

Kagan (1992) argues that the crucial experience for student-teachers is to get in touch with the reality of pupils' experience of learning, in effect to attain sociality with them (Salmon, 1995). Through this, student-teachers can discover that their assumptions and expectations are at times inaccurate or inappropriate. In this way, their personal theories are contradicted by surprises, new insights into learners' experience which provide a stimulus to rethinking and change: *'It is a novice's growing knowledge of pupils that must be used to challenge, mitigate and reconstruct prior beliefs and images'* (Kagan, 1992: 142).

This can be achieved by assignments such as learner profiling and obtaining feedback (e.g. Richards and Lockhart, 1994; Pennington, 1996). (McLaughlin, 1996, makes a similar point regarding the need for providers to gain insight into the thinking of future training staff; see Appendix 7.6.)

ITE structures: Partnership schemes

Partnership schemes provide a structure which is capable of integrating reflection and experience. State schemes in England and Wales are required by law to place student-teachers in school for two thirds of their course time. Other schemes could operate effectively with a different distribution of time. Below, we summarise principles and corresponding structural features of Partnership design (see section 6.2 for a more detailed account).

Principle	Feature of design
1. Access to the thinking of established teachers	Student-teachers spend at least two thirds of course time in schools
	Teachers are trained and released from other duties to serve as mentors while they are in school (Wilkin, 1990; McIntyre et al., 1993);
2. Personal experience is needed to mediate, test out and personalise theory	Two thirds' course time in school; time intervals between student-teachers' HEI and school-based experiences are kept short, e.g. with split weeks in the HEI and school
	Use teaching experience as a basis for the mutual testing out of HEI-based theory and school-based craft knowledge
	Assessment should include assignments which test theory against classroom experience
3. Coherence between HEI and school curricula	School and HEI staff collaborate on course planning and monitoring
	Staff roles in university and school are complementary
4. Students' images of teaching mediate 'input'	Students reflect on their personal images and beliefs
5. Diversity in student-teachers' personal theories; their learning is focused by their own concerns	Assessment needs to be flexible enough to respond to diverse student-teacher agendas

6. Student–teachers lack classroom management skills	Provide early training in basic, consensual teaching skills
	Offer graded and extensive classroom experience
7. Survival concerns block risk-taking	Offer enough classroom experience to allow time for mistakes; offer some unassessed teaching practice
	Assessment is broadly based (section 5.3)
	Have an assessment 'watershed' before the end of the course (see section 6.2)
8. Perception of self as competent can inhibit development	Focus on areas of future development at the end of course, leaving time for individual inquiry
	Provide skills which enable further development (e.g. self-evaluation, observation)

The integration of school and HEI curricula, such as the split weeks in section 6.2, may not be possible for logistical reasons. In this case, an alternative strategy can be to make the courses under a provider's control as relevant to pedagogy as possible. This could be done by structured observation and analysis programmes linked to methodology courses or by focusing microteaching on issues arising in school (Sharkova, 1996; Mace, 1996).

Providers' expectations

Imitation or personalisation

Research shows unambiguously that while novice teachers come to an ITE course with deficits in knowledge and skill, they are not merely empty vessels waiting to be filled. While providers may be misled by novices' skilful use of 'display lessons', they need to recognise a basic condition of ITE: that they will 'confront classes composed of students who possess varying definitions of good teaching' and who 'adopt diverse models of the occupation' with the result that they 'will not find it easy to develop consensual standards of practice' (Lortie, 1975: 66). As he also observes, 'in such circumstances instruction can easily move to a superficial level of discourse' (1975: 66). In other words, there may be a lack of communication due to lack of sociality, unless student-teachers are given the chance to explore their own biographies, test out input in the classroom for themselves, and present their own interpretations of input and personal experience in discussion and writing (see also sections 5.1, 6.2 and 6.3).

No one theory

The general lesson of research is that teacher learning is too complex to be reduced to a single paradigm: 'At present, we have no one theoretical framework to account for these different areas of development and to provide us with an overview of the complex processes and interactions involved' (Calderhead, 1990: 155).

For providers, this indicates the need to avoid limitation to a single paradigm or theory (section 3.3) and to adopt a design that integrates the different dimensions of teacher learning by means of cycles of related activities (sections 1.1.5 and 4.3, Box 4.3 and Table 8.4).

Student-teachers' lack of personal experience

Student-teachers lack the experience to make personal sense of specialist concepts and terms. This suggests that:

- concrete experiences and exemplars are essential for them to build concepts;
- teaching practice and input are best provided in closely integrated cycles (not separate blocks) so that student-teachers can test one against the other (see sections 2.2.3 and 6.2);
- theoretical input in ITE courses can be weighted relatively lightly as compared with later in the teaching career when teachers have the experience to make sense of it (as is implied by the UCLES scheme of qualifications, section 6.3).

Student-teachers are likely to recognise their own lack of experience, which suggests:

- supervisors should display credibility and provide concrete guidelines in early stages of ITE;
- students may be too ready to develop false certainty by clinging to supervisors' prescriptions.

A difficult task for supervisors is therefore to move from directive to non-directive roles. The transition can be helped along by assignments which require independent analysis and reasoned pedagogic decisions (see section 6.3).

2.5   The new language teacher

The circumstances of language teachers in their first post after they qualify vary enormously. Some have to complete an assessed probationary year, while others are considered fully trained on graduation. Some receive support and a reduced timetable, others will go straight in at the deep end. Whatever their circumstances, it is generally agreed that the first school strongly influences a teacher's development.

2.5.1   How does a new teacher's thinking develop?

Self and the school

Zeichner *et al.* (1987) suggest that new teachers' development is affected by their response to the relative congruence between school culture and their own values (see also section 1.1.4). A match will tend to confirm and reinforce their personal theories. In the case of a mismatch, their response will determine how their theories then evolve: they may retain their values covertly and 'play along' with the school ('strategic compliance'); or they may fit in with the system and begin to rethink in line with the school ('internalised adjustment'). Alternatively, new teachers might affirm their values by maintaining their teaching style in spite of the school ('strategic redefinition'). Zeichner cites such a case, which had a reciprocal effect on the culture of the whole school. As Zeichner *et al.* put it: 'first year teachers, under some conditions at least, can have a creative impact on their work places and survive' (1987: 51). We should note, however, that it takes a determined and self-confident teacher to persist in the face of resistance from colleagues.

Match

- Adjustment in personal theories as they are confirmed and developed by consistency with school.

Mismatch

- Strategic compliance: fit in as the situation demands but keep to own theories.
- Strategic redefinition: hold out against the school and carry through one's own practices.
- Adjustment in personal theories to conform with the norms and values of the school.

A tendency to privatism

Lortie (1975) observed that, for teachers in his study, early experience was largely 'sink or swim': there was inadequate grading in teaching responsibilities, a lack of peer support, and limited time with other teachers to become aware of alternative perspectives, or to tap into an existing 'professional vocabulary'

(Lortie, 1975: 73). He argues that as a result the first few months of work tended to be a largely *private* ordeal. He argues that this experience strongly reinforced privatist attitudes in later career. He contrasts this with the *shared* ordeal of some occupations (such as medicine) which he argues produces stronger identification with a group culture (section 1.1.4).

This suggests that the collegiality and support teachers experience in their first post are likely to contribute to their attitudes to learning from colleagues in future. Teacher development staff would therefore do well to try to develop support systems in schools that are receiving new teachers.

2.5.2   What do new teachers learn about their subject?

Shulman (1987) suggests that a particularly important area of development lies in pedagogic content knowledge (PCK): the restructuring of subject knowledge to make it accessible to pupils. He suggests it contains:

- knowledge of the communication of subject matter;
- knowledge about pupils relevant to the communication of content (their preknowledge and what they find relatively easy or difficult).

It is suggested that the transformation of content knowledge is an area of special concern and development in the first few years of teaching. It is also suggested that control over curriculum content frees the teacher to attend to pupil learning, and so gains in PCK imply that the teacher can become more capable of adaptive teaching. Unfortunately, the writer is unaware of language teacher research in this interesting area. We can only speculate that language teachers also build a repertoire of planning criteria, examples and tasks which restructures their knowledge of the TL.

2.5.3   What are the concerns of a new teacher?

Kagan (1992) observes that ITE concerns tend to carry over to the first job. This is perhaps to be expected, given the evolutionary nature of teacher development and the need to maintain esteem in a new school.

The experience of the new language teacher will be affected by her status in the school. In some contexts a well-trained graduate with good competence in the target language would immediately enjoy high status and independence. However, it seems that some new teachers often report frustration at their powerlessness in school hierarchy, surrounded as they are by established teachers who can get smoothly through the day and senior staff who determine school policy (Wragg, 1982). Also, it is commonly reported that placements are not necessarily those trained for or even as initially advertised. The new teacher might be saddled with responsibilities the school needs to offload rather than those s/he is trained for.

2.5.4   What does ITE contribute?

Research on some state ITE courses reported inadequate practical preparation (Turney *et al.*, 1982a; Chisholm *et al.*, 1986; Department of Education and Science, 1987). Two features stand out:

- discipline: many ITE courses in the UK failed to provide training in classroom management (leading to a demand for INSET in this area; see section 8.6);
- utopianism: as Lortie observed, university-based courses endorsed the 'highest values', as in progressive approaches, without seriously confronting the resistances and tactical difficulties involved in implementing them.

'Marginal teachers'

Kennedy (1995) draws attention to a significant subgroup of 'marginal' English-language teachers, whose needs are best met in the first years of their school career. Kennedy defines them as teachers 'who operate consistently on the margin of effectiveness' (1995: 10) whose needs reflect the social conditions of their entry to teaching, identified as eased entry to teaching because of shortages, a decline in teachers' prestige and conditions of work due to cuts in government spending, and the absence of alternative secure employment.

On the basis of supervisor diaries and critical incident analysis, Kennedy identified four general areas for development: professional awareness (being aware that there is a problem that demands a decision); professional judgement (recognising when it is necessary to intervene); professional knowledge (knowledge about language systems and teaching strategies); and procedural skills ('knowing how'). She argues that these needs should be addressed in ITE or soon after, not in the later career where training seems only to benefit already competent teachers (McDonald, 1982; Avalos, 1985; Cooke and Pang, 1991).

Later development activities (such as trainer training) will be a waste of resources if teachers' basic knowledge and skills are lacking. The plight of marginal teachers indicates the need to reform ITE or to provide compensatory training *in the first few years* of their career.

2.5.5   What are the implications for a new teacher?

The above research findings suggest strategies for the reform of ITE and for support in school, as summarized below. The 'implications' column on the left suggests ways in which ITE can prepare the new teacher for the first year(s) of work. The right-hand column illustrates school conditions where there is access to support from peers and from outside the school. We have no one case study to illustrate all these characteristics. However, section 8.3 describes a school climate where there is a commitment to dialogue and development; section 8.5 reports an off-site structure (i.e. away from the school) which could support new language teachers. Also the package summarised in section 8.6 has been designed to provide compensatory skills training and support in schools for teachers whose ITE programmes failed to provide classroom-management strategies.

Finding	Implications for ITE design	Implications for schools
Concern with survival	Provide school-based practice	Offer support from senior staff
Tensions with school culture	Develop awareness of school conditions as they are	Support from within and and outside school
	Provide experience of more than one school	Provide help in adapting ITE to school conditions
	Set school culture analysis tasks	
Lack of validity in the ITE curriculum	ITE programme designed with input from schools;	Access to INSET and exchange with other teachers (e.g. Teachers' Centres)
	Need for formative feedback from schools on programme design	Support from senior staff
		Access to reading materials
Pedagogic content knowledge	Adequate classroom experience and responsibility for planning and teaching lesson sequences; materials analysis tasks focusing on pedagogic grammar; coherence between courses on language description and pedagogy	Access to INSET focused on language systems and pedagogic grammar
Lack of power in the system	Do not expect student teachers to act as agents of innovation	Do not expect new teachers to act as agents of innovation
'Marginal' teachers	Improve selection	Provide additional training in early career
	Give training in practical skills	

2.6   Learning as an established teacher

In this section we outline evidence on INSET relevant to design. Factors relevant to INSET design are also discussed in sections 7.1 and 7.2.

2.6.1   How do adults learn?

As long ago as 1913 Thorndike established that training was more effective if trainees were committed to the occupation and to improvement; if they saw training as relevant to personal goals; and if they were aware of a need that training could meet. Drawing on subsequent research on differences between adult and child learners, Knowles (1984) proposed the following preconditions:

- self-direction: adults see themselves as responsible for their own lives and so will resist perceived impositions by others;
- prior knowledge: adults have rich role experience which will mediate inputs from others;
- relevance: adults become ready to learn when role demands present them with a need to know (e.g. system-wide curriculum changes);
- problem focus: adults frame learning in terms of a perceived practical problem at hand, rather than as a more abstract gain in knowledge.

Research on adult learning (e.g. Knowles, 1984; Hopkins, 1986; Cline *et al.*, 1990) suggests clear guidelines for INSET design:

- teachers should be involved in identifying what their learning needs are;
- their learning experiences should build on their current knowledge and experience: teachers' personal craft knowledge is an important learning resource;
- INSET programmes should provide experiences optimally related to teachers' current practice;
- a curriculum problem or project is a good medium for teacher development; theorising arises naturally from making sense of incidents and problems that are important to teachers.

Adult learning theory needs some qualification when applied to teachers. First, many teachers are likely to differ from adult learners in general because they have spent more time in higher education, and so are more likely to have definite expectations and preferences regarding their own learning. Then, their socialisation into teaching produces powerful personal theories specific to teaching and learning (section 2.3.1). It follows that the beliefs bound up in their own practice about knowledge, teaching and learning will strongly affect their orientation to course content. It is for this reason that explicit attention to their experience of instruction is an important strategy in the design of all teacher learning activities whereas it may be less pressing in other branches of adult education (e.g. Day *et al.*, 1990; Griffiths and Tann, 1992; Tann, 1993; sections 5.2, 8.2).

It also follows that the knowledge of experienced teachers should be pooled and built on (see Appendix 7.4) and also that teachers' preferred modes of learning should be used as a means of effective communication (e.g. Pennington, 1996).

These general principles are realised in several other sections: in approaches to needs assessment (section 7.3.1); in the case study of an award-bearing course with an action research component (sections 8.2 and 8.4); case studies of curriculum inquiry (sections 8.3 and 8.4) and an on-site (i.e. in-school) training package (section 8.6 and Appendix 8.5).

2.6.2   What is effective INSET?

General principles

Influential research in the late 1970s and early 1980s (e.g. Rubin, 1978; McLaughlin and Marsh, 1978; Fullan, 1982; Hopkins, 1985) suggested the following principles for INSET design:

- teachers possess important and valuable practical knowledge;
- teacher learning is adaptive and heuristic, in that it departs from assumptions based on past experiences and proceeds by trial and error;
- teacher learning is long-term and nonlinear i.e. it is evolutionary and accretive and may pass through phases of calm and turbulence; it is not a simple matter of progressively 'bolting on' new information and practices;
- professional learning should be tied to school-based curriculum development, i.e. teachers learn through experience and participation in curriculum development, not from abstract principles alone;
- professional learning is critically influenced by organisational factors in the school (school climate, opportunities for contact and exchange of ideas with peers) which are affected by school leadership and wider policy.

Each of these principles is reflected in our case studies (sections 8.2–8.6), notably the importance of adequate timescales, relevant and practical training inputs, and school- and classroom-focused work supported by dialogue with peers and process leaders.

In reviewing effective INSET programmes, Fullan (1982) comes to conclusions that confirm these general principles. As he was drawing on US-based research, which is 15 years old at time of writing, his conclusions should be seen as suggesting design and evaluation criteria rather than a description of existing programmes. We summarise his account of negative and positive programme features.

Negative features:

- topics for INSET are often decided by people other than those for whom it is intended;
- follow-up support in the use of ideas and practices presented in the INSET experience rarely occurs;
- most INSET programmes fail to address the positive and negative factors within each teacher's school that will affect the teachers' attempts to apply them;
- evaluation of INSET by assessing its impact on schools rarely occurs;
- INSET programmes rarely address individual needs of teachers;
- there is no conceptual basis for the planning and development of INSET programmes.

Positive features:

- where complex changes in practice are the objective, school-based programmes are more effective than those off-site;
- programmes which include demonstrations, supervised trials and feedback are more likely to meet their objectives than those in which teachers are offered theoretical or generalised input and in which they are simply expected to store up ideas for future use;
- teachers contend that they learn best about job-related skills and practices from other teachers but that they need some outside help from consultants to offer demonstrations, rationale and feedback;
- programmes where teachers share ideas and offer each other help are more likely to be effective;
- programmes which offer a variety of training experiences that suit individual variations in learning style are more likely to be effective;
- programmes where teachers participate in planning and decision-making about their own INSET are more likely to succeed;
- teachers are more likely to benefit from an activity (e.g. a specific course) if it is part of an overall development plan, and if it is focused on a curriculum project;
- approaches which enable teachers to reflect on and discuss their work seem to have positive effects on teacher thinking and their ability to synthesise from public theory and their own experiences.

We can reasonably assume that these findings can be applied to language teacher education.

LTE is very often characterised by its cross-cultural context, with resulting perception gaps between providers and teachers (most clearly where providers are L2 mother tongue specialists and teachers have another first language). This has led to cases of INSET which have failed to take teachers' personal theories and classroom culture into account, and so have not attained the sociality necessary for effective communication. Lamb (1995) summarises the consequences as:

- limited take-up of training;
- confusion and poor recall of the intervention;
- superficial labelling of old practices with new names;
- 'appropriation': the reinterpretation of new concepts in terms of the current system of ideas;
- abandonment of new strategies when they do not work.

Lamb goes on to argue that two crucial elements in effective INSET in ELT lie in:

- initial work on developing teacher awareness of their implicit beliefs;
- follow up during a teacher's early attempts to apply new strategies, which is when misunderstandings and practical difficulties are often revealed for the first time (Fullan, 1982).

The first principle is exemplified in sections 8.2, 8.3 and 8.6; the second in sections 8.2, 8.5 and 8.6. In sections 8.3 and 8.4, teachers are offered regular support while engaged in trying out new classroom strategies.

Successful planned change

The above findings are consistent with Fullan's resumé of the research on effective innovations (Fullan, 1982: Chapter 5). Particulary significant for INSET policy are his findings in terms of the change itself, the school, and beyond the school. Planned innovations tend to be implemented effectively when the change itself is recognised as necessary and relevant by teachers. At school level, change is supported where the head teacher gives active and visible support; where there are collegial teacher relationships (where they exchange ideas and offer mutual support); and where teachers have the skills necessary to implement the new curriculum. Beyond the school, innovations are supported by positive previous experience of innovation by insiders; by the perceived support and involvement of central authorities; by the integration of the change with staff development needs; by a high level of teacher participation, at least in dealing with implementation issues; and the perceived use of evaluation findings to fine-tune the innovation. At a wider level, positive forces included the general disposition of the community to change; support and resources from national administration; and external assistance when needed.

Support during implementation

A particularly significant finding of innovation and INSET research is that teachers need support in the early stages of 'going it alone' with a new practice. Fullan (1982) and Lamb (1995) note that teachers often hit unexpected difficulties in the early stages of introducing changes in the classroom. This is because the training situation cannot possibly anticipate the particular difficulties, confusions or misunderstandings that will be revealed once each teacher goes back to his/her own class. If s/he is not helped to get past this 'critical hump' s/he is likely to abandon the innovation and fall back on familiar ways. This indicates that teachers need a social framework of support and discussion, a design which keeps in touch with them as they begin to introduce changes. Fullan summarises this key design principle as follows:

> ... training approaches ... are effective when they combine concrete, teacher-specific training activities, ongoing continuous assistance and support during the process of implementation and regular meetings with peers and others. ... *Research on implementation has demonstrated beyond a shadow of doubt that these processes of sustained interaction and staff development are crucial regardless of what the change is concerned with* (our italics)
>
> (Fullan, 1982: 67)

This view is supported by Olson and Eaton's research (1987) which suggested that in introducing an innovation teachers are concerned about maintaining control and the esteem of others. They are concerned about the perceptions of pupils, parents and colleagues, in that they want to be seen as up to date but also as staying in control. As a result they typically introduce changes by gradual trial and error, attempting to integrate the novel with the routine and minimising risk. This account is consistent with the view that INSET design should offer teachers ongoing support either on site (Ghani *et al.*, 1997; also sections 8.3 and 8.6) or off site (sections 8.2, 8.4 and 8.5).

2.6.3   Three INSET strategies

We summarise research on three common INSET strategies: off-site courses, coaching and curriculum development projects. Issues relating to off-site courses, and their integration with on-site work, appear in sections 8.2 and 8.4. The role of curriculum inquiry in teacher development is particularly relevant in sections 8.2–8.5. The integration of courses and self-directed inquiry is explored in case study sections 8.2, 8.3 (option 2 workshops) and 8.6.

Courses

We refer here to short off-site courses, summarising Henderson (1979), Rudduck (1981), Fullan (1982) and Hopkins (1986).
  Conditions for effectiveness seem to be:

- 'one-shot' workshops are widespread but ineffective;
- short courses are effective when complementary to school-based activity;
- a supportive school climate is needed for post-course application;

- the course input needs to be tested out by participants: 'good training requires that members constantly test what goes on in the in-service programme against the events of the training situation, and vice versa' (Miles and Pasow, 1957: 360); they must be able to experiment with training 'when the chips are down', at once and directly;
- there is a need for links between training and job demands to be made explicit to learner-teachers.

Expectations of participating teachers appear to be:

- evidence of good preparation by providers (materials ready, room arranged);
- good course management: providers keep to the schedule, do what is announced; build variety into sessions;
- relevance to their own setting;
- providers start from where participants are;
- providers value participants' knowledge;
- time is allotted for response, discussion and application that is equal to input time.

Common problems of short off-site courses tend to result from inadequate resources, providers' insufficient knowledge of good practice, staff overload, and logistical constraints. Some reported failings (Rudduck, 1981) are:

- 'casualness of purpose': teachers attend courses for many motives some of which may have nothing to do with the course content;
- lack of follow-up: courses are delivered 'one-off' with no attempt to support teachers in implementation;
- providers overprepare or overload content, which leads to 'one-way' interaction (i.e. they lecture);
- feedback and evaluation are nonexistent or perfunctory.

The value of off-site courses appears from the research (e.g. Rudduck, 1980; Hopkins, 1985) to include:

- contact between teachers from different schools makes for stimulus and rethinking: colleagues from the same school tend to get along by establishing 'truces', agreements not to raise contentious issues;
- time out from teaching promotes critical thinking;
- courses can increase propositional knowledge;
- courses may boost morale as they are seen as confirmation by the administration of teachers' value.

It seems that an effective strategy is to combine the positive features of off-site and on-site work. This can be done in courses which move from off-site to on-site blocks (section 8.2) or by 'two-stage' courses or workshops where teachers can try things out between the two off-site sessions (see option 2 in section

8.5). Where a course is on site, then it is possible to work through closely linked cycles of classroom trials and course-based reflection (section 8.6).

Coaching

Coaching refers to practical classroom support by a trained and experienced fellow teacher, over a period of weeks or months (Joyce and Showers, 1980). It was developed to improve the implementation of curriculum innovations. It was not originally designed from a constructivist perspective, but pragmatically as a form of effective dissemination.

Joyce and Showers make an important distinction between changes which 'fine-tune' the curriculum and those which are 'new', where a radically different set of principles and values underlie new practices. Coaching is seen as desirable to introduce 'new' practices. They argue their case by recognising the limitations of conventional skill training, as follows:

presentation
    description and rationale of the new practice: this alone will not lead to transfer of training but is effective combined with other procedures;

demonstration
    this supports presentation; it is appropriate to 'fine-tuning' where rationale is unnecessary;

practice
    develops skills; transfer occurs if feedback is provided, but training 'washes out' when feedback ceases;

coaching
    individual planning, reflection and discussion with a skilled peer 'hands on' at school; offers best conditions for the transfer of 'new' training.

They conclude that these elements were most effective under the following conditions:

- the integration of rationale (theory), demonstration, practice and feedback;
- practice in simulated conditions helps teachers' fluent control of new skills;
- individual and concrete help with implementation sustains long-term implementation;
- on-site coaching helps develop knowledge about implementation to feed back into training programmes;
- coaches have to be trained to provide help.

According to Joyce and Showers, coaching proved to be very effective. Unfortunately it is too expensive for many systems to provide. However, interesting attempts have been made in ELT to implement teacher development schemes based on the same principles, by occasionally releasing effective teachers to give support in schools (e.g. Ghani *et al.*, 1997) or to provide regular offsite workshops (section 8.5).

Curriculum development projects

Teacher/curriculum development (TCD) refers to activities that integrate teacher development with curriculum improvement. Typically they consist of curriculum inquiry by teachers in their schools: materials, methods, tests or some other aspect of the curriculum are tried out, their implementation is monitored, and outcomes are assessed (e.g. Burns and Hood, 1995; Matthew and Eapen, 1996; Allwright and Lenzuen, 1997).

TCD assumes that curriculum development and teacher development are interdependent: '. . . unless the teacher is developing, development in schooling will not occur. The corollary is that teachers will develop only when there is a need and an opportunity to develop . . . ' (Gibbons and Norman, in Wideen and Andrews, 1987: 105–106).

It also assumes that, to be effective, curriculum development should involve teachers, as they are closest to implementation issues: 'only if teachers were centrally involved in research, and thereby able to engage with the implications of classroom practice for students' learning, would it be possible to develop the curriculum in any meaningful way' (Somekh, 1995: 344).

It is now widely accepted that effective INSET locates teacher learning within curriculum projects (Day *et al.*, 1987; Day, 1990), and that teacher professionalism can be developed by means of TCD: 'the outstanding characteristic of the extended professional (teacher) is a capacity for autonomous professional self-development through systematic self-study, through the study of the work of other teachers and through the testing of ideas by classroom research procedures' (Stenhouse, 1975: 144).

The initial case for TCD arose from a diagnosis of the failure of centrally planned innovation attempts (Stenhouse, 1975; Elliott, 1981). This was allied to the view that personal and professional change require change in tacit beliefs underlying day-to-day action which could be achieved by teachers monitoring and evaluating their work (Day, 1987; 1990; Elliott, 1981; 1991; Shulman, 1987; 1988; Griffiths and Tann, 1992; Somekh, 1993; Richards and Lockhart, 1994; Lamb, 1995; Karavas-Doukas, 1996).

Action research has been seen as a vehicle for TCD (Elliott, 1991; Somekh, 1993). However, there has been a recent critical reassessment of action research as a means to teacher development (Adelman, 1989; Griffiths and Tann, 1992; Elliott and Sarland, 1995), arguing that it does not produce 'hard, joint theorizing on the relationships of values, action and consequences prior to the devising of fresh options for action' (Adelman, 1989: 177). It has been argued that structured awareness-raising activities are needed to complement curriculum inquiry because: 'reflection relies on an ability to uncover one's own personal theories and make them explicit' (Griffiths and Tann, 1992: 71).

Methods and issues in uncovering tacit beliefs are discussed in Denicolo and Pope (1990), Day *et al.* (1990), Pennington (1990), Diamond (1991), Yaxley (1991), Morine-Dershimer (1993), Calderhead and Gates (1993) and Richards and Lockhart (1994). McGill and Beaty (1992) provide a detailed account of the processes and skills involved in self-directed group activity.

Participation in TCD does not *guarantee* development in teacher thinking. Apart from the need for structured reflective activities, it also seems that the nature of the curriculum project will strongly affect personal theory development. Day (1990: 215) identifies the conditions under which projects are likely to promote teacher development:

a) projects should centre on an important school issue, . . .
b) projects should be collaborative . . . participation . . . should be regarded as an important outcome in itself . . .
c) projects should lead to . . . an actual change . . .
d) project teams should be deliberately and clearly linked to the normal . . . processes and bodies which . . . 'manage' curriculum maintenance and review
e) projects should clearly relate . . . to classroom interactions . . .

These findings are highly significant for the design of TCD projects. They indicate that the curriculum issue should relate closely to teachers' concerns and that teacher participation must be genuine, in that their practical findings are seen to contribute to larger-scale decision-making (see case study, section 8.4). There is little point in setting up a TCD project if curriculum decision-makers will ignore the findings, or if the agenda for exploration is determined by outsiders. Therefore, if an administration wishes to involve teachers in TCD it must be prepared to share some power and responsibility with them, to give them a voice (sections 8.2, 8.3 and 8.4).

2.6.4   Non-native speaker language teachers

In the case of ELT, the term 'non-native speaker' (NNS) is controversial. It could refer to a school-leaver with virtually no functional English who is teaching in an EFL context; or to a graduate of a five-year literature and philology course; or to bi- and trilingual teachers educated in the medium of English and teaching in a bilingual culture. NNS levels of language competence and analytic knowledge of the English language therefore vary greatly, as does the role of English in their various settings. Given this extreme diversity, it is not possible to generalise about NNS teachers as a homogeneous group.

We are short of empirical research into INSET for teachers of languages which are not their mother tongue, even if they outnumber native-speaker (NS) teachers worldwide. In spite of this we speculate that they may have some of the following characteristics relevant to their learning needs.

- NNS teachers may lack confidence in their English language ability and give their own language improvement a high priority.
- NNS teachers may undergo an erosion in their English language performance through its restriction to classroom discourse.
- They may not have NS intuitions about the language and may need linguistic rules as a source of security; they may avoid classroom activities which demand unpredictable language use and where rapid and intuitive assessment of accuracy and appropriacy are needed; they may need the support of a textbook more than NS teachers.
- They have the personal experience to understand their learners' difficulties.
- Where teachers and learners share a common culture, group norms may exert a powerful influence on their behaviour, whereas NS teachers may be exempt from such norms.
- Language teaching behaviour cannot be separated from pedagogic models inherited from the mother tongue culture (Koranic, Confucian, African etc.) in such attributes as institutional culture, attitudes to authority and knowledge, adult–child relationships etc.
- The place of English in society at large has a profound influence on the purposes of English language education, the English language curriculum, and therefore the nature of the teacher's work.

Richards and Nunan (1996) report valuable work on the perceptions and concerns of non–native-speaker teachers. Case studies in sections 8.2, 8.3 and 8.5 are also relevant to the non–native-speaker teacher.

2.6.5   What are the implications for INSET design?

INSET as process

General and specific lessons are suggested by the above research. A general insight is that INSET and teacher development should be perceived as a concerted, long-term process, not as a series of discrete events. Another is that the *process* of INSET is as much if not more significant in determining outcomes as is its content: process determines the degree of teacher participation, perceived relevance and integration of INSET with teachers' concerns (see sections 7.1 and 7.3.1).

Negotiation and participation

Teachers are uniquely well placed to resist imposed change attempts. They work in isolation, often in a privatist culture, and are led by diverse, stable personal theories. They learn from INSET if they genuinely engage with it, if they understand its basis and recognise a need for change. As Rudduck concluded: 'I suggest that professional development may be most dynamic when personal commitment to change is strong and when its basis is understood by the teachers concerned' (1988: 205). Ownership can be promoted by such processes as participative needs assessment (section 7.3.1), the negotiation of INSET content and procedures (section 8.6), and support in self-directed collaborative work (sections 8.2–8.6).

INSET as an adaptive cycle

Teacher concerns do not stand still, but evolve over time. They develop as teachers become more experienced in carrying out the curriculum. Once initial concerns are met, such as familiarising with new tests or materials, others arise, such as shortfalls in time or gaps in the material. No INSET plan can be based on a single long-term decision about teachers' needs. Therefore INSET provision should be able to match teacher needs as they evolve: design should work through adaptive cycles much as does effective learner-centred language teaching (Nunan, 1988). This adaptiveness depends on effective 'macro' processes of needs assessment and formative evaluation, built into the structure of INSET sessions (section 7.3). It also applies in 'micro' designs, as for example Tillinca's (1996) account of 'micro-planning' (discuss and plan – try out – report back – discuss) with fellow teachers and support staff. This enables progressive attention to teachers' concerns in secure social settings (see also sections 8.3, 8.4 and 8.6).

Sustainability

The importance of process implies that providers should earmark resources (money, space, time, duplicating facilities, additional staff etc.) to ensure that each phase of the INSET cycle can function properly, particularly the less visible activities which promote effective INSET. These would include needs assessment, monitoring, dissemination of information to participants, collection of evaluation data, discussion of and decision-making from evaluation data. All phases of the cycle of planning, orientation, implementation, support and feedback need adequate resources.

Summary

Table 2.1 summarises conditions for effective INSET suggested by research (left column) and their practical implications for the design of training and development activities (right column).

Table 2.1 Findings and INSET design

Condition	Implication
Recognition of the need for change	Present and discuss needs assessment data (section 7.3.1)
	Try to present teachers with feedback from learners (e.g. section 8.3; Pennington, 1996)
Ownership improves implementation of changes	Focus on issues of high priority to teachers (sections 8.3, 8.5 and 8.6)
	Use needs assessment techniques which promote teacher participation (section 7.3.1)
	Curriculum projects are based on an issue agreed with teachers (section 8.2–8.3)
	Involve teachers in monitoring and evaluating new materials and syllabuses (section 8.5; also Mathew and Eapen, 1996)
	Demonstrate that teachers' findings are fed into larger-scale decision-making (section 8.4; Day, 1990)
Awareness of personal theories	Beliefs 'need first to be articulated, and then analysed for potential contradictions with each other, the teaching circumstances, and the beliefs of the learners ... the focus of the short INSET course, where experienced teachers already have well-developed mental constructs of teaching, should be the teachers' beliefs themselves' (Lamb, 1995: 79; see also section 7.4 and Appendices 8.1 and 8.5)
Support from colleagues or process leaders	Establish structures offering regular discussion and support e.g. sections 8.3, 8.6 (on-site) and 8.4 (off-site workshops)
	Follow up INSET courses at school (8.2)
Integrate modes of learning	Time allowed for discussion and processing input (8.6)
	Integrate classroom experience and course-based work (8.2 and 8.6)
	Use a low-intensity or two-stage design, interspersing training sessions and school experience (8.5)

Table 2.1 Findings and INSET design (*continued*)

Condition	Implication
Realistic timescales needed	Whole school/department plan is designed over an extended time period (minimum one year) (7.3.1 and 8.3)
Incentives	Cover expenses; provide incentives: qualifications, points on pension scales etc. (8.2)
	Skills acquired through INSET contribute to career growth (8.2–8.6)
Teachers learn best from active participation	Base sessions on experiential activities linked to reflection and input (8.6)
	Teachers decide which new techniques they will try (8.6)
	Choice of curriculum development issue negotiated with teachers (8.2, 8.3 and 8.6)
	School ensures logistical support for teachers, e.g. some release from teaching, duplicating facilities (8.5)
Input from specialists available	Long-term plan to enable specialist input when needed (7.3, 8.4 and 8.5)
	Provide specialist information in accessible form, e.g., short readings (8.5 and 8.6)
Alternative perspectives should be available from peers or process leaders	Provide video samples of teaching for analysis and discussion (8.6)
	Provide activities for reflection and values clarification (Appendices 7.4 and 8.1)
	Provide team-building activities (8.3 and 8.6)
	Process leader structures discussions to maximise group effectiveness (8.3 and 8.6)
Teachers value learning from each other	Ensure that participating teachers' knowledge is pooled (Appendix 7.5)

In the next chapter we move from specific research findings and proposals to a more general perspective: the assumptions and paradigms underlying views of the LTE curriculum. The reader may prefer to move on either to our case studies or to more specific matters of LTE design (Chapters 4, 5 and 7) before considering these more abstract issues.

3

Approaches to the teacher education curriculum

3.1 Introduction
3.1.1 The curriculum as a system
3.1.2 A simple framework: approach, design, procedure

3.2 Assumptions about teaching and teacher education
3.2.1 Models of teaching and LTE objectives
3.2.2 What do teachers know?
3.2.3 What is teaching?
       Routines
       Routines and reflection
       Uncertainty
       On display
       Isolation
       Perceptions
       Teaching a second language

3.3 Knowledge-centred and person-centred paradigms
3.3.1 The paradigms in contrast
3.3.2 Positivism: a knowledge-centred view
       Positivism and the transmission of knowledge
       A sufficient guide for action?
       False dependency?
3.3.3 Phenomenology: a person-centred view
3.3.4 The value of paradigms
3.3.5 Paradigms of teacher education: some health warnings.
       Paradigms are simple, the real world is complex
       Oversimplification of factors in design?
       Oversimplified terms?
       Irrelevant paradigms?
       A single dimension

3.1   Introduction

3.1.1   The curriculum as a system

An LTE programme is part of a network of interacting systems: the learner, the teacher, the classroom, the school, the local community, and national education. One characteristic of a system is the ripple effect: change in the relationships between some of its elements will affect others (Bowers, 1983). Also, big and small systems interact with each other so that big policy and resource decisions affect the choices of individual teachers and LTE providers. For example, in a national system where resources are very limited, a lack of textbooks tends to limit teachers to formal 'chalk and talk' modes of teaching, because they are the only source of input for learners. If each pupil has a book, then the teacher has more classroom options. In the same way, a provider's options are affected by bigger policy decisions, such as available time and provider-teacher ratios. In this way relationships in classrooms and contexts of training are intimately affected by the bigger systems. LTE providers need to recognise the impact of other systems on teachers and on their own design decisions (see sections 4.2 and 7.2).

3.1.2   A simple framework: approach, design, procedure

We can usefully apply the notions of approach, design and procedure to LTE (Richards and Rodgers, 1982; White, 1988; Appendix 4.3).

Our *approach* consists of assumptions which help us to define target competence, goals and teaching strategies. A language programme is based on a model of linguistic competence ('what is it to know the foreign language?') and language acquisition ('how is it learnt?'). In the same way, an LTE programme is based on a model of teaching competence ('what is teaching?; what do teachers know?') and a model of acquisition ('how do people learn to teach?').

In *design* (planning) we decide programme objectives and structures by trading off between our approach, the purpose of the programme and the immediate, often conflicting, variables in our situation. High-priority variables include: purpose ('what do the people providing the funding want; what are the criteria for qualifications?'); time ('how long is the course?'); resources ('how many staff do we have, how many participants, how much room?') and the known or anticipated characteristics of learner-teachers ('will they need any language improvement work?'). In design we make decisions on goals and objectives; the selection, sequencing, weighting and integration of programme elements; the content of courses; methods and staff-student roles; learning tasks and materials; assessment and evaluation.

In *implementation* (carrying out plans), the provider will go through short-term cycles of planning, working with learner-teachers, monitoring and assessing their reactions. Implementation is where the video breaks down, participants surprise us, or a brilliant idea takes a session off in unexpected directions. It is marked by constant adjustments as we meet the unexpected and revise our perceptions of learner-teachers and ourselves.

In this chapter we are concerned with general perspectives, approach and design. In Appendix 4.3 we suggest a checklist to accompany the assessment or design of a programme. It is only an *aide memoire*, and cannot guide decisions on priorities and context-specific needs as required in real-world design. Aspects of design are discussed in more detail in Parts 2 and 3 of this book.

3.2   Assumptions about teaching and teacher education

3.2.1   Models of teaching and LTE objectives

A model of linguistic competence informs the categories we use to design a language syllabus or a textbook. Similarly, models of teaching influence the definition of LTE goals (Table 3.1). In an 'operative' model the teacher is restricted to meeting the requirements of a centralised system, such as the delivery of a textbook as planned, to a set timescale. Such a limited role, limited to that of curriculum transmission, implies training objectives based on mastery of a set of competencies determined by the centralised syllabus.

In the case of the 'problem solver' model, a decentralised curriculum gives teachers greater autonomy in making educational decisions (see sections 8.2 and 8.3). A diversified language curriculum, characterised by adaptation to learners' needs, requires teachers to be able to diagnose problems and adapt materials and design original learning activities (e.g. Nunan, 1988). In this case the function of an LTE programme will be to prepare the teacher as a free agent. The LTE syllabus is therefore likely to include a category of enabling skills (e.g. of materials development and evaluation) which support independent, context-sensitive decision-making. It is also likely to emphasise learner-teachers' participation and personal responsibility as is consistent with their role in the curriculum (see sections 6.2, 8.2 and 8.3).

The model of teaching implicit in an LTE programme may be determined by the language curriculum (centralised-predictable as compared with diversified-unpredictable) or by teachers' relative autonomy (as servants of the system or as independent professionals).

3.2.2   What do teachers know?

Teacher knowledge can be analysed as a system of knowledge bases (Wilson *et al.*, 1987: 113; Calderhead, 1988a; Eraut, 1994), which suggests the main categories for an LTE syllabus (Box 3.1).

Content knowledge refers to teachers' knowledge of target language (TL) systems, their TL competence and their analytic knowledge.

Table 3.1 Models of teaching and goals of teacher education

Model of teaching	LTE objectives
Curriculum operative The language teacher delivers a prescribed textbook as intended by central planners	**Initial training** Teachers' language competence levels are set by the school language syllabus
	Essential teaching skills are defined by textbook content and tasks
	Teachers' planning skills are limited to textbook delivery, and exclude, e.g., materials selection, testing
	Inservice education and training Remedial training in language or methods is needed if teachers are unable to deliver the textbook as intended
	The inservice agenda is set by the demands of delivering a new textbook. Inservice training is needed if and when the textbook or exams are changed
Problem solver Teachers' role is to support independent learning. Curriculum is decentralised	**Initial training** Teachers' language competence needs to be good enough to enable independent materials selection and adaptation
Teachers diagnose the unique needs of learners	Teachers need diagnostic and planning skills
Teachers can make decisions about the syllabus, materials and tests	Their language competence should be good enough to cope with varied and unpredictable learner needs
	Teachers' skills repertoire should be broad enough to meet diverse learner needs
	Inservice Focus on teachers' 'process' skills as well as any necessary language and methodology 'content', e.g. problem framing, conducting needs analysis, developing learner collaboration and self-evaluation

Content knowledge Knowing target language systems, text types etc.	**Curricular knowledge** Of the official language curriculum (exams, textbooks etc.) and of resources
Pedagogic content knowledge (Content restructured for purposes of pedagogy) Adapt content and means of communicating linguistic knowledge according to learners' needs	**Contextual knowledge** Learners: knowledge of their characteristics; appropriate expectations
	School: norms of behaviour in class and with colleagues Legal accountability Community: expectations and accountability
General pedagogic knowledge Principles and strategies for classroom management Planning and formative evaluation Classroom management Repertoire of ELT activities Aids and resources Assessment	**Process knowledge** Ability to relate to learners, peers, parents Study skills Team skills Observational skills Classroom inquiry skills Language analysis skills

Box 3.1   Expertise: types of language teacher knowledge

Pedagogic content knowledge refers to the knowledge of language we need to teach it. It includes our awareness of what aspects of the target language are more or less problematic for our learners; a personal stock of examples and activities by which to communicate awareness of systems; and a sense of what aspects of the TL system to present now and which to leave for later. *General pedagogic knowledge* refers to classroom management skills: a repertoire of language learning activities appropriate to different situations; the use of aids; monitoring and feedback; and formal assessment of learning. *Curricular knowledge* refers to, for example, awareness of materials that are available and the nature of examinations. *Contextual knowledge* refers to awareness of the characteristics of learners, schools and the wider system which guide one's conduct and help anticipate the reactions of others. The last category, *process knowledge*, consists of a set of enabling skills, that is skills and attitudes that enable the development of the teacher. These apply within and beyond courses: academic study skills, collaborative skills (such as teamwork, active listening and constructive criticism), inquiry skills (such as observation and self-evaluation); and finally 'meta-processing': the skills and attitudes of self-awareness and self-management (section 1.2). These categories are reflected by 'proto-syllabus' in Appendix 4.2 and in UCLES CELTA topics in Appendix 6.2.

3.2.3   What is teaching?

A typology of teacher knowledge is a useful starting point for design, but it does not capture the real nature of teaching, which we would characterise as essentially social and dynamic, an exercise of intention rather than certainty (Brown, 1975; Doyle, 1986; also section 1.1.5).

Routines

Teaching is a social activity, realised in discourse built jointly by learners and teachers. It makes complex simultaneous demands on the teacher. While interacting with individual learners, s/he also has to monitor time, scan the whole class. She has to manage the group and to think ahead, adapting plans for later in the lesson or after it. Over time the teacher is involved in many thousands of individual interactions with learners: questions, answers, instructions and responses. To cope with these repeated interactions and simultaneous demands on her attention, she has to develop routines: set ways of giving instructions, eliciting language, responding to learners and so on.

Routines have two benefits. They free the attention of the teacher from the detail of repeated interactions to enable more strategic thinking. They also provide familiar patterns which offer a secure social structure for learners and teachers alike. These routines therefore develop a wider meaning, in that they hold the group together and also reflect the beliefs underlying the classroom exchanges, for example about the respective roles of learners and teachers, or the nature of the TL. These beliefs are usually tacit rather than consciously thought out.

Routines and reflection

Teacher competence has its automated and deliberative aspects. In classroom interaction established teachers use their smooth interactional routines and respond appropriately to classroom situations in an apparently intuitive manner. Compared with novice teachers (who seem more dependent on all-purpose recipes) they seem to have a more differentiated perception of teaching situations so that they can respond quickly and appropriately to classroom incidents. They seem to have a tacit knowledge of variables such as the type of learner involved, the task, the time of day, and even their own mood, an apparently intuitive craft knowledge built from day-to-day experience (Berliner, 1987; 1988). However, we should not assume that all teaching routines are principled. As Maingay points out, some of these routines may in fact be unthinking rituals: 'this kind of teaching is ritual in the sense that, although there may be principles behind it, the teacher has never known, or has lost sight of those principles, and is consequently going through the motions in the same way as a child will recite multiplication tables' (1988: 119). The highly structured and limited nature of discourse in elementary-level language learning, and a dependence on textbooks, can promote these theory-free classroom routines. This suggests that not all routines are grounded in tacit theory: they may simply be done 'because that is what teachers do'.

The reflective aspect of expertise comes into play as we identify, analyse and resolve problems in teaching, drawing on all the knowledge types outlined in Box 3.1. Another level of reflection lies in self-awareness and self-assessment, characterised by Eraut as meta-processing: 'the thinking involved in directing one's own behaviour' (1994: 115); and by Bell and Gilbert (1996) as meta-cognition: 'learner's awareness of their thoughts, beliefs and ways of coming to know about the processes of learning and teaching' (1996: 61).

This suggests that the agenda of LTE is to help the learner-teacher develop the smooth routines they need for day-to-day effectiveness, but to be able to stand back from these routines to assess their usefulness (section 1.2).

Uncertainty

Teaching differs from many other occupations because it is characterised by intention rather than certainty. We give input, explain, set tasks to cause learners to change. Because learners vary, the effects of these interventions are essentially unpredictable (Williams and Burden, 1997). Therefore a teacher's practice is characterised by ongoing trial and error rather than certainty about learners' reactions and individual learning outcomes.

On display

Teaching is also highly public: our teaching self is on unrelieved display to learners. All of a teacher's actions become potentially meaningful because they set precedents and create expectations for the future. Additionally, because the subject *is* the discourse of the class, the language teacher's own mastery of the subject is on permanent public display, a reason for its high priority for those teachers for whom it is not a mother tongue.

Isolation

Teaching is an unusual occupation in that much of the work goes on cut off from peers. It is for this reason that the social organisation of school has been described as an 'egg box': for much of their working day teachers are contained in a school but are separated from each other, one to a compartment. This can promote a privatist, go-it-alone teaching culture which may rationalise this isolation, but also seals off teachers from colleagues, a potential source of learning.

Perceptions

Teachers' behaviour in class depends on their perceptions of the incidents which make up classroom life (Brown, 1975; Doyle, 1977; Carter and Doyle, 1987; also section 1.1.3). To understand a teacher's actions we have to understand how s/he perceives classroom events. If one hopes to change teachers' behaviour then one first has to understand these perceptions. For example, only by understanding teachers' perceptions of pairwork could we expect to attain sociality and work with them on its use in their classrooms (see also section 2.2).

However, teachers' perceptions of the classroom do not develop in isolation. Classrooms are also test-tube samples of school and local culture (e.g. Philips, 1972; Omokhodion, 1989; Kramsch and Sullivan, 1996; also section 2.2). Teacher-pupil relationships, the boundaries of acceptable behaviour, the classification of learners as weak or strong – all are framed by cultural expectations from outside the classroom. Also, a teacher's behaviour is affected by the responses of learners and by subtle interactions with colleagues outside the classroom. Through informal social behaviour, teachers transmit expectations of their occupational culture which create expectations in the individual (Somekh, 1993). School climate and occupational culture therefore influence teachers' thinking and behaviour in and out of class (section 1.1.4).

Teaching a second language

Perceptions of the target language (TL) will influence LTE objectives. To some the TL may be a medium for information, to others a system of rules, to others a social experience to be enacted in class. Each perception of language learning will tend to produce different classroom priorities, a very different methodology, and a different agenda for LTE.

The learning and teaching of language will also be affected by the perceptions of learners and teachers as to its place in the curriculum. It may be seen as an essential means of entry to an elite or for good career prospects. In this case, the subject may be associated with other priority subjects such as science or maths. In other cases it may be seen as relatively marginal, as it seems some pupils in English schools see modern languages. Additionally, there may be strong associated issues of identity and control where the language taught is dominant or international in nature. In the case of English in postcolonial societies, issues of personal identity and the status of the home culture are likely to be inseparable from English language and ELT issues (e.g. Phillipson, 1992; Widdowson, 1994; Hyde, 1995).

The LTE provider may not share the assumptions and beliefs of learner-teachers as regards the nature of the TL, language learning or its place in the curriculum. Their first task therefore is to respect these perceptions and try to understand them, that is to attain sociality. Also, change in teachers' thinking and behaviour requires work to help them to uncover and analyse their own implicit beliefs and routine practices, especially with reference to the nature of language and its place in society (Shulman, 1988; Griffiths and Tann, 1992; Bolitho and Tomlinson, 1995; also sections 1.2.3, 7.4 and 8.2).

The themes of routine and reflection, uncertainty and experiment, isolation and collegiality recur in our account of teacher learning needs (Chapter 2) and in our case studies (Chapters 6 and 8).

3.3   Knowledge-centred and person-centred paradigms

The models of teaching and of LTE we refer to in section 3.2 reflect distinctions which are fundamental in our culture: different paradigms of knowledge, how knowledge is obtained and how it guides our actions. Our argument here is that these paradigms serve as necessary compass points in our thinking about knowledge and learning, such as in the views of the person discussed in section 1.1. However, paradigms are too simple to guide the design of LTE programmes.

Our starting point is, therefore, that:

> The paradigms, slogans and beliefs that we use to justify particular approaches to teacher education tend often to be relatively simple and contrast sharply with the complex picture of learning to teach that is currently emerging from research on student teachers and on comparisons of experienced and inexperienced teachers.
>
> (Calderhead, 1990: 154–55)

Our perceptions of teaching and teacher knowledge are orientated by fundamental distinctions, which underpin such contrasts as the 'What?' and 'How?' orientations in the language syllabus (see section 3.3.4), and models of teacher as operative or teacher as problem-solver. Such contrasts are derived from two opposing traditions, respectively the positivist ('knowledge-centred') and phenomenological ('person-centred') paradigms of knowledge. These traditions are part of our culture and inevitably form part of the landscape within which each of us constructs our knowledge of the world. The social constructivist perspective tells us that each of us draws on traditions available in society from which to construct our own view of the world and of ourself. The role of these paradigms in orientating our thinking nicely demonstrates the social constructivist view.

Box 3.2 summarises the realisation of these traditions, in views of the curriculum, the person, the teacher and LTE. We suggest that the 'knowledge-centred' paradigm underpins the notion of person as 'input-output system', and model-based learning (section 1.1.1). The person-centred paradigm underpins humanistic and constructivist perspectives (sections 1.1.2 and 1.1.3).

Paradigm	Knowledge-centred	Person-centred
	The natural science paradigm: positivism	Humanistic paradigm: phenomenology
	'External' perspective: behaviour is determined by environment	'Internal' perspective: behaviour is self-determined
	Focus on objective knowing	Focus on personal knowing
View of curriculum	Type A: ends focus (e.g. grammatical syllabus)	Type B: process focus (task-based syllabus)
View of person	Person as input-output system	Person with self-agency
View of teacher	Operative/employee	Professional/'free agent'
Aspect of LTE	Model-based LTE	Nondirective intervention
		'Whole person' change and affective reactions Person as constructivist
		Focus on change in thinking
		Reflection on personal models and direct experience

Box 3.2   Paradigms, views of the person and LTE

3.3.1   The paradigms in contrast

All description is selective. If you were asked to look out of the window and describe what you saw, your first question would be: 'Why; what is the description for?' Knowing the reason for the description, you would have an idea what to attend to and what to ignore. Similarly, scientific description is based on decisions about what is significant to describe. A scientific *paradigm* consists of mutually consistent decisions about what to describe (what aspects of human behaviour are important) and how to describe it (appropriate methods). As they are based on assumptions about what is meaningful in human behaviour, all paradigms therefore make assumptions about what people are like: they start from an assumed *model of the person*. Put in another way, a scientific paradigm focuses on the aspects of the person that are most significant for its purpose (see sections 1.1–1.4).

In this section we outline two traditions in the construction of knowledge: the *positivist* paradigm and the *phenomenological* paradigm, which frame these views of the person.

The positivist view values knowledge which is objective and from which we can safely make generalisations. Such knowledge is, by definition, independent of and external to individual perceptions. On the other hand, the phenomenological position values the meaning which each person makes of the world. The positivist seeks general and reliable truths that are free of subjective distortion; the phenomenologist seeks to understand behaviour by understanding the person's inner life, perceptions and expectations. The former aims to produce generalisations unaffected by context, whereas the latter addresses the unique combination of features that provide the context for personal meaning.

Similarly, positivism approaches behaviour as determined by some features of the context *external* to the person (section 1.1.1) while the phenomenological position views our *internal* representations of the world as determining our actions and as of central importance in explaining them (section 1.1.3).

An acid test of the difference between the two paradigms lies in their approach to unique contexts of situation (such as the classroom situations in which teachers have to take action). Positivist ('natural science') knowledge is intended to make generalisations that are true across different contexts. Therefore, priority is given to such truths as can be generalised across contexts, such as some general rules for effective classroom teaching. We should note therefore that any generalisations about teaching and learning have to assume that local differences between classrooms, teachers and learners do not invalidate the general truth.

A phenomenological view would stress the particular meaning of events to the participants, and also the difficulty or impossibility of applying all-purpose generalisations to unique combinations of circumstances. Such an approach would tend to emphasise the variable or unpredictable nature of the situation (Parlett and Hamilton, 1977). These contrasting views appear throughout this book in a variety of guises. We can refer to them as 'external' and 'internal' perspectives on the person, in that positivism places knowledge outside the individual and phenomenological/humanistic approaches view knowledge as each person's inner representations of the world (section 1.1.3). We could also refer to public knowledge (produced by empirical natural science, available in books and lectures) and private knowledge (the personal knowledge of individuals, built from experience and interpretation of public knowledge).

When discussing professional education and the use of knowledge to influence practice, we can suggest the same distinction by referring to a positivist 'applied science' view (that public knowledge can and should determine effective action) and a 'reflective' view that reflection on public and personal knowing determines action (Wallace, 1991; section 1.2).

The two traditions reflect ethical and political differences, most clearly seen in their approach to individuals, their right to self-determination and their uniqueness. The positivist deals with groups (in order to make safe generalisations) whereas the phenomenologist is concerned with individuals (in order to understand their perceptions and motivations). The positivist view implies that action can best be guided by general and reliable truths, while the phenomenologist's view implies that action is determined by the nature of the individuals engaged in the action and the unique combination of circumstances met in any given setting. In short, one view gives priority to general truths (a knowledge-centred view) while the other focuses on the role of the individual (a person-centred view).

As an example of this distinction, a positivist/natural science approach to the explanation of snooker works well to predict the relative direction and speed of the snooker balls: the balls are all the same weight and size, the surface the same, and there are general laws that predict their motion. Similarly, it would try to describe general truths about the effects of fatigue and stress on concentration, reaction times and muscle control, whoever the player might be.

A phenomenologist would be interested in the players, and the perceptions and expectations which explain their actions. S/he therefore has to take into account the special circumstances of the individual and of the context (the time, place and conditions of the game). S/he would also be interested in the social meaning of taking part.

It should be clear from this example that positivists and phenomenologists have different priorities, different purposes, ask different questions, and have a different view about what is worth describing and explaining.

3.3.2   Positivism: a knowledge-centred view

The positivist view asserts that: 'the aims and methods of natural science should be applied to all realms of knowledge, including the study of people' (Roth, 1990: 829).

Positivism developed as a reaction to mentalism (introspection and mysticism as roads to knowledge) and so its goal is to establish objective truth, in the form of general natural laws, built from empirical observation and free from superstition and false beliefs:

> the only significant statements about the world were to be based on empirical observation, and all disagreements about the world could be resolved, in principle, by reference to observable facts. Propositions which were neither analytically [i.e. logically] or empirically testable were held to have no meaning at all.
>
> (Schön 1983: 31–32)

The experimental method is the essential tool for a positivist approach to the creation of knowledge. In terms of human learning, behaviourist psychology is the classic example of a positivist approach to making knowledge about human behaviour. It is constructed from empirical observation in the framework of experimental research designs and is intended to produce general laws about human behaviour.

In teacher education, a positivist approach is represented by curricula which assume that the presentation of generalised knowledge about teaching is an adequate form of professional preparation, and which view 'practical knowledge of anything (as) simply a matter of relating the most appropriate means to whatever objectives have been decided on' (Wallace, 1991: 8). We can therefore see model-based LTE (section 1.1.1) as consistent with a positivist/external paradigm of knowledge.

Positivism and the transmission of knowledge

It is argued that knowledge made by the natural science method is most likely to be transmitted, by 'imposition from above and from outside' (Dewey, 1938: 18), because it is external to and independent of the personal knowing of individuals and because it is the property of an elite (researchers, academics, teachers, experts). It is for this reason that we can refer to a positivist approach to professional education as an 'applied science' model (also referred to by Schön as 'technical rationality'; section 1.2.2).

There are two main criticisms of this form of knowledge: that it cannot be a sufficient guide to action, and that it leads practitioners to overdependence on experts.

A sufficient guide for action?

One danger of a positivist view of knowledge is that it suggests that human problems can be treated in merely technical terms, and can be resolved by using general scientific truths. It suggests that a professional's actions are best guided by objective knowledge. It is this view which Schön (1983) characterises as the technical rationality (TR) view of how knowledge can guide effective professional action.

When Schön (1983: 30–37) refers to technical rationality (TR) as the positivist epistemology of professional practice, he means that TR views effective social action (practice) as guided by a form of knowledge that is scientific in nature (a positivist epistemology). Professional knowledge in a TR view exists as a body of objective and empirically validated laws external to and independent of the professional person which s/he will then bring to bear to solve problems by the best technical means (hence 'technical rationality'). An example would be a doctor drawing on objective scientific knowledge to diagnose and treat a disease. Schön's criticism is that conditions for action are always unpredictable and unique, and so practical action is guided not only by general truths but also by a unique act of judgement. Therefore, he argues, expertise consists of an ability to identify and solve unique and novel problems, not the acquisition and deployment of scientific knowledge.

It is important to note that Schön refers throughout to the knowledge of 'major professionals' (as in medicine, engineering and architecture) whose training had been based on a TR view. We discuss Schön's critique of TR and his views on expertise in more detail in section 1.2.2.

False dependency?

By implication, a TR approach to action 'created the illusion of objective reality over which the individual has no control, and hence to a decline in the capacity of individuals to reflect upon their own situations and change them through their own actions' (Carr and Kemmis, 1986: 130). In other words, teachers accepting a TR view would assume that their work consisted of the deployment of safe, all-purpose prescriptions sanctioned by the knowledge of experts. Problems and difficulties would be resolved by calling on expert knowledge.

This transfer of responsibility can be seen as problematic for a number of reasons. First, it places the teacher in a socially subordinate position and denies her capacity for autonomous action. However, it is the teacher and not the expert who has to take ultimate responsibility for her work. Second, because teaching is done under highly variable conditions, the outsider/expert may not be able to modify generalised knowledge to meet these conditions. Third, the expert may not understand what conditions affect the teacher's work and may offer knowledge that is irrelevant to the task at hand. Finally, it disregards the fact that the teacher will construe teaching and her self as teacher in personal ways (Freeman, 1992; section 1.1.3).

The adoption of a positivist view will lead to an approach to teacher education in which prescribed and reliable knowledge is provided on the assumption that it will be a guide to effective action. Therefore authoritative models will be required to lead teachers' future practice.

3.3.3   Phenomenology: a person-centred view

To a phenomenologist, the task of description is to explain the meaning people give to their own experience. It is 'concerned with understanding conscious experience, personal meaning and the experience of what it is to be human, rather than explaining behaviour through general laws' (Roth, 1990: 830). In summary, its characteristics are:

- it presents a picture of persons as self-determining because their own representations of the world guide their actions;
- it tries to understand behaviour by understanding the perceptions of the person;
- it recognises the unique configuration of factors that provides the real-life context for us to think, act and learn;
- it accepts that people act in settings that are variable and unpredictable.

This view supports an approach to teacher education which will emphasise the preparation of teachers to cope with the unpredictable: to recognise unique combinations of circumstances and to act effectively within them. It denies any approach to LTE based exclusively on the imitation of models.

Humanistic and constructivist theories are within the phenomenological tradition, because they embrace 'the individuality, awareness, agency and self-determination of people' (Roth, 1990: 830). The essence of humanistic theory is its notion of 'self-agency', the self-determining power of persons (section 1.1.2). The essence of constructivism is that it views each person building a mental representation of the world which guides their learning and behaviour (section 1.1.3). This private representation overlaps with others (the basis for communication and social life) but not entirely. This implies that individuals act differently in part because they have perceived the world differently.

There are at least two ethical implications of the humanistic and constructivist positions:

- we should recognise each person's self-determination, their right to internally motivated actions;
- we should accept the legitimacy of each person's interpretations of the world rather than dismiss them as untrue or merely subjective or idiosyncratic.

However, these notions cannot be applied in LTE design without considering teachers' cultural and political worlds. Knowledge-centred and person-centred perspectives naturally associate with different political and moral beliefs. Conservative or authoritarian systems, especially those which implement centralised curricula, are unlikely to be sympathetic to principles of pluralism and independent decision-making by teachers (see section 8.2).

Political/cultural climate and LTE policy are not readily separated. A centralised or authoritarian system will tend to endorse a positivist approach to knowledge and the related assumptions about teacher learning we have suggested above. On the other hand, democratic capitalist cultures provide a climate favourable to a phenomenological view. Their emphasis on individualism gives value to each person's unique perceptions of the world (see section 1.2.1 on the work of Dewey). In contrast, group-orientated cultures might reinterpret the individual's exercise of autonomy as license, irresponsibility or, at the least, a threat to harmony (e.g. Kramsch and Sullivan, 1996).

3.3.4   The value of paradigms

Design requires us to formulate objectives, and to do this requires us to ask some difficult questions:

- what do experienced teachers know?
- what does their work consist of?

- how do they learn to teach?
- how does public, objective knowledge affect teachers' actions?

These are issues of epistemology. Decisions about types of knowledge; how it is acquired; how it is communicated (i.e. transmitted between social groups); how individuals construct their personal knowledge of the world; and how it guides action: *all* require epistemological assumptions which are also inseparable from moral assumptions. As a single example, if we believe that what teachers know about using new materials has value, and that this knowledge should be taken into account by central curriculum planners, it would suggest INSET by means of curriculum inquiry (see section 2.6.3). This would be to adopt a political stance as regards the power teachers should have in the curriculum they implement.

Therefore, the nature of teacher knowledge is not merely an 'academic' matter (i.e. irrelevant and self-indulgent!). All providers need to reflect on the assumptions which underlie the teacher education curriculum they are helping to shape and transmit. Issues in epistemology are not limited to the concerns of academics, in their ivory tower up on the 'hard high ground' (Schön, 1984: 42), while practitioners try to cope with the messy confusion of real situations, the 'swampy lowlands' where they have to make day-to-day decisions (1984: 43). These issues are of deep personal importance to teachers because they determine the basis of professional training, the respective status of teachers' knowledge and that of experts, and the extent to which we expect teachers to take control of their own learning.

In the field of ELT, positivist and phenomenological views of knowledge underlie contrasted views of the syllabus and the roles of teachers and learners (Breen, 1987a) as summarised by White (1988: 44–45), as follows.

Type A What is to be learnt? Interventionist	**Type B How is it to be learnt?**
External to the learner	Internal to the learner
Other directed	Inner directed or self-fulfilling
Determined by authority	Negotiated between learners and teachers
Teacher as decision-maker	Learner and teacher as joint decision-makers
Content: what the subject is to the learner	Content: what the subject is to the expert
Content: a gift to the learner from the teacher or knower	Content: what the learner brings and wants
Objectives defined in advance	Objectives described afterwards

Subject emphasis	Process emphasis
Assessment by achievement or mastery	Assessment in relationship to learners' criteria of success
Doing things to the learner	Doing things for or with the learner

White's distinction can be useful in clarifying one's general approach to language instruction. However, when we look at real life, we find that we cannot, as it were, sort all the features of teaching and the curriculum into either one box labelled 'What?' or another box labelled 'How?'! Rather, we can associate each feature more or less closely with one pole or the other, at some point along a scale. For example, when we characterise a syllabus, it is far more likely that we will see it as putting relatively more emphasis on grammar or method, and not as exclusively focused on one or the other.

The picture is made more complicated because people are not as logical and consistent as are abstract paradigms! We are quite capable of associating some features closer to one pole (such as seeing self as facilitator) but other features closer to the other (such as seeing teachers as selecting the content to be taught). We are all capable of containing such apparent contradictions in our thinking.

In summary, we construe elements of our experience (such as syllabus, teacher or assessment) by association with polar constructs. We do not construe events in terms of only 'black and white', and we are not as logical or consistent as abstract paradigms (see section 1.1.3).

While it is more appropriate to see opposing paradigms as compass points rather than absolute descriptions of the world, they are useful in reminding us of the ethical dimensions of what we do. We have to make practical decisions which contain assumptions which have ethical and political meaning. This is because the positivist and phenomenological traditions reflect fundamentally different value positions, respectively the appeal to authority and continuity, and the appeal to individual self-determination and pluralism (Parlett and Hamilton, 1977; Schön, 1983). There is a danger for LTE that the adoption of these mutually exclusive ideological and moral positions may lead to a 'partisan' approach to LTE design, where a single dimension of teacher learning is given overriding priority. It is what Schön referred to as 'the dilemma of rigor or relevance' (Schön, 1984: 42) that is the appeal to prescription and certainty on one side, or the appeal to the idiosyncrasies of individual teachers and classrooms on the other. Our view is that while we must be aware of the fundamentals represented by paradigms, design should not and could not be framed by paradigms, nor by dichotomies such as rigour or relevance, theory or practice, private or public knowledge, training or development, craft or reflective. We prefer to approach LTE by recognising that teachers' learning needs are complex and multidimensional, too complex to be met by designs based exclusively on single paradigms or dichotomies (section 1.1.5). We develop this point in the next section by suggesting some health warnings about 'paradigm dependency'.

3.3.5   Paradigms of teacher education: some health warnings

Discussion of teacher education (TE) in the literature has referred to underlying paradigms, which provide a consistent view on teaching, teacher expertise and teacher learning. As an example, we summarise below paradigms of teacher education proposed by Zeichner (1983) and Wallace (1991).

behaviourist	TE as mastery by imitation of scientifically validated behavioural skills (e.g. micro-teaching)
personalistic	TE as growth of the whole person and assertion of the self (e.g. counselling-based approaches)
traditional craft	TE as mastery of inherited craft knowledge by means of apprenticeship to a master teacher (e.g. whole school-based ITE)
inquiry	TE as development in attitudes and skills-orientated enabling teachers to analyse novel pedagogic problems and arrive at contextually appropriate solutions Zeichner (1983)
craft model	the young trainee learns by imitating the expert's techniques, and by following the expert's instructions and advice
applied science model	professional education seen as the acquisition of empirical scientific knowledge as the basis for effective practice, a theory-into-practice approach
reflective model	develop expertise by direct experience and conscious reflection about that experience; enable development by exposing assumptions that underlie routine behaviour and considering alternatives Wallace (1991)

Zeichner suggested four orientations to teacher education, in turn focusing on learning as mastery of behaviourally defined practical competencies; as personal realisation; as acquiring the craft knowledge of an experienced teacher; and as becoming an independent problem-solver. In a similar analysis, Wallace suggested three orientations: the craft model; the applied science model; and a reflective model in which development is enabled by critical and conscious reflection on one's practice.

Paradigms are helpful because they make us aware of principles underlying day-to-day practice. However, they can become restrictive if they are used uncritically, the more so if they are used to justify polarised and value-loaded positions about teachers and teacher learning.

Paradigms are simple, the real world is complex

Teacher education (TE) raises complex issues in approach, design and implementation. This is due to the internal complexity of the types of knowledge deployed by established language teachers: behavioural (classroom skills), cognitive (perceptions and beliefs, tactical and strategic decisions), affective (relationships with others and emotional reactions to learning and change); and social (meeting occupational norms and the expectations of others, making working relationships).

It is also due to the diversity of social variables: the nature of the language curriculum, classroom and school culture, the social context of the school, and the impact of policy and resource decisions.

> Research on learning to teach would seem to suggest that becoming a teacher involves complex changes and development not only in behaviour but also in cognition, affect and knowledge, and that these changes occur within a powerful ideological context. Learning to teach involves acquiring a repertoire of pedagogical behaviour, but it also requires the development of ways of thinking about children, the curriculum and the task of teaching, resolving certain commitments and beliefs about teaching and about one's role as a teacher, acquiring knowledge related to the teaching task, and adapting and interacting with the pressures that school and the educational context bring to bear upon teachers' work.
>
> (Calderhead, 1990: 155)

LTE for English teachers is diverse for discipline-specific reasons relating to the social meaning of teaching English: internationalism and the role of the language. ELT teacher training is international, with circumstances that vary in almost every respect: purpose, political control, funding, structure, staffing, and cultural traditions. The nature of English language classrooms and schools similarly varies: in size, resources, learner characteristics, roles and interaction types. As a result, training and development opportunities are hugely variable between different contexts, producing great variety in English language teacher education (ELTE) programmes.

The role of English in curricula also diversifies the role of English language teachers. In some societies, English is a true foreign language, restricted to use with native speakers. Elsewhere, such as in Singapore, South Africa or India, it is one code in a bilingual or multilingual culture. Furthermore, there are many Englishes to be taught (Widdowson, 1994; Bisong, 1995). In some contexts British Standard English (BSE) may be appropriate to language syllabuses, but elsewhere, a local variety may be preferred because it asserts the local identity of users in the face of the global power of BSE. Some teachers may have to make a choice of variety, and may find the use of BSE places them in a sensitive no-man's-land between local culture and learner identity on one hand and on the other the global forces represented by English and the need to learn it (Hyde, 1995).

We therefore suggest that no one paradigm, nor crude dichotomies between paradigms, is or are adequate to account for the complex, variable and context-specific nature of language teacher learning: 'At present, we have no one theoretical framework to account for these different areas of development and to provide us with an overview of the complex processes and interactions involved' (Calderhead, 1990: 155). Thus, any attempt to classify a teacher education programme as belonging to one of a few distinctive types or paradigms is bound to oversimplify the case:

> The paradigms, slogans and beliefs that we use to justify particular approaches to teacher education tend often to be relatively simple and contrast sharply with the complex picture of learning to teach that is currently emerging from research on student teachers and on comparisons of experienced and inexperienced teachers. Detailed accounts of teacher educators' own experiences tend also to confirm that learning to teach is a complex and variable process. Zeichner's four paradigms, for instance, are, on closer examination, far from the discrete analytical categories that they first appear. It may well be that all four paradigms are more or less appropriate in different contexts, in relation to different aspects of teachers' work, or at different stages in a teacher's career.
>
> (Calderhead, 1990: 154–55)

It is quite possible for one LTE programme to contain objectives and activities consistent with different paradigms. As Freeman and Richards (1993: 211–12) observe regarding ITE, model-based paradigms (craft or behaviourist) 'might be taken as appropriate for novice trainees who lack the depth of classroom experience to pursue ... improvisational forms of instruction' while a more inquiry-based approach becomes appropriate 'when trainees are in professional settings in which they are encouraged to think philosophically about the reasoning which underlies their teaching'. They go on to suggest a 'developmentalist' view, that at early stages in teacher learning a model-based approach is most appropriate while at later stages an inquiry orientation is best.

We would suggest, however, that even this view is an oversimplification. As Sendan (1995b: 9) observes: 'it seems to imply a simple linear progression ...

(in teacher learning) . . . and fails to address both the complexities of teaching, and the highly complex, idiosyncratic nature of an individual trainee's or teacher's personal and professional development' (see also section 2.4.6). Therefore, an LTE programme cannot be expected to be consistent with only one paradigm; nor should we expect to apply only one paradigm at a given point in a programme or a teacher's career.

Oversimplification of factors in design?

Institutional history tends to produce hybrid curricula. As Calderhead (1990: 153) points out: 'The form that any particular course of initial training takes can be attributed to a variety of factors, including historical development, organisational factors within the institution, staffing levels, national policy restrictions and, of course, the views, preferences and values of individual tutors.' Thus any LTE design has to make trade-offs between theoretical assumptions, institutional history and local conditions, and as a result we are more likely to come across programmes that are hybrids rather than 'paradigmatically pure'.

Oversimplified terms?

Labels such as 'reflective teacher education' (a virtual buzzword in the past ten years) are in fact extremely vague. Munby and Russell (1993) reviewed seven TE programmes in the USA claiming to be reflective, but found almost no common features between the seven: 'there is no shared sense of "reflection" to give direction to future developments' (1993: 431). Colclough (1996) reached a similar conclusion in a small-scale study of the UCLES CTEFLA.

Vague and generalised notions are not likely to be helpful when working with the complex, multilevel needs of real learner-teachers. The more clearly we conceptualise our objectives, and the more clearly we can share them with learners and colleagues, then the more effective our work can be. As Freeman and Richards (1993: 194) put it, the need for awareness of 'embedded conceptions of teaching is crucial to the maturation of the field of second language instruction'.

Irrelevant paradigms?

Schön (1983) proposed a dichotomy in the definition of expertise: technical rationality (TR) where practice is guided by objective knowledge, and the reflective practitioner, where it is guided by creative reframing of problems. The key process in this reframing is, he argued, reflection in action ('thinking about what we do while we do it'; Smyth, 1987: 3).

His work is highly persuasive, especially in his critique of positivist approaches to practice, and is supported by a brilliant use of metaphor, which perhaps distracts the reader from an absence of fact. In section 1.2.2 we have already made some criticisms of his view. Two points are made here. One is that his dichotomy was not intended to apply to teaching. The other is that it cannot reflect the complexities of learning to teach.

Schön's position is grounded in controversy over professional education for doctors, engineers and lawyers in the USA in the 1970s. Schön himself explicitly *excluded* teaching from consideration as a major profession, because it lacked a homogeneous body of theoretical knowledge and professional practice. He therefore excludes teaching from his discussion of professional education. Schön is quite consistent in this. In discussing the reflective practitioner, his examples are in contexts quite unlike teaching, and he actually goes into detail (1983: 329–36) to argue that conventional school culture militates against reflection-in-action. To this we can add our own scepticism that teachers, while actually teaching, can 'reflect in action': 'think critically about the thinking that got us into this fix or this opportunity; and we may, in the process, restructure strategies of action, understandings of phenomena or ways of framing problems' (1983: 28). We accept entirely that we can reflect on action, after the event, a notion no different from reframing or Dewey's notion of reflective thinking (section 1.2.1).

In spite of Schön's exclusion of teaching from his argument, the notion of reflective practitioner has been widely cited as the basis for teacher education programmes. The inappropriateness of the TR/reflective distinction to teaching might be one reason why there are such diverse ranges of activities described as being 'reflective'. In the case of LTE it would be more accurate to reduce the term to the common factor all these meanings seem to have: a cognitive view of teacher learning.

A single dimension

In section 1.2.2 we suggest that Schön's account of expertise is too narrow: it applies only to creativity, not to expertise as a whole. We cannot compress teachers' professional development into a single dimension of 'reflection'. Important as self-awareness is in teacher learning, it is only one dimension of change. Teacher development involves multilevel changes which therefore demand multilevel experiences (as section 1.1.5, Box 4.3, Figure 6.1 and Table 8.4). Apart from processes of reflection, we all need access to theory and new ideas, and we often need to practise skills to understand the ideas underlying them. The complexity of teacher learning suggests that a complex of related activities are needed to help teachers develop their sense of 'the teacher I am now' and 'the teacher I want to be'.

In this chapter we have argued that we need to be aware of fundamental distinctions which frame our practical thinking. However, we also argue that paradigms and dichotomies are not an adequate guide to design. Paradigms, and contrasts between paradigms, are generalised and oversimple. Because of the complexities of teacher learning, providers should expect to offer diverse and integrated learning activities to address the multiple dimensions of learning to teach (section 1.1.5, Box 4.3 and Table 8.4), adapted to context and the people they work with (see sections 4.2, 6.2, 6.3, 7.2, 8.2–8.6).

Part 2: initial teacher education

4

Two aspects of ITE design

4.1 Introduction

Initial ITE courses vary enormously: from a four-week intensive course for private-sector teachers to a five-year degree course in the state system; from emergency training to meet a shortage in secondary schools to education for a lifelong career in language education.

A particular complication is that a clear-cut distinction between ITE and INSET only applies to teachers, usually in state systems, who have followed the conventional sequence of school-ITE-teaching-INSET. In ELT, in contrast, many teachers have done other jobs before turning to teaching, while others start teaching with no ITE and take their first course after some years' experience (section 6.3). Their approach to ITE will certainly be different from that of an inexperienced school-leaver (see section 6.3 discussion). We cannot really address all the possible variations, and so have to discuss design in general terms, backed up by examples in our appendices and case studies. Therefore in this chapter we consider two issues: the effect of pre-existing factors on design choices (see Box 4.1) and the principle of coherence, the integration between different course components (Wallace, 1991: 153). In Appendix 4.1 we summarise the main types of activity to be integrated. In Appendix 4.2 we suggest an ITE 'proto-syllabus'

Accreditation requirements

Intake: numbers, full/part-time involvement, characteristics	Geography
	Income and costs
Course duration and structure	Staff conditions of work: full/part-time, nature of role

Staff weaknesses, strengths and attitudes

Box 4.1   ITE design parameters

of possible objectives based on the frameworks in Part 1. In Appendix 4.3 we provide a general design checklist. In Chapter 5 we discuss ITE from the standpoint of a provider's concerns: input, feedback and assessment.

4.2   Preconditions and design

Design is affected by preconditions which are often beyond the control of individual providers. At the broadest level, the goals of an ITE programme are determined by its place in the education system as a whole, and by its social purpose. Regarding its place in the system, we should distinguish clearly between the state and private systems. In the state sector an ITE programme will be part of the general teacher education structure of the country. It will take forms that are determined by history and educational traditions, the resources available, and the status of teachers. A critical feature of state-system LTE is that it is bound by government policy and a legally enforced framework of requirements (e.g. section 6.2). The function of private-sector LTE is to meet the needs of private-sector schools (though there are cases of state funding being provided for access to privately run courses), and, again in the main, it is funded by fee-paying trainees. As such, the requirements of employers and the constraints of operating on a fee-only income will influence design preconditions (see sections 6.2 and 6.3).

The purpose of an ITE programme will depend on such structural factors as the occupational status of teachers in society and the demand for teachers in schools. We illustrate a complex picture with two extreme cases. If there is a crisis of teacher supply in state schools, perhaps because of civil war or lack of resources, then the priority will be to provide large numbers of adequately competent teachers. This may require emergency programmes, such as apprenticeship schemes, or 'eased entry' schemes, or shortened programmes so that the intake can be deployed back in school as quickly as possible. In a situation where teachers' social status is high and there are no shortages, then programmes are likely to be relatively lengthy and with demands equivalent to any other higher-education qualification. Therefore providers in the two situations will be working with entirely different training agendas set by these preconditions.

In Box 4.1 we summarise the main preconditions, whose effects on design are discussed under the subheadings below. Of course, in the real world, each context will produce a unique mix of these preconditions, requiring a series of unique decisions.

Accreditation and accountability

Accreditation requirements usually fix basic design parameters such as course hours, time for teaching practice, compulsory and optional subjects and assessment. While these requirements are non-negotiable, they may be relatively restrictive or open in different situations (see section 6.3 for an example of the latter). The degree of official monitoring and accountability can similarly vary. Accrediting bodies may leave staff relatively free of oversight (as in section 6.3), or, alternatively, they may impose strict conditions which impinge on providers' work. For example, in the programme described in section 6.2, staff are subject to no fewer than seven different forms of scrutiny and accountability, a combination of internal quality assurance procedures and the legally enforced external demands of a government agency.

Geography

The relative physical concentration or dispersal of participants directly affects design. Concentration enables at least two course structures: long-term drip-feed (e.g. one half-day a week for a year) or long-term intensive (e.g. resident students on a one-year degree course).

In contrast, if participants are widely dispersed and if travel is difficult, then courses either have to be dispersed (as in 'cascade' schemes) or offered as infrequent blocks (e.g. two two-week blocks in a year), or, as is increasingly popular, as distance programmes with occasional course-based sessions.

These different structures are bound to have profound effects on objectives, staff roles, and the use of contact time. To illustrate this point, the advantages and disadvantages of block and drip-feed structures are summarised in Table 4.1.

Intake

The characteristics of teachers entering the ITE course will set fundamental limits to design. These would include such factors as their levels of TL competence, their general education, and their motives for entry. For example, with a school-leaver intake, part of the function of an ITE course is to complete their general education. With a graduate intake, on the other hand, a course would be geared specifically to pedagogy (section 6.2). In LTE, the existing language competence of entrants is certain to affect design, in that it will determine the proportion of course time devoted to language improvement and the analysis of language systems. The general standards of English in the secondary system will therefore impact on design. For instance, in a four-year degree programme for non-native-speaker teachers, the first year at least could be devoted to language improvement; in some cases this could also constitute a significant component throughout the whole course.

Part-time/full-time

The source of funding will determine whether student-teachers are part-time or full-time. Typically, self-funding students will attend either low-intensity courses as working part-timers or short intensive courses as full-timers. Full-timers can commit themselves to course activities with relatively few

Table 4.1 High- and low-intensity courses

Short intensive	Drip-feed
Advantages	
Continuity of focus between sessions enhances coherence	Allows 'digestion' and reflection time between sessions
Energy can be sustained throughout the course	Input can be in the form of readings between sessions, so contact time is freed up for discussion, experiential activities etc.
	Integration by means of repeated cycles which alternate classroom experience and course activity
	Fee payment may be spread over a longer period
Risks	
Insufficient reflection time	Loss of momentum, dropouts due to overload
Insufficient linkage to place of work	If dispersed: lack of study resources
No contribution to longer-term development	
Content limited to consensus areas only because adaptation to participant needs demands negotiation and preparation time	
Best context	
Where participants can only be brought together for a short period (e.g. if widely dispersed)	Where all participants are from the same institution
Where training objectives are agreed and clear-cut	Where objectives can be adjusted to the distinctive needs of the participants

distractions. Courses can be designed in integrated whole-day, whole-week and whole-term blocks. However, with part-timers, especially on long drip-feed courses, participants are at greater risk of dropping out because their circumstances change, or because they cannot sustain multiple demands on their time. This is balanced by the possibility of integrating courses with their teaching. Of our case studies, section 6.2 describes a one-year full-time course, while in 6.3 we discuss the contrast between more and less intensive initial training courses.

Funding and structure

Course structures are determined by an equation that balances accreditation requirements, course objectives, income, costs and staffing levels. The connection between these can be exemplified as follows (see also section 6.3). In the case of a short course for self-funded trainees, an intensive course structure offers around 30 hours' contact a week for four weeks (6 hours a day × 5 days × 4 weeks = 120 hours). If staffing and other fixed weekly costs demand a break-even income of about £2,500 a week, then a total cost of £10,000 can be met by 13 students paying around £800 each.

Many providers are aware that a longer and less intensive course might be desirable (e.g. six weeks × 25 hours a week). However, this would either raise fees to a point the market could not bear, or force an increase in group sizes which staffing levels could not support. Therefore, intensive courses are usually four weeks long. Alternatively, longer-term drip-feed courses can be provided for participants who can pay as they go, by staff released from their normal teaching duties. It should be added that organisations offering courses such as the UCLES CELTA (section 6.3) usually aim only to break even financially and also intend to optimise standards by keeping ratios as low as possible.

In other contexts, as in state systems, limited central funding can lead to large student numbers and high staff-student ratios. In this situation, student-teachers can receive a high number of course hours, but only in forms determined by these ratios. Activities have certain desirable group sizes: a plenary session at a maximum of around 60, workshop around 15, teaching practice around six, supervision two, and so on. Where ratios are high and resources are limited, then providers may be forced into lecture mode to transmit information. Also, low-ratio activities (such as regular individual feedback and supervision) may have to be abandoned or devolved to other structures, such as to self-help groups of students or co-operating school teachers. This transfer of responsibility can aid participation of students and other teachers, but cannot be effective unless it is supported administratively and by adequate preparation and training (see section 6.2). Thus fairly simple calculations of income against cost will determine some basic parameters for a design: duration, intensity, and staff-student ratios. It follows that the programme objectives will have to be modified according to these parameters.

Staff: conditions of work

Design is strongly affected by the employment conditions which determine staff roles.

Full-time or part-time staff

The presence of full-time, established staff indicates adequate and stable funding of an institution. The employment of part-timers as a proportion of an institution's staff is quite normal, and in fact is often a good deal for the employer. However, over-reliance on part-timers is usually caused by cost-cutting, or inadequate conditions of employment. Part-timers, especially if they are casualised and on short-term contracts, are liable to be in the institution only in paid time and as a result may not overlap with other staff (Weir and Roberts, 1994; Chapter 5). The institution may seem very busy, but in the same way as a station concourse: staff are running from one classroom to another, with no time for more than hello and goodbye. As a result, formal liaison (as in staff meetings) becomes extremely hard to maintain. Key activities to further course coherence and peer learning such as joint supervision or collaborative course development become hard to arrange, and impossible if teachers' timetables do not match. At worst, when dependence on part-timers is associated with rapid staff turnover, then staff may feel little commitment to the organisation, to occupational affairs or to the development of the curriculum. As a result the programme's quality and potential for development can be severely limited. Therefore, employment conditions are fundamental to the quality of an ITE programme. A stable full- or part-time staff is needed to maximise commitment and continuity. Timetabling to allow staff to meet is essential to enable course coherence and development.

Mixed or specialised roles?

ITE providers may specialise as a course tutor or they may have a mixed role (language teacher and course tutor as in section 6.3, mentors as in section 6.2). In the case of a mixed role, the possible advantages and disadvantages are outlined below.

Advantages

- Greater credibility with learner-teachers on matters of pedagogy.
- More in touch with classroom reality and so able to justify and criticise theory from a practical standpoint.
- More able to communicate practical teacher thinking.
- Better able to provide demonstrations and input on methods.
- Better able to give feedback on the appropriacy of teaching to context.
- More likely to engage in an equal power relationship with learner-teachers, so opening up communication with them.

Disadvantages

- May lack specialised knowledge relevant to the curriculum (e.g. on aspects of learning theory or language systems).

- May have a strong investment in their own style of teaching and be less open to learner-teachers with different personal styles.

Specialist teacher trainers, particularly those who have not taught for some time, may suffer from the reverse of the advantages of a mixed role. For example, they may lack credibility on practical issues because of their time out of the classroom. However, they may have corresponding strengths:

- to develop the specialised knowledge needed for the ITE curriculum;
- to develop the specialised skills required of supervision and feedback;
- to develop complex course administration skills.

The role of specialist trainers can also vary significantly: some might teach only one type of course (e.g. theory only, language improvement only, methods only) or they may teach courses of different types (e.g. some theoretical, some on methods). According to the range of courses they teach, they will relate to learner teachers in either relatively narrow or relative broad ways (e.g. as lecturer, as teaching practice supervisor, as process leader).

A narrow role means that staff see learner-teachers in only one context. This can prevent them from seeing connections between their own course and others, and from seeing student-teachers' responses to the whole ITE curriculum. As a result they may be unable to select the content of their own course to integrate well with others. Also, they will not be able to see what use student-teachers are making of their course in teaching and other requirements of the programme. As we also suggest in section 4.3, broader staff roles contribute to the overall quality of courses because they enhance coherence between courses and the selection of relevant content. It is for this reason, for example, that UCLES expects staff to be involved in both input/methods courses and teaching practice. However, broad involvement of staff is limited by practical constraints (such as timetabling) and their own capabilities and preferences.

Staff attributes

The attributes of staff must be taken into account in a design, and are certain to determine the quality of its implementation. The experience, education, personal theories and preferences of staff will determine their teaching and supervision contributions, how they relate to each other and to learner-teachers.

A critical attribute is the attitude of staff to each other: institutional culture may be collegial or individualist. If the former, there is more likelihood of a coherent approach to the ITE curriculum and of sustained programme development (section 4.3). Then, their competence in TL and also their personal theories about its nature (e.g. as a medium of communication, as a library language, as a discipline) will affect their approaches to teaching, to methodology, and to supervision and practical feedback. Finally, as teaching practice supervisors, their response to the classroom style of learner-teachers is likely to be skewed by its match with their own (Cook and Richards, 1972; section 5.2). However, these predispositions are rarely considered by staff themselves. They may never be required to confront their personal theories, their views of the curriculum and their relationships with learner-teachers. Therefore the implementation of an ITE may be subject to the unexamined and diverse personal theories and ideologies of staff. The greater the mismatch between these personal theories and those implicit in the ITE design, the less likely is effective implementation. Similarly, the greater the differences between the personal theories of staff, the less easy it is to achieve overall course coherence (section 5.2).

4.3   Coherent design

By coherence we mean 'how far are the course designers going to try and ensure that the different elements in the course will be seen as relevant to one another and forming a coherent training experience?' (Wallace, 1991: 153). Coherence between course elements is important in any curriculum, the more so in ITE because the curriculum can contain such diverse but interdependent knowledge bases (section 3.2.2). Evidence on effective teacher education courses suggests that they are characterised by coherence, as realised by: a thematic approach; cohort groups; a context for practice that is compatible with inputs and consensus among staff (Graber, 1996).

Coherence can be longitudinal (an appropriate order of learning experiences) or simultaneous (appropriate grouping and integration between course elements in the same period). Longitudinal coherence can be achieved by effective sequencing (see below and sections 6.2 and 6.3).

Developing practical skills

Teaching practice can be organised to maximise coherence between input and classroom experience. There are two common designs (Box 4.2): block practice or cycles with relatively short intervals between practice and course-based activity (as in partnership schemes and intensive UCLES CTEFLA courses, sections 6.2 and 6.3). A third option not discussed here, internship, entails the placement of teachers for a whole year in schools after full-time college courses, but with a reduced load and some supervision (Wallace, 1991).

In long programmes, both options could be used (see section 6.2). Each structure has its implications for course coherence. Block practice allows extended

| course with occasional block practice | OOOOOOOOOOOOOOOOOOXXX |
| course and school experience in integrated cycles | XXOOXXXOOXXXXOOXXXXOO |

Box 4.2   Teaching practice structures

practice under the supervision of a teacher, but risks lack of liaison between school and the ITE course (section 2.4.5). Linked cycles can integrate practice and input very effectively, but demand close liaison between the tutor and class teachers, which demands effective organisation and constant monitoring.

Grading practical experience

As student-teachers lack confidence and the skills needed to manage a whole class, they need to start teaching in relatively sheltered situations. At the same time, teaching practice needs to be as realistic as possible, to offer the best conditions for novice teachers to learn from their own direct experiences (see sections 1.1.3 and 1.1.5). This suggests a progression from observational learning to full responsibility for a class, optimising the genuineness of experiences at each stage.

Observation

Structured description and contrast between incidents, teachers' styles and schools can help the development of a specialist vocabulary and of concepts for the analysis of teaching (e.g. Maingay, 1988; Day, 1990; Wajnryb, 1993; also sections 6.2 and 6.3).

Peer micro-teaching

This rehearses basic skills in preparation for the real thing. It can be made more realistic by the introduction of foreign language teaching or teaching nonsense-word vocabulary.

Genuine micro-teaching

This enables rehearsal of classroom skills (e.g. section 6.3) and can also be used developmentally by experienced teachers (Mace, 1996). It offers the most realistic conditions if micro-classes are stable, are homogeneous in composition, and follow a textbook or syllabus over an extended time period. 'Free classes' for any student who happens to turn up are unlikely to provide these conditions, so that students will not be able to address real learning needs and will be reduced to offering display lessons to please the supervisor.

In a large language school one option is to set up special language classes for teaching practice which are taught jointly by training course tutors and trainees. For example, the tutor could teach the class for two sessions a week, with the third taught by trainees. This enables tutors to increase demands on students in small steps, informed by the progression of the whole training course. For example, in a low-intensity course, such as one spread over a year, the trainer can begin by assigning lesson plans based on four five-minute segments, each of which is taught by a different trainee. This can be adapted to two trainees teaching 20 minutes each, then one teaching the whole short lesson. Similarly, the guidelines for the lesson can be made progressively looser, first with team planning but then moving to individual responsibility for planning and teaching.

Teaching practice

Student teachers are placed in classes, either within the training institution or in co-operating schools. A comprehensive account of research findings and design issues in the 'practicum' can be found in Turney *et al.* (1982a; 1982b) which, even though some 15 years old at time of writing, and referred to state systems, continues to be relevant to all forms of teaching practice (TP). These issues are also discussed in Wallace (1991: Chapter 7). TP can be graded, according to tasks of progressive challenge set by the class teacher/supervisor. In cases of poor liaison between the training staff and teachers, however, student-teachers can be put in situations which seriously compromise the value of TP (such as being left with classes with no support, or simply left to watch). Designs which maximise contact between course providers and class supervisors are exemplified in section 6.2 (Partnership structure) and in section 6.3 (closely integrated timetables within a language school).

Coherence between courses

Coherence can be achieved by two other strategies. One is to build part of a programme around a theme, so that one can bring together elements such as theory, materials, methods and testing. For example, by focusing a course block on receptive skills one can integrate input on comprehension theories, the analysis of reading materials, observation of materials in use and teaching practice focused on the needs of particular groups of learners. This integration would be reflected in assessments requiring students to describe and discuss connections between these components.

Another strategy is to integrate two particular courses (for example on theories of language processing and on skills teaching) either by means of one person teaching both courses or by two staff designing a single assessment that requires some synthesis of the courses (Wallace, 1991).

Coherence between related activities

Coherent sequencing and grouping of learning experiences is essential to help learner-teachers to make their own sense of the diverse inputs and experiences an ITE course can offer (section 1.1.5 and Table 8.4). In Box 4.3 we outline the main elements in a concerted design which integrate activities of different types. It suggests that learning cycles could consist of combinations of direct experience (as in teaching practice), indirect experience (as in classroom observation), input of new information (as in readings and lectures on learning theory), and activities to develop self-awareness (as in journal-keeping). These core activities are processed by each person privately (as in reflective writing

---

Direct experience   **Second-hand experience**
Teaching experience   Classroom observation
(controlled skill   Classroom inquiry
practice/experiment)   Readings
Language learning
    Processing by reflection
    Reflective and analytic writing
    (diary, assignments)

    Processing by dialogue
    Seminars/group tasks/supervision
Self-awareness: **Input of new information:**
of own models   on the curriculum
of personal theories and values   on TL learning theory
of knowledge relevant to input   on language
                                          on good classroom practice

---

Box 4.3   Concerted design

assignments) and in dialogue (as in post-teaching 'debriefing' and discussion). These cycles are supported by the development of enabling skills, such as listening and feedback. An example of concerted learning activities appears in section 8.6, a package of materials which can be used for ITE or INSET.

Coherence in roles

In section 4.2, we have already noted the effect of employment preconditions on liaison and coherence. To summarise, we suggest that staff liaison can be promoted by such strategies as:

- involving staff across course components;
- ensuring staff are released for liaison meetings (preferably on issues they perceive as important and with a practical and productive focus, such as materials production);
- keeping all staff informed about the results of reviews, formative evaluations and course development;
- involving staff in cross-course review and development;
- engaging staff in team teaching (e.g. plenary input/separate groups/ plenary review);
- staff preparing cross-component assessments jointly.

An example of coherence strategies can be found in the case of a large language school in Brazil which runs a year-long drip-feed CTEFLA course. Many teachers are involved as tutors but for relatively limited components. Coherence is promoted by sharing resources and holding timetabled liaison and development meetings. All tutors contribute to a general course file (notes, hand-outs, over-head projection transparencies etc.) and also attend fortnightly meetings, which focus on the development of the file. Apart from the development of a coherent set of materials for all staff to use, task-focused work of this kind benefits professional development and peer support.

In this short chapter we have discussed the powerful effect of preconditions on design, and the need to apply the 'coherence criterion' to ITE design. In our case studies (sections 6.2 and 6.3) we have cases of design affected by preconditions, particularly of funding and accreditation. The issue of coherence is central to the design of the programmes described in sections 6.2 and 6.3. In the next chapter we go into some detail on provider roles which are of central importance and are often problematic: input, feedback, assessment.

Appendix 4.1   Activities summary

(See also Box 4.3.)

Direct experience

- Foreign language learning experience (e.g. Woodward, 1992).
- Micro-teaching and teaching practice (e.g. Wallace, 1991).
- Role play and simulation (e.g. Woodward, 1992).

Second-hand experience

- Observation: classroom, demonstrations, video (e.g. Day, R. 1990; Wallace, 1991; Allwright and Bailey, 1991; Waynryb, 1993; Richards and Lockhart, 1994).
- Readings: transcripts, description of incidents, case study (e.g. Day, R. 1990; Richards and Lockhart, 1994; Harrington *et al.*, 1996).

Input of new information

- Lecture/ette combined with demonstration (Doff, 1988, Woodward, 1992).
- Readings (Doff, 1988; Ur, 1996; section 8.6).

Self-awareness

(See also section 1.1.3 and Appendices 5.1, 7.4 and 8.1.)

- Criticism of public knowledge: e.g. discussion tasks, Appendix 8.5.
- Recall own 'learning history' (e.g. Bailey, 1996).

- Linking input to self (e.g. Appendices 5.2 and 8.5).
- Discrepancy confrontation: getting surprises (e.g. pupil questionnaire, section 8.6; Fanselow, 1987).
- Language awareness (Bolitho and Tomlinson, 1995; Britten, 1996).

Processing experience and input by reflection and dialogue

(See also Appendices 5.1 and 5.2.)

Of direct experience	logs, diaries (e.g. Bailey, 1990); shared description, compared interpretation (e.g. Fanselow, 1990)
Of new information	summarising, mindmapping, notemaking, presentations, seminar papers, assignments
Of the language curriculum by curriculum studies	curriculum development project, including learner profiling/linguistic analysis/interaction analysis/ materials analysis (McNiff, 1988; Nunan, 1989; Ashton *et al.*, 1989; Day, 1990; Wright, 1990; Richards and Lockhart, 1994; Wallace, 1996)
Of dilemma-based cases	written assignments (e.g. Harrington *et al.*, 1996)

Appendix 4.2   A 'protosyllabus' of objectives

This syllabus is no more than a checklist of possible course objectives. Decisions on which objectives are most important, which have to be excluded and so on have to made 'locally' in the light of factors outlined in section 4.2. The main categories used here reflect a construction of the main knowledge bases of language teaching suggested in Chapter 3: content knowledge of the language; theoretical knowledge about language structure and use; contextual knowledge of the curriculum and schooling; pedagogic skills, planning, evaluation and classroom management; immediate enabling skills; and skills and attitudes promoting further development after qualification.

1   The English language

1.1   The nature of communication and linguistic systems

Systems

- Understand and use terminology for description of English formal systems (syntax, vocabulary, phonology, text types, discourse above the sentence etc.).

- Understand form–meaning relationships (speech functions, grammatical concepts etc.).
- Understand and use terminology for description of English language skills and subskills (productive and receptive).
- Understand and use classifications of language competence relevant to syllabus and materials design (structure, topic, skill, lexis, task etc.).
- Understand and apply to own use of English major differences between English in structure and use and own L1 and other relevant languages.
- Know of and be able to use reference material on English language as relevant to learners' needs.
- Be able to apply systems of analysis to texts and samples of classroom interaction.

Variation

- Understanding of language variation: aware of the nature of personal language variety; aware of language variation according to its context and purpose; awareness of text types and genres.
- Awareness of relevance of textual variation in the curriculum.
- Appreciation of characteristics of authentic language and idealised text for language teaching uses.

1.2   Pedagogic grammar

- To translate linguistic description into material for student learning.
- To anticipate and analyse the nature of learner difficulties with aspects of the system of English (grammar, vocabulary, phonology, discourse, meaning–form etc.).
- To prepare explanations/tasks to resolve learner difficulties with language.

1.3   Language in society

- Understand the status and role of English in one's own country (in EFL settings); its significance in education and the L1 culture; the effect of its social role on the expectations and attitudes of learners; the role of English in its major areas of use, e.g. trade, tourism, science and technology.
- Understand the status and role of English in a range of different countries and communities; its significance in education and the L1 culture; the effect of its social role on the expectations and attitudes of learners.
- Be aware of variations in L1 and TL social functions: dialect, creoles, lingua franca, bilingualism, code mixing and code switching.

1.4   Personal language competence

- Be able to meet standards appropriate to the context of employment in speaking and writing (accuracy, intelligibility, fluency, expression of meaning by appropriate stress, intonation and rhythm, style) and listening and reading (recognition of intention, of formal and stylistic error).
- Demonstrate adequate oral English competence for pedagogic purposes: e.g. telling a story; reading dialogues; giving instructions; explaining concepts and other aspects of English systems; monitoring learners' English; use of prompting and encouragement; identifying errors in form and meaning; offering appropriate and accurate corrections.
- Be able to recognise native English speech (prepared and spontaneous; formal and informal) in a range of voices and major dialects.
- Have an adequately wide receptive and productive vocabulary, including idioms.
- Have command of strategies for the inferencing of unfamiliar words from context.
- Demonstrate adequate literacy in providing examples of written English as appropriate to the curriculum and learners' level (e.g. notices, letters, comprehension questions, test items and rubrics, short dialogues, short narratives, summaries).
- Be able to prepare classroom materials (e.g. adapt and simplify texts).
- Be able to assess and give feedback to learners' written English.
- Demonstrate the ability to use appropriate published texts on English teaching as input to their own planning or implementation.
- Show the ability to identify the type and purpose of a text; to recognise implicit and inferential content relevant to teaching requirements.
- Be able to write comprehension questions appropriate to the text.
- Be aware of own language variety (according to L1 and idiolect).
- Demonstrate adequate study skills to enable English medium study (see 5 below).

2   Theory

2.1   Language learning

- Be aware of past and current theories of formal language learning and natural acquisition as relevant to the language curriculum.
- Understand and compare major approaches to language teaching (grammar translation, audio–lingualism; task based etc.).
- Understand the implications of approaches for the personal concerns of individuals and the curriculum in general.
- Understand differences between young and adult learners.

3   The context of teaching

3.1   Learners' needs

- Understand the characteristics of learners being worked with (in teaching practice or elsewhere), with special reference to their expectations of ELT instruction based on their prior experience of education; expectations may be social (how classes are run); affective (nature of relationships) or cognitive (the manner of formal language learning).
- Appreciate the significance of English for learners' general development and educational concerns.
- Appreciate the significance of working with monolingual and multilingual/mixed-culture classes.
- Adapt teaching strategies in the light of the composition of the class (mono-/multilingual).
- Understand the purposes and motives of learners as regards English instruction.
- Understand and apply to teaching differences between both individual learners and types of learners.
- Understand cognitive and emotional needs of learners.
- Relate the above variables to different styles of instruction that may be appropriate (directive/nondirective).
- Appreciate the needs of learners of different ages: children, young adults, working adults.

3.2   School conditions

- Understand and apply to teaching relevant aspects of the learning situation: resources, physical conditions on class, school culture; parental relationships with the school etc.
- Appreciate the effect of class size on teaching: from one to one, to small groups (to around 15), to large classes (40+).
- Understand how a school is managed and administered, including the roles of senior staff.

3.3   The curriculum

- Be able to recognise the basis for the design of a syllabus or textbook materials.
- Be aware of different genres of ELT syllabus (general English; English for special purposes (ESP); business English.
- Understand the connection between variations in ELT curricula and contextual variations (learners' needs, culture, social function of English, institutional conditions etc.).

- Be aware of learning-to-learn activities to improve learners' strategies.
- Be aware of the function and methodology of curriculum evaluation as it affects practice.
- Be aware of relationship between the English curriculum and other aspects of the curriculum followed by learners (e.g. in state systems or higher education), with potential use of cross-curricular activities.
- In EFL settings, know the history of education in one's own country, and the basic principles and structure of the present system.
- Understand the nature of the national education system as it affects learners: examinations, the syllabus.

4   Language pedagogy

4.1   Planning and evaluation

- Understand the value of planning to meet learner needs.
- Take into account learners' predispositions, language learning needs, interests and prior knowledge (of language and general knowledge).
- Identify the assumed level of language and other knowledge of learners on which planning of objectives is based.
- Apply criteria to the setting of objectives: the range of categories that can be used; clarity; measurability; feasibility; loading.
- Apply criteria for the selection of appropriate teacher roles, lesson focuses and lesson types.
- Be aware of a range of options in the development of learning activities within a lesson and between lessons (PPP; and alternatives), balancing topic, task and language.
- Apply a series of decision points: establishing aims, objectives, selection of language focus, selection of skills, expected difficulties, timing, differing teacher/learner roles.
- Be able to give a coherent explanation of the objectives of the lesson, and the rationale for these objectives.
- Assess and select materials and resources.
- Have access to and select appropriately from a repertoire of exercises, activities and tasks, with consideration of learners' needs in language learning, cognition and affect.
- Demonstrate the ability to develop sequences of classroom activity to support language learning (e.g. by effective skill integration).
- Be able to plan units of work ranging from a single lesson to a term.
- Be able to modify or translate a general syllabus into a programme adapted to the needs of a particular group of learners.
- Monitor appropriate aspects of the lesson while it is in progress.
- Evaluate lesson as planned and lesson as it occurred, using both personal reflection and feedback from others.

- Use the evaluation of lessons for subsequent lesson planning.
- Be able to adjust units of planned work in the light of progress tests and other feedback.

4.2 Classroom management

General classroom management skills

- Physical organisation: can arrange classroom to suit the lesson and the learners; can manage whole, group and pair work.
- Presence: exhibit rapport with learners.
- Climate: develop a positive learning atmosphere and show awareness of group dynamics and interactions between learners.
- Show effective management of time in learning activities: variety, staging, weighting and pace.
- Keeping learners on-task: application of strategies to maximise on-task behaviour and learner co-operation.

Managing learning outside the classroom

- Be able to prepare and set appropriate homework tasks.
- Devise appropriate homework marking schemes for normal and large classes.
- Foster independent language learning outside class according to opportunities available.

Personal

- Teacher use of English: adjust own use of English to the level of the class; give effective instruction; employ appropriate forms of correction; convey meaning; develop a consistent position as regards the place of L1 and TL in classrooms; limit amount of teacher talk to an appropriate level.
- Be able to check on learners' understanding.
- Use of materials and resources: appropriate use of wide range of materials and resources (blackboard, tape recorder etc.).
- Adjust teaching strategies to match state of resources available.
- Monitoring and evaluation in class: be able to identify where the whole class and individuals have made progress; identify where whole class or individuals need additional work; use informal and formal methods to do this (monitoring, learner self-assessment, achievement testing etc.).
- Monitoring: identify and keep adequate records of individual learner progress.
- Demonstrate flexibility (the ability to respond appropriately to unpredicted incidents and learner responses).

- Be able to offer and receive feedback on personal performance in teaching.
- Be able to evaluate own performance by reflection and feedback from others.
- Be able to apply self-evaluation to subsequent teaching.

ELT procedures and techniques

- Understand the rationale of classroom procedures and criteria for appropriate use in different contexts.
- Recognise and implement effectively an appropriately varied repertoire of classroom procedures for the support of language learning (aspects of language systems, skill development, fluency and self-expression).
- Meet learners' needs at phases of presentation of concepts or materials; establishing and checking understanding; leading controlled forms of language practice; forms of skill practice; giving opportunities for self-expression.
- Employ effective types of activity; involve all learners, when of different levels.
- Correct students' language appropriate timing and strategies.

4.3   Formal assessment

- Understand the purpose and nature of formal assessment methods: placement, achievement, diagnostic tests etc.
- Be able to recognise good and bad language tests.
- Be able to select, adapt or prepare valid language tests and marking schemes appropriate to their purpose and context (progress tests, achievement tests).
- Prepare learners for public examinations, both local and internationally recognised.
- Be able to interpret test results: as evaluation data; as diagnostic data for subsequent teaching.

4.4   Resources and materials

- Develop criteria for the evaluation and selection of materials according to variations of learner need and context.
- Be aware of sources for commercially produced materials and locally produced noncommercial materials (learner materials and teacher materials, including testing).
- Be familiar with media and literature relevant to learners' interests and language needs.
- Be able to adapt existing materials to meet the needs of particular groups of learners.

- Be able to prepare, evaluate and revise supplementary materials (aids, tasksheets, texts, tests etc.).
- Be able to select and edit as necessary appropriate authentic materials.
- In limited resource settings, adapt materials where students have no textbooks.
- Understand the value of organising classroom resources and displaying information and language materials.
- Understand function of self-access materials and learning centres, and support learners to use such facilities.

5   Immediate enabling skills

Observation

- Observe other teachers and use systematic methods.
- Relate observations to their own assumptions and practice.
- Relate observations to theory on language learning.

Self

- Reflect on personal experience of second language learning and self as language learner.
- Monitor personal use of English in the classroom (e.g. by recorded excerpts) and assess the need for change.
- Be able to identify a personal change in practice (use of English, procedures, testing etc.) and use appropriate means to monitor the change, draw conclusions on its outcome in the classroom and relate these to future practice.
- Develop skills of inquiry for use in further independent development by means of, e.g., classroom analysis, linkage to public theory, learner profiling, systematic curriculum development by means of piloting and evaluation.

Study skills

To be able to meet the requirements of participation in an English medium ITE programme:

- to demonstrate functional reading skills of speed, reading selectively for relevant information, knowledge of specialised lexis; ability to inference lexical meaning from available clues; to inference implied meaning; to recognise connections above sentence level;
- to be able to make coherent and economic notes from reading;
- to be able to make coherent and economic notes from lectures;

- to be able to participate in course activities: to give oral presentations (with visual aids); discussions; role plays; questioning and responding to others;
- to be able to write in a range of styles as needed, e.g. formal academic; narrative; letters; informal;
- to be able to prepare assignments:
  - to use a library referencing system;
  - to select relevant information from abstracts and full sources (e.g. journals, books);
  - to plan and draft with coherence;
  - to self-edit drafts;
  - to recognise and avoid plagiarism;
  - to apply conventions of presentation (e.g. referencing, quotations, bibliography).

6   Further independent development

Self-awareness

- Be able to assess personal strengths and weaknesses.
- Appreciate the nature of training to date.
- Be orientated to reflect critically on personal practice, in the light of monitoring and assessing learners; self-management (awareness of assumptions).
- Be aware of pedagogic traditions affecting other teachers and a range of learners.

Language

- Be able to recognise native English speech (prepared and spontaneous; formal and informal) in a range of voices and major dialects.
- Be able to initiate and participate in conversation with native English speakers and those of other dialects.
- Be able to access published texts contributive to further professional development (e.g. professional journals; the media; literature).

Career

- Appreciate the importance of further professional development.
- Be aware of opportunities for further development.
- Be aware of aspects of employment (conditions of contract etc.) and career prospects.
- Be aware of recognised EFL qualifications for both teachers and learners.

Sources of development

- Be provided with understanding and skills for classroom research, including collaborative curriculum development.
- Be aware of sources of professional information and exchange of ideas (associations, journals etc.).
- Be orientated to reflect critically on personal practice, in the light of public theory on teaching and the curriculum.

Professional conduct: role in school

- Meet occupational standards of conduct, e.g. personal organisation, responsibility, confidence, self-presentation, co-operation with colleagues.
- Be able to deal with learners in terms of their personal needs and feelings; demonstrate interpersonal skills towards learners and colleagues (respect, attention etc.).
- Be orientated to attend to feedback and professional views of others.
- Be orientated to collaborative work with fellow teachers.
- Be orientated to attend to feedback from peer observation and appraisal procedures.
- Be orientated to offer support and practical suggestions to colleagues regarding their teaching.
- Appreciate the qualities of learners' mother culture, and be alert to cultural norms and expectations in and out of the classroom.
- Show commitment to equality of opportunity for all students.
- Be aware of legal conditions applying to teaching, including copyright, statutory aspects of examinations and curriculum.

Management functions

- Resources: be familiar with principles of managing teaching resources (cataloguing, controlling use, evaluating) and be able to set up systems of use.
- Be able to keep class and student records as appropriate.
- Be able to hold effective meetings with colleagues, students and parents.

Appendix 4.3   A design checklist

Approach

Model of competence (what is teaching? what is language teaching? what is effective ELT?).

Model of learning (how do people learn to teach?).

Protosyllabuses (general categories of content/process).

Design

Requirements of the education system

General conditions, e.g. religious cultural and political imperatives.

National mission, e.g. English standards as access to economic development or as gateway to higher education; associated skills and competence demanded of English teachers.

National legal requirements, e.g. syllabus, range and choice of textbooks, examinations, medium of instruction, leaving age.

National pragmatic requirements: relative shortage or sufficiency of teachers; political needs of government to satisfy interest groups.

Resources

In the education system: per capita spending on pupils, teachers, and teacher education programmes (affects design in terms of materials available, teacher-pupil ratios, setting mixed-ability TL classes); teachers' pay levels and hours per week teaching (which affect staff numbers, staff-participant ratio, location of programmes, facilities).

Teaching situation(s)

School characteristics: physical dispersal; resources, institutional climate, rules and norms; management styles, role of teachers, teacher-teacher relationships.

Learner characteristics: mother tongue(s); exposure to the TL out of school; perceptions of subject.

Teachers' work characteristics: role in the curriculum; classroom conditions (ratios, resources); expectations from peers and students; expectations from the community; official teaching load; additional workload.

Providing institution

Legal imperatives (e.g. assessment, teaching practice time etc.).

Institutional culture: leadership style; rules and norms; expectations of staff and staff relationships.

Resources: staff-participant ratios; group sizes, staff/participant mobility; duration and structure of programmes, options in supervision styles, availability of space, reading materials, 'hardware', teaching practice opportunities, opportunities for follow up after immediate training.

Providers and participants

TL language competence; previous education. Perceptions of own role, of relationships with participants, of the language curriculum.

Role-related experience and skills.

Predispositions as providers or as participants: expectations of directiveness; receptiveness to change; flexibility; reflectiveness; attitude to collaboration with peers.

Current workloads and available programme-related time.

Personal priorities.

Expectations of future work.

Needs assessment

Formal or informal identification of participant needs; target situation analysis, learning situation analysis.

Programme goals and objectives

Choice of categories when writing objectives, according to the model of teacher competence adopted.

Priorities: determined by most pressing local factors, e.g. government policy; recent curriculum change; teacher shortfall etc.

Selection of objectives.

Timetabling: sequencing, weighting, integration.

Specific course design: content, method, roles and relationships, materials and task design.

Role descriptions

ITE: e.g. providers to offer input in varied modes and at appropriate level of challenge; set tasks; organise training activities; observe and give feedback; offer support; assess progress; make summative assessments; be fully knowledgeable in TE curriculum content and requirements; conduct selection procedures;

design whole or part of ITE programmes; manage or collaborate with colleagues.

INSET: e.g. conduct needs assessment; provide input; support independent collaboration and reflection; offer support; conduct evaluation and programme revisions.

Assessment: meet legal requirements and programme objectives.

Forms of evaluation: input to formative and summative evaluation; structures for the consideration of evaluation data.

Procedure (implementation)

Cycle: plan, perform, monitor.

Nature of discourse: types of interaction between participants and providers implied by objectives.

Formative adjustments: short-term changes.

Summative evaluation: review, assessment of slippage, longer-term changes.

5

Provider roles in ITE

In this chapter we focus on three key provider roles. In section 5.1 we discuss input, in 5.2 feedback and supervision, and in 5.3 summative assessment. In our case studies, the linkage between input and teachers' prior knowledge is addressed in section 8.6; difficulties in supervision and a flexible and broad-based assessment scheme are both discussed in 6.2.

5.1   Input and self-awareness

The need to present new information is an essential feature of ITE courses because of the gaps in novice teachers' knowledge and experience (section 2.4.1). A broadly social constructivist view of teacher learning suggests that new information will be 'personalised': processed and interpreted by learner-teachers according to their current personal theories, and then tested against direct experience and social exchanges (sections 1.1.3 and 1.1.5; Williams and Burden, 1997). Personalisation activities are summarised in Appendix 5.1.

All teachers, whatever their level of experience, bring their prior knowledge and personal theories to new information. However, learner-teachers are likely not to be fully aware of their prior knowledge (Argyris and Schön, 1974; Eraut, 1994) and so personalisation of new information can be enriched by enhancing self-awareness. This can be by means of private reflection (as in journal writing, e.g. Bailey, 1990; Jarvis, 1992; or in reflective assignments, e.g. section 6.2) and by dialogue (as in discussion of teaching incidents with learners, peers and supervisors, e.g. Newell, 1996; Bailey, 1996). Activities which try to integrate input and prior knowledge appear in Appendices 5.2 and 8.5.

In summary, the implications of this view for the presentation of new information to learner-teachers are that:

- the manner of presenting input needs to take the learner-teachers' current ways of learning into account, and where appropriate should try to capitalise on them (Lamb, 1995; Pennington, 1996);
- the uncovering of prior knowledge and of personal theories is an *essential complement* to presenting new information, so that the provider can

try to 'start from where the teachers are'; and so that student-teachers can become aware of the difference between their current practice and ideas and the new information presented to them;

- new information needs to be represented by concrete examples and cases as well as more abstract description and explanation;
- all new information needs be complemented by appropriate direct experience, either in the classroom or in training sessions: the more unfamiliar or challenging the concepts presented the greater the need for appropriate experiential activities;
- experience alone is not enough for learning to take place; it needs to be made sense of by private reflection and dialogue;
- it is essential to provide time for discussion and other processing tasks that is *no less* than the time allotted to presentation itself. Also, different social contexts in which new information may be communicated and exchanged require different discourse (academic, staffroom, classroom). As a result, time for talk in *each context* is needed to personalise new information fully (Eraut, 1994).

This suggests an input and processing cycle of three phases, as follows.

Phase 1

- Uncovering: articulating existing practice, personal theories and knowledge relevant to the new information (Shulman, 1988; Lamb, 1995);
- Receiving input: presentation of new information by appropriate means (readings, lectures, demonstrations, experiential activities etc.).

Phase 2

- Processing input through talk and writing: relating new information to prior knowledge and beliefs; formulating and re-presenting the new information to others (in both academic and teacher talk; in talk and in writing); comparing others' interpretations of the new information; criticising the new information; assessing its relevance to one's own context.

Phase 3

- Relating to practice: discussion and testing out of practical applications; assessment of new information in the light of classroom testing; assessment of changes in the light of observation and reflection. For examples see Parrott (1993) and also sections 6.2 and 8.2–8.6.

ELT has proved particularly creative of interactive teacher training techniques, often inspired by communicative methodology. We recommend the reader to more detailed ELT sources on activities which link prior knowledge to input: these include Wallace (1991), Freeman (1991), Woodward (1992), Parrott (1993), Richards and Lockhart (1994), Bolitho and Tomlinson (1995), Lamb (1995), Thornbury (1997) and James (forthcoming). It is also well worth referring to ideas from higher education teaching, such as Brown (1978), Gibbs (1981), Gibbs *et al.* (1987) and Wallace (1991: Chapter 3).

While practising teachers will have crystallised their personal theories through classroom experience, student-teachers will lack the experience which helps them to be critical. Therefore the ITE student in particular may need to be encouraged to adopt a critical stance towards input (presented as it is by people who can affect his or her future prospects). To do so s/he needs to value the prior knowledge that s/he brings to professional education and also the insights gained from classroom experience. To do so requires a combination of structural opportunities (section 4.3), positive supervisor relationships (section 5.2) and appropriately integrated activities (sections 1.1.5, 4.3 and 8.6; Appendices 5.1 and 5.2).

5.2   Supervision and feedback

'In giving feedback the supervisor provides information to students about their progress in teaching. Feedback assists recall, analysis and interpretation of observed teaching sequences. It entails holding regular conferences with the student and systematic collection and use of information to indicate strengths and diagnose weaknesses' (Turney *et al.*, 1982b: 164).

The impact of feedback on learner-teachers seems not to be as powerful as supervisors might wish it to be (Turney *et al.*, 1982a). The evidence suggests that the experiential learning of the student teacher, filtered by their personal theories and focused by their perceived priorities, will be the most powerful influence on their development (section 2.4.3). The influence of a supervisor is likely to be greatest if:

- there is sociality, mutual understanding of each other's perspectives on teaching and classroom incidents (Salmon, 1995);
- there is a match in values between supervisor and student-teacher (Tillema, 1994);
- supervisors try to influence by channelling and focusing teaching experiences rather than merely by telling and advising (McIntyre, 1988).

5.2.1   Role analysis

Feedback

Feedback, 'a response or reaction providing useful information or guidelines for further development' (*Chambers Concise Dictionary*, 1991), is essential in all learning. In ITE, its purpose is to give students an idea of where they stand vis-à-vis programme objectives and criteria. The feedback role consists of a cycle of observation, feedback, reflection and planning, and further observation (Fig. 5.1). The reader will note an assumption that effective supervision relies on repeated cycles of contact which enable the development of trust, a degree of mutual understanding and the negotiation of the purpose and focus of the next TP. The feasibility of such cycles depends on the course structure (see Fig. 5.1; also sections 4.2, 4.3, 6.2). The approach taken to supervision will also depend on the attitude of both parties to prescription and collaboration (Wallace, 1991: 108–12).

Role flexibility

Supervision can be seen in terms of mutually exclusive models (e.g. Gebherd, 1990). However, in practice a supervisor is likely to enact a number of roles which cut across theoretical categories. At times a counselling role may be appropriate (attending, accepting emotional states, reflecting back and clarifying the person's

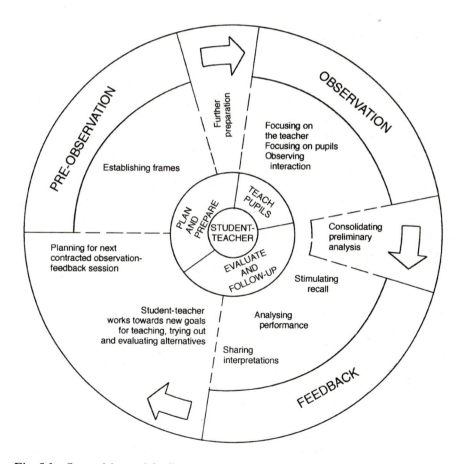

Fig. 5.1   Supervision and feedback cycle, adapted from Turney *et al.* (1982b)

perspectives) while at other times a supervisor may need to be directive (e.g. by making specific suggestions for new procedures and skills). Heron (1986) provides a helpful framework for a flexible approach, as follows.

Prescriptive: direction to teach in a certain way.
Informative: provide alternatives and information.
Confronting: present evidence of teaching strategies that have been effective and those which have been ineffective; particularly in the case that the teacher seems unaware of dysfunctional aims and techniques in their teaching this can be the most powerful and disorganising intervention, and one that will require positive subsequent support.
Cathartic: reflect how the person is feeling.
Catalytic: stimulate by open questioning, regarding rationale, context etc.
Supportive: positive attending to the teacher which 'is really a precondition of using any other intervention in any other category' (Heron, 1986).

To these roles we should add one more: 'structuring' or 'process leader', where the tutor provides a framework for self-directed experiment and discovery. This would apply to ITE programmes in which the student-teacher, on attaining a level of basic competence, is able to then move into forms of curriculum inquiry more usually associated with INSET programmes. For example, Ashton *et al.* (1989) report in detail the inclusion of structured inquiry into ITE programmes; and in section 6.2 there is provision for some student-teachers to engage in development activities at the end of their year. We refer to this role as 'process leader' because the tutor is not concerned with content and instead focuses on maintaining processes of collaboration and inquiry. The only input is provided to maintain independent work by teachers, such as introducing structures and ground rules (see sections 8.3 and 8.6) and enabling skills (e.g. section 8.6) and modes of classroom inquiry (Appendix 8.2). Case studies in sections 8.3 and 8.6 describe teacher development supported by a process leader. McGill and Beaty (1992) and Heron (1993) provide valuable guidelines for process leaders.

5.2.2   Some obstacles to constructive feedback

Supervision and feedback represent an intervention in the sensitive process of learning to teach, which 'requires a journey into the deepest recesses of one's self-awareness, where failures, fears and hopes are hidden' (Kagan, 1992: 164). It demands fairness, respect, discretion and self-awareness because, in offering feedback and making assessments, we are intervening directly in the lives of others to change them in ways they would not change themselves, on the grounds that it will help them to something better (Scriven, 1981; Peterson, 1995).

For the supervisor, there are two key difficulties in giving feedback: what to focus on, and how to communicate her perceptions to the student-teacher. The student-teacher's problem is to make sense of feedback in terms of her own recall of the lesson, her personal theories about teaching and her view of self.

Humanistic insights

Feedback is an interpersonal event with a potentially high emotional temperature. One's teaching self cannot readily be separated from one's whole self: 'people's self-images are strongly bound up with their values and beliefs, and their attachment to them is highly emotional' Somekh (1993: 35). For this reason, feedback, potential criticism of and change in one's teaching, carries a powerful emotional charge, with the result that emotional and interpersonal 'noise' can jam feedback.

It is common for student-teachers to be initially concerned with their sense of personal worth. This fear factor has to be overcome, because it leads to defensive coping strategies such as risk avoidance, display lessons rather than real trials of teaching skill, and denial of problems: a 'hedgehog strategy' which hinders genuine dialogue and also prevents the student teacher from focusing on the learner (section 2.4.3).

Another effect of the high emotional temperature can be that student teachers often find it hard to take in feedback immediately after a lesson. S/he can't remember what happened and may be recovering from nerves. The use of written notes and delayed feedback discussions can help communication.

The insights of humanistic theory help us to be aware of the affective dimensions of supervision and feedback, of learner-teachers' need for support. However, as Lansley has pointed out, models derived from counselling apply to work with people in distress such as 'bereavement, terminal illness, alcoholism, mental problems, stress or other psycho-social problems' (1994: 50). In these cases a skilled helper is needed to offer support and uncritical understanding. Learner-teachers need support but they also require a framework of clear expectations and critical challenge to stimulate reflection on their assumptions and behaviour. This need for normative judgements distinguishes ITE supervision from therapeutic contexts (Cogan, 1995).

Talking past each other?

Each supervisor has her personal theories: about the nature of the TL; effective teaching; her image of herself as a teacher; how student-teachers should behave; and relationships with them. These theories affect all aspects of supervisory behaviour: how they interpret and evaluate the teaching they see and how they relate to the student-teacher. The degree of match in personal theories between the two parties determines the initial basis for mutual understanding. Without sociality, the common ground of recall and interpretations will not be available with the result that rather than communicating new insights, 'we may do things to them but we cannot relate to them' (Bannister and Fransella, 1980: 28).

Therefore it is essential to try to work towards shared understanding, for example, on what actually took place in the lesson, and which incidents were the most significant. To do this requires regular and reasonably frequent supervision sessions, the provision of which raises major issues of course structure, funding and staffing (sections 4.2, 6.2 and 6.3). Observation and analysis activities can also contribute to this by developing a common shared vocabulary (see Appendix 4.1).

Organisational problems

Liaison

Organisation problems can harm communication. Lack of liaison between different supervisors can make for confusion, divided loyalties and conflict. These issues are detailed in section 2.4.5. Structures such as Partnership schemes (e.g. section 6.2) are designed to minimise such problems.

Role conflict

Many supervisors are expected to combine educator and assessor roles. They may want feedback sessions to provide support and encouragement and to lead student-teachers to examine their own weaknesses and strengths. However, the student-teacher will be aware that this same person will also decide their final grades, their future prospects. Not surprisingly, many will approach staff defensively, with priority to creating a good impression. Therefore it is highly desirable to separate assessment and support roles if it organisationally possible.

5.2.3   Some principles in giving feedback

There are no blueprints for the way a supervisor and student-teacher may relate to each other. However, some of the following principles and strategies may be worth considering given the obstacles discussed above.

Communication

Awareness

The supervisor needs to be aware of his or her personal theories to avert bias and inappropriate expectations of student-teachers. Training activities could include the following.

- Role-switching: supervisor enacts the student-teacher's position in a simulated feedback session and then reflects with others on each party's perspectives.
- 'Cultural homework' on student-teachers' context and learning styles (Richards and Lockhart, 1994; McLaughlin, 1996; Appendix 7.6).

- Reflection on personal theories: supervisor reflects on her criteria for effective teaching, by means of 'blind' group assessment sessions where the grounds for assessments are discussed.
- Reflection on personal autobiography, on formative experiences and their effect on one's work (e.g. 'snakes', Appendix 7.4).

Communication skills

The quality of communication between supervisor and student–teacher depends on sociality: each understanding how the other perceives the practice lesson and the feedback conference. As a supervisor, one cannot set out to win over student–teachers or to convert them; one needs to understand how they are perceiving a situation to decide where to start the discussion of their teaching.

Attending

It takes considerable discipline to listen properly, rather than begin formulating the next question or comment while the other person is still speaking. For this reason it can be helpful for both parties occasionally to 'reflect back', that is to summarise what the other person has just said (e.g. King, 1983). The supervisor also needs to be a good watcher to attend to the body language of the student–teacher: often the real feelings of a person are reflected in their posture and movements rather than what they say.

Flexibility

The supervisor needs to enact different roles rather than become stuck in one intervention style (e.g. mostly directive or mostly 'hands-off'). At any point, some student–teachers may need guidance before attempting another lesson, while others may be able to proceed to more autonomous planning and self-assessment. Self-awareness is needed for the supervisor to use an appropriate and flexible range of interventions with different student–teachers at one time and at different stages of a course (Heron, 1986; and above).

Ground rules

'When supervision begins with an understanding between supervisor and student about each other's expectations and there is shared agreement about what ought to be observed and analysed, feedback will have a chance to operate positively in the supervision cycle' (Turney *et al.*, 1982a: 165). Therefore, from the outset, supervisors need to establish a clear framework for supervision which is explained to student–teachers. To support this, many courses now provide students with a course handbook detailing course structure, rationale, assessment methods and criteria and a description of the responsibilities of staff and students.

Pre-observation phase

Ideally, a pre-observation meeting should identify the focus for the next teaching practice. This will require the elicitation of the student-teacher's priorities in the lesson and agreement on what to observe: 'a tutor who encourages a student to focus on the competence statements before an observation session found that the resulting discussion could be more meaningful than if an agenda had not been set . . .' (Davies and Macaro, 1995: 31).

This clear agenda-setting depends on establishing clear teaching objectives for the upcoming session which can then be related to the evaluation criteria which are most relevant. Once this is done the supervisor and student-teacher have a common frame of reference with which to monitor and assess the lesson.

Timing

The conventional view is that feedback should be offered as soon as possible after observation. However, delayed discussion or written feedback with later discussion can both be helpful, especially if the student has had a difficult practice lesson.

Trust and a mutual understanding need time to develop. Therefore supervision cycles need to be as frequent as possible, and time for them needs to be protected. To ensure this may require structural changes, such as reduced staff-student ratios and timetable changes to enable regular cycles of practice teaching and supervision.

Learner focus

Turney *et al.* (1982a) and Kagan (1992) strongly suggest that student teachers need to be released from their concern with self-presentation by focusing on the effects of their behaviour on learners (Turney *et al.*, 1982b: 122; Kagan, 1992). Therefore feedback should focus on the learners' experience of and reaction to the teacher's actions, not only on the teacher's behaviour.

Information not opinion

Concrete objective information is of far more value to the student-teacher than a global judgement (e.g. 'I think they used Spanish after they'd finished the task'; compared with 'I liked that lesson'. The former suggests what happened, the latter what the supervisor's values are). Information can be based on recall alone but will be more convincing and useful if data-based (e.g. video, detailed checklists, verbatim notes).

Quantity and selection

The tutor should not overload the student-teacher. As much information should be offered as the student can take in. It should be selected according to what s/he can be expected to change at that point in her/his development. This demands a decision, often intuitive, as to what the student can and cannot change at that time. This is further reason for frequent practice-feedback cycles to help the supervisor make such judgements.

Forward focus and co-operation

In a prescriptive approach, the purpose of feedback is to show student-teachers how close they are to mastering required techniques or strategies. The prescriptive approach is viable only if:

- the prescribed model of teaching matches the personal theories of the student- teacher;
- future teaching conditions are predictable;
- student-teachers do not expect the freedom to make pedagogic choices.

In a collaborative and developmental approach to ITE, feedback is needed to develop consensual teaching skills but it also aims to encourage self-evaluation. It should be based on the joint identification of priorities for the practice classes. This means that student-teachers and supervisors need to agree on the focus for the *next* practice, with a mutual understanding of its relationship to teaching objectives and the development of the student. This enables increasingly independent judgement by student-teachers.

Résumé

Attempting to influence learner-teachers by offering feedback on their teaching is recognised by most supervisors as a sensitive and difficult business. Research has shown that it can be ineffective (Turney *et al.*, 1982a; 1982b; Tillema, 1994). Feedback should be in the most accessible and relevant form that a student-teacher can use. The difficult balance for a supervisor to strike is to build the most open and supportive relationship possible while also applying course criteria and challenging student-teachers.

5.3   The assessment of teaching

'The assessment of practice teaching for the purposes of certification is a very problematic subject' (Stones, in Dunkin, 1987: 683). We only outline the main issues in assessment here. The reader can refer to Scriven (1981), Turney *et al.* (1982b), and in particular a challenging and excellent account from Peterson (1995).

5.3.1   Purpose of assessment

The function of ITE is to accredit teachers. The purposes of ITE assessment therefore include:

(i)   giving students accurate information about their standing in the course;
(ii) meeting institutional requirements for evaluation information to grade and rank students;
(iii) carrying out a professional responsibility to ensure that only fit, proper and competent teachers enter the profession; thus being accountable to parents, employing authorities, and the community for the standard of entrants to teaching.

(Turney *et al.*, 1982b: 200–201)

The accrediting institution in effect protects pupils/paying clients, parents and employers from incompetent teachers. Given their responsibility to these parties and to the teachers themselves, providers should be aware of factors that can prejudice fair assessment.

5.3.2 Problems in defining good teaching

The literature on effective teaching suggests that it is not possible to identify a single style, set of practices, behaviours or strategies as effective: there is no one best way to teach. Effective learning can be produced by various combinations of characteristics and conditions (Stones and Morris, 1972; Peterson, 1995). Therefore prescriptive assessment criteria based on a limited set of classroom strategies cannot encompass all the ways of teaching effectively. It follows that because 'there is no one standard in which effective teaching can be evaluated, diversity in teaching styles is to be advocated' (Braskamp, 1980: 63). The reasons for this conclusion are summarised below.

Values and assessment

A prescriptive approach to assessment assumes that a limited and precise set of criteria can be safely applied to assess the performance of teachers. This view assumes that certain methods of language teaching are best; and that criteria applied to student-teachers' classroom performance will be appropriate to all possible future teaching contexts. Neither is a safe assumption.

The effective assessment of teaching depends on the development of a model of effective teaching. However, such models derive from values and ideology, not from certainty:

> Good teaching is a direct function of the judge's value systems. And judges do not always agree . . . Both good and successful teaching are inescapably value-laden, involving, as they do, the selection of criteria and modes of assessment which are shaped by our values. Some values are deeply embedded in our culture and are therefore held by most teachers, some are accepted by groups of us, and some values are predilections of a few individuals.

(Brown, 1975: 10–11)

Uncertainty

Prescription assumes we can predict the response of learners to a teaching strategy, such as peer correction or the use of 'warmers'. However, learners vary in their intake of and interpretation of teaching inputs (Williams and Burden, 1997). They may not perceive the purpose of activities as does the teacher, they may only take up some of the input offered, and they may not enact the learning processes that the teacher hopes they will use in completing her tasks.

Additionally, an action or strategy may have highly diverse meanings for and effects on learners, between classrooms and even between learners in the same classroom. For example, research by Saka (1995) showed that within one class, weak and strong students reacted quite differently to teacherless and teacher-led activities.

Some aspects of teaching behaviour have predictable results (e.g. 'if you mutter the back row won't hear you'), but it is by no means true of all (e.g. 'if you put students in groups the stronger ones will help weaker ones'). Therefore:

> ... while it is sensible to presume that there are a few, but only a few, skills that a beginning teacher must be able to demonstrate, such as being able to write clearly on the blackboard and to project the voice to the back of the classroom, once beginning teachers move beyond these to questioning or motivational skills, there are no established procedures that they must adopt in order to teach effectively.
>
> (Diamond, 1991: 9)

Context

No model of good teaching can be framed in terms of an individual teacher abstracted from social context. Teachers' actions and the outcomes of these actions are a complex product of their training; their knowledge and competencies; interaction with their students; the organisation and norms of their school; their occupational culture; the syllabus, textbook and examinations (sections 1.1.4 and 1.1.5). Good teaching is never separable from setting: 'the definition of teaching effectiveness is contingent upon the expectations and instructional goals of the institution, the type of students enroled, course goals, and the instructor's teaching style' (Braskamp, 1980: 64).

Therefore, effective teaching occurs when we achieve our goals by means of procedures that fit the social context of the classroom. The strategies effective in one context (e.g. a non-native speaker teaching large secondary school classes) may not fit another (e.g. a native speaker with small groups in a private school). Unfortunately, much ELT and TL training input (in books on methodology) is based on conditions which can apply to only some of its audience, only describing strategies effective under a particular set of conditions.

Effective teaching is that which best fits purpose, learners and classroom situation. While we can reach consensus on some basic characteristics of effective teaching and apply them in our assessment criteria, we cannot claim that one particular style can be effective in all situations.

Master teachers?

Stones and Morris (1972: 8–10) suggest further criticisms of prescriptive models of teaching that are based on the notion of the 'master teacher'. Apart from arguing that 'there are no universally accepted criteria to help us to identify master teachers' (1972: 8–10), they point out that the student-teachers' values, experiences and personality may differ from those embodied in the 'master'. If practices inconsistent with their teaching self are imposed on them, in effect they are asked to change themselves and their beliefs. As a result, the student-teacher may give display lessons in imitation of the given model to satisfy the supervisor, but these may not engage with their true teaching selves. While they may manage to smooth their way through the course in this way, this will inhibit any constructive dialogue based on their true perceptions of teaching (Lortie, 1975; Sendan, 1992; sections 2.3.1 and 6.2). It is also likely that after qualifying they will abandon the practices they felt to be imposed on them.

Also, by trying to master a model the student-teacher may copy isolated bits of teaching behaviour which actually need to be implemented coherently. In the absence of a consistent underlying point of view, the bits of behaviour, 'when fragmented and adopted by another ... may be ineffective or even harmful' (Stones and Morris, 1972). In a skill subject such as ELT, learners need long-term consistency, not an assortment of strategies pulling in different directions.

Stable or changing society?

Prescriptiveness reflects social conservatism. In stable societies a traditionally sanctioned model of teaching is sustainable. However, it becomes problematic when major social and curricular change is taking place. This is because established teachers' knowledge will not necessarily be relevant to a language curriculum based on revised assumptions and objectives. This has happened widely over the past two decades as language teaching goals have shifted from a focus on content and form to communication skills.

Reductionism

A prescriptive approach relies on unambiguous 'low inference' criteria, precise competencies such as clear speech, eye-contact and so on (see also section 1.1.1). While it is desirable for practical objectives to be as clear as possible to reduce assessor bias and to offer student-teachers unambiguous learning targets, there are great problems in trying to define effective teaching in narrowly behavioural terms:

- it limits teaching to overt, relatively low order features;
- it ignores less visible longer-term consequences of teaching, notably higher order cognitive learning;
- there could be a backwash effect which leads supervisors and student-teachers to devalue higher order teaching objectives, such as a focus on learners' long-term needs;
- listings of competence in behavioural terms tend to be too long, detailed and inflexible to be of practical use;
- because detailed inventories of competencies are unwieldy and inflexible, very specific criteria may have to be conflated in broader categories (e.g. section 6.2).

Lists of behavioural competencies continue to be popular in the USA and are gaining ground in the state system in England and Wales. They meet the needs of a bureaucracy in establishing clear accountability and conformity to central criteria, but their use denies the variable and context-specific professional knowledge of teachers and providers. However, used flexibly, with room for interpretation and negotiation according to context, competencies can be a helpful feature of LTE design. For example, see section 6.2 where staff adapted a detailed list of competencies for use in a flexible and individualised scheme of assessment.

5.3.3 Bias

Given that personal theories of effective teaching vary and are often tacit (Zeichner and Tabachnik, 1982; Eraut, 1994), it is not surprising that research confirms that supervisor judgements tend to inconsistency and bias.

Supervisor inconsistency

If assessment is not biased, assessments should vary according to the teachers who are observed, not according to the person doing the observing. In a well-conducted and significant study, Cook and Richards (1972: 11) found that, when 236 teachers were rated on 23 schedules by supervisors and principles, the most consistent results were, according to the rater: 'the rating scales generated data that were more a reflection of the rater's point of view than of a teacher's actual classroom behaviour.'

Mackay (1989) came to the same conclusion when analysing RSA DIP TEFL assessments. It seems that bias arises because supervisors assess according to the match they perceive between their own style and that of the person observed, 'rating highly those students who reflect their own approach and personality' (Turney et al., 1982a: 27; also Stones, 1987: 683). It is manifestly unfair for a student-teacher's assessment to depend on a chance similarity between their style and the observer's.

Bias is compounded if assessors are unaware of their own beliefs; for example Zeichner and Tabachnik (1982) suggested that university supervisors for an elementary student-teaching programme seemed unaware of their own beliefs and did not share beliefs with each other.

5.3.4 Problems in observation

Direct observation is still the most common form of assessment in ITE courses. Peterson confirms that in the USA there is a 'vast preponderance of observation-based systems in current teacher evaluation practice' (1995: 154). Its appeal is that it provides direct, first-hand information about a teacher's actions in a classroom. However, its use is fraught with difficulties, unrecognised by bureaucracy and accrediting agencies, to the extent that Scriven, on the basis of a series of 'staggering objections' (1981: 252) was to conclude: 'using classroom visits . . . to evaluate teaching is not just incorrect, it is a disgrace' (1981: 251).

We can only summarise issues dealt with in much greater depth elsewhere and refer the reader to Hook (1981), Open University (1981), Scriven (1981), Turney *et al.* (1982b), Stones (1987), Nunan (1989), Allwright and Bailey (1991), Weir and Roberts (1994) and Peterson (1995).

General characteristics of classroom observation

- All observation is selective. An observer cannot describe everything that is available for description: in classrooms, there are a huge number of possible cues an observer can attend to (e.g. teacher body language, voice, movements, teaching tactics, use of aids, types of language used; teacher-learner interactions; learner behaviour; group time on-task; quality of learner talk; physical conditions). Therefore the observer must select according to what s/he perceives to be relevant.
- Some observational data are of concrete events, and so are low inference in nature; and the observer has to make no inferences when recording a description. For example, if an observer reports that *the teacher replied 'Not now'* or that *learners moved into groups of six*, these are low-inference observations. On the other hand, some observations depend on interpretation of mental states and intentions. For example, a description might read *teacher replied not now, impatiently* or *teacher has good rapport with a class*. Here the teachers' attitude is inferred and not known. Many judgements of teaching derive from high-inference observations and are therefore susceptible to bias.

  Bias can also result from selective attention to low inference data (attending to things that confirm the observer's prejudices or expectations) as well as subjective high-inference interpretation. Selection and 'skewed' interpretation are usually unconscious: in most cases an observer would deny being biased.

- Judgement can be affected by interpersonal reactions between observer and observed, for example according to expectations (a teacher who already has a certain track record) or stereotyping (expectations based on class, gender, race or culture).

- Observation systems vary in degree of structure. Unstructured observation (where description is selected entirely at the choice of the observer with no prior categories or headings) leaves the observer free to attend to any aspect of the classroom s/he considers significant and to record it in any form s/he wants.

  Structured observations are predetermined by a set of observational categories (which may be low-inference or high-inference in nature) and sampling rules, as in checklists or rating scales.

  Structured instruments are therefore not necessarily objective, even though they make for better agreement between those using them. The selection of categories is theory-driven, and will only obtain data presumed important by the designers of the instrument. As Long commented about interaction analysis instruments: 'observational instruments are, in fact, no more (or less) than theoretical claims about second language learning and teaching' (1980: 12). Similarly Peterson (1995: 154) observed: 'every evaluation system has an inherent value system that produces the judgement to use it. The choice of a particular set of topics to observe is a subjective act, not the purported objective, hard data gathering so often claimed by classroom observation advocates.'

  Thus a decision on what is relevant must derive from a prior theory, set of assumptions and implicit values. Therefore even data obtained by objective, structured methods are skewed by the prior assumptions which determine what data are obtained and what are not.

- Any category-based system can produce *quantitative* data, that is a record of the relative frequency of categories. Frequency data is useful in indicating the relative distribution of certain categories of talk or behaviour in a class. However, what these frequencies signify requires interpretation and an understanding of the teachers' goals and of classroom conditions. Therefore numbers should be supplemented by *qualitative* data, i.e. verbal or narrative description to explain the quality or meaning of actions in context.

ITE assessment affects the future of the teacher, and the interests of learners, paying clients, parents and employers. It follows that equity and fairness are essential. For the above reasons, observation alone is an unsafe basis for summative teacher assessment.

Summary

Advantages of observation

- Observation provides direct evidence of teacher behaviour, interactions with students and general classroom climate (King *et al.*, 1987; Weir and Roberts, 1994; Peterson, 1995).
- It offers first-hand formative information for teachers as a means of personal and professional development.

Disadvantages of observation

- Routine teacher performance and learner behaviour are rarely seen during a one-off observation, as it disrupts normal class activity.
- Obtaining accurate data requires observer training and appropriate instrumentation.
- Observation data is extremely time-consuming to get and analyse.
- Obtaining a fair sample of a teacher's performance requires more classroom visits than is usually feasible.
- There is no consensus on effective language teaching to validate the selection of observation categories.
- Teachers' qualities may not be revealed by an observation. Their effectiveness might be due to non-observable causes, such as the quality of their preparation, selection of materials or assignment setting and feedback.
- Proactive behaviour by a teacher may not be recognised by an observer at all.
- Observer bias is inevitable; the fact that two observers agree does not *necessarily* mean that their descriptions and judgements are accurate or fair. However, this is the best proof of fairness which we have, along with tests for the initial validity of categories (Weir and Roberts, 1994).
- The immediate events in a classroom do not inform us as to the past history and external forces which give them meaning. An activity might succeed or fail because of some previous incident or because of interpersonal or cultural factors observers are unaware of. The time and opportunity needed to pick up on such causes is beyond the resources and skills of most ITE supervisors.
- What determines the course and quality of learning lies within the learner and the teacher. How learners perceive and construe their own learning will almost certainly *not* be the same as the perceptions of 'short term adult guests in the classroom' (Peterson, 1995: 154). However, understanding of teacher and learner perspectives is essential before one can interpret observable classroom events.
- A teacher may be effective in one class but not in another. Research has shown that teachers vary their strategies according to such variations

as subject and learner levels, and that teachers are effective with some classes but not others (Stodolsky, 1984).

- Observation systems are often used just because they are there and have been used before, without consideration of the purpose for which they were originally designed or for their built-in limitations.

Principles in ITE observation for summative purposes

The implications for assessment of these characteristics can be summarised as follows.

- Caution: observation-based assessment is subject to bias, much of it unintentional and unconscious.
- Systematic observation: unstructured observation leaves so much room for personal bias that focused and structured methods are preferable, even though they will delimit the scope of observation.
- Limited data: it is safer to collect less observational data that is objective and is of definite relevance, than more data that is not controlled for bias.
- Consensus: it is the responsibility of staff in any institution to monitor the consistency of their observations and assessments, and to standardise their observations (Weir and Roberts, 1994: 199).
- Appropriate choice of system: the choice and design of observation methods depends on purpose. Criteria for a choice of method include appropriacy, reliability, validity, adequate sampling and simplicity of use. Helpful sources on structured observation and choice of method include Boehm and Weinberg (1977), Hook (1981) and Weir and Roberts (1994).
- Transparency: all methods of assessment should be understood by those assessed. Therefore observation instruments should be familiar to teachers under observation.

Given the problems, one could conclude with Scriven that many conventional forms of assessment (such as 'one-off' visits by a lone observer) can only be justified if they have some ritualised social purpose other than of fair and constructive assessment. However, as long as there is accreditation there will have to be summative assessment. Our comments imply that assessment should draw on a much broader base of information than a few observed lessons (Scriven, 1981; Peterson, 1995).

5.3.5   Good practice in the assessment of teaching

Criteria for effective assessment

On the grounds of equity and validity, methods and procedures for assessment should meet the following criteria:

- they are fair to student-teachers;
- they represent training objectives;
- they are appropriate to classroom conditions;
- criteria and conventions of assessment are public, known to student-teachers, and not withheld by those in authority;
- they are applied consistently;
- judgements are reached on a fair sample of the student-teacher's performance, that is, on adequate evidence of what they can do;
- they are flexible enough to take into account contextual and personal variations;
- assessment should serve a developmental function as well as a purely summative function;
- if the ITE course values the autonomy of student-teachers, then they should be able to participate in assessment processes as fully as possible (e.g. by gathering relevant evidence see section 6.2);
- if unfavourable action can result from assessment (such as failing a course, or loss of employment), then it is ethically desirable to use the fairest and broadest methods of assessment; to allow teachers to review and react to evidence about them; to allow them to scrutinise the chain of reasoning from evidence to conclusion; to give them advance warning and a clear indication of what improvement is needed; and to log encounters between teachers and assessors, preferably jointly signed off by both parties (Scriven, 1981).

General implications

Evidence

Valid and fair assessment should be based on the widest possible information about the student-teacher.

Process

Assessment criteria should be open to student-teachers from the outset of the course. They must understand the assessment system and the criteria to be applied to them.

Student-teachers should have the right to regular and clear feedback on their standing vis-à-vis summative assessment criteria. Also, there should be an appeal procedure for student-teachers dissatisfied with their teaching practice grades.

The pre-observation phase should include discussions which link assessment criteria to the specific objectives and conditions of the lesson.

Observation-based assessment should be conducted by paired staff, who complete ratings blind (i.e. unable to see the other person's ratings until they are both completed).

Insiders' opinions need to be moderated by some shared assessments with visiting outsiders.

Grades

It is desirable to abandon differentiated passing grades such as A/B/C because there are no agreed criteria by which to predict whether a student-teacher will prove later to be outstanding, above average or average. Grading is most justifiably based on the principle of filtering out unsuitable teachers. This would suggest a simple pass/fail system, supported by qualitative information to represent the particular strengths, weaknesses and potential of each person.

Systems of assessment in ITE

Checklists

A checklist provides a list of behaviours or other criteria to focus the attention of the observer. A rating scale is a checklist with a scale on which the assessor estimates the frequency or quality of occurrence of each category. Examples and further discussion can be found in Brown (1975), Hook (1981), Turney *et al.* (1982b) and Wallace (1991: 162). A checklist or a rating scale summarises assessment criteria and, by implication, course objectives.

Checklists and rating scales are designed to control high-inference judgements by supervisors. They have the following advantages:

- they provide a standard instrument for all to use, which improves consistency between assessors;
- they are public, open to assessor and student-teacher alike;
- because they are public there is some potential for the negotiation of categories.

Each category in a checklist can represent either very specific acts (e.g. 'uses pair work') or broad categories which contain complex sets of individual acts (e.g. 'varies lesson activities'). This presents its designer with the problem of how many categories to use, and of what type. The more categories there are the more precise and comprehensive the instrument might become, but it also becomes much harder to use. However, the fewer categories there are the broader they are and the more open to different interpretations by supervisors and students. The known drawbacks of rating scales are:

- rating is affected by personal bias;
- the 'halo' effect: student-teachers who start well go on being rated well, in that positive rating on one characteristic early in a lesson tends to carry over to the others;
- low-inference and hence reliable categories (e.g. 'teacher faces class when writing on the board') have the drawback of being overly detailed

and potentially trivial, in that they do not deal with higher-order concepts, such as attainment of teaching goals, or appropriacy of
materials;

- Categories such as 'rapport' are undeniably important, but are high-inference, global and interpretive in nature and so are liable to subjective and inconsistent interpretation by assessors;
- Difficulty: 'the awarding of marks on a scale for each item of the schedule is in most cases extraordinarily difficult and depends a great deal on the assessor's ideas and values' (Stones, 1987: 684). The objectivity implied by a rating scale may be more apparent than real. In practice, rating decisions are interpretive and subjective.

Checklists and rating scales are convenient and promote a degree of consistency between observers. However, for them to be fair and accurate, they should meet the following design criteria.

- Use standard instruments which contain all the categories of competence to be assessed.
- Derive the content from course content and objectives.
- Validate their content with reference to theory, other existing schedules and the realities of student-teachers' future teaching and context.
- Design rating scales to include space for evidence or incidents which support the judgment reached by the supervisor (Turney et al., 1982a).
- In using rating scales, hold team standardisation meetings in which staff rate blind a series of video-recorded lessons, and then compare and discuss their ratings to arrive at a reasonable level of consensus. This helps to make explicit the personal values implicit in the criteria applied to assessing teaching.
- Support checklists with other data.

Profiling

In response to objections to conventional assessment methods, some institutions have introduced more broadly based systems of assessment (Peterson, 1995; also section 6.2). For example, a student-teacher assessment profile might contain:

- a curriculum vitae;
- a personal opening statement (expectations, needs, past influences);
- an assessment record;
- summative statements by staff;
- a portfolio of assignments;
- a personal closing statement (including targets for further development).

For the assessment record, relevant evidence could include a completed competency record, method-related assignments (including classroom studies, and practical teaching and self-evaluation exercise), a record of lesson observations and a teaching file.

An assessed teaching file may consist of lesson plans, self-evaluations, observations, analyses of learner work, notes of discussions and so on. It could also include school- or class-related materials on such matters as whole school issues, school policies, the pastoral system, and work as a form tutor.

In a flexible profiling system, competencies can be 'signed off' at any point in the year, rather than at a single period at the end of the course. This has great developmental advantages because profiles are flexible and broadly based, seem fairer to the student-teachers and can develop their planning and decision-making skills (see section 6.2).

5.3.6   Conclusion: taking a stand on assessment

ITE assessors face a dilemma. On the one hand, there seem to be relatively few safe generalisations about effective teaching on which to base assessment, particularly if these are expressed in behavioural terms. However, one must make judgements for purposes of accreditation. Clear and agreed criteria for accreditation have to be set, because all learner-teachers deserve fair and equal treatment.

Consensual, essential teaching skills are a common-sense starting point for ITE assessment and practical teaching objectives (Kyriacou, 1991; Wragg, 1993). To meet principles of fairness, these criteria need to be arrived at collectively by staff. However, once we move from the relative certainty of these essential teaching skills, both student-teachers and providers have to adopt more open, flexible and contextually sensitive criteria.

Assessment should be broadly based and flexible enough to admit individual variations, be representative of programme objectives and be as free of supervisor bias as possible. Ideally it should also be carried out by assessors who are aware of their own beliefs and potential for bias, and aware of the inherent limitations of assessment methods they use. In spite of the administrative workload it creates, profiling seems to meet criteria of fairness and equity far better than a system based on observation alone.

In the next section we outline two ITE programmes, one a full-time one-year PGCE for all disciplines (section 6.2), the other an intensive 'survival' course for ELT (section 6.3). Both cases highlight issues of assessment, supervision and structural coherence.

Appendix 5.1   Input and processing

We divide presentation strategies into propositional (talking about) and experiential, and then outline some processing tasks to help learners to 'personalise' new information, that is to construct their representations of it. Our broadly 'social constructivist' approach to LTE (see section 1.1.5) indicates a central role for dialogue, in conjunction with private reflection and inputs of new information. An emphasis on experiential learning has in some cases tended to reduce the value given to formal input. Our approach indicates the importance of formal inputs, but also recognises that learner-teachers will vary in their expectations and preferences for the manner of input and in the meaning they construct from it. This argues for a flexible and integrated use of input and processing activities.

Input

Propositional

Directed/free reading

A tutor's selection and sequencing of readings is helpful to the learner in a new field. An open choice of reading is more suitable to courses aiming at self-directed development (e.g. Doff, 1988; Wallace, 1991; see also sections 6.2 and 8.6).

Lectures/talks

The lecture can consist of description, an account of theory, explanation, examples and cases. It may pose questions and issues. There are varieties of lecture according to purpose and personal style: one-way and relatively long (around 40 minutes); or punctuated with 'buzz' activity; or informal with audience participation throughout (Brown, 1978; Wallace, 1991: Chapter 5).

Experiential

Enact language learning tasks

Direct foreign language learning is a most powerful resource for experiential teacher learning (e.g. Willis, 1983; Woodward, 1992). Genuineness can also be simulated by the use of nonsense words to represent new lexis (e.g. Williams, 1994: 225). The more genuine the learning, the more powerful the potential of the experience.

Loop input

In loop input 'a process for the session ... exactly matches the content' (Woodward, 1992: 48). Where it is possible to find ways of matching process and content, loop input effectively combines presentation, demonstration and direct experience.

Language awareness tasks

Language awareness work involves practical analysis and interpretation of linguistic systems, and as such is a basic skill required by language teachers. It is particularly helpful for those unfamiliar with linguistic concepts and for non-native speakers who need to develop a working vocabulary about English in English. It is also a means to challenge assumptions about the nature of language and communication which can lead to reflection on teaching styles (Bolitho and Tomlinson, 1995).

Processing

Learner-teachers need active processing time to make sense of new information and experiences.

Private thinking time

Before group discussion each person can be given some private thinking and processing time to clarify her thinking and so improve the value of discussion. This can be done by offering input at the end of a session, with discussion in the next, or by providing pre-readings with reflection tasks so as to release contact time for discussion (e.g. section 8.6). In the longer term, logs and journals can give learners a useful record of their immediate reactions to the course (Porter *et al.*, 1990; Jarvis, 1992). The occasional 'silent thinking period' during a session can be very helpful in giving participants time to digest new information and focus on issues that concern them.

Structured dialogue

Conditions needed for productive discussion include: active listening; respect for the views of others; equal opportunities to speak; individual control over self-disclosure; and interpersonal trust (Bramley, 1979; McGill and Beaty, 1992; Bailey, 1996; also section 8.6). Where groups meet long term, initial activities to develop these attributes are highly desirable. Discussion is often most productive when it is structured by a process leader. 'Free-for-all' unstructured discussion should be reserved for small and well-integrated groups.

Paired discussion

Where learner-teachers are dealing with unfamiliar ideas or information, an initial paired summary/comment can be a useful preparation for more public discussion, especially for participants who may be shy or who need a chance to 'rehearse' their ideas in a safe context.

Buzz groups

Small groups are given a short time, perhaps 3–5 minutes, in which to summarise the content of input and list immediate reactions to it, which are then very briefly presented to the whole group. It is a useful way to 'activate' a group during a lecture, or to pick up first reactions from a whole group.

Pyramiding

Views are first exchanged in pairs and then in larger groups. This helps participants to articulate their ideas, and also gives each person a 'friend' in the larger group, so supporting their readiness to talk. In some cases, groups may be split and regrouped so that ideas can be discussed in detail by a larger number of students (i.e. 'cross-over' groups). In larger groups, creative discussion is better conducted in small groups with plenaries used to elicit summaries from each group which the provider can comment on.

Pooling

A topic or question is introduced (e.g. 'How have you reacted to the first week of this course?') and participants are invited to take turns to speak with *no interruption* from the others, whose task is to listen. Observations and questions can be invited after everyone has spoken. Participants have the right to 'pass' if they do not wish to speak. Pooling is a very effective way to take stock and to hear out a whole group on a well-focused issue. Pooling at the right time can have positive effects on personal reflection, mutual understanding and group climate because it is gives each participant an equal voice, attends to each, and does not subject what they have to say to 'censoring' by the questioning or reinterpretation of others.

Fishbowl

A subgroup conducts a simulation or a discussion in the centre of the room, with the rest of the group listening to them. It gives participants a good chance to think through issues without immediately having to present and defend a point of view.

Group discussions are most productive if they are well focused and related to ongoing work. Therefore they should be set up with a clear task, and with a definite time limit, which is kept to. Roles in the group may be pre-assigned (e.g. chair, secretary). Having to produce a concrete product is a very good way of focusing a group (e.g. to produce a poster, a set of notes etc.). After the discussion, a trainer can usefully summarise group contributions, on a poster for example, but should resist rephrasing or interpreting what has been said, as this effectively imposes his/her perceptions on those of the group. On no account should a trainer use the opportunity of group work to leave the room without explanation. It will be noticed and may be seen as evidence of lack of interest.

Not all learners are happy to disclose opinions or perceptions to others to order rather than when they feel ready. Adequate warning and preparation time are helpful. Also, participants should have the right to opt out of activities that they find emotionally difficult.

Appendix 5.2   Input and self-awareness

A constructivist approach to language teaching conventionally explores the prior knowledge of learners and links it to new material. In reading comprehension, 'pre-reading' activities are now standard methodology, designed to relate the learners' knowledge of the world and language to the new topic or text type (e.g. Grellet, 1981; Barr *et al.*, 1981, Williams and Moran, 1989: 221). Similarly, the purpose of activities here is to offer learner-teachers 'a framework in which to reflect on and analyse beliefs, assumptions and experience' (Parrott, 1993: 8) which can be related to new information.

Here we separate tasks according to focus, but in practice they can be combined and integrated with input and other activities in a flexible manner (e.g. Parrott, 1993: 116).

What you already know

Record what you know about the topic to be introduced, for example in notes, or as a 'mind-map' (Woodward, 1992: 52).

- It may be done as private reflection; or in a 'buzz group' to pool knowledge; or as a combination of the two.

Clarify your point of view

Propositions on the new topic are presented with an agree–disagree rating scale, for example that 'we can learn a language without knowing any grammar rules' (Williams, 1994).

- Providing a four-point scale prevents rating at a midpoint, and so requires the participant to take a positive point of view;
- The activity may be done as private reflection; as a 'pooling' activity to display diverse views; or as a consensus-reaching activity to promote discussion.
- Instead of a rating scale, participants may simply be asked to agree or disagree with a set of propositions (e.g. Parrott, 1993) or select

propositions they agree with from a list shared with colleagues (e.g.
Richards and Lockhart 1994: 48).

Naming

Participants are presented with a list of key terms to be included in the lecture/
readings and given time to research their meaning (Woodward, 1992).

- Before the lecture, participants discuss the word meanings and anticipate the lecture content.
- After the lecture they may discuss their revised understanding of
  terms, illustrate their meaning with examples, and also suggest other
  related terms.
- The activity is likely to be particularly helpful for non–native–speaker
  teachers, for whom conceptual development and naming in English
  can work together (Brown, 1990).

Language awareness

Assumptions about the nature of language often cluster with assumptions about
language teaching and learning. As learning about English is of top priority to
so many teachers, language awareness activities can be a critical means for
teachers to explore their assumptions, beliefs and experiences. Good examples
can be found in Bolitho and Tomlinson's (1995) activities on 'myths and mis-
conceptions' about systems in English.

Uncover and contrast assumptions

Participants are asked to select a metaphor which represents an aspect of their
teaching, or language learning (for example 'My classroom is a garden'). They
then draw it, elaborate on its meaning and present it in poster form (e.g.
Stofflet, 1996; James, forthcoming; also Appendix 8.1).

- Drawing helps participants to express notions that they might otherwise be unable or unwilling to express; they may be surprised by contrasting their own metaphors with those of others; and they may be
  helped to face up to assumptions that are normally submerged by
  routine.

Uncover images of teaching

Participants are asked to identify teachers whom they recall as particularly effective, or ineffective, or important to them personally; they can then explore their
characteristics, and how they might influence their current views and teaching.

- This may be done by guided recall (Woodward, 1992; Weintroub, 1993) or by structured contrast and identification of their distinctive features (Sendan, 1995a; Pope and Keen, 1981)

Reflect on your current teaching

Participants are asked to recall and note down aspects of their present practice relevant to the new information, as, for example, in section 8.6 (this should be as concrete and focused as possible).

- These reflections may be kept private; alternatively they may be 'pooled' (see above).

6

Case studies of ITE

6.1   Introduction

In this chapter we describe two very different ITE courses: one is a state-sector programme, non–ELT but including modern languages; the other is for private-sector ELT. In section 6.2, the Reading University partnership scheme, we report a revolutionary structure for state postgraduate teacher training across all secondary-school subjects, including modern languages. We focus on two issues: the need for coherence and integration between elements of the course (particularly assessment, course structure and styles of supervision); and some problematic features of student-teacher/supervisor relationships. The Partnership scheme for the secondary PGCE was introduced in 1993. We describe the year 1995–96, as the first implementation data were beginning to emerge. This case study illustrates:

- a structural alternative to conventional 'block practice' designs;
- the practical realisation of current theories of teacher learning;
- coherence between objectives, staff roles, styles of supervision, and assessment methods;
- issues arising from implementation.

In section 6.3, we discuss the UCLES Certificate (formerly CTEFLA, CELTA from October 1996), which is a widely recognised initial training programme. We focus on developments in the new CELTA (Certificate in ELT to Adults) scheme, and some of the implications of an intensive structure: the pressure towards a prescriptive approach, problems of assessment, and the question of further development of teachers once they have qualified. The general characteristics of the scheme are described, illustrated by a CTEFLA course run in Tokyo.

There are common themes in both descriptions:

- the tension between meeting the survival needs of learner-teachers (LTs), and the need to promote abilities leading to self-directed development and independent practice;
- the recognition of individual variation among language teachers as they develop their personal theories and pedagogic skills;

- the crucial importance of structure in providing positive learning opportunities;
- the need for coherence in course design;
- the importance of interpersonal relationships for constructive discourse between LTs and supervisors.

In each case study (also sections 8.2–8.6) there is a short section ('Connecting up') where we point to connections between it and our theoretical framework (Chapter 1) and summary of research evidence (Chapter 2). Space restrictions exclude many other significant ITE programmes such as 'fast-track' programmes in nations formerly part of the eastern bloc (e.g. at the University of Pilsen, Czech Republic); the development of teacher training colleges (e.g. in Zambia); large-scale university schemes in China.

6.2   University of Reading/Schools Partnership: the 1995–96 PGCE secondary course

6.2.1   Background

The Partnership model was introduced as an experimental initiative by pioneering universities in the late 1980s, and then introduced as law by the Department for Education and Employment in the early 1990s. PGCE students are required to spend a minimum of 24 weeks of their 36-week course 'on the premises of partner schools' (Department for Education, 1992: 4; also HMI 1991; Department for Education, 1993). Thus the relationship between higher education institutions (HEIs) and schools has been decisively changed.

While HEIs may realise a Partnership model in different ways, its key features are:

- student-teachers spend at least two thirds of course time in schools;
- time intervals between student-teachers' university and school-based experiences are kept short, e.g. with split weeks in the university and school;
- student experiences in the two sites are carefully integrated;
- staff roles in university and school are complementary, with collaboration on course planning and implementation;
- teachers are released from other duties to offer support and direction as needed ('mentors'), i.e. to supervise the students while they are in school (Wilkin, 1990; McIntyre *et al.*, 1993; Moon, 1994);
- student-teachers are placed in school to access the craft knowledge of experienced teachers;
- resources are transferred from HEIs to schools in recognition of their contribution to training.

In this model, new role demands are made of students, tutors, teachers, and of schools as organisations.

The change to School-based Teacher Education (SBTE) was motivated by government concerns over school standards. Also there had been concerted attacks on university-based ITE from right-wing political circles (e.g. Lawlor, 1990). Indeed, the case for greater school responsibility in teacher training was used in some circles to argue for a wholesale transfer of responsibility to schools and a regression to an associated apprenticeship model of teacher education (O'Hear, 1988; Hillgate, 1989).

From within HEIs, change arose from a widespread recognition of the need for reform, and from profound shifts in theory (see below). An administrative change which has enabled direct contractual arrangements between the HEIs and individual schools has been local management of schools (LMS). Under LMS each head teacher controls the school budget and is accountable to the governing body and the wider community to balance the books and to justify the use of money.

Research findings

Research from the early 1970s in England and in comparable systems in Scotland, Australia and the USA pointed unambiguously to a need for reform. It revealed a lack of clarity and coherence in many teacher education programmes; serious curricular disjunctions between schools and HEIs; and the insufficient preparation of students in classroom skills (Stones and Morris, 1972; Turney et al., 1982; Wragg, 1982; Chisholm, 1985; McIntyre, 1988). A worst-case summary set of problems, which did not necessarily appear in all programmes, is summarised in section 2.4.5.

Reform

Proposals for wide-ranging reform had appeared throughout the 1980s and early 1990s (Department of Education and Science, 1982; 1987; Alexander et al., 1984; Hopkins and Reid, 1985). They included the introduction of quality assurance of ITE; the prescription of good practice to clarify course objectives and practical assessment; the participation of experienced teachers in courses; the introduction of structured classroom inquiry into block practice (Ashton et al., 1989); and the adoption of student-centred modes of supervision (Stones, 1984).

Research clearly suggested greater school participation in ITE courses (Wilkin, 1990). Proposals included increased course time to be spent by student-teachers in schools; closer linkage between theoretical studies and practical experience; and renewed teaching experience for training institution staff. The first systematic realisation of these proposals occurred in 1987, with the launch of the Sussex and Oxford University schemes (Benton, 1990).

Partnership and the theory of learning to teach

School-based ITE could be implemented in different ways according to different approaches. For instance, a prescriptive apprenticeship model of learning could be applied to such a structure. However, Partnership/Internship[1] schemes in the UK commonly assume that integration and partnership should enable students to test theory and practice against each other and thereby develop their personal theories and practical skills in concert (Alexander, 1984; McIntyre, 1988; Haggerty, 1995).

This approach is based on the changing view of the nature of teacher knowledge and its acquisition (e.g. Alexander, 1984; Hopkins and Reid, 1985; Calderhead, 1988a; McIntyre, 1988). The design and implementation of Partnership schemes such as those at Oxford, Reading and many other HEIs in the UK are based upon key principles.

The first rejects the notion of prescription: 'there is not, nor can there be, any systematic corpus of theoretical knowledge from which prescriptive principles for teaching can be generated' (McIntyre, 1981: 296).

Secondly, they adopt an essentially constructivist model of learning to teach. For example, McIntyre cites research by Lacey (1977) and MacLeod (in McIntyre *et al.*, 1977), also supported by Griffiths (1977) which:

> showed how student-teachers in a microteaching context depended heavily on their own repertoires of concepts and criteria for construing and evaluating their teaching, only very gradually over time incorporating the concepts in terms of what they were being taught about teaching.
>
> (McIntyre, 1988: 103)

McIntyre concludes that students will acquire knowledge about teaching through the development of their own theories and perspectives: 'whether we like it or not, interns [students] will make their own judgements about what matters in teaching and about how best they can teach' (1988: 106).

Progressive ITE in the UK has been widely influenced by this constructivist model of student learning, which emphasises individual conceptual development by testing theory and practice against each other:

> Learning to teach must be a continual process of hypothesis testing framed by detailed analysis of the values and practical constraints fundamental to teaching. The 'theory' for teacher education should therefore incorporate (i) speculative theory (ii) the findings of empirical research (iii) the craft knowledge of practising teachers, but none should be presented as having prescriptive implications for practice: instead students should be encouraged to

---

[1]'Partnership' and 'Internship' are terms for essentially the same model of school-based ITE (Benton, 1990).

approach their own practice with the intention of testing hypothetical principles drawn from the consideration of these different types of knowledge.

Alexander (1984: 146)

The mission of such training is to prepare teachers for self-direction, to teach
them how to make decisions under conditions of uncertainty.

6.2.2   Description

The Reading University Partnership scheme was launched in 1992. At the time
of writing it is still evolving and implementation concerns are still emerging.
We report the 1995–96 PGCE secondary course, one of three courses at
Reading University leading to qualified teacher status (QTS).

Participation and funding

Under LMS, schools can choose for themselves whether to opt in to a partnership agreement. Placement of students in schools is funded by a financial
arrangement between the university and school which receives an annual sum
per student to pay for school tutors' (ST) and professional tutors' (PT) release
time. In 1995–96, 45 schools had signed such agreements with the university,
mostly for a period of 3 years. The university paid the schools £918 per student, which for a typical school would total about £7,344. The total paid to secondary schools for the 1995–96 PGCE secondary course was £209,304.

The university also pays for student and staff travel expenses. As schools are
widespread and public transport expensive, this adds greatly to costs (in
1995–96, travel expenses for primary undergraduate, primary postgraduate and
secondary postgraduate courses totalled £157,000). Finally, the administration
of all three courses requires 3.5 full-time equivalent administrative staff.

Model of learning to teach

The approach to student learning is presented in the Student Handbook as an
ability to make appropriate decisions taking into account the considerations
unique to each setting, as outlined in Fig. 6.1. It indicates that each teacher is
expected to work from her own prior knowledge, drawing on generalised knowledge such as of good practice and language learning theory, and context-specific
knowledge of the school, as well as external imperatives such as centrally determined requirements in the curriculum and the law.

Students are expected to access teachers' craft knowledge by observation and
discussion with them. Time in school allows the student to learn about its special circumstances and their effects on practice. Students can also differentiate
cases where teachers have choice and where not because of school policy or the
law.

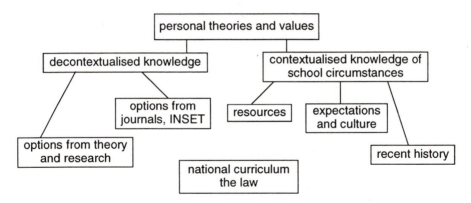

Fig 6.1   Factors in teaching decisions

Students should apply their awareness of teachers' reasoning to their own progressively less-sheltered teaching tasks. They reflect on and explain their own choices in the light of the considerations above: when planning; when monitoring and adapting teaching in class; and when evaluating their actions after class.

The constructivist and experiential nature of this learning model is recognised in the Handbook. Referring to the plan, teach, evaluate cycle, it says: 'this broadly based reflection lies at the heart of the course model of student-teacher learning' (p. 10); while students are invited to 'pay attention to changing your thinking as well as improving your actions' (p. 10).

Thus, student teaching is not seen as the re-enactment of proven blueprints for action, as in a prescriptive approach. Students are seen as making choices, testing them out and reflecting on these experiences to develop their thinking and practical skills. This reflection draws on the widest possible range of sources: decontextualised knowledge sources of theory and research, personal experiences, and practical models. It is realised in teaching decisions, critical discussions with peers and tutors, and through reflective assignment writing.

The student needs support and clear expectations. Support is available from regular discussions with supervisors and peers. The clear framework of expectations is supplied by the consensual professional criteria applied in assessment. To prevent this framework from becoming a prescriptive straitjacket, a flexible profiling assessment system has been adopted.

Tutors need to support students to realise the 'intention of testing hypothetical principles' (Alexander, 1984: 146) by taking part in discourse which explores options and reasons for choices rather than providing prescriptions. The learning model implies an exploratory mode of supervision, as is recognised in the government's investment in staff training for mentor skills during the transition to the new scheme (McIntyre *et al.*, 1993).

One consequence of this approach is that participants will have conflicting views about best choices and so the student–teacher will have to cope with staff who do not agree with each other. Novice students cannot be expected to cope with uncertainty until they are ready. Therefore, practical experience is graded from work in sheltered settings, with an agenda set by consensual criteria, to more open settings where contradictions arise and where a student can follow a more individual learning agenda.

Objectives

The learning objectives of the course are detailed in the student's competency record (Appendix 6.1). The goals of the course relate to five areas, for which students should draw on theory and practical experience:

1) Students should understand the model of student-teacher learning upon which their course is based and acquire the skills needed to work within this model and thus become creative and reflective practitioners, open-minded and questioning, able to appreciate the importance of theory and of local circumstances in decision-making in the school and the classroom.

2) Students should acquire knowledge and understanding of factors relating to whole school issues ... and should demonstrate competence in the wide range of activities which are expected of teachers in the whole-school context ...

3) Students should acquire knowledge and understanding of factors relating to classroom practice and should demonstrate competence in the wide range of activities which are expected of teachers in the context of the subject classroom ...

4) Students should recognise that the model for student-teacher learning provides a mechanism for long-term professional development, and should demonstrate that they are taking first steps towards such development.

5) Students should define some personal goals, and take steps to attain them.

Structure

On admission, the 1995 intake of 228 PGCE secondary students were placed in groups of two kinds: a cross–disciplinary complementary studies seminar group, normally of 16 students and led by a complementary studies tutor (CST); and method groups ranging in size from 16 to 38 working with two or more method tutors (MT). They were grouped by subject, including modern languages.

University	School	Focus
Complementary studies tutor (CST)	Professional tutor (PT)	Whole school/ professional issues; liaison

STUDENT-TEACHER

Method tutor (MT)	Supervising teacher (ST)	Language teaching issues and liaison

Throughout, the curriculum is divided into method and complementary studies (CS) areas. The CS group is the basic unit of course planning. It is split into two matching groups, which swap schools when the course requires it (see 'Year structure' below).

Students are paired by subject, and normally four different subject pairs are placed in each school. Pairing enables team teaching, peer observation or other appropriate forms of collaboration.

Roles

Each role is detailed in the Student Handbook and the partnership contract. MTs and STs deal with directly subject-specific questions. The CST and PT are concerned with wider issues such as school organisation, children with learning problems, school policy on discipline and homework etc.

The role of university tutors is defined by programme objectives (above) and also includes developing STs' enabling skills such as the observation and analysis of different ways of teaching; investigation of alternative types of schools organisation; the development of inquiry techniques; accessing the craft knowledge of experienced teachers; becoming aware of their own personal theories; and opposing tutors' views.

School-based tutors' responsibilities include making arrangements for practice; grading students' responsibilities; specifying what they must do by law or school policy; presenting teaching strategies for investigation; supporting student-teachers' inquiry into their own teaching; and discussing their own practice, revealing the reasoning which shapes it.

The ST works with a pair of students on subject-specific matters. The PT co-ordinates students' work in school and works closely with the CST in a weekly tutorial focused on whole-school issues (such as language development across the curriculum, the European dimensions and environmental education). The PT also works closely with MTs on each student's programme of classroom work.

University tutors work with the school to plan each student-teacher's programme (i.e. from sheltered settings to full responsibility) and to conduct assessment.

Year structure

(Three terms of 12 weeks.)

Term 1
Week

1–2	First university-based phase Orientation to course and preparation for initial school placement
2–4	Initial full-time placement in school A Guided observation and enquiry in school
4–5	Second university-based phase Method and complementary studies work, and preparatory work on school B
6–12	First '2+3' phase Mon–Tue at university, Wed–Fri at main placement school (school B) The programme is jointly planned by university and school staff. Theoretical aspects of an issue can be explored in the university and explored by observation and in collaborative teaching with the ST and some sheltered individual teaching. Lecture notes and other details of university input are shared with STs and PTs

Term 2

13–18	'2+3' phase continues Responsibilities increasing to teaching whole lessons and lesson sequences; complementary studies shift in focus from fact-finding to investigation and development of cross-curriculum issues
19	Study week in university
(half–term)	Discuss assessment (method and complementary studies) and prepare for main placement 2.

Term 3

25-29	Main full-time placement 2 (school B) Teach *c*. 50 per cent normal timetable (in pairs and alone), carry out form tutor duties and prepare assignments related directly to own teaching One lesson in three observed by ST; MT visits minimum of four times

30–32	University-based phase
	Tutorials and private study time (feedback on block practice, prepare complementary studies assignment, orientate to final school-based phase)
33–35	Final School A phase: three weeks' block experience
	Focus negotiated with ST and PT and action plan presented to MT. Students develop a specific aspect of teaching, the subject negotiated with school and university staff
36	Final university-based phase
	Complete assessment requirements and produce plans for further professional development in following year

Some notes on the structure

- Two thirds of course time is spent in school.
- Student-teachers' awareness of local school conditions is developed by the contrast between two placements. This enables experience of contrasting school conditions.
- 'Split weeks' enable short time intervals between personal experience in school and the wider frame of reference of university-based discussion and reflection.
- The second review at week 30 attempts to release the students from the survival concerns that often block more exploratory thinking and practice, and so to enable developmental curricular work and a focus on personal agendas for future professional development.
- The Reading scheme faced conditions different from the Oxford scheme (Benton, 1990). In terms of locations, participating schools are in four LEAs, so making co-ordination more problematic. Also as the partnership area is larger, travel time and travel costs are greater. A wider range of subjects are taught at Reading than Oxford, so in some 'minority' subjects it is more difficult to find co-operating departments and an adequate pool of co-operating teachers.

Assessment

Reading students are assessed by a competency-based profiling system designed to meet three conditions. First, as with any assessment system, it should make valid distinctions between students and should be fair to all. Second, it should meet official requirements at government and institutional level. Thus, the Secretary of State's criteria (Department for Education 9/92) are included within the competencies defined by the Partnership. Finally, it should be consistent with course goals, in this case to develop 'creative and reflective practitioners, open-minded and questioning, able to appreciate the importance of theory and of local circumstances in decision-making in the school and in the classroom' (Handbook 1995–96: Appendix 1). A central characteristic is the joint responsibility taken by assessor and assessed (Scriven, 1981).

Competencies

Ministry initiatives (Department for Employment, 1992) required HEIs to detail their course objectives and their assessment criteria in terms of competencies that should be exhibited by a new teacher in school. While seen by some as risking a return to an approach based on behavioural models of teacher education (Frost, 1993), this has had considerable benefits. It clarifies objectives for all by offering staff and students explicit statements of standards to be applied; it specifies the evidence needed to meet standards and procedures to be followed in awarding pass grades. After much work by staff and students, the original Reading course competencies have changed from being detailed and behavioural to a broader and more flexible set of categories (Appendix 6.1).

The competency record consists of the categories of competence, the evidence which justifies the award of a competency, and tutors' dated signing off of competencies. In Appendix 6.1 we include the basic course requirements as presented to the student-teacher and also an extract from the record. We have selected two pages from the competence record which relate to 'knowledge and approach', 'planning' and 'teaching'. Each competence is briefly exemplified to help shared interpretation. The competencies are framed in global terms, to allow context-specific interpretation. This inevitably leaves more room for different interpretations of the competence. Thus part of the work for supervisors and student-teachers is to arrive at common interpretations of the competencies in practice.

Responsibility

The responsibility for maintaining the competency record and keeping written evidence lies *with the student*. For summative assessment, the student must assemble and submit the whole profile.

Awarding a competency

Students have to present the evidence which they consider merits the award of a competency, from a broad range of sources (coursework, class teaching, a teaching portfolio, discussions with tutors) and discuss this with the teacher and the tutor in three-way meetings. School or university staff can sign off competencies if they are satisfied with the evidence.

The profile

Each student's profile contains:

    a) a curriculum vitae;
    b) a personal opening position statement;

c) a copy of the complete signed record of competencies;

d) summative comments from tutors and teachers;

e) a portfolio of assignments and other written evidence supporting the attainment of competencies;

f) a personal end-of-course position statement, including targets for further development.

Flexibility and individualisation

There is flexibility in assessment: any competency can be awarded at any point in the year if tutors accept there is enough evidence. Once awarded it is not normally withdrawn. This individualises each student's agenda through the year: 'you can therefore use your developing record of competence to plan the focus of your later work – e.g. concentrating on competencies not yet secured' (Student Handbook: 41).

It is also hoped to tell students as soon as possible (e.g. by week 26) when they pass the practical element of the course so that they can work 'further on a competency which is of particular interest to you once all are in place' (Student Handbook: 41).

For observations, students can ask in advance for a specific competency or number of competencies to be addressed. Also, feedback indicates which competencies are being addressed, and whether they are considered to have been attained. Early warning is also given to students at risk.

Formal reviews are held in the middle of the second term before the main school placement and early in the third term. Staff discuss the evidence for each student's attainments of competencies, and then meet them individually to review competencies signed off and to help set targets for those still to be awarded. After the second review, there are some six to eight weeks in which passing students can engage in further development and inquiry, while those with competencies outstanding have an additional teaching programme focusing on the problem areas, such as the level of TL use being demanded of pupils.

Summative assessment

On completing assessment requirements and submitting their profile in the last week of the course, students are awarded pass or fail grades.

Evidence

For the rest of this summary, we focus on methods assessment. The requirements are:

- a short assignment dealing with theory-practice links, due week 12;
- a longer assignment analysing an aspect of subject teaching (due week 18) which is then explored and evaluated in the student's own teaching, due week 31;

- leading a seminar 'describing and evaluating ways of teaching a topic and exploring the relationship between these approaches and theoretical insights', and then producing a report discussing the preparation and evaluation of the seminar in the light of tutor feedback;
- a teaching file (information on the department, teaching done, lesson plans and evaluations, notes of discussion on lessons taught or observed, and a summary of personal targets post-course), due week 31;
- a record of lessons observed by tutors and copies of written feedback (based on a minimum of 10 visits during the main block experience, four by the MT and six by school supervisors).

Assessments focus consistently on the interaction between personal experience and decontextualised theories (such as on motivation, error correction etc.).

Maintaining the approach

As school staff turnover is quite high, and schools rotate their involvement, university staff are responsible for maintaining the approach of the course. School staff participate in university quality assurance systems. They are represented on course design teams, and the monitoring and evaluation group. STs meet MTs three times a year in Faculty and there is an annual summative meeting for PTs and tutors to review the course. Course co-directors are advised by a Partnership Joint Steering Group of eight head teachers and seven senior faculty members, including the Dean. One head teacher represents the schools on the Faculty Board for Teacher Education which is responsible for quality assurance across all initial teacher education courses in the Faculty.

6.2.3   Issues and lessons

Course coherence

For reasons of history or institutional inertia, it has been the case that ITE courses have contained contradictory elements within their own curriculum, and between the HEI and the school (Calderhead, 1989; section 2.4.5).

In contrast, the Reading PGCE demonstrates coherence between course elements. In structure this is achieved by means of integrated curricula, contact time between university and school staff, student time in schools for analysis and experimentation, time with tutors, and structured experience of contrasted schools.

Assessment is a key aspect of coherence: it should be consistent with course objectives. It has a profound effect on how students approach their studies and their relationships with supervisors. If course objectives require students to take responsibility, then it must be possible for them to do so in the process of assessment. Similarly, if objectives stress personal development, then assessment must allow for individual student differences and the development of personal agendas. It seems that the flexibility of the Reading system does enable student responsibility, reflection, experimentation and some individualisation.

Implementation of roles: some issues

Changes in institutional culture and role perceptions do not happen overnight (McIntyre *et al.*, 1993: 8). Evidence on implementation at the time of writing suggests that while Partnership schemes have had considerable successes in the integration and planning of curricula, there may be some difficulties in supervisor/student-teacher discourse. The possible scope of this discourse is suggested by a large-scale qualitative study (Wildman *et al.*, 1992: 208–9) which suggested eight mentor roles: encouraging reflection; directing and supporting beginners' actions and plans; providing direct assistance; providing a menu of information; providing ideas to help beginners solve a problem; personal support; beginner helping the mentor; and mediating between the beginner and other staff.

Other evidence seems to be limited to small-scale studies: the early years of the Oxford scheme (Haggerty, 1995b); an analysis of conversations between five STs and 10 students (Haggerty, 1995b); and an analysis of the views of 32 prospective STs (Saunders *et al.*, 1995). Therefore, rather than generalising findings, it is more appropriate to present them as issues that seem central to the Partnership model.

To what extent can students uncover the practical knowledge of experienced teachers?

McNamara and Desforges (1978) were disappointed in their attempts to help students uncover the sophistication and complexity of teachers' contextual craft knowledge. Subsequent research which revealed that 'what teachers have been able to tell us has often surprised and excited them as much as it has excited us' (McIntyre, 1988: 102) also suggested conditions under which this uncovering could occur. Apart from a concrete focus on aspects the teacher perceives as successful, McIntyre suggested that a further condition was that 'the teacher is encouraged and helped by *a skilled, sympathetic and mature researcher*' (1988; author's italics).

Given our knowledge of the routinisation of teacher knowledge, the status of routine practice as ritual, its closeness to self, and the power of group culture (Somekh, 1993; section 2.2) it seems that there may be considerable obstacles to the same uncovering occurring in student-ST discussions. A number of obstacles suggested by the research are:

logistical: some supervising teachers may be under time
                               pressure, so curtailing time for analysis.

analytic/observational:	students may not be able to recognise the complexities of teaching situations and so appreciate the reasons for decisions made in them (for example the influence of school culture, or of a teacher's prior knowledge of particular pupils).
student attitudes to the ST:	politeness constraints may prevent probing of the ST's practice; mismatches between theory and observed practice may be left unexplored, as they imply criticism of the observed teacher; students may not value the help or practice of the ST (perhaps because of rivalry; or incompatible personal theories; or the known tendency of some students to affiliate with pupils rather than staff); the student may not accept the priority teachers give to practicability in terms of resources, workload and personal energy saving.
ST attitudes:	some STs may prefer not to discuss the work of other teachers; STs may not discuss the complexities of practice in context, instead referring to more general decontextualised theory (perhaps because of the tacit nature of their practical reasoning, or perhaps because of a perception of their role as a surrogate HEI tutor which might be due to their accountability for assessment (Frost, 1993); STs may be reticent about discussing what they regard as having done well.

This suggests the need for careful selection and training of supervising teachers. As Lortie (1975: 71) presciently observed of a quite different context: 'there is no assurance that the supervisors are selected for their ability to explain underlying rationales for decision making'.

Do STs' personal theories conflict with a reflective role?

STs may bring role expectations from previous personal experiences as pupils and students which may be at odds with their intended role as a source of craft knowledge. For example, in a study of prospective STs' role expectations, Saunders et al. (1995) identify a common 'hands-off' orientation to the role.

Observation and feedback figure strongly, but there is no reference to sharing with the student on an equal and open footing. Such an orientation might well preclude discussion of their own reasoning and so exclude students from a central means to learn about teaching.

Are all teacher decisions complex?

We speculate that an effect of group and institutional culture may be that teachers' decision-making is not always based on such sophisticated or complex decisions as some research has suggested. As Somekh (1993) suggests, an effect of affiliation with the occupational culture may lead teachers to take on a job-lot of practices because they are the conventional and accepted way to behave in the institution. In such a case, a teacher's analysis that 'I do it because it works/it's just what I do/it's the way things are done' really does explain that practice. In other words, it may be that some teacher actions are not based on thought-through decisions, but are simply 'the normal thing to do'. If this is true, then the challenge for the Partnership model would be to identify such of an ST's practice, observed by a student, that *was* the product of choice according to competing considerations as identified in the course model of learning.

If students cannot uncover the practical knowledge of experienced teachers, what are the consequences?

If students fail to understand why particular decisions have been made in the school, then they may not bring as broad a set of considerations to the analysis of their own choices in the same school when taking on less sheltered teaching duties. Also, without an available account of practical reasoning, students may not be able to test practices against theory or to challenge theory with effective but theoretically unsanctioned practice.

When will students take an exploratory orientation to their teaching?

It seems that students will resist an exploratory orientation to their work if it threatens their personal priorities. These seem to be the priorities of survival: achieving control in class and passing the course satisfactorily. Until the student feels that these priorities have been addressed, s/he is most unlikely to take the risks inherent in exploration. As Maynard and Furlong (1993: 83) point out, one way *not* to become an expert swimmer is to 'learn with an expert who expects you to refine your stroke while you are struggling to stay afloat'.

Weak and strong students can have good reasons to avoid risk: the former may prefer to mask their difficulties with failsafe coping strategies; the latter may see no need to compromise their previous successes and good assessment and references.

We do not claim that all these difficulties will be found in any one Partnership scheme. However, they usefully suggest areas for attention while evaluating and developing school-based schemes. More generally, they suggest that the attitudinal shifts that accompany deep role changes will only occur over time and by means of consistent collaborative work.

Connecting up

In approach, the Partnership PGCE is highly consistent with social constructivist principles of student-teacher learning (see sections 1.4 and 1.1.5). A constructivist view is implicit in its appeal to learning by means of reflection on a broad base of experiences and 'inputs' (Figure 6.1), and an assessment design which recognises that each learner teacher will progress through the programme at different rates and with different concerns. Also, the inclusion of opening and closing 'position statements' in assessment focuses explicitly on the evolution of personal theories over the year, and awareness of these personal theories.

The social dimension (attention to context and conceptual development by interaction with others) is central to the design: in its awareness-raising about school contexts; in the team basis of its organisation; in the extensive opportunities to learn more about learners' perspectives; in the regularity of supervisory support; and in the role of dialogue with mentors.

As our discussion above suggests, dialogue is by no means a simple process of 'downloading' the knowledge of others. On the contrary, the evolutionary and incremental model of development we endorse (section 2.4.6) suggests that the knowledge of others will never just be 'bolted on' to a person's prior ways of understanding. However, support and dialogue are essential for the values and understandings of each learner-teacher to be challenged, clarified and evolved. Perhaps the richest developmental experiences this design offers are the better understanding of learners' perceptions, and relationships with peers and mentors who inform student-teachers' sense of 'the teacher I want to be'.

As regards research data, in section 2.4.5 we suggest explicit connections between research and Partnership designs. We also summarise activities under the headings of awareness, feelings and skills which can be matched against our account.

Applying the Partnership model

SBTE will take different forms in different settings. However, certain conditions seem to be necessary to sustain a true partnership scheme, with an integrated curriculum and adequate liaison between staff and adequate supervision of students.

Logistics: there should be enough schools within one day's
                            travel of the HEI for student placement;

student–teacher ratios in the schools should enable adequate supervision time.

Transition:
there should be genuine participation by schools and other interest groups at the planning stage (Benton, 1990);
whole-school staff training for prospective STs should be available, including values–clarification activities.

Ongoing funding:
STs' supervision time should be taken as paid release time from their other duties;
training of STs new to an ongoing scheme should be funded.

Attitudes:
HEI staff have to be ready to work on an equal footing with teachers and be ready to accept school side initiatives;
STs need a role concept consistent with course objectives;
students have to accept responsibility and self-direction.

Positive incentives:
teachers' incentives might include some release from teaching and the enhancement of career prospects by additional responsibility;
school incentives might include the addition to school funds and access to educational innovations;
HEI staff incentives may include opportunities to pursue academic issues in context; however, there may be serious disincentives if promotion and professional development are based exclusively on research and publication, which time-consuming MT/CST duties would hinder.

Institutions:
the HEI must be ready to place school staff on university boards;
HEIs should be ready to accept forms of assessment appropriate to an exploratory model;
school staff should be positively orientated to the partnership agreement and aware of its full implications;
schools should enjoy sufficient slack in staffing for release of STs in paid teaching time.

A complex Partnership scheme may well be too demanding on resources and administration to be sustainable in a poorly resourced or loosely administered system. Conditions for transfer include:

- a large enough pool of teachers with competence in classroom management to be drawn on for supervisors;
- adequate additional resources in college and schools (personnel, materials, time);
- selection procedures capable of identifying those who are suitable for a supervisor role;
- adequate and ongoing supervisor training, with a strong element of self-awareness and reflection as well as interpersonal and feedback skills;
- systems to monitor the scheme and respond to short- and long-term concerns;
- the optimum participation by supervisors in the formative development of their scheme;
- staff liaison and syllabus co-ordination between participating institutions.

There is already some evidence of slippage in a comparable scheme, in which probationary-year student-teachers were supported in school by co-operating teachers and by teams of mobile supervisors (Woolger, 1989).

Acknowledgements

Special thanks are due to Mike Weller, Chair of the Board for Teacher Education, geography methods tutor and complementary Studies tutor, Faculty of Education and Community Studies, University of Reading, for his help and detailed additions and corrections; also to his colleagues, Ernesto Macaro and Martin Parsons.

The work of the course Co-directors, Mr James Hall and Dr Keith Postlethwaite, underpins this whole case study: they wrote the Student Handbook and directed the course from its introduction in 1993/94 until 1995/96. The rationale, aims and objectives, structure, content and assessment of the course were developed initially by a joint working party of colleagues from the Faculty and from schools approved by a Conference of Headteachers as well as the University Senate, who also jointly approved subsequent revisions.

6.3 The Cambridge/RSA Certificate in English Language Teaching to Adults (CELTA)[2]

6.3.1 Introduction

In this section we outline the UCLES initial teaching qualification, the CELTA (formerly CTEFLA). We do so because it is part of a highly significant

[2]Special thanks to Rosemary Wilson for her detailed help on the description of the CELTA.

international ELT training scheme, CILTS (Cambridge Integrated Language Teaching Schemes). It is an interesting case of an essentially introductory form of ITE as described in section 6.3.2 and discussed in 6.3.3.

From the early 1980s to 1996 the qualification was entitled the CTEFLA, but a long process of consultation and piloting culminated in the launch of the CELTA in October of that year.

At the time of writing, the CELTA scheme was new and all UCLES schemes were undergoing comprehensive review and development (e.g. UCLES 1992; 1995; 1996) leading to new course titles and revised structures, syllabuses and forms of assessment. Readers needing up-to-date information or advice can obtain it directly from UCLES.

There is remarkable diversity in the structure, intake and setting of Certificate courses. The one brief example below cannot be representative of the whole scheme. Additionally the issues discussed are necessarily selective. However, we try to report the key changes made in the new CTEFLA, and also to focus on issues of concern for providers of *any* introductory ITE course.

6.3.2 Description

Background

Among private ELT institutions, the UCLES Certificate and Diploma awards come closest to recognised or accrediting teaching qualifications. This has been reinforced by their inclusion as accepted qualifications in the British Council-administered ARELS/FELCO scheme for the recognition of schools meeting its standards of efficiency.

The awards are a large-scale enterprise. In 1995, for example, some 600 full- or part-time CTEFLA courses were run for about 7000 candidates at some 130 centres worldwide. For the DTEFLA, some 60 centres provided courses for about 700 candidates. By 1996, at International House (IH) alone an estimated 30 000 teachers had taken the IH short course/CTEFLA since 1962.

It is important to note that UCLES is an examining board (as was the former awarding body the RSA) and not a curricular or educational institution. Its functions are to define the syllabus, set assessment requirements, appoint and monitor assessors and inspect centres awarding qualifications. Its key task, therefore, is to set and maintain standards: 'UCLES approves courses but does not run them' (CTEFLA brochure, 1994).

Considering its function, its self-funding intake and the private sector employment of those qualifying, CILTS are very different from educational qualifications in England and Wales such as the BA (Ed) and PGCE in intake, philosophy, context, and means of control.

History

Development in the scheme since the 1960s has derived from the dramatic worldwide growth of ELT and from the development of TEFL as a major service industry and as an independent discipline.

In 1967 the Department of Education (with British Council support) suggested the introduction of a postgraduate ELT qualification for native speakers, characterised by its combination of theoretical and practical content (the RSA 'Certificate in Teaching English as a Second or Foreign Language'). In the early 1980s, the scheme was retitled the DTEFLA, to distinguish it from the Preparatory Certificate.

In 1962, International House had introduced a short initial teacher training programme, initially intended for the induction of its own staff, including those going on to affiliated schools overseas. Over time it was increased in length from two to four weeks. It was designed for people with no prior teaching experience and had a strongly practical orientation. It provided a high proportion of teaching practice time, continuous practical assessment and demanded no theoretical written assignments. The assumption of the IH scheme was that those qualifying would go on to its own schools where further support and training would be provided. The IH scheme was very much the model for the 'Preparatory Certificate in TEFLA', introduced in 1975. In the early 1980s it was retitled the RSA CTEFLA.

During the late 1970s and early 1980s qualifications were introduced for teachers of English outside the UK who were not native speakers (the DOTE and COTE). The intake for these courses was never as great, largely due to their nonrecognition by national education authorities. In 1988, UCLES took over the administration of the four awards.

As Morrow (in RSA/UCLES, 1992: 1) observed: 'There is a history in the scheme of development by evolution and new Certificates and Diplomas have been devised in response to perceived needs. In addition a variety of new syllabus areas and assessment procedures have been introduced over the years. It is, however, fair to say that this development has been piecemeal and often ad-hoc.'

He went on to assert the need for 'the development of a coherent and systematic framework' and to describe the process of comprehensive consultation and review with course providers and other stakeholders which had been under way since 1991.

At the time of writing UCLES has launched the new CELTA after 'a long process of consultation with the ELT profession, and an extensive piloting phase' in which 'a conscious and deliberate effort has been made to ensure that the new developments are in line with the perceived needs of centres, employers, candidates and ELT professionals internationally, and that they reflect and extend the best of current practice' (UCLES, 1996: 4).

Nature of the award

We can summarise the key features of the CELTA award as follows (UCLES, 1996).

Admission

An educational standard enabling entry to higher education; minimum age 20; 'an awareness of language and a competence in English, both written and spoken, that enables them (candidates) to follow the course' (UCLES, 1996).

Duration

A minimum of 100 hours full- or part-time contact with tutors; part-time may last from eight weeks to a year.

Objectives

The minimum objectives for candidates are summarised in the 1996 Syllabus as:

1   Develop an awareness of language and a knowledge of the description of English and apply these in their professional practice;
2   Develop an initial understanding of the contexts within which adults learn English as foreign language, their motivations and the roles of the teacher and the learner;
3   Develop familiarity with the principles and practice of effective teaching to adult learners of English;
4   Develop basic skills for teaching adults in the language classroom;
5   Develop familiarity with the appropriate resources and materials for use with adult learners of English for teaching, testing and for reference;
6   Identify opportunities for their own future development as professionals in the field.

Practical preparation

Each candidate should have equal practice time. Each is required to 'practice teach in a class of the relevant age group, for a total of 6 hours ... at a minimum of two levels' (UCLES, 1996) with supervision; micro-teaching using foreign students is included in practice teaching; candidates are also required to 'observe experienced teachers for a total of 8 hours' (UCLES, 1996); and to 'maintain and submit a portfolio of all course work including all written assignments and materials related to teaching practice' (UCLES, 1996). Groups should be no smaller than 10, and two levels should be taught, one elementary.

Staff

A minimum of two staff are required, with a ratio in teaching practice of at least 1:6; a minimum number of eight candidates per course is normally required for approval by UCLES.

Tutorials

A minimum of one tutorial should be given.

Fees

These vary according to the centre, but in the UK the norm at the time of writing is *c*. £700 or higher.

Assessment

Candidates are internally assessed, based on the continuous assessment of their teaching, with the course tutor keeping ongoing records during the course and weekly summaries as appropriate. All courses are moderated by an assessor who visits the course, checks standards by observing teaching practice and looks at written work. Cases of disagreement or complaint can be referred to the TEFL Unit at UCLES.

Written work of up to 3 000 words is also required. Three types of assignment are required: work on the language system of English; 'reflection on classroom teaching and the identification of action points' (UCLES, 1996); and exploration of English learning and teaching with a focus on adult learners and their context and on learning materials

Grades of fail, pass, B and A are awarded. In the CTEFLA about 2–3 per cent of candidates failed, 70 per cent received a pass, about 25 per cent a B and 2–3 per cent an A.

External validation

An assessor reports on each course, based on documentation provided by the centre and a two–day visit (or equivalent) in which some teaching practice is observed and student work reviewed. The assessor also participates in grading decisions. This is to ensure standardisation and also to provide feedback for areas of development in course delivery.

Syllabus

This is notable for the room for interpretation given to centres, though in practice courses tend to be quite similar. It focuses on the pedagogic abilities to plan, identify learner needs and lead skill development activities.

It is organised according to six topics matching its core objectives.

- Language awareness.
- The learner, the teacher and the teaching/learning context.
- Planning for effective teaching of adult learners of English.
- Classroom management and teaching skills for teaching English to adults.
- Resources and materials for teaching English to adults.
- Professional development for teachers of English to adults.

In Appendix 6.2 we include two of the six topics: Topic 4 'Classroom Management' and Topic 6 'Professional Development'. We should note that classroom skills are considered to include learner assessment (4.6) and reflection (4.7). In this context, reflection consists of a readiness to attend to feedback and to apply self-evaluation guided by course criteria to subsequent lessons. The course therefore attempts to develop an 'attitude of self-evaluation' to enable future effectiveness. In Topic 6, there is a further emphasis on attitudes to self and development which enable growth (6.1), on attributes which improve working relationships (6.2) and knowledge of the means for further learning (6.3).

Centres are required to have suitable library resources in order to obtain course approval.

A list of recommended books is also provided, and centres are expected to have these available.

A CTEFLA course at the British Council, Tokyo: a thumbnail sketch[3]

The course lasted 13 or 14 weeks, part-time (Tuesdays, Thursdays and Saturdays). It had an intake of about 15 learner-teachers (LTs), consisting of some novices but mostly of experienced teachers, who had from one to 15 years' experience in private lessons, private schools, and Japanese high schools. This reflects the Japanese situation, characterised by a huge demand for native-speaker teachers.

There were four training staff, teachers at the BC who had originally become trainers either by putting themselves forward, or by being seen as good teachers. Trainers were approved by UCLES and had to follow guidelines laid down by UCLES for their training. They did not necessarily have the CTEFLA themselves, but had other qualifications. They were allotted six hours a week of their contract to work on the course, time which was fully committed to input, observation and feedback.

Incentives for the institution to run the courses were not financial: they did little more than break even. However, they contributed to the overall quality of the institution, while trainers gained a sense of worth and challenge and improved career prospects.

[3]Thanks to Michèle le Roux for this summary, provided in 1993.

To complete the course, LTs went through the following experiences:

- application;
- interview (where likely fail candidates and unsuitable applicants were filtered out);
- a pre-course task (usually language awareness exercises; the task was not assessed but group feedback was provided early in the course);
- the course itself:
  - input sessions;
  - supervised lesson planning;
  - teaching practice (six hours) with feedback from trainers;
  - peer teaching;
  - observation of experienced teachers (8 hours);
  - two individual counselling sessions with trainers;
  - maintenance of a course diary (unassessed);
  - a whole-group course feedback session;
- completion of a final assignment (a needs analysis of a real group of learners; the overall aims, objectives and teaching procedures for them; three detailed lesson plans for actual lessons);
- the award of provisional grades which became finalised at the end of the course when they were endorsed by the assessor. Most candidates received pass and B grades.

The course was timetabled as follows:

Tuesday	Thursday	Saturday
1.30–3.00	1.30–3.00	10.00–12.00
Input	Input	Teaching practice (TP)
3.00–4.30	3.00–4.30	12.00–1.00
Input	TP: Setting up	TP: Feedback
		2.00–5.00
		Input
		(×2 in course)

Input

This was done by all four trainers using varied means and formats. Topics were weighted by assigning about one quarter of input time to language awareness; one quarter to skills teaching; one quarter to phonology, classroom management, error correction and teaching lexis; one eighth on the 'PPP' model, lesson planning and drills; and one eighth to extras such as uses of video, CALL, literature, songs etc.

Experienced teachers were observed in British Council classes according to availability and convenience of timing.

Teaching practice (TP)

This was based on four free language classes at three levels for specially enrolled students. LTs were placed in groups of three or four and taught two of the three levels: every four weeks they were likely to be teaching different students and also to be with a different group of LTs. The teaching followed a textbook, though not necessarily its order of units.

In setting up TP (i.e. assigning practice teaching tasks), the trainer stayed with the class and the LTs rotated. TP tasks were graded, from following a detailed lesson plan at the beginning to almost independent work by the end. Similarly, practice lessons built up from 30 minutes to 60 minutes in length.

Feedback was provided in groups. The LT first commented on her/his own performance, then received peer feedback. The trainer then offered feedback, which was also written.

Assessment was based on the written TP feedback from the last six weeks of the course, according to a shared checklist of criteria. The final assignment and an overall impression were also drawn on.

Comment

The relatively low intensity of the Tokyo course offered positive learning conditions. It allowed for a degree of pre-input preparation and reflection on feedback. It also allowed for more thinking time than would a four-week course.

As most LTs were experienced, we could anticipate some tensions between their own beliefs and the demands of the course. However, we have no data on the extent to which their personal theories were challenged and any reactions to the degree of stress this may have caused.

Features of the new CELTA

Notable features of the CELTA syllabus that have emerged through the evolution of the old CTEFLA programme and consultation with stakeholders can be summarised as follows.

Sensitivity to context

Candidates need to develop an awareness of appropriacy: that strategies and materials have no guaranteed all-purpose merit, but must be chosen according to context. This awareness is developed in Topic 2 of the Syllabus (Appendix 6.2) and in assignments focusing on learners and materials.

Explicit focus on the learner

Teachers' decisions need to be led by the needs of the learner, not by the logic of the subject or the order of the textbook. To develop an awareness of learner needs, candidates are presented with issues of individual differences (Topic 2) and prepare an assignment with a focus on their particular group of learners (see also section 2.4.3).

Development after the course

One mission of all ITE providers is to prevent their trainees from assuming that their learning is effectively completed by the award of their first teaching qualification. A theme in other ITE syllabuses is to foster an individual's sense of areas in need of development. This is addressed in Topic 6 of the syllabus (Appendix 6.3.1) and by the requirement to produce an assignment which includes action points for future development.

Broader assessment

Reliance on observed lessons for assessment provides a push towards prescription and the provision of display lessons. Also, the difficulty of assessing classroom performance teaching is now widely recognised. A response to this is to broaden the scope of assessment by means of:

- the requirement to produce a portfolio;
- the use of continuous assessment;
- the requirement for an assignment exploring teaching and learning in terms of particular learners and teaching materials;
- the inclusion of the criterion of professional awareness in assessments.

6.3.3   Discussion

A basis for development?

The CELTA is an initial, almost survival-orientated form of training. A minimum experience of six hours' practice could be nothing else. Its aim is to help candidates to cope, by providing basic management skills and some guidelines for further development. It is reasonable to question whether it can be expected to provide a basis for independent development.

In considering this, we should separate true novices from those with several years' teaching experience (in ELT or another subject). Novices have not had the chance to develop any confidence in classroom management nor personal theories about language teaching. In their case it seems reasonable to hope that they develop an *orientation* to reflection on personal assumptions and practice rather than to expect them to employ reflection as a central means of learning. This is because reflection on existing practice seems to require a threshold level of confidence and classroom competence (McIntyre, 1993). Also, novice teachers consciously plan every step of their lessons, so reflection on their own reasoning is hardly needed (McIntyre, 1988; Calderhead, 1989).

While taking part in courses, novice candidates are far more likely to be orientated to meeting course demands than to exploring assumptions underlying their own personal approaches to teaching. They have not had the time or experience to develop a strongly held personalised style of teaching. Therefore 'reflection' in this context may have a very different meaning from work with experienced teachers: essentially to be conscious of one's classroom actions and apply course criteria to them rather than depending on a supervisor.

For further development to occur, such teachers would need follow-up and support at work, for example in the form of constructive supervision or contact with fellow teachers in short courses and workshops. Otherwise their isolation from other teachers could restrict them to a reliance on coursebooks to guide their teaching. While coursebooks are invaluable in supporting teachers, they may also push the teacher towards following recipes and routines (i.e. by following the book) and away from decision-making processes.

The isolated teacher can certainly educate herself, usually by reading and reflection. However, reading alone does not offer chances to talk through ideas or provide any challenge to assumptions which the teacher uses in filtering and interpreting the reading.

In contrast, experienced candidates are far more likely to have developed personal theories and routines which will be central to their perception of themselves as a teacher and as a person. In this case, there may be tensions between these personal theories and those implicit in the course. There is a possibility that for some candidates, there might be a mismatch between their personal theories and the requirement to pass. In this case, they either have to comply with, negotiate with, or even resist the criteria applied in the course.

Knowledge is still limited in this area. In one view, it is argued that trainees may filter in or filter out inputs according to their congruence with their own beliefs (Kagan, 1992; Tillema, 1994). Tillema (1994: 601) argues that 'the greater the correspondence between teachers' beliefs and what was presented in training, the more likely learning was to take place'. In the case of those trainees whose beliefs do not match the training, Tillema suggests that while trainers need to diagnose their trainees' beliefs, this process alone does nothing to *alter* the beliefs.

A very small-scale study of a CTEFLA group by Sendan (1992) suggested that, rather than selectively filtering training, some experienced candidates chose to shelve or suspend their personal theories for the duration of the course. It seems that some experienced candidates are unlikely to maintain practices at the cost of a poor grade. This suggests that, for some experienced candidates, the short training course may exert little influence on their later development.

A further point to note is that of some 7000 who obtained the CTEFLA each year only about 10 per cent went on to obtain the DTEFLA, a more theoretically orientated course designed to support reflection, rethinking and professional development. We can only speculate as to why: perhaps some candidates already had other types of teaching qualification (such as BEds or equivalent) and did not need it; perhaps some could not afford the additional cost.

However, it seems reasonably clear that quite a high proportion of people who enter TEFL leave it again after five years or so, having used it as a means for travel and overseas experience. Given this, one can question the relevance of reflective and professional models of pedagogy and teacher development to them, given a probable lack of long-term commitment to what Lortie (1975) called 'occupational affairs' (section 1.1.4). Therefore the goals of syllabus item 6.3 (see Appendix 6.3.1) may only be relevant to a subset of qualifying teachers.

Prescription

In the past, some CTEFLA courses were characterised by the display lesson and a rigid adherence to fixed lesson formats: typically the 'PPP' format (presentation, practice, production). It is probably true that now there is more emphasis on skills development and on the selective use of coursebooks as a basis for teaching practice.

Most tutors would probably reject the notion that recent CTEFLA courses were prescriptive, and that assessment was based on merely a display of approved behaviours. It has been felt that it is possible to lead candidates to consider what happened in the lesson, why it happened, how else it could be done, and what to expect if it were done differently.

However, there may tend to be a difference of perception between tutors, who rightly wish to develop independent reasoning and awareness in teaching; and candidates, who above all need to pass and get a job.

Given limited time and the pressure to get the award, candidates are likely to cope by impression management, in short to provide what they think tutors want and expect. In this way, courses may be prescriptive in effect if not in intent.

The main objection to prescriptive and model-based training is not that it 'brainwashes' future teachers. Constructivist theory tells us that each learner-teacher's personal theories and concept of self will 'filter' course input, even if their similar display lessons seem to suggest that the course is producing a set of pedagogic clones. The key objection to prescriptive initial training is that it fails to prepare novice teachers for conditions of uncertainty after the course: skills of analysis, diagnosis and self-management are not developed. It is very difficult to predict the extent to which learner-teachers will develop the kind of self-evaluation skills intended in course objectives (Appendix 6.3.1). It will vary according to the disposition and commitment of the person in question.

Assessment

Assessment of teaching is never simple (section 5.3). In the case of the CTEFLA, some particular difficulties have arisen:

- the enormous pressure on tutors to pass candidates, and also provide a grade that would improve employment opportunities;
- in the case of intensive courses, the short time interval between input and assessment, and the expectations that were fair to candidates in such conditions;
- candidates who were clearly improving but did not reach a passing standard after four weeks;
- candidates who began well but showed no change over the four weeks: could it be assumed that they would fail to develop afterwards?
- candidates who met practical criteria, but showed little evidence of critical thinking about learners or teaching;
- candidates who did not teach very effectively but showed good awareness of what they were doing and how it should be improved;
- the difficulty of defending distinctions between pass, B and A grade candidates, given the above considerations and the known limitations of such forms of grading.

Given these difficulties, one obvious solution would have been to simplify grades to pass or fail. However, there was considerable market pressure against this: employers want to be able to identify teachers who will be able to cope well and candidates want the chance of good jobs. This seems to create a tension between best practice and the demands of the marketplace.

Developments in the CTEFLA

A challenge to the revised CELTA has been the constraint of cost and duration ceilings. Working within these constraints, the following developments have emerged by experimentation in centres operating the old CTEFLA. They are likely to become more common practice with the introduction of the CELTA. In general, developments were based on optimising independent study time and developing a role for supervising teachers:

- provide a one-day pre-course observation of two or three teachers, with a task sheet: in order to affirm the notion of differing personal styles;
- provide pre-course readings: to help focus observations, and offer an advance organiser for course input;
- provide one day a week with a supervising teacher with whom to plan and team teach: to raise awareness of decision-making processes;
- provide short pre-input readings and tasks during the course: to provide a frame of reference for new concepts and strategies;

- place candidates in pairs or teams: to enable critical discussion and provide peer support.

A radical structural solution would be to link Certificate and Diploma awards as part of a single qualification, to bring out the essentially preparatory nature of the Certificate. It would then have an equivalent status to the early survival phase of longer and more developmentally orientated courses (e.g. section 6.2).

This would meet considerable obstacles. Candidates might be unable to pay for two courses, and they might resent the requirement to do so. As a result, a revised two-stage award might only appeal to the 10 per cent or so of entrants who stay in the ELT field for more than five years or so. In fact, a ladder approach to the CILTS schemes has been resisted by UCLES.

Another radical solution, of a post-course probationary period, can only apply where qualifying teachers stay on in the same system as their initial training, impractical for most UCLES schemes.

Connecting up

If an ITE course aims to provide a 'toolkit' of techniques, then it implicitly denies a constructivist view of teacher learning (the personalisation of inputs and the evolution of personal theories). In particular, it would seem that the notion of reflection in such courses should be realistically limited to review and assess your own actions in class according to given criteria. This would contrast with a potentially wider range of reflective activities (section 1.2) enabled by the duration and structure of the programme we describe in section 6.2.

However, we can make a sensible 'constructivist' interpretation of such courses. Where the teacher is inexperienced then s/he may be quite prepared to adopt the techniques on offer, and will set about personalising and incorporating these inputs into a sense of 'the teacher I am' *after* the course, once at work. It is as if s/he dresses in borrowed clothes at first in the absence of anything else. For some these will turn out to suit very well; for others they may be set aside at once: 'just not me'; and for others, some items will be kept, some thrown away, and still others altered to fit. However, for such personalisation to take place, it is probably helpful for ITE courses to develop an attitude of self-awareness, at least at the level of monitoring one's classroom practice and questioning its usefulness for one's objectives and its appropriacy to context.

In the case of experienced teachers entering a CELTA course, it seems that they will adopt practices that fit their prior constructions of teaching and self, but where there is a mismatch between these and course requirements, they may well 'play along' for the qualification and revert to familiar ways afterwards. However, exposure to other ways of teaching offers alternatives which may be adapted and used, or called on much later as the teacher or her context changes.

Highly intensive courses tend to limit chances to 'personalise' inputs. However, we can see that attempts to redress the balance ('Developments in the

CTEFLA' above) offer the thinking time, dialogue and contextual awareness consistent with a social constructivist model.

Endnote

In spite of the critical tone of some of these comments, the positive features of the Certificate qualification should be kept in mind. It is firmly practical and classroom-based. It is often located in language schools, where LTs are surrounded by working teachers and learners (though it is also offered in further education colleges and some university language departments overseas). LTs are constantly focused on teaching real groups of learners and on their reactions to teaching. Personal pedagogic skills are scrutinised and immediate feedback given. There is exposure to a range of personal teaching styles, both other LTs and experienced teachers. Assignments focus on real learners, their needs, and how they can be met.

There are many ITE courses in existence which, in spite of far more hours in the timetable, fail to provide any such authentic experience of language teaching.

A further point is that the pattern of providing practical training first (CELTA) and then opportunities for more self-directed reflection and theorising after some experience (DTEFLA) is consistent with much current thinking on teacher development. It argues that basic classroom competence and a body of personal experience are required as a prerequisite to further professional development, particularly to reflection on values and assumptions embedded in one's practice (McIntyre, 1988; 1993). The CELTA training could thus explore issues of principle as well as of practice but it is more appropriately in the Diploma that personal theories developed through practical experience can be explored.

So long as we accept their essentially *preparatory* nature, we can recognise the many strengths of the CTEFLA/CELTA schemes. However, all survival training contains an inbuilt dilemma with which many tutors have struggled. Long ago it was put by Dewey (1904: 28) as follows:

> ... criticism should be directed to making the professional student thoughtful about his work in the light of principles, rather than to induce in him a recognition that certain special methods are good, and certain other special methods are bad. At all events, no greater travesty of real intellectual criticism can be given than to set a student teaching a brief number of lessons, have him under inspection in practically all the time of every lesson, and then criticise him almost, if not quite at the very end of each lesson, upon the particular way in which that particular lesson has been taught, pointing out elements of failure and success. Such methods of criticism may be adapted to giving a training-teacher command of some of the knacks and tools of the trade, but are not calculated to develop a thoughtful and independent teacher.

Dewey sums up the dilemma of 'survival' training in a single memorable sentence: 'immediate skill may be got at the cost of power to go on growing' (1904: 15).

Ultimately, the issue for any 'survival training' is whether it should aspire to train thoughtful and independent teachers or simply to produce enough competent teachers to meet the needs of employers and schools. In some situations the priority, very reasonably, is to have a teacher in every classroom, able to deliver a curriculum effectively. The alternative would be no teacher, or an entirely untrained one. In such a case, a survival approach is justifiable. However, in the long term, an education system can only be strengthened by maintaining the longer-term development of its teachers. The readiness or ability of a system to support the further development of its teachers is ultimately a political, economic and ethical issue.

Appendix 6.1: Competency record: extract

Basic course requirements	Date	Signature	
Method assignments completed			(MT)
Attendance at method sessions 'complete'			(MT)
Complementary Studies assignments completed			(CST)
Attendance at Complementary Studies sessions 'complete'			(CST)
Attendance at school 'complete' (First Second A Phase)			(PT)
Attendance at school 'complete' (School B 2+3 Phases)			(PT)
Attendance at school 'complete' (School B, Main Placement II)			(PT)
Attendance at school 'complete' (Second School A phase)			(PT)

For a definition of the term 'complete' see Handbook Section E

Competency	Examples	Evidence	Initials & Date
Area 2 continued			
2i) know what subject-specific experience the pupils will have had in primary school and recognise the implications of this for the secondary school	Lessons for Year 7 should, for example, pay attention to the requirements of KS2		
2j) appreciate the part their subject plays in the general education of the pupil	Discuss role of your own subject with students from other subjects (CST/PT may be able to indicate evidence for this competence)		
2k) be able to plan units of work in a way which fulfils subject-specific and cross-curricular requirements, including those of the NC and of appropriate syllabuses	Relate work to other subject areas; plan lessons which address NC cross-curricular themes		
2l) understand and demonstrate the notions of continuity and progression in their subject	Plan sequences of lessons in which there is continuity and progression. Relate work with one year group to that with another		
2m) plan work taking account of the range of resources available to support classroom practice and be able to present their own classroom materials well	Presentation of material may involve the efficient use of IT. IT may also be one of the types of resource used in class		
2n) be able to identify specific learning objectives for pupils of different ages, attainments and abilities, and plan lessons appropriately to meet those objectives	This may include the selection of resources and equipment. It will involve using assessment of pupils' previous work to guide planning		
2o) plan work taking account of a range of teaching strategies	This should include strategies for whole classes, groups, pairs and individuals. See also notes for 2p		

Knowledge and approach — Planning

Competency	Examples	Evidence	Initials & Date
Area 2 continued			
2p) be able, effectively, to use a range of resources and strategies to teach and support the learning of all the pupils in each class	This means, for example, use of group management techniques, practical work, demonstration, discussion, role play, IT, display, appropriate use of teaching space, of resources of all kinds, of questioning skills, appropriate responses to pupils questions and ideas, appropriate timing and pacing. It should include attention to differentiation		
2q) be able to communicate clearly with pupils in ways that encourage learning and generate interest	This may include verbal and written communication and non-verbal communication		
2r) be able to help pupils develop their own language and communication skills	This may include the skills of listening, talking, writing and reading and may involve pupils' use of IT		
2s) be able to draw on their own, and their pupils' interests in their planning and teaching	This may include following up pupils' leads during lessons		
2t) know about the range of approaches used to teach controversial issues and select the approach appropriate to the circumstances.	Various techniques can be used to ensure that pupils' experience of a topic is balanced. Although this competence will normally be addressed through classroom work it could be met through work as a form tutor		
2u) understand health and safety regulations and implement them in the classroom	Know your departmental safety policy and the whereabouts of safety equipment in your department		
2v) be aware of the need to identify pupils with special educational needs (SEN) in their classes (including more able children) and have some knowledge of the strategies appropriate for their development	Work successfully with all pupils (incl sen pupils) through, say, changes in emphasis, different examples, different materials, different media. Liaise with sen staff over identification and provision for sen pupils in your classes		

Appendix 6.2: Syllabus extracts: Topics 4 and 6

Topic 4 Classroom management and teaching skills for teaching English to adults

Syllabus content	Course objectives *To enable candidates to:*
4.1 The effective organisation of the classroom	■ arrange the physical features of the classroom to suit the learners and the type of lesson; ■ set up and manage whole class work, pair work and group work as appropriate.
4.2 Classroom presence and control	■ have a good rapport with learners at all times and foster a constructive learning atmosphere.
4.3 Teacher and learner language	■ adjust their own use of language to the level of the class; ■ give clear instructions in a supportive way; ■ choose appropriate moments, and appropriate strategies, for correcting learners' language.
4.4 The use of teaching materials and resources	■ make appropriate use of a range of materials and resources in relation to specified aims; ■ teach with limited resources.
4.5 Practical skills for teaching at a range of levels	■ work successfully with learners at different levels, in the same or separate classes, using appropriate types of classroom activity; ■ involve learners of different ability levels in the work of the class and enable them to feel a sense of progress.
4.6 The monitoring and evaluation of adult learners	■ identify areas, after lessons, where the class as a whole and individual learners have made progress and where additional support or supplementary work is necessary.
4.7 The evaluation of classroom management and monitoring teaching skills	■ evaluate their performance in this area by monitoring and reflection during and after lessons, and by taking note of comments from tutors and colleagues; ■ take account of this evaluation in planning future lessons.

Topic 6 Professional development for teachers of English to adults

Syllabus content	Course objectives
	To enable candidates to:
6.1 Self assessment: understanding weaknesses and developing strengths	■ assess their strengths and weaknesses, and make practical use of that assessment; ■ recognise and acknowledge the initial nature and scope of their training so far, and understand the importance of continuing professional development.
6.2 Working in context: preparing to be a teacher, colleague and employee	■ listen to, take note of and act on comments by tutors, colleagues and learners on their abilities and performance; ■ help colleagues by observing and commenting constructively on their lesson plans and lessons; ■ develop accurate and appropriate record-keeping skills; ■ take part in a variety of teaching situations and co-operate when being observed by colleagues and supervisors.
6.3 Professional development: support systems, publications, and courses for teaching English to adults	■ find out about opportunities for further professional development in teaching English to adults; ■ develop a practical working knowledge about appropriate professional associations, magazines, journals and publications for teachers entering the field of teaching English language to adults.

Part 3:   inservice education and training

7

INSET: focus on design

7.1 Diversity

7.1.1 Definitions

We define INSET as:

> education and training activities engaged in by . . . teachers and principles,
> following their initial professional certification, and intended primarily or
> exclusively to improve their professional knowledge, skills and attitudes in
> order that they can educate children . . . and learners of all other ages . . .
> more effectively.
>
> (Bolam, 1986: 18)

The reader is recommended to refer to section 2.6. Further reading is recommended: on INSET in general we suggest Dove (1984), Hopkins (1985), Edge and Richards (1993); on school management we suggest Everard and Morris (1985), Wideen and Andrews (1987) and White *et al.* (1991); on the role of curriculum development in teacher development, Lomax (1989; 1990), Day *et al.* (1987), Nunan (1989), Burns and Hood (1995), Bell and Gilbert (1996); on specific INSET activities, see Newstrom and Scannell (1980), Oldroyd *et al.* (1984), Cline *et al.* (1990), Miller and Watts (1990), Woodward (1992) and Britten (1996).

If the message of this chapter can be summed up in a phrase, it is 'horses for courses'! Teachers' needs vary, and the challenge for INSET is to identify and respond to needs which vary between individuals and which change in individuals over time.

7.1.2 Training and development

INSET can address *training* or *development* needs. Training is characterised by objectives that are defined by a deficit in language, teaching skills, curricular knowledge or some other area of expertise. Typically they are defined by the gap between the teacher's current level of skill or knowledge and the level required by their role in the system. A training orientation to INSET can be associated with the concept of teacher as operative/employee, which implies that the employer controls his or her learning (see section 3.2.1).

Training needs can persist after ITE either because of inadequacies in training programmes (section 2.3.5) or because of systemwide curriculum changes which demand new teaching routines (Kennedy, 1995). In the former case, the absence of basic competence acts as a severe obstacle to effective INSET in later career (Avalos, 1985) and suggests the need for 'deficit training' for working teachers. In the latter case, research on effective innovation confirms the need to involve teachers in INSET processes (see section 2.6.2).

The notion of development implies more divergent objectives, which allow for teachers' individual differences and which are determined by teachers' sense of their own learning needs. It also presupposes competence in basic skills and knowledge. It can be associated with the notion of a teacher as professional/independent problem-solver, who takes responsibility for personal and professional development (see sections 8.3 and 8.5 (Option 2)).

7.1.3   Provider roles

In the context of training objectives, INSET provider roles will be similar to those in ITE (see introduction and section 5.2.1). In the context of development activities, particularly where teachers are involved in self-directed problem-solving, then an additional role is to act as a 'process leader', to help teachers focus, structure and sustain their work. Our case studies in sections 8.3 and 8.6 include the work of process leaders. In section 8.3, two tutors introduced teachers to action research, negotiated an agreed structure to meetings, supported discussion and self-questioning, and provided means for self-assessment. They also offered individual discussion and support. In section 8.6, the process leader is released from providing content by the readings provided by the training package. His/her role is to introduce, discuss and maintain group ground rules, and to structure discussions (see Appendix 8.5). Section 8.5 describes an interesting shift in the role of support staff. Initially their task was to provide teachers with materials, direct experience as language learners and background principles. Later, as teachers became more experienced with communicative and authentic materials, sessions became more problem-orientated (in 'phase 2' workshops) where the tutor's role moved toward that of a process leader. McGill and Beaty (1992: Chapter 6) give a very helpful account of the role and skills in facilitating groups in addressing their own concerns; also see Heron (1993).

7.1.4   Needs and types of programme

We can suggest four types of INSET, according to how they are initiated and their purpose.

- Programmes in **co-ordination with ITE**, where elements of ITE are built on once teachers have had some experience (e.g. in a staged system of qualifications).
- **Centrally determined** programmes, controlled by a central authority, usually to attain long-term educational outcomes set by government policy. Central initiatives are often required by curriculum innovations, systemwide changes which may demand changes in teaching style (as section 8.4).
- **Locally determined content, with local control**: emphasis on system needs, met by local providers with a clear brief set by the administration but with attention to local conditions (e.g. courses offered by a teachers' centre; also cascade schemes – see section 8.5 discussion).
- **Determined by individual needs**: emphasis on the personal or professional development of teachers (e.g. by following higher degrees; flexible needs-led workshops; self-directed self-help activities, as section 8.3; learning activities beyond teaching).

In all INSET there is tension between the needs of the system and those of the individual. The key task for the INSET provider is to address both and to negotiate between systemwide and personal needs (as section 8.4).

Another cause of diversity of needs is that each teacher's work context will vary according to a unique mix of circumstances: school culture, working relationships, past history, physical layout and pupil characteristics all create a novel 'cocktail' of conditions. For example, in a small town in Nepal, two secondary teachers were trying to implement a course on methodology. One new activity was to have pupils act out examples of grammar points ('he has opened the window, he has eaten the sweet'). Both teachers were enthusiastic, committed and competent, used the same textbook, taught to the same exams. One school was in the centre of town, in a modern building, with a middle-class intake that could afford higher attendance fees. Classrooms were well lit, wider than they were long. The other school was in a beautiful old building with a temple in the school yard, on the edge of the town and with a more socially mixed intake. The classrooms were dark, long and narrow. In the first school, activities in which pupils came to the front worked well, while in the other it was very hard to involve more than the front half of the class. In this way, school conditions made for different implementation concerns for the two teachers.

Another fundamental cause of diversity is that individuals vary in their perceptions of their own needs. In the context of curriculum innovations, for example, Roberts and Roberts (1986) suggest that the involvement of teachers will vary within a group at one time, and also in an individual over time. Some may perceive their work as in no need of change; others may be open to information about change but have no intention to get involved; some may be struggling to implement new strategies in their own classrooms; some may be focusing on the reactions to change of others and attempting to influence them.

7.1.5 Ways of learning

Teachers may learn in many ways, only some of which are offered by formal pro-grammes (Newstrom and Scannell, 1980; Oldroyd *et al.*, 1984; Britten, 1996). Working from Cline *et al.* (1990) we suggest that these means of learning could include:

Teaching

- development of skills through experience
- guidelines from highly structured textbooks and/or accompanying teachers' books
- experimenting with the curriculum, or taking on a new role at work
- developing a specialism
- secondment to a new task
- placement in another institution/job swapping

Professional collaboration

- work with a skilled fellow teacher
- work with other professionals
- curriculum development: formative evaluation and 'fine-tuning'
- collaborative curriculum development: developing and evaluating new courses
- watching someone else
- discussing practice with colleagues
- access to specialist knowledge of colleagues
- peer supervision or support
- being a member of an interest group/working party/action learning group/action research group
- observation, role play and feedback with peers
- responding to and discussing needs assessments

Innovation and research

- writing and presenting a paper
- working on a policy statement
- developing and evaluating materials
- doing research for a higher degree

Helping others learn

- providing a course/skills work for others
- giving talks, workshops
- helping prepare training materials
- presenting an aspect of one's practice to peers

- collating and disseminating information to others
- supervising student-teachers or novice teachers

Courses/formal situations

- higher education courses
- short courses (on-site/off-site)
- conferences
- practical workshops/seminars
- distance learning

Self-study

- reflecting on current practice
- study leave
- reading

Language learning

- learning a new language
- ongoing language development and awareness of learner perspectives.

This rich variety of learning experiences indicates that different teachers can go about learning in very different ways. This suggests that providers could usefully find out how their 'clients' are currently learning and try to build them into their programmes (e.g. Pennington, 1996). It also suggests that they should try to offer as varied a programme of structures and activities as resources allow.

Considering the diversity of teachers' needs and classroom circumstances we suggest that there cannot possibly be a single all-purpose form of INSET.

7.2 The importance of social context

7.2.1 Levels of policy

State system INSET may be planned at four levels: national, regional, local and institutional. In the private sector, INSET may be planned at similar levels, either through professional associations (e.g. IATEFL) or private employers.

In state systems each layer of the system above the school will be led by a key decision-maker (minister, regional director, local director) who will be supported by bureaucracy and a professional staff of inspectorate and/or advisers.

Policy decisions at each level will concern aims, finance, staffing, delivery, needs assessment, monitoring and evaluation, and dissemination of information. Staff at each level in the system will have to communicate with those at other levels. At their own level, they may have to work with:

- professional associations/unions;
- providing agencies external to the school (such as universities, inspectors, advisors, teachers' centre staff, specialists, private agencies);
- schools, both as receivers and in some cases as providers
- individual teachers, heads etc.

Within the policy boundaries set by key decision-makers at higher levels and at their own level, providers are responsible for the design and implementation of programme activities (content, method, staffing, resourcing, liaison work etc.).

This rather obvious analysis shows that an individual INSET provider works within interdependent systems, and that the boundaries to her field of action will be set by larger-scale policy decisions in ways we exemplify below.

7.2.2   Point of decision and political conditions

INSET has strong political significance, reflected by the location of spending decisions. For example, in a centralised/authoritarian system, key INSET decisions will be reserved for politicians or senior bureaucrats. This enables INSET to be kept under political control and to be geared to national priorities. In pluralist systems, money might be committed per capita or per school, with its use decided locally, so empowering teachers and schools to control the course of their own development. INSET structures will reflect the politics of the educational system and cannot be separated from wider political and occupational issues.

7.2.3   Funding levels

Most of an INSET budget is spent on salaries and salary replacement. The level of funding therefore determines provider-teacher ratios, release time and travel time, all of which create preconditions for design.

Where funds are limited, design may have to go for maximum coverage for minimum cost. This can lead to programmes appropriate to transmit information, for example an annual mass briefing on the syllabus. While these can communicate information, they are unable to influence classroom implementation (section 2.6.4).

Better funding enables more frequent contacts and better provider-teacher ratios. It can provide local teams to work with smaller groups of teachers, perhaps with frequent in-school contacts. Such a structure makes possible, but does not ensure, needs-led, diversified and long-term INSET design (see section 8.5).

7.2.4   Provider roles

A key aspect of policy is to determine providers' roles. A system may offer a single INSET structure or a number of structures in parallel with a variety of providers' job descriptions. The pros and cons of four such roles are summarised here.

A *full-time mobile trainer* can work with teachers on-site or off-site. S/he can develop specialist skills which can enrich the system. However, there is a risk that specialists may be lost to better employment elsewhere. Also, the creation of an elite of trainers may isolate them from teachers' day-to-day concerns.

Part-time 'cascade' trainers receive training from an inner expert team and then disseminate this training to teachers or to other trainers-to-be. The cascade principle implies that an inner core of specialists will be supported by cascade teams, usually of split-role teacher-providers. It is cost-effective because expensive central training can be disseminated to increasingly large numbers of providers, who in effect retransmit the content and methods of the training. Additionally, split-role providers are more likely to be in touch with teachers' concerns and to be credible. However, there is a risk of 'dilution' due to reinterpretation of the initial training inputs, since at each link in the chain of communication the cascade trainers are bound to filter and reinterpret the original training 'message' according to their own assumptions and personal theories (Dove, 1986; Williams and Burden, 1997; also sections 1.1.3 and 8.5).

In the case of *part-time local trainers*, skilled teachers are trained and then released occasionally from their normal duties to support teachers in other schools. In this way permanent INSET staff can build up a pool of skilled local support teachers. This has the advantage that only occasional release from school avoids the need for paid teacher replacements. Also, the support teachers can be very close to classroom realities. The main drawback may be that the new role greatly adds to the part-time trainers' workload, and, without additional payment or reduced teaching, such staff might eventually burn out. Alternatively, their own schools may be disrupted by losing an effective member of staff and head teachers may put pressure on for their support work to stop. Ghani *et al.* (1997) report an interesting school-based project in Malaysia involving such trained part-time support staff, running in parallel with other support structures. Section 8.5 reports the development of a pool of skilled part-time tutors in Latvia.

In a split role to *teach and give on-site support in one school*, skilled teachers are trained to conduct in-school needs assessment and INSET support work in their own school (e.g. half a day per week INSET throughout the year). The quality of INSET support is likely to be high, due to continuity over time and the possibility of good liaison with school management and the staff. It is costly because nonteaching time has to be paid for. Therefore, pressure on school budgets is likely to squeeze out an in-house specialist of this kind, as has happened in the UK.

7.2.5   The social dimension

A person's sense of a need for change will be influenced by social climate. A context of economic and political renewal can carry teachers along on a tide of

228 LANGUAGE TEACHER EDUCATION

change: 'Life is changing very rapidly and you must keep up with it' (Latvian teacher, Ellis, 1994). INSET effectiveness often depends on this 'following wind' of change as much as providers' expertise and enthusiasm.

Similarly, at school level, energetic and positive leadership can create a climate that promotes development in teachers and the curriculum. Much recent INSET work has placed staff development in the context of whole-school improvement rather than simply treating transfer of training as an individual matter (Hopkins, 1985; Wideen and Andrews, 1987).

School culture serves as a powerful influence on personal and curricular change (Schmuck, 1974; Henderson, 1979; Fullan, 1982; Easen, 1985; Rudduck, 1988; Somekh, 1993; section 1.1.4 and 2.5.1). One fundamental feature of teacher work is isolation from colleagues, with work time spent alone with one's classes. Isolation is greatly reinforced if there is a culture of individualism or 'privatism' in the school (sections 1.1.4 and 2.5.1). It seems that in contrast a positive climate for teacher development is one in which teachers can and do talk to each other about teaching (Fullan, 1982). This climate seems to be closely related to the politics of the school, in that a structure that encourages teacher participation and responsibility sharing tends to support dialogue and collaboration (see section 8.3).

A culture of individualism can be costly for teachers. It weakens the ability of the group to bargain effectively, relying instead on individual accountability and individual rewards. It can also greatly add to stress: Lortie (1975) observes that the burden of a perceived individual failure or shortcoming is very great because there can be no recourse to colleagues or to a body of generally accepted practice to justify the actions under question.

However, the picture is perhaps more complex than a simple distinction between privatist and collaborative cultures. Lortie suggests that individualist occupational culture is not characterised by absolute lack of contact between teachers but by their *selective* intake of ideas, conditional on a match with their personal theories. He suggests that teachers seek help from peers all the time, but do so selectively, only taking up a practice if 'consistent with the receiver's personality and way of doing things' (1975: 77). Thus, teachers' personal theories filter peers' influence, so that the 'teacher mediates between ideas and their use in terms of the kind of teacher he [sic] is' (1975: 78).

Thus teacher learning from colleagues, as from other sources, is mediated by their personal theories: 'practices which suit the person of the teacher become candidates for admission to his [sic] kit of regular behaviours and are then tried out. The personal nature of such selection is even more manifest when teachers justify their practices on the basis of their individual experience as students. What worked on me, they say, despite its possible uniqueness, will work on others' (1975: 78).

The power of Lortie's analysis is that it shows that exchanges of ideas between peers do not necessarily have any impact on the fundamental assumptions on which a teacher bases her work, though they may help her to work out her own ideas more clearly. This suggests that while dialogue is critically important in teachers' development, it needs to be complemented by their uncovering and assessing their current routines and 'ways of seeing' (Easen, 1985; Griffiths and Tann, 1992).

This analysis suggests two general INSET strategies. One is to focus on communication within the school and to strengthen its capacity for self-development (see section 7.2.6). The other is to integrate off-site and on-site work, so that teachers can bring their classroom concerns to fellow teachers away from their own, so freeing them from some of the inhibitions created by the need to 'rub along' with colleagues. Such structures are exemplified in sections 8.2, 8.4 and 8.5. An alternative structure is for teachers to work in school on issues of immediate concern to them with the help of skilled support staff (as sections 8.3, 8.6 and Ghani *et al.*, 1997).

7.2.6   Focus on the school or the individual?

The organisation development (OD) perspective on teacher learning recognises the interdependence of personal change and social forces in the school. We briefly summarise the key features of OD and its implications for teacher education here and recommend further reading (e.g. Hopkins, 1986; Wideen and Andrews, 1987). It is argued that planned reforms often fail because they do not attend to the context of implementation: the school. Therefore, to improve LTE, we should aim to develop whole schools and not teachers in isolation (Easen, 1985). Schools are complex social systems that perpetuate themselves through role expectations and working relationships. Individuals behave and monitor each other's behaviour according to school norms. This collective enactment of norms makes school culture highly resistant to change (Somekh, 1993).

The purpose of OD is to teach schools how to become self-modifying, by helping staff in collective review and change. Thus the staff: 'with the aid of OD consultant, examine current difficulties and their causes and participate actively in the reformulation of goals, the development of new group process skills, the redesign of structures and procedures for achieving the goals, the alteration of the working climate of the school and the assessment of results' (Schmuck, 1974, in Hopkins, 1986: 280).

OD interventions focus on subsystems (groups within the school) and how they relate to each other, not on individuals. Interventionists use two key strategies. One is to confront the school with discrepancies between its goals and its achievement. The other is to make each 'subsystem receptive to information from every other subsystem, including the external environment' (Schmuck, 1974, in Hopkins, 1986), in other words to open up communication between individuals and groups that is obstructed by daily routines. Finally, the interventionist works to help the school to maximise its resources and set about its own problem-solving. This will be through strategies such as monitoring and review, leading to an action plan which could include curriculum development by action research (sections 8.3 and 8.4), staff training (8.6) or professional exchange with other schools.

Schmuck proposes seven objectives for an OD strategy:

- staff develop more open communication with each other;
- they clarify and share their objectives;
- they uncover and confront areas of conflict and interdependence;
- they improve the ways meetings are run;
- the school develops its problem-solving skills;
- schools learn to use decision-making methods which maximise the commitment of those who implement them;
- schools develop and use systems to evaluate changes.

Thus school development focuses on working relationships, mutual expectations, dialogue and collective action.

OD represents a whole-school approach to development. It emphasises the need for teachers' participation in INSET activity and the integration of development with normal school activities (Allwright and Lenzuen, 1997; see also sections 7.4.1, 8.5 and 8.6). Unfortunately we have no case studies to illustrate whole-school development (although section 8.3 is a good case of a learning school). However, the principles of whole-school involvement are reflected in section 7.3.1 and in methods appearing in Appendices 7.1–7.3).

Other social and contextual influences on teachers which affect their approach to INSET including the following.

- Nonteaching priorities: if teachers are underpaid, they may perceive occupational improvement primarily in terms of a better work situation or better pay, rather than change in their practice. Also teachers may be unconcerned with occupational issues because they have entered teaching unwillingly, or because they see it only as a temporary occupation. In this case, they may see INSET initiatives as personally irrelevant.
- Time: where pay is poor (particularly if overtaken by inflation) teachers may be too busy getting extra income, for example giving private classes or farming, to give time to INSET. In this case, they would need positive incentives to take part, such as in pay or pension points.
- Morale: where work and employment conditions are poor or if teachers are held in low esteem, morale may be too low for them to engage seriously with work-related development activities.

7.3   The INSET cycle

Teacher learning takes time; it is gradual and cumulative; it requires a mix of experience, reflection, discussion and input; its focus changes as teachers' thinking, practice and self-awareness change (sections 1.1.5 and 2.6). Therefore, INSET needs to be sustained over time. It should be seen as a process, not as a series of one-off events (Fig. 7.1).

Needs assessment and evaluation are of central importance in sustaining INSET. They enhance the continuity of INSET programmes in the face of forces that oppose it: funding changes, teachers move on, staff leave. They enhance relevance because they monitor teachers' needs as they evolve over time (see sections 7.3.1 and 7.3.2, and also sections 8.4 and 8.5 for examples of evolving teacher needs). Helpful practical guidelines on needs assessment and evaluation appear in McMahon *et al.* (1984), Cline *et al.* (1990) and Sanders (1992).

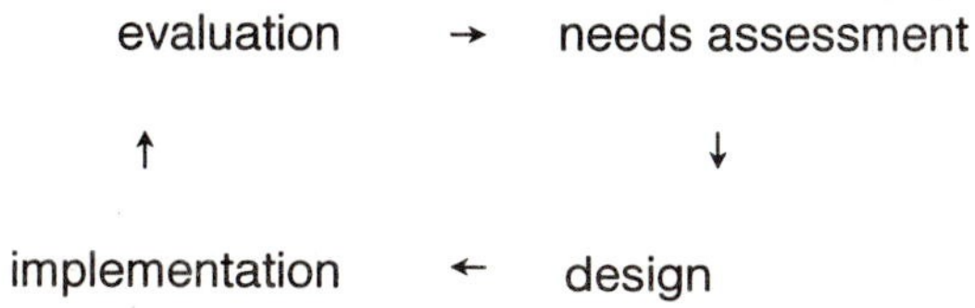

```
    evaluation      →    needs assessment

        ↑                       ↓

    implementation   ←    design
```

Fig. 7.1   The INSET cycle

7.3.1   Needs assessment

Real and apparent needs

Teachers' participation in courses does not necessarily mean that they are fully relevant to their needs. Given the chance to attend a course related to teaching (or to have a sabbatical), a teacher will usually take it. It may well be that they follow courses because they are available rather than because they address their most salient needs. For example Ben-Peretz *et al.* (1990) found that teachers attended 'content' courses which they valued but which did not meet their highest stated priorities, for personal enrichment and active learning. This suggested that, in their context, there was not a wide enough range in INSET programmes available (section 8.3 exemplifies such teachers adopting this style of INSET on a self-help basis).

Professional development

Models of professional learning have particular relevance for needs assessment. In particular, the notions of ownership and participation have generated structured consultative needs assessment methods (Miles and Pasow, 1957; Howey and Joyce, 1978; Rubin, 1978; Fullan, 1979; Hopkins, 1986). There is a direct link between teacher commitment and ownership, and needs assessment methods:

Teachers need to be involved in the identification and articulation of their own training needs whenever possible. This does not mean 'knowing what they need' in all respects but the process of articulation, with resource help, is a major way of securing involvement and commitment to personal growth.

(Rubin, 1978: 136)

Other assumptions about professional learning which have implications for needs assessment are summarised in Table 7.1 (see also section 2.6).

Table 7.1 Teacher development and needs assessment

Assumption	*Implication*
Ownership: a sense of participation maximises effectiveness at work and in professional learning	Participation can develop with the use of consultative needs-assessment methods (section 7.3.1)
Teacher learning is 'adaptive and heuristic', i.e. it takes place as a series of trial-and-error experiences	It is essential to incorporate action planning with the assessment of needs (see GRIDS Appendix 7.1)
Teacher learning is evolutionary and nonlinear	Perceptions of need will evolve as the teacher experiences INSET activities (section 8.5)
Teacher learning should be linked to curriculum development in school	Both systemwide and individual needs can be addressed through participation in curriculum development with 'local' support (sections 8.2–8.5)
Teacher learning is critically influenced by school and local constraints and opportunities	Needs assessment must reflect the real conditions of teachers' work (section 7.3.1)
Teachers possess 'important clinical expertise', i.e. teachers know their classroom best	Teacher development actvities should maximise the use of teachers' own resources (sections 8.3, 8.4 and 8.5; Appendix 7.5)

We should be aware that these principles derive from a Western cultural context, as the research is from the USA, Canada and the UK (e.g. Fullan, 1979; 1982; McLaughlin and Marsh, 1978; Hopkins, 1985). Research from such liberal-capitalist, democratic contexts tends to perceive learner-teachers in individual terms. Autonomy and self-determination are taken as the good, for example:

We are describing a paradigm shift in our whole approach to (staff development). . . . The essence of that shift is changing the perspective that sees all decisions, plans and programs being determined by authorities outside the school to a perspective which sees them as being determined by teachers who in reality do decide what and how their students will learn. Our recommendation is based upon our extensive experience with self-directed learning for students and with self-directed professional development for teachers.

(Gibbons and Norman, 1987: 110)

These assumptions may not apply in more centralised, hierarchical or authoritarian systems, within which pupils, teachers and external agencies may have a very different orientation to their roles. In such systems, a top-down approach might be the only ecologically viable approach to INSET design, because teachers are restricted to an 'employee' role in which the employer determines occupational learning needs. However, it is possible for centralised systems to set up support systems for individual teachers in schools, often in parallel with centralised structures (e.g. Ghani *et al.*, 1997).

Planning a needs assessment: key considerations

- Providers should recognise that different participants may have different needs, which have to be traded off against each other. Tensions and conflicts of interest have to be addressed and resolved, e.g. between those of pupils, teachers, the department/groups of staff, the school, the local authority and beyond.
- Therefore, a needs assessment should be seen by all parties as fair, open, and capable of reflecting the needs of all and not just of those in authority.
- Needs assessment in a participative approach to INSET integrates review with planning for action: 'the focus is on review leading to development for improvement and not on something that stops short at the review stage' (McMahon *et al.*, 1984: 7). It is essential to design needs assessment and planning for action as part of one process (Appendix 7.1).
- In carrying out needs assessment, practical considerations include:
  - what the focus of the needs assessment should be (individual, group, school);
  - relative economy in methods of obtaining and analysing information;
  - adequate time to obtain information;
  - adequate time for the analysis and dissemination of results;
  - a match between procedures and the administration's policy on consultation with staff;
  - which interest groups might be affected;
  - how feasible it will be to meet needs once they have been expressed.
- In general, one should consider the dynamic consequences of needs assessment on colleagues:

- the process by which needs assessment is carried out will signal the attitude of the school/provider to teachers' involvement in their own learning;
- teachers should not feel 'railroaded' by lack of time or lack of access to information;
- there may be tension between personal, occupational and institutional needs, which will have to be addressed;
- once a needs assessment is done, there is an implied commitment to action, which should be seen to be met.

● Needs evolve: when we are first consulted about our needs, we may not be able to give immediate clear guidelines for design: 'areas where we feel ourselves in need of some help are not likely to be areas about which we know enough to analyse precisely what help we need' (Wray, 1989: 146).

Needs broadly described at the outset (e.g. 'I want ideas on how to teach writing') become more precise and evolve as the teacher's perceptions of classroom issues develop.

Needs and objectives should therefore be reviewed in regular stoc-taking sessions during an INSET programme. A comparable concept of language programme development based on evolving learners' needs is to be found in Nunan (1988).

Appendix 7.1 includes a summary of the main stages of a school-wide review and assessment exercise developed by McMahon *et al.* (1984) through collaborative work with schools. They give special attention to the political and interpersonal dynamics of review and assessment, and the need for careful planning before taking action.

Methods

Needs assessment methods are common to research, evaluation and syllabus design: watching (observation) and asking (questionnaire, interview). Helpful guidelines on observation can be found in King *et al.* (1987), and Nunan (1989); see also section 5.3.4. Guidelines on questionnaires can be found in Oppenheim (1992) and on interviewing in Powney and Watts (1987). In Box 7.1 we outline methods in terms of number of informants and economy of data collection. In the case of one-to-one data collection, which is time-consuming and appropriate to smaller groups, open-ended interviews, questionnaires with open questions (Appendix 7.1), and structured classroom observation may be appropriate. With larger numbers of teachers, structured group discussion (such as nominal groups, Appendix 7.1), structured questionnaires and selective checklist-based observation are more appropriate. In general, pressure of

Individual	Group
Interview	Group discussion
	e.g. Nominal group technique
	Focus groups
Questionnaire	Questionnaire
	e.g. DELPHI, GRIDS
Checklist	Checklist

Box 7.1   Needs-assessment methods

time suggests that systematic large-scale observation is often impractical because it makes great demands on staff time.

7.3.2   Evaluation

Once an INSET cycle is under way, the distinction between needs assessment and programme evaluation disappears. The evaluation of one activity indicates needs for the next. Similar technical and interpersonal issues arise. Evaluations are never neutral, often uncovering tensions, rivalries and conflicting interests in an institution, and so it is essential to plan carefully before introducing them (Sanders, 1992; Weir and Roberts, 1994: Chapters 1 and 8). Above all, an evaluation can improve teacher participation and ownership if real consultation and information sharing take place (Weir and Roberts, Chapters 1 and 8). Helpful

What to evaluate	Focus evaluation on the purposes and specific objectives of the INSET activity
Why	Determine how information will be used, by whom and with what tangible outcomes
	Evaluation data are likely to identify developments in teachers' perceptions of their needs and priorities
Who does it	Identify who is responsible to collect and distribute data
	Involve other participants by sharing information
How	In principle, methods are the same as for needs assessment (interview, discussion, questionnaire etc.)
	Considerations of economy and time are vital: evaluation findings should be provided on time so they can contribute to decisions

Box 7.2   INSET evaluation: major decisions

sources for planning evaluation are: Herman *et al.* (1987), Fitzgibbon *et al.* (1987), Sanders (1992), Weir and Roberts (1994). Key principles are summarised in Box 7.2 and exemplified in Appendix 7.2 where we present a table and two figures from Sanders (1992). While these refer to school programmes, they exemplify a systematic approach to evaluation. Table 7.3 is an example of a proforma designed to guide evaluation decisions. It shows the need to identify clear questions, and to justify why they are important. The proforma then requires us to decide, for each question, what information is needed, and how it will be collected and analysed. In Figures 7.3 and 7.4 we see an example of the careful planning and time management needed to bring an evaluation in on time so that it can be used to inform decisions.

7.3.3   INSET design

Assumptions

Design decisions derive from assumptions about teachers' learning. We summarise some propositions, advising the reader to treat them critically and not as certainties (see also sections 1.1.5 and 2.6).

Teacher learning

- Teacher learning is essentially evolutionary, with the development of new ideas and practices built from preceding systems of perception and thinking.
- It arises from the synthesis of opportunities for experiential learning (determined by classroom context), access to public theory, private reflection, and discussion with others.
- Teacher learning is characterised by a rhythm of successive phases of certainty/stability and uncertainty/instability.
- In coping with deep role changes, experienced teachers will have to 'unlearn', a difficult process causing uncertainty and confusion (Eraut, 1994).
- Professional change and personal change are interdependent, at least in cases where teachers' work is central to their sense of self.
- Personal change demands practical and personal support, talk, and trial and error implementation.
- A conducive group/school climate is highly important for teacher development.
- Big systems plan for big changes, whereas teachers typically introduce changes in practice gradually, by trial and error. It would be wrong to dismiss such changes as insignificant. Adjustment to the running of a class within the rules of a school has to be done with care, in small steps. If you want to overhaul an engine, you stop it. If you have to change it while it is running, you can only fine-tune it.

- Learner-teachers' personal theories mediate developments in their perceptions and constructions of the world; their personal theories may not match those of providers. Therefore establishing *sociality*, arriving at an understanding of the other person's perceptions, is an essential first step in any attempted intervention (see McLaughlin, 1996, and Appendix 7.6).
- What is of core concern to one person might seem insignificant to someone else. If a person reacts strongly to change, then an issue central to their self must be in play: we should accept its importance for the other person, even if it may seem to be a side issue to us.

Design decisions

In this section we draw on Cline *et al.* (1990: 130–40) and the work of Binstead (1980) who argues that design should work from fundamental decisions (issues affecting the total learning event); to shape and sequence decisions; and then to fine-detail decisions. These are comparable to decisions in approach, design and procedure (section 3.1). It is particularly important to begin with fundamentals rather than immediately making decisions on detail such as on materials and activities, which can be arrived at because of availability or habit rather than their relevance to overall purpose.

Helpful guidelines on planning courses and workshops appear in Britten (1996) and in Appendix 7.3, which presents the checklist Cline *et al.* (1990) developed for the preparation of an INSET course. It shows the amount of forward thinking needed to provide an effective INSET experience.

The checklist should be complemented in one respect: by noting the special importance of the final session of a course/workshop. This should invite teachers' assessment of the achievement of their personal objectives. It should also invite teachers to forward plan applications of the course/workshop to their own school. In particular they may need to identify the 'first steps' they need to begin introducing changes, and who it is in school that they need to involve in order to do so effectively.

Following Binstead, we now summarise the three levels of INSET decision-making: fundamental, shape and sequence, and fine detail.

Fundamental decisions

Maintenance or change?

Fine-tuning established skills or preparation for deep role change? The personal and cognitive challenge of deep role change is far greater than fine-tuning. It therefore requires far more support, discussion, demonstration and long-term 'on-the-job' support.

Focus on problems or solutions?

Is your goal developmental, working collaboratively with teachers who will work out their own solutions, or will you provide a training which offers ready-made solutions?

The provider's role

Will you be a provider of knowledge and skills; or facilitate others in devising solutions; or will you initiate change yourself? Each role demands distinctive skills and should be clearly agreed with participants at the outset.

The learners

Are they already working as a group, are they peers, or strangers? Groups of strangers need to work to establish effective communication on group processes, such as by agreeing ground rules and sharing ice-breaking activities, before other more work-related tasks (see section 8.6). Groups known to each other may have to overcome tensions or even factions brought in from work.

Location: in the classroom, at home, off-site?

If courses are based outside schools, providers may have to complement the course content by a number of 'linking' strategies (see also sections 5.2, 8.2 and 8.5):

- basing work on cases provided by learner-teachers;
- supporting teachers in experiment and monitoring in their own classrooms;
- eliciting issues of high priority to them;
- negotiating with school management to support implementation (e.g. administrative or timetabling help).

Shape and sequence decisions

Start and finish points

What is the current state of learner-teachers in terms of their perceptions, competence, knowledge and skills? How does this compare with a desired end state? How will they move from one state to the other?

Flexibility

How far will teachers contribute to and modify the INSET events? This will be proportional to the extent that objectives focus on development rather than training, and on exploration of problems rather than providing solutions.

How long do we have?

Considering the time available helps determine where you can expect to be by the end of the programme.

Fine detail decisions

Type of learning activity?

What combination of modes will you use? Broadly, these are reflective (internal clarification and rethinking of perspectives); experimentation (e.g. learning from classroom inquiry); and reception (input of new information). A course or any other framework should provide combinations of these modes in flexible cycles (Box 4.3 and sections 1.1.5 and 8.6).

Grouping?

We all tend to reuse familiar techniques, because we feel secure with them. However, it is as well to ask if they actually match the purposes we have. Table 7.2 summarises the relationship between group size (plenary, small group, pairs and individuals) and purposes. Plenary grouping is suitable for the transmission of information and for demonstrations. Smaller groups (eight or less) are effective for the pooling and generation of ideas and for teachers to contrast their personal interpretations of inputs and experiences. Pair work can be suited to

Table 7.2   Groups and purposes (Cline *et al.*, 1990: 139)

	Whole group	*Small group*	*Pairs*	*Individual*
Efficiency of transfer of trainer's ideas	High	Low	Low	Low
Visibility of learning process in oneself and others	Low	High	High	High
Generation of many ideas	Low	High	Medium	Low
Realisation of personal goals	Low	Medium	Medium	High
Feeling involved and active	Low	Medium	High	High
Becoming aware of own prejudices	Low	High	Medium	Low

deeper exploration of different perspectives and values, especially for participants who are uncomfortable in larger 'arenas'. Individual work provides high levels of activity, and opportunities for private reflection before or after other types of activity.

A social constructivist approach indicates the central function of dialogue in teacher development, integrated with complementary opportunities for reflection, experience and input (sections 1.1.5, 6.2 and 8.2–8.6; Newell, 1996; Bailey, 1996). However, dialogue needs to be carefully structured and matched to immediate purposes.

Order

The order of activities has to be decided in view of:

time:	the whole time available, the length and frequency of sessions, intervals between sessions;
coherence:	the need for variety;
	the need to integrate experience, reflection and input;
	the need for participants to see the logic of course activities.

Examples of integrated activity sequences can be found in section 8.6.

Notes on group activities

First and last sessions of a course or workshop are of particular importance. It is important to make members feel welcome (personal greetings, coffee), and for the provider to establish credibility by evidence of good preparation (folders ready, name badges etc.).

Then, the group needs to serve as an effective environment for learning. Opening activities set a tone for the group which is difficult to change afterwards. If we want maximum teacher participation, then it is much better to begin not with a conventional talk or mini-lecture but with an activity that focuses on the participants and encourages equal participation and active listening. These could include activities to promote effective communication (see section 8.6) and some self-disclosure and pooling in areas of relatively low risk, such as personal experiences as learners and teachers (e.g. Woodward, 1992). 'Metaphor' activities can have a similar effect, in that they encourage sharing of teachers' perceptions in a 'light' and unthreatening way (see Appendix 8.1). Such activities can also help to establish trust and openness. In a first session (and after a long interval between sessions) there should also be a structured discussion of needs and objectives, in terms of both system needs and those of participating individuals (see section 7.1.1).

In the case of regular meetings, but where the group composition changes, the first activity of each session similarly needs to re-establish a group climate. A participative activity, such as pyramid discussion, can help achieve this. Similarly, a brief plenary to end a session is advisable to summarise what has been done, to look forward to intervening activities and the focus of the next session.

In the case of experienced teachers, we should pool the resources of the group itself, each teacher's knowledge and experience. This can happen informally at any time, but it can be helpful to elicit this knowledge in a structured manner when tackling a new topic. This is to help the provider establish suitable starting points with teachers, and also to ensure the participation and ownership of the group. A simple procedure is described in Appendix 7.5 (see also Appendix 5.1 on 'pooling').

A final session is most important and should leave participants feeling that things have been rounded off effectively. This can be done by pooling what each particpant feels s/he has gained, and also by planning their next steps on going back to classroom.

In sections 8.2–8.5 we report some ELT INSET programmes and the lessons which we can learn from them: a Diploma course for teachers in the Basque country; collaborative curriculum inquiry in a secondary school in Israel; centrally co-ordinated action research in Australia; and a teacher support network in Latvia. The case studies are intended to reveal the conditions which promoted effective INSET and to demonstrate general principles of effectiveness: participation, relevance, adequate timescales, constructive working relationships, integration of learning modes; and starting from where teachers are.

We end by outlining a teacher development package on classroom management (section 8.6). It is not specific to any particular subject, but is most relevant to teaching in state schools. It is chosen because it demonstrates certain key principles of INSET design. It shows that activities should be designed in concerted cycles which address distinctive dimensions of teacher learning: input, reflection and self-awareness, discussion, analysis of learners' experience and perceptions, skill recognition and practice, and experiment in class. It also demonstrates the need for a facilitator who can introduce and sustain group conventions and develop communication skills. Finally, it shows that each teacher should control the process of introducing changes to his/her classroom, in the context of support from and accountability to supportive colleagues.

Appendix 7.1   Needs assessment methods

In this section, we focus on participative methods of needs assessment. This is not to dismiss conventional questionnaires, but their use is well described elsewhere (e.g. King *et al.*, 1987; Bell, 1987; Henerson *et al.*, 1988).

Small group needs assessment and negotiation of objectives: nominal group technique

Nominal group technique provides a structure to elicit the perceived needs of a group, to put them in order of priority and so enable an agreed plan of action. It requires face-to-face discussion and is suited to relatively small groups (compare with DELPHI below). Descriptions can be found in Miller and Watts (1990) and Weir and Roberts (1994).

Whole-school needs assessment and information sharing: GRIDS

GRIDS (Guidelines for Review and Internal Development in Schools, McMahon *et al.*, 1984) is a procedure for whole-school internally initiated review and development which was developed through trial and consultation in schools. It consists of five stages, each divided into steps (Fig. 7.2). Its five stages are fully explained in McMahon *et al.* (1984): potential users must refer to this and not just to this short summary.

GRIDS is based on seven principles:

(a) the aim is to achieve internal school development and not to produce a report for formal accountability purposes;

(b) the main purpose is to move beyond the review stage into development for school improvement;

(c) the staff of the school should be consulted and involved in the review and development process as much as possible;

(d) decisions about what happens to any information or reports produced should rest with the teachers and others concerned;

(e) the head and teachers should decide whether and how to involve the other groups in the school, e.g. pupils, parents, advisers, governors;

(f) outsiders (e.g. external consultants) should be invited to provide help and advice when this seems appropriate;

(g) the demands made on key resources like time, money and skilled personnel should be realistic and feasible for schools and LEAs.

(McMahon et al., 1984: 7–9)

Lessons that have emerged from using GRIDS include the following.

- The needs assessment and planning phases are crucial to effective 'bottom-up' INSET: 'to be effective, school-focused ... in-service education ... must be as participative and collaborative in its pre-planning procedures as is reasonable given the hierarchical traditions pertaining within the educational system' (Nixon, 1989: 155)
- 'Upstream' planning of time and resources is essential.
- Procedures that are clearly structured, rule-bound, and understood by all are needed in order to ensure equal staff participation.
- Senior staff must initiate the process, and see it through in a politically consistent manner.
- The manner of consultation will determine relationships for the rest of the process.

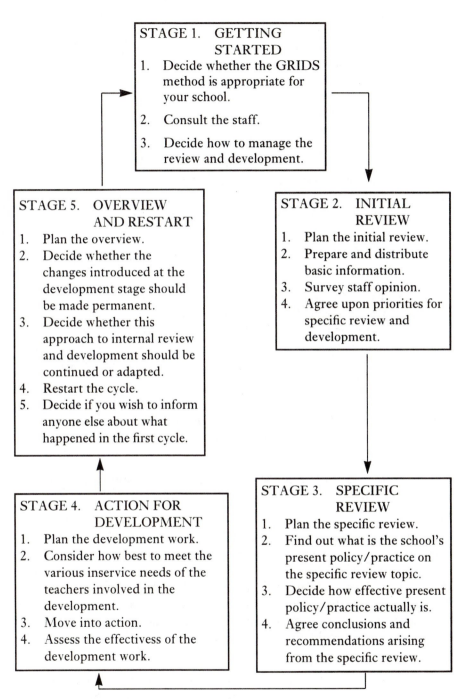

STAGE 1. GETTING
           STARTED
1. Decide whether the GRIDS
   method is appropriate for
   your school.
2. Consult the staff.
3. Decide how to manage the
   review and development.

STAGE 5. OVERVIEW
           AND RESTART
1. Plan the overview.
2. Decide whether the
   changes introduced at the
   development stage should
   be made permanent.
3. Decide whether this
   approach to internal review
   and development should be
   continued or adapted.
4. Restart the cycle.
5. Decide if you wish to inform
   anyone else about what
   happened in the first cycle.

STAGE 2. INITIAL
           REVIEW
1. Plan the initial review.
2. Prepare and distribute
   basic information.
3. Survey staff opinion.
4. Agree upon priorities for
   specific review and
   development.

STAGE 4. ACTION FOR
           DEVELOPMENT
1. Plan the development work.
2. Consider how best to meet the
   various inservice needs of the
   teachers involved in the
   development.
3. Move into action.
4. Assess the effectivess of the
   development work.

STAGE 3. SPECIFIC
           REVIEW
1. Plan the specific review.
2. Find out what is the school's
   present policy/practice on
   the specific review topic.
3. Decide how effective present
   policy/practice actually is.
4. Agree conclusions and
   recommendations arising
   from the specific review.

Fig. 7.2 GRIDS: the five stages (McMahon *et al.*, 1984)

- Needs tend to be identified progressively not as absolutes from the first round of consultation.
- There is a benefit in receiving outsiders' perspectives and input, but on terms decided by the receivers, in this case the teachers.

Consultation at distance: DELPHI technique

DELPHI is a procedure for consultation and negotiation of priorities suited to larger groups and organisations in which participants cannot easily meet. It also aims to give informants feedback on how their views compare with those of colleagues and provides an opportunity for them to rethink and change their preferences. It is fully explained in Cline *et al.* (1990).

This technique is in contrast with a questionnaire, which is essentially a ready-made inventory with categories provided by outsiders. As items in an inventory are standardised, it contains the inherent problem that the content of statements may be irrelevant or meaningless to the particular teachers being consulted. Also, in terms of process, the inventory approach can be criticised because by completing ready-made checklists teachers are not contributing the essential content of their own needs assessment, and so are 'not challenged to rethink their beliefs by being asked to engage in a more thorough going process of research' (Elliott, 1981: i).

Using the DELPHI technique for inservice needs analysis: one example

Step 1
Ask all staff to complete questionnaire **A** attached and return to you within three days.

Step 2
Make a list on questionnaire **B** of all the topics identified by staff. As there may be duplication and overlap, you may have to rename some of the topics but be careful that by doing this you do not change what is being said. Leave some blank spaces for them to insert any extra topics. Use a second sheet if necessary. Photocopy for all staff, write their names on the questionnaire and ask them to return to you within three days. You cannot make this questionnaire anonymous.

Step 3
Use form **B** to add up all the ratings for each topic, tally them using a tick system and then total each. At the right of the form for each topic, write down the median rating chosen by the staff – the mid-point. You can calculate this by counting the tally marks from the left until you reach the middle one (that being the number of half the staff).

Example:

Rating

	1		2		3		4		5		Median
	Tally	Total	Tally	Total	Tally	Total	Tally	Total	Tally	Total	
Topic 1	✓✓✓✓ ✓✓✓✓	9	✓✓✓✓ ✓✓✓✓	10	✓✓	1	✓	9	✓	1	2
Topic 2	✓✓✓✓ ✓✓✓	8	✓✓✓✓ ✓✓✓	8	✓✓✓✓ ✓✓	7		0		0	2
Topic 3	✓✓✓	3	✓✓✓ ✓✓✓✓	3	✓✓✓✓	4	✓✓✓✓	4	✓✓✓✓	9	4

For any topics added to the list by staff, you will not be able to work out a median, only one person may have mentioned it. For these cases leave the median column blank.

Step 4

Write on to questionnaire **C** the list of all topics from form **B** and insert where possible the median rating in the column headed 'median rating of all staff'. Now make enough copies of questionnaire **C** for all staff. Before you give them out write on to each their name and circle the rating **that they originally gave this topic**. This allows them to compare their rating if they wish and give a rationale if it differs from others. Explain that it is important to find out why there are differences of view, so that the best possible choice can be made.

Step 5

Summarise the results of the new ratings on form **C**, work out the median ratings and select one or two topics with the highest rating for inservice training.

Deciding priorities: nine-card diamond

A challenging aspect of a participative INSET is to move from teachers listing their concerns and priorities to agreeing what to do, and formulating it as a plan of action. Discussion on what to do can be structured in a variety of ways, one of which is the 'nine-card diamond'. Individual items (which may be problems, needs, or actions) are written one to a card. The group task is to lay the cards out in a diamond shape, with the top priority at the top of the diamond, second and third priorities as the next row, three equal priorities as the next, two as the next and the lowest priority at the bottom. While this is in one sense an artificial task, it serves to structure discussion and projects attention 'outwards' to a collective and concrete outcome rather than 'inwards' to personalities. It is not a descriptive needs assessment procedure, but is used to decide priorities for action.

Appendix 7.2 Planning an evaluation

From Sanders (1992).

Table 7.3 Evaluation information collection and analysis worksheet (all columns completed)

Evaluation questions	Why the question is important	Information needed to answer the question	When and how the information will be collected	Analysis and interpretation
1. What are the expected student outcomes of the science curriculum?	1. We need to have goals.	1. What each teacher of science expects; what our curriculum guides say.	1. In October, each teacher of science will be asked to list the ten most important outcomes for students in science this year.	1. A grade-by-grade listing of what teachers provided will be produced and distributed to teachers. These listings will be compared to curriculum guides and will be evaluated by the science committee.
2. How well are students performing on the expected outcomes?	2. We need to know how well we are meeting our goals.	2. Achievement of students in science.	2. In May, each science teacher will be asked to list strong and weak outcomes of their students. In March, standardised science achievement scores and state assessment science scores will be compiled.	2. A grade-by-grade listing of strengths and weaknesses of students in science will be prepared in June by the science committee.

3. What topics are covered by grade level, and how much time is spent on each?	3. We need to know what we are doing to meet our goals.	3. What each teacher covers; what our curriculum guides say.	3. In January, each science teacher will be asked to list topics and time allocations for each for this year.	3. & 4. A grade-by-grade listing of topics, time spent on each, methods, and materials will be prepared in March. This listing and teacher's judgments about needs in methods and materials will be evaluated by the science committee.
4. What methods and materials are used for each topic, and how good are they?	4. We need to analyse our instruction to identify targets for improvement.	4. What each teacher uses; teachers' judgements of strengths and weaknesses of methods and materials.	4. In January, each science teacher will also be asked to list methods and materials for each topic and to evaluate each.	
5. To what extent is the curriculum meeting our expectations?	5. We need to be clear about our standards and the extent to which we are meeting them.	5. What others (e.g. NSTA, AAAS, state department of education, our curriculum guides) say about standards.	5. In November, curriculum standards from different sources will be compiled.	5. The curriculum will be compared to known standards by the science committee in June. A final report of strengths and weaknesses will be prepared by the committee after reviewing all of the evaluation information collected during the year.

Evaluation Question	Activity	Aug	Sep	Oct	Nov	Dec	Jan	Feb	Mar	Apr	May	Jun	Jul	Aug
1.	a. Create survey form		//////											
	b. Survey teachers			//////										
	c. Compile results				//////									
	d. Get comments					///								
	e. Compare to curriculum						///							
	f. Committee review											//////		
	g. Prepare report											//////		
2.	a. Create survey form									//////				
	b. Survey teachers									//////				
	c. Compile survey results										///			
	d. Compile test results								//////					
	e. Committee review											///		
	f. Prepare report											///		
3–4.	a. Create teacher survey form					///								
	b. Survey teachers						///							
	c. Compile results							//////						
	d. Committee review											//////		
	e. Prepare report											////		
5.	a. Compile standards				/////////									
	b. Compare curriculum to standards						/////////							
	c. Summarise strengths and weaknesses						/////////							
	d. Prepare report											//////		

Fig. 7.3 'Gantt Chart for Program Evaluation' (Sanders, 1992: 55)

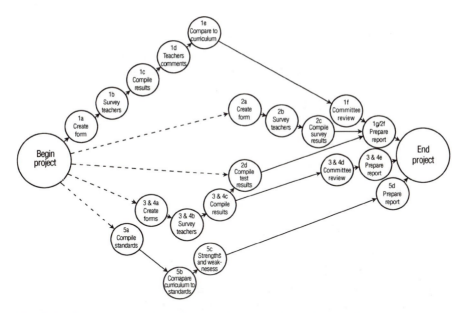

Fig. 7.4   'Activity Network for Program Evaluation' (Sanders, 1992: 56)

Appendix 7.3   Activity planning: checklist

('Suggested Checklist on Course Organisation and Administration', Cline *et al.*, 1990: 257.)

SUGGESTED CHECKLIST ON COURSE ORGANISATION AND ADMINISTRATION

This checklist starts from the point when a needs assessment has been completed and a course proposal approved. There is an outline, a named organiser, and some guidance on a maximum budget. What next? This list gives a great deal of detail. Even so it is not exhaustive. Would you omit anything? What would you add?

Course organisers will not take personal responsibility for everything in this list, but they will ensure that a system exists for someone to do so and will fix deadlines and provide support where needed.

A. Finalise course programme and planning schedule
- course tutors' responsibilities
- course title
- course length

- residential or not
- dates and times
- minimum and maximum number of participants
- range of qualifications and experience of participants
- open invitation
- formal or informal methods of applying to come on the course
- range and order of activities in programme
- room requirements
- lectures
- practical demonstrations
- practical activities
- group activities
- reception area
- exhibition space
- area for lunch and refreshments
- check on wheelchair access
- finalise venue to meet these requirements for the numbers involved (taking account of room sizes, facilities, comfort, noise, and travelling convenience for expected participants)
- for school-based courses and other venues where training is not the principal function double-check availability of rooms on planned dates
- speakers and group leaders
- number required
- rates of pay
- likely expenses
- possible names
- availability
- collaboration with other departments/agencies
- consider options for course evaluation and take any advance action needed (e.g. if outsiders to be involved)
- prepare schedule of deadlines

B. Briefing of speakers and group leaders

- give information on course objectives, participants, rest of programme, how their session(s) fit(s) into overall plan
- discuss venue and timetable, giving particular attention to any possible problems, including potential conflicts/overlap between speakers
- discuss session objectives and content with the aim of reaching agreement on a clear definition of both, confirming conclusions in writing
- check their requirements for audiovisual aids and other equipment

- invite their comments on plan for course evaluation
- give information on arrangements for paying fees and expenses

C. Publicity
- finalise contents of publicity sheet/leaflet
- agree design
- arrange printing
- update addresses on circulation list
- special circulation for this course?
- notice in Teachers' Centre booklet
- notice in LEA or other newsletter
- notice in *TES* or other journals or papers
- notice in publications of related groups/professions
- include application forms in publicity material or send out on request
- set deadline for applications

D. Planning exhibition and/or bookshop
- contact Teachers' Centre and/or Library for relevant materials
- circulate relevant publishers and equipment manufacturers

E. Accommodation
- if residential, estimate number of bedrooms needed and check recreation facilities, availability of warden, contact person for urgent problems arising outside office hours
- finalise room bookings for course work after checking access, size, furniture and general suitability
- order any special furniture that is required (e.g. exhibition screens)
- arrange booking of audiovisual and other equipment
- any special security arrangements or security clearance?

F. Catering
- morning and afternoon mid-session refreshments
- location
- timing
- speed of service
- breakfast and dinner if residential
- lunch
- bar opening hours
- availability of vegetarian food
- special meals for first or last days of course

G. Selection of participants

- set criteria for acceptance on to the course
- arrange for queries to be dealt with
- system for invoicing successful applicants, processing fees that are received, and sending receipts
- replies to unsuccessful applicants

H. Despatch of course information to participants and speakers

- programme
- map and details of venue (plus domestic arrangements for residential courses)
- pre-course assignments
- details of speakers and participants (can wait till first session)
- check on special diets, wheelchair access, nos for outings/activities

I. Course material

- preparation of slides and transparencies
- typing and duplicating of course notes, etc.
- pre-viewing and purchase or hire of video material
- preparation of certificates of attendance
- folders
- name badges
- finalise arrangements for exhibition
- preparation of evaluation material

J. Last-minute preparations

- phone check to visiting speakers week before session
- notices for routes to and through building
- notices for rooms indicating their function during the course
- check seating and equipment in each room
- check where MRO or technician will be if needed
- welcoming arrangements for participants and guest speakers

K. During course sessions

- the successful organiser has nothing to do?

L. Follow up

- issue certificates of attendance
- who needs formal and informal thinking?
- authorising payment of speakers' fees and expenses
- analyse and report on evaluation

Appendix 7.4   A reflection activity: snakes

(From Denicolo and Pope, 1990: 158–59.)

Our participants, who were already alert to our interest in personal constructions of life events in general and professional role in particular, were asked to
participate in an exercise which would involve them in thinking back over their
life experience to elicit particular incidents and experiences which influenced
their career paths. They were asked to reflect in private, visualizing and drawing their lives as a winding snake in which each 'twist' in its body represented a
change in direction of, or intention for, their career. Brief annotations were to

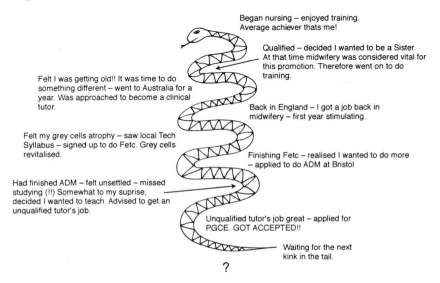

Began nursing – enjoyed training.
Average achiever thats me!

Qualified – decided I wanted to be a Sister.
At that time midwifery was considered vital for
this promotion. Therefore went on to do
training.

Felt I was getting old!! It was time to do
something different – went to Australia for a
year. Was approached to become a clinical
tutor.

Back in England – I got a job back in
midwifery – first year stimulating.

Felt my grey cells atrophy – saw local Tech
Syllabus – signed up to do Fetc. Grey cells
revitalised.

Finishing Fetc – realised I wanted to do more
– applied to do ADM at Bristol

Had finished ADM – felt unsettled – missed
studying (!!) Somewhat to my suprise,
decided I wanted to teach. Advised to get an
unqualified tutor's job.

Unqualified tutor's job great – applied for
PGCE. GOT ACCEPTED!!

Waiting for the next
kink in the tail.

?

be included, for each twist, about the experience or incident which precipitated
the change. No instruction was given about *when* in their lives to start considering whether experiences influenced career and it is of interest to note that the
majority of participants who subsequently submitted their 'snakes' to the
researchers in conditions of confidentiality mentioned incidents from pre- or
early school years which continue to contribute to the 'why' and 'how' of their
role. Two of those whose snakes began later in life were among the original
eight chosen for in-depth interview from those who expressed willingness to
discuss their reflections in greater depth. In interview they recalled earlier
experiences which at least acted as predisposing factors to later 'twists'.

Appendix 7.5   A knowledge-sharing activity

Our example refers to a short course on the teaching of writing, for group of
twelve secondary-level English teachers from France.

Step one

Explain the need to pool our knowledge and also not to waste time by introducing activities already known to the group.

Step two

Ask each teacher to think of the writing activities which they currently use with all their classes (not techniques they feel they *should* use); ask them to jot down a private list of activities, and which classes they are used with (3 minutes).

Step three

Ask teachers to pool activities and to write them down on a file card, one to a card (15/20 minutes).

Step four

Ask teachers to lay them out on a table top and sort them into a pattern, according to the level and other important factors (15 minutes).

Step five

Ask teachers to review each other's patterns; discuss the best framework to use (usually by level).

Step six

Display a summary of activities (on board/overhead projection transparencies/poster) and ask teachers to comment on any gaps or strengths they notice. With this group, they noticed a big gap between paragraph level writing based on a model at the lower level, to free essay writing with advanced classes.

Step seven

Teachers were asked to comment on the writing skills they wanted to develop and the activities they currently use. With this group, they felt that the gap they noticed was too big, and that their activities did not prepare properly for free writing.

Step eight

The tutor previewed some activities and materials which could be presented; some teachers volunteered to do some library research by reviewing writing materials.

Note

The use of cards is not optional: they externalise the topic, and make individual contributions common property. They also make it easy for teachers to recognise an overall pattern in activities they might use. The tutor has to be fully prepared with resource materials on teaching of writing, to be drawn on as needed.

Appendix 7.6   A provider's 'cultural homework'

(From McLaughlin, 1996.)

Student journals

For another unit, students ($N = 15$) were requested to maintain a 'learner's journal'. Students were asked to write one entry each week of about one page in length. The theme of the entry was the students' own choice. However over the period of a semester, they were asked to include the following prompts when they believed it appropriate.

Journal themes

How do I go about reading for assignments?
How do I go about collecting information?
How do I go about writing an assignment?
My experiences of reading in English
How can lecturers help students learn?
What are your problems at UPNG?
Relationship with academic staff
Group work versus individual work
Teaching at UPNG

Forums and informal interviews

Three 'forums' were held over the year with interested, volunteering students. The themes of the forums focused on learning difficulties. Participants numbered approximately twenty. From these forums, a number of students were identified as helpful and articulate informants. They were approached and asked if they would be willing to participate in a fortnightly interview with the researcher for approximately 15 minutes' duration. It was stressed that students should maintain a commitment for the fortnightly interview, otherwise it would be better not to volunteer. Twelve students finally accepted the invitation to be interviewees. Below is the informal interview schedule that formed the basis of data collection. Quite often a single question/theme was pursued over a number of interview sessions.

Informal interview schedule

Reasons for task
What have you been studying lately?
What have you found out? (choice in its selection)?
How did you feel about assignment before start?
How did you attempt to answer the question?

Reading
Did you get help from lecturers?
Did you ask for help?
Obtaining information from books difficult?
How did you go about it?
How do you go about note-taking?
How difficult is reading for you? (explain).

Writing
While you were doing your assignment, how did you feel towards your task?
What problems did you experience?
What did you feel you learnt?
Do you ever rush assignments?

Assessment
Do you usually get good marks?
How do you go about getting good marks?
(a) Is there any subject that you are doing in which you particularly like the assessment?
(b) You don't like the assessment?

Teaching
For you what are good lecturers?
Tell me about good lecturers and the way they run
 – their course;
 – their relationship with students.
Bad lecturers

8

Case studies of INSET

8.1 Introduction

Table 8.1 provides a summary of the case studies presented in this chapter.

In the Basque Country Diploma programme, we have a case of a well-funded central initiative to upgrade the qualifications and professional skills of English teachers. In the description we focus on the positive factors supporting the aims of the course (general political climate and the leadership of central authorities); and aspects of course design (opportunities for reflection on assumptions, past experiences and present practice; a degree of individualisation; the integration of off-site and on-site experiences; the support given teachers when exploring their own teaching).

Table 8.1 Summary of case studies

Location	Scheme	Issues
Basque Country	Diploma in ELT	Part-time upgrading for state-sector primary-school teachers; integration of off-site and on-site experiences
Israel	A self-directed action research project	Secondary-school teachers explore issues of mixed-ability teaching
Australia	A co-ordinated action research project (AMEP)	Teachers explore issues raised by the introduction of a centralised curriculum; with external support and co-ordination
Latvia	Support of a local INSET framework (PDP)	Part-time tutors support local groups in the context of systemwide change
	PAD: materials to develop classroom management skills	On-site skills development for secondary-school teachers; integration of input, discussion and experiment with teacher control over processes of change

The action research project in an Israeli secondary school which we report was, at the time, one of the earlier action research projects in our field. It represents a self-directed teacher development activity which shows the importance of structure, support and school climate for collaborative action research.

Next, we outline the AMEP action research study (exploring the implications of a reformed curriculum framework in AMEP programmes) as it illustrates a larger-scale externally supported project (Burns and Hood, 1995).

Then, we sketch out the Professional Development Programme (PDP) project which took place at a historic moment of social and education renewal in Latvia. Its purpose was to develop a network of local tutors and it illustrates a low-cost initiative, the effectiveness of which derived from a clear vision of what was possible and the long-term support of local tutors as they developed their new skills.

Finally we outline a training resource pack designed for on-site use by secondary-school teachers: Preventive Approaches to Disruption (PAD). Its purpose is to offer teachers of all disciplines a framework in which to develop classroom management strategies which their initial training has failed to provide. It demonstrates two key principles. One is that teacher learning is multilevel in nature, and that design should address each of these dimensions by integrating and relating activities of different types (see Table 8.4 and also section 1.1.5). The other is that providers should respect the autonomy of working teachers, who should be given responsibility and control in the process of their own learning. The provider has a crucial role to play in this transfer of responsibility, that of a *process leader*.

With only five case studies, we make no claims to comprehensiveness. We try to engage the readers' professional interest, and to illustrate some of the general issues explored in other chapters.

The case studies suggest that teacher development is best supported through long-term involvement of support staff; optimal participation by teachers; and the relevance of programme concerns. From the point of view of a provider, they demonstrate the principle that 'inservice is a process not an event – a process of role change which involves new knowledge, new skills, new behaviour, new theories or conceptions and new attitudes' (Fullan, 1979: 277). To help the reader relate the case studies to principles of teacher learning, these are restated in summary form in Appendix 8.5.

8.2   Professional development for primary-school teachers of English in the Basque Country[1]

Introduction

In this case study we describe a Diploma course developed collaboratively by the Basque Government, the University of the Basque Country and the British

[1] The author wishes to acknowledge the detailed and generous help of Peter James, Course Leader at the British Council DTE, Bilbao, 1991–94, and Stephen Halden, for his valuable evaluation study; also Sr Jesus Arzamendi, Instituto Pedagogico de Lenguas, San Sebastian, for his support in publishing this account.

Council DTE, Bilbao. It began in 1991, and has evolved each year since then. We focus on one course (year 1992–93) but also describe later changes.

A key feature of the design was its intention to support the *individual* development of each participating teacher, by means of such activities as reflection and discussion, self-directed reading and action research.

8.2.1 Description

Summary

Context	Centrally initiated large-scale language curriculum reform Commitment of state authority to the empowerment of schools, teachers and local communities
Purpose	Prepare English language teachers to work with children aged 8–14 Prepare teachers to interpret a new English language curriculum Produce qualified ELT staff in primary schools
Providers	University of the Basque Country Department of Education, Universities and Research, the Basque Government British Council DTE, Bilbao
Clients	Experienced primary-school teachers Basque Government
Objectives	Develop English-language skills and knowledge of methodology Enable teachers to take responsibility for curriculum plans Enable further personal development Enable collaboration with and dissemination to other teachers
Incentives	Teachers seconded for three months Teachers receive University Diploma, recognised within and outside the Basque Country Teachers' level of English raised Teachers enabled to fulfil new responsibilities
Resistance	Tacit models of teacher-centred instruction Challenging new role demands Lack of self-confidence
Intake	Varies year by year; around 40 in year of case study Experienced primary-school teachers with existing specialisations

Location	On-site and off-site combined	
Structure (1992–93)	Phase 1:	Modules 1–3
		First term: full-time, off-site
	Phase 2:	Module 4
		Second term at school + off-site weekly seminar (10 weeks × 3 hours)
		Module 5
		Third term at school: classroom enquiry with tutor support
Content	Module 1:	Language improvement activities
	Modules 2 and 3:	Activities to stimulate development in teachers' personal theories
		Methodology and language study (conventional activities)
	Module 4:	Issues in and practice of classroom data collection techniques related to teaching plans (weekly seminar)
	Module 5:	Classroom enquiry and personal supervision
Duration	500 hours	
Assessment	Module 3:	Lesson plan and scheme of work
	Module 5:	Action research project
Liaison	Regular meetings between the University, the Basque Government and British Council	
Staffing (1992-93)	Four British Council staff (full-time, one course leader and one assistant; a maximum of around nine part-time tutors)	
Costs	British Council staff salaries, resources and premises University staff time Salary of replacement teachers	
Accountability	British Council to Basque Government British Council to University Teachers to schools, community and Government	

Context

In the late 1980s, the Spanish Government initiated fundamental, legally binding changes in state education (the *Reforma*). Autonomous regions such as the

Basque Country were empowered to reinterpret the *Reforma*, which was then disseminated to schools and communities by means of the state *Boletin Oficial del Pais Vasco*. The priority given to communicative ability in the guidelines represented a major innovation in behaviour and thinking for many of the teachers in question. Furthermore, the Basque Government interpreted the *Reforma* in terms of a progressive curriculum model disseminated through a cross-disciplinary central initiative which gave priority to empowering teachers and schools in the design and delivery of the curriculum, by means of devolving detailed curriculum preparation to them.

Authorities committed major support to the implementation of this initiative by means of documentation and INSET funding. English language education benefited alongside a simultaneous and much greater commitment of funds by the authorities to Basque language education, Basque medium schools and Basque language teacher training.

Curriculum guidelines in the *Boletin* were global in nature. As a matter of policy, as part of the devolution to schools of curriculum planning responsibility, school staff were expected to interpret them in their own school curriculum plans. This was intended to enable the interpretation of large-scale goals according to local conditions, and to maintain local autonomy. This process of interpretation and planning was supported by advisers and the dissemination of cross-curricular information. Additionally, approved materials were made available by collaborating publishers.

Teachers and schools were therefore presented with a major professional and educational opportunity but also a new challenge. Schools could control language syllabuses and assessment and also had opportunities to negotiate with stakeholders such as pupils, teachers and parents. However, teachers were often anxious in the face of such new responsibility, perhaps feeling that they were left in limbo as to what to actually do! Therefore, a priority of the Diploma was to equip teachers to fulfil these new responsibilities.

Another purpose of the Diploma was to provide qualified staff at the primary level, as the starting age for English had been lowered to eight.

In response to these needs, the Basque Government funded a postgraduate Diploma programme for primary-school teachers, starting in 1991 and offering three-month full-time secondment for eligible teachers and paid replacement teachers.

The government wanted to set up its own qualification, hence the involvement of the University of the Basque Country and the approach to the British Council in Bilbao for specialist input. The Basque Country structure consisted of a full-time off-site phase integrated with a low-intensity on-site phase in which the teachers focused on their own implementation of the new curriculum, a model also used in other disciplines such as physical education and music. A 500-hour structure applies throughout Spain as an INSET framework eligible for a postgraduate award; the organisation of off-site and on-site elements varies considerably between authorities.

Incentives

Teachers volunteer for the course. Take-up has been good, in part because there are good incentives to do so. The intrinsic value of obtaining a higher degree is backed up by practical benefits: the degree is recognised throughout Spain, so teachers are able to apply for jobs in other autonomous regions, very helpful for teachers unable to find jobs within the region.

Programme philosophy and objectives

The priority of the course was to focus on the *Reforma* from the personal perspective of each participating teacher. The decision to adopt an assessed classroom enquiry project as the principal means for teachers to apply and interpret course input was central to the purpose of the course. To produce action research reports helped teachers meet their new responsibilities: to interpret general curricular goals in terms that would be meaningful and effective in their own schools, and to be publicly accountable for their work (James, 1996).

The action research had to focus on a relatively narrow aspect of the curriculum but all projects were planned to establish explicit links between classroom 'micro' strategies and 'macro' goals. Teachers were required to explain how their project related to the official curriculum (for example, by making a connection between learner autonomy and 'teacherless' classroom strategies). Thus, the action research experience was intended to develop the thinking of each teacher; to encourage their personal syntheses of theory and practice; and to make explicit connections between global goals in official curriculum documents and their own practice.

Objectives

The stated objectives of the course (for year 1992–93) were:

Language
(i)   develop teachers' awareness of English as a system
(ii) develop teachers' general and course-specific language skills
(iii) develop teachers' linguistic confidence and their ability to use English for professional purposes (minimum target of CEELT 1 level)

Methodology
(i)   develop teachers' personal theories of teaching and learning by exploiting individual and collective experience
(ii) provide an up-to-date overview of language teaching developments
(iii) help teachers to interpret guidelines provided in official curricular documents
(iv) enable reflection, discussion and evaluation of (i) to (iii)
(v)   encourage teachers to apply course learning to their own practice

Preparation for the future
(i)   develop teachers' ability to make informed and principled professional decisions
(ii) help teachers co-operate with each other and colleagues in school
(iii) prepare teachers for language curriculum developments in the nineties.

The programme has been developed through close collaboration between the Basque Government, which administers, funds and monitors the scheme; the University of the Basque Country, the awarding body; and the British Council, the course provider. Course development has been a joint effort between British Council staff and University school syllabus specialists. The three bodies meet regularly for liaison and development.

The participating teachers have had diverse previous training, are experienced at primary level, if to varying degrees, and have different specialisations. The English language admission requirement is set by an agreed score on the Oxford Placement Test. In general, teachers' experience of formal language learning has been through translation-based and teacher-centred forms of instruction. The intake has varied over the years which has required adaptation in course structure but in the year of this case study at this location it was around 40, so enabling teaching in two sets, and a staffing ratio of around 1:10.

It should be noted that participating teachers were not observed teaching at any point in the course, for reasons of feasibility rather than principle. The teachers were quite widely scattered over the region, and the 1:10 tutor-participant ratio was too high for systematic visiting. As a result, the teachers were required to self-direct, self-monitor and self-evaluate their implementation of the course.

Developments in the programme

The course has developed organically since 1991. It has been run at a variety of sites, with different start and completion times, varying group sizes and different arrangements of the off-site and on-site phases.

By 1994, some 300 teachers had completed the course. In the first year (1991–92) there was an intake of 120, in six cohorts of 20 starting and ending at different times, at a number of sites (in Bilbao, Vitoria and San Sebastian). Intake numbers have dropped to some 40 per year, and courses now end in July. The British Council staffing for an intake of 40 consisted of a full-time course leader, a full-time assistant and four or five part-time tutors. A smaller intake enabled more opportunities for individual supervision and guidance. Also, the original modular structure, required by the diversity of course timing and location, came to be simplified as a two-phase structure. It usually consists of an intensive phase at the beginning and end of the course in which participants are released from teaching duties, and an extensive phase of fortnightly seminars when teachers are back at school. However, there are variations according to local circumstances.

Providers have changed, and academic responsibility has come to be shared between the University and the British Council. Similarly, assessment requirements have developed to include a language component and formal assessment requirements have been increased. Other significant changes include greater support given to teachers on testing and assessment issues and on assignment writing.

It is important to note that course development by the British Council staff was collaborative in nature, with tutors discussing and revising drafts produced by the course leader (who strongly emphasises the importance of the collective contributions of *all* staff). Thus the principle of ownership and responsibility sharing was replicated in course development processes. It is desirable for working relationships between providers to be consistent with the anticipated relationships between them and participating teachers.

The 500-hour course in 1992–93 was designed in modular form to accommodate groups with different start dates, as is summarised in Table 8.2.

Phase 1 – Modules 1–3

The design adopted the view that course objectives and working relationships should be consistent. Therefore, participants were given a voice from the earliest feasible point in order to develop the self-esteem to cope with their new responsibilities, and for them to begin to uncover their personal theories (Shulman, 1988; Pennington, 1990; Griffiths and Tann, 1992; Parrott, 1993; section 1.1.3).

The first module was devoted exclusively to language practice, a top priority to enable teachers to cope with the rest of the course and with reflective activities in English.

In the second module, teachers began working on the review of their own pedagogy. It takes time for teachers to uncover and assess their beliefs and personal theories. Talking about their own situations and values in this phase of the course began a process that culminated months later in individual action

Table 8.2   Course description (year 1992–93)

| Phase 1: First term | | | Phase 2: second and third terms | |
Module 1	Module 2	Module 3	Module 4	Module 5
Language development (100 hours)	Language development and methodology (100 hours)	Language development and methodology (100 hours)	Seminar: implementation and classroom research (10 weeks × 3 hours) Supervision (estimated 100 hours)	Individual classroom research project (estimated 100 hours)

research projects. It was in this module that explicit attention was given to developing a metalanguage in English for the discussion of teaching. The process of naming key features of language teaching served both as a means of language development and of conceptual development (Brown, 1990). Thus teachers looked at key terms and built up personal professional glossaries, containing their own denotations of terms such as 'communication', 'utterance' and so on. To encourage teachers to read extensively and critically was a further object of this module.

In one activity participants were asked to describe their classrooms and schools, some of which experience considerable social problems. This was intended to encourage realism in considering theory and curriculum planning issues, and to value the teacher's place of work. Participants also began to uncover their pedagogic values in this module, through visualisation and discussion activities (example in Appendix 8.1). It is increasingly recognised that one way to tap teachers' tacit beliefs and assumptions is by their exploration of personal metaphors, for example of the classroom, language learning, or their approach to teaching. A metaphor allows freer self-expression and an element of play in what otherwise can be an unduly 'heavy' activity. In the example, teachers were asked to draw, compare and discuss a visual metaphor for their own classroom. This was not an isolated or 'one-off' activity, but was related to discussion, and long-term reflective writing. James (forthcoming) who provided the example in Appendix 8.1 explores in depth the use of metaphor in teacher awareness raising.

Each teacher also produced a personal pedagogic manifesto, a statement of principles and beliefs, which peers could read and discuss. This manifesto served to crystallise implicit personal theories and also to provide a baseline against which to compare personal development at a later stage, such as during the action research project in Module 5.

Learning through reflection was not seen as a one-off or short-term process: course providers tried to initiate reflection early in the course, and then worked consistently to support individual developments in thinking throughout (James, 1996).

In all three modules, conventional activities were used to convey principles, demonstrate language teaching/learning strategies, and encourage teachers' reactions (e.g. demonstrations, short lectures, directed reading, workshops and seminars).

Diary-keeping was an important element but it was done in a series of short bursts rather than throughout, as it can become rather tedious and subject to a law of diminishing returns (see also Jarvis, 1992). Thus for 7–10 days in Phase 1 participants were asked to keep a diary to record personal reactions to course activities. Notes taken from diaries were brought to sessions for comparison and discussion. Diaries were also kept during individual action research data collection in Module 5, and submitted before tutorials to help discussion.

The agreed form of assessment for Phase 1 consisted of an assignment describing a scheme of work with a lesson plan. This was done in pairs to promote collaborative skills, important for the course and for subsequent curriculum development work. The lesson plan was based on Phase 1 input and was intended to be taught, evaluated and reported in Phase 2.

Phase 2 – Modules 4–5

Phase 2 lasted for six months, with participants back in school. Its purpose was to support the critical implementation of the Phase 1 syllabus and the personal interpretation of curricular guidelines.

In Module 4 (10 weeks × a weekly three-hour seminar) participants tried out the lesson prepared in Phase 1 and reviewed it in seminars. The seminar enabled further input from course providers and enabled exchange between peers about implementation. It provided support as well as practical help in the trial and error business of implementing changes (Olson and Eaton, 1987).

The module was also designed to prepare for Module 5 by practising the collection of classroom data and helping teachers to identify an area for individual classroom enquiry.

In Module 5 teachers worked by themselves, supported by personal tutors, and conducted classroom inquiries following an action research model (using Hopkins, 1985; see section 2.6.3). Diaries and field notes were used for classroom monitoring, and pupil feedback was collected. These data were then used in the final assessed assignment which described and evaluated their enquiry. In the project teachers were required to include a statement of beliefs (with possible back-reference to the Phase 1 pedagogic manifesto) and explicit reference to the implementation of the curriculum. They were also asked to write guidelines for the form of the inquiry for future course participants. University and British Council staff assessed the assignments.

The action research project represented the culmination of the course. It aimed to help the teacher to develop a personal realisation of the curriculum in terms of her own classroom. It served to uncover and develop personal theories, and helped teachers to interpret public theory (explanatory theories or theories implicit in materials and curricular guidelines) in areas such as language acquisition, learner roles, error and language as communication. In this way, teachers were able to draw on the reading they had done in the course.

Action research has been much criticised for the absence of theorising exhibited by teachers (Adelman, 1989; Elliott and Sarland, 1995), and in this course tutors also experienced difficulty in leading teachers to go beyond description and to analyse the implications of the data they collected. It is not surprising if teachers find it very difficult to move from description to analysis and interpretation: it is an unfamiliar task, demanding a new kind of discourse. There is likely to be a tension between tutors and teachers, in that this lack of experience (and self-confidence in some cases) leads teachers to want the tutor to do the work of critical analysis for them.

The goal of the tutor is to guide teachers through the action research stages: selection of topic; description of classroom events; the analysis and interpretation of these data in terms of wider theories and personal theories; forward planning. This takes time and regular contacts. Tutors need to give teachers permission and time to make mistakes and to allow inquiries to evolve.

It is interesting to note the dynamic effects of teachers publishing their action research reports. Year on year, they are available to new intakes and are read as part of the course literature, a most powerful statement to participants that the action research task is serious; that their work is valued; and that it can be done by people like them! Some project titles appear in Appendix 8.2.

Evaluation

Evaluation of the Diploma programme has been positive (e.g. Halden, 1995). The results suggest the following outcomes: a high level of impact upon the teachers' classroom practice (including the use of a wider range of EFL techniques and less dependence on course books); changed attitudes towards pupils (a more active role of pupils in language learning and a greater awareness of their feelings); and an increase in curricular knowledge and terminology.

Some teachers expressed greater confidence in putting forward their own ideas. There are also indications among some of the teachers of a more open and reflective disposition towards their teaching: 'it was a very good opportunity for reflecting on my own teaching. I have started thinking about how I do things and I realised I had a lot to learn. . . . Now I think I'm more open to any new teaching ideas from other teachers . . .' (Halden, 1995: 151).

It is worth noting that many teachers attributed their development to the discussions and exchanges of experiences they were able to have with fellow teachers (Halden, 1995).

These positive evaluations should be treated cautiously. There is no *direct* formal evidence on training impacts, such as could be obtained by observation. However, the overall impression among all participants is of a well-received and effective course. Accepting this, what general lessons can it offer?

8.2.2   Discussion

Positive preconditions

A well-conceived course design will be undermined by negative preconditions. The Diploma programme has benefited from positive preconditions. Involvement in the programme offered teachers strong incentives: a period of full-time secondment; the award of a higher degree; improved job prospects, security and mobility; and the adoption of a high-status specialisation within the school. A further incentive lay in the improvement of participants' own English.

The authority not only provided incentives but also demonstrated that it *valued* teachers sufficiently to commit resources to them without imposing a prescriptive change agenda.

Design fits its context

The design of the programme may not have been consciously led by the Basque authority's curriculum development model, but it certainly provided a back-drop and a context for the thinking of course designers. The recognition of individual learning needs and the absence of an inspectorial element to the pro-gramme are associated with respect for autonomy. Autonomy is a far-reaching concept, and in this setting an autonomous education authority has endorsed the autonomy of teachers in respect of their learning.

The place in the system which teachers were assigned by central policy did, however, determine the goals of the programme in that an emphasis on partici-pants' autonomy would be consistent with their role once back in school. In their approach, course designers were certainly aware of 'horror stories' of other training programmes, if not in Spain, that failed because of the imposition of unacceptable values, inappropriate role expectations or impractical teaching strategies. It was a case where knowledge of INSET theory and good practice contributed to their design.

In other political/cultural settings, such as those in which central authority is dominant or even coercive, and in which teacher learning is required to be in terms of a single officially endorsed pathway rather than diverse pathways, it is to be expected that a more prescriptive and inspectorial mode of course provi-sion would be applied. Also, in such a context the need for incentives may be seen as less relevant than sanctions and top-down direction.

Centralisation is not to be condemned a priori. There are cases where the exercise of centralised authority is the most effective option available and where the orientation of teachers towards their own learning is less in terms of self-direction than of approximation to the models determined by higher authority in their system. Teacher education programmes have to be ecologically viable: the literature is full of accounts of programmes that have set full sail for an edu-cational El Dorado only to be wrecked on the submerged rocks of cross-cultural incomprehension, of incorrect assumptions about how particular teacher-clients learn most effectively and of false assumptions about the opportunities and constraints afforded teachers by the role their systems offer them (e.g. Phillips and Owens, 1986; Kramsch and Sullivan, 1996).

Valorisation and self-esteem

Prescriptive INSET programmes intrinsically deny the value of participating teachers' personal theories and craft knowledge. In development-orientated programmes, it is essential that the first message they get from course providers is that they are valued for what they are and for what they already know. Many of the activities early in this Diploma are designed to achieve this.

Direct experience and participation

Phase 1 provides direct language instruction which offers participants a set of shared experiences. This provides a concrete and *shared* basis for teachers to develop their understanding of terminology and to contrast their own perceptions and reactions with those of fellow teachers. It also enables greater insight into pupils' experience of instruction and provides concrete rather than abstract models of pedagogy.

Exchange insights and perceptions

Participants prize discussion with their peers, for a number of reasons. First, fellow teachers speak the same practical language, framed by the realities of school. Then, experience sharing brings support, the sense that 'I thought I was the only one, but I feel a bit better knowing others have been there too'.

The formulation and crystallisation of personal theories is promoted by exposure to colleagues' perceptions and interpretations, offered without an attempt to *impose* change on the part of tutors. This is supported by Fullan's view that social support is an essential element in enabling teachers to implement innovations, observing:

> ... training approaches ... are effective when they combine concrete, teacher-specific training activities, ongoing continuous assistance and support during the process of implementation and regular meetings with peers and others.... Research on implementation has demonstrated beyond a shadow of doubt that these processes of sustained interaction and staff development are crucial regardless of what the change is concerned with.
>
> (Fullan, 1982: 67)

The clarification of personal theories is supported by discussion and writing, while opportunities for rethinking are offered but not imposed (also section 1.2.3).

Opportunities for reflection and taking stock

Reflection has been defined as: 'making explicit some of the tacit knowledge embedded in action so that the agent can figure out what to do differently' (Argyris *et al.*, 1985: 51).

We conceive of tacit knowledge as the teacher's personal theories which are reflected in her routine actions and largely intuitive pedagogic skills. As Argyris and Schön put it, 'we know more than we can tell and more than our behaviour consistently shows' (1974: 10). In order to make this knowledge explicit, it appears that one needs to *take stock* of one's current practice as it actually is and work to uncover and make explicit the personal theories that underlie it. It has been convincingly argued that work to uncover personal theories is a pre-requisite for their development (sections 2.2.3, 2.2.5, 4.2.3 and 4.5; also Day *et al.*, 1990; Griffiths and Tann, 1992).

It seems that development in personal theories may be triggered by the experience of *dissonance* (a discrepancy or mismatch of some kind between what is and what one expected). The discrepancy may be between what one assumes to be in one's classroom and what actually is, or, less threateningly, between one's interpretation of an incident or activity and that of another person.

Taking stock of current practice is promoted indirectly in Phase 1 of the course by means of returning to the learner's role; by participants exchanging experiences and views with each other; and through recording their responses to the course by reflective writing. It is encouraged directly by means of visualisation and discussion tasks (Appendix 8.1). Then in Phase 2 it is done directly by conducting structured classroom enquiries demanding self-monitoring and self-evaluation (Appendix 8.3).

Dissonance may be experienced by means of the contrasting perspectives offered by colleagues. In Phase 2 it may also be experienced more directly by surprises that arise from a close study of the reality of classroom life. It is unusual for such enquiry not to reveal discrepancies between expectation and reality (Roberts, 1993). However, their contribution to reflection and development in thinking seems to depend on extended social exchanges (with peers and tutors) and a full menu of concerted learning experiences that address all dimensions of teacher learning (section 1.1.5).

We should note that awareness raising and reflection in this programme was gradual, drew on a variety of activity types and was introduced early and sustained throughout the course. It may be that cases of reflective activities failing to produce any conceptual or attitudinal change might be explained by providers applying them over too short a period, not using them incrementally, and being of too narrow a range to appeal to the different expectations and dispositions of learner-teachers. A further point is that reflection activities were not used continuously. Reflection is demanding, and there is 'other business' to be addressed. Therefore periodic reflection and stock-taking seems to be the most effective.

The role of theory

Experience of dissonance is not the only means to change. It is equally true that 'big ideas' (e.g. on the significance of learners' errors as an indication of acquisition processes) have an essential function in the development of teacher thinking. They challenge existing assumptions, provide an alternative way of telling the story of what goes on in class, and can provide impetus and enthusiasm. Such explanatory theories (of teaching, methodology, competence, language etc.) generate a descriptive lexicon, offer explanations of personal experience, and can propose departures from routinised practice. As such they contribute to rethinking and personal change (Ur, 1992).

Explanatory theory can contribute to personal theory development. In this course it was realised through readings and lectures, the adoption of a specialist terminology, and the writing of classroom studies for purposes of assessment.

We should note that, in this course, there has been great variation between individuals in the degree of reflectiveness and conceptual change thinking they show (Lennon and James, 1995). This is explained by personal differences and the different career points at which individuals might be when attending the course (Huberman, 1989). Lennon and James (1995) detail some of the processes of change which teachers experience on a programme such as this, which they propose can be explicitly discussed with participating teachers.

Control

Participants were in control of self-disclosure. They could tell peers what they chose, withhold what they chose. No authority figure/inspector ever entered their classrooms to impose external criteria upon them. The degree of control and self-direction that this programme offers (for logistical as well as principled reasons perhaps) actually supports self-monitoring and self-evaluation by placing initiative and responsibility with the teacher, supported by regular seminars and tutor visits.

Relevance

By committing Module 1 to English language improvement, the course providers were aiming to improve teachers' English so they could best engage in the course and deliver the English curriculum. Additionally, they were dealing from the start with the top priority of almost all non-native-speaker teachers everywhere: their own English competence. As such, it demonstrated an awareness of teachers' needs and optimised the perceived relevance of the course from the outset. Other activities were designed to lay the ground for the action research project and the curriculum planning tasks awaiting teachers (e.g. objective methodology iii).

In Phase 2 of the course, teachers self-selected the focus for their action research and the occasions on which they would make experiments. Choice in exploring one's own classroom is a most important means by which to maximise ownership and the perceived relevance of the course (sections 7.4.1 and 8.6).

Support during change

The implementation of an innovation is not a simple matter of replacing materials, or expecting to train teachers to change their practice from 'old' to 'new' like respraying a car. Teacher change is typically evolutionary and heuristic in nature. It seems that most teachers introduce new practices by a step-by-step trial-and-error approach (Olson and Eaton, 1987). During these trials they need support because they are sure to run into unpredictable problems, dilemmas and blocks, with attendant self-doubt and confusion (Fullan, 1982; Eraut, 1994). This is because implementing innovation involves entirely new practical problems (for example for a highly directive teacher to try to introduce pair or group work) and also demands new ways of thinking, not just new ways of acting. The help needed at this stage is to work with the realities of the teacher's own classroom; generalised advice is of no particular help (Joyce and Showers, 1984).

The second phase of the programme has been designed to provide the support needed during the teachers' experimental attempts at implementation. To begin with, Phase 2 is comparatively long: six months to the three months of Phase 1. Then, throughout Phase 2, *support* is available to teachers in the form of seminars with peers and staff in Module 4, and then individual supervision during Module 5. This support enables discussion in concrete and individual terms of the difficulties and successes teachers meet, and also provides much-needed encouragement during the difficult phase of going it alone. Other courses have been relatively ineffective either because they stop at the input/Phase 1 stage altogether or provide a relatively cursory follow-up phase, usually because of lack of funding, a lack of awareness of implementation needs, or both.

Integrate off-site and on-site experiences

Off-site courses have been criticised because they fail to engage with the norms, relationships and ways of acting that operate in the school. However, there are good reasons to build an off-site component into teacher education programmes. First of all, an off-site course, particularly on secondment as this one is, gives teachers time out. When at the chalkface, it is hard, even impossible, to distance oneself from the short-term imperatives of the job, and from the routines which ensure daily survival. By definition, to reflect upon one's current practice implies revision of that practice, and teachers in the daily round of delivering a curriculum need certainties upon which to base their actions, not second thoughts. By removing the need for immediate action, reconsideration of current practice is made more possible and less threatening. Second, all work groups operate according to certain tacit norms and rules of behaviour (Somekh, 1993). Removal from the work group and involvement with another set of peers enables a more distanced view of school norms; and distance adds perspective. Finally, daily work in institutions is often helped along by the adoption of truces, by the avoidance of issues which are potentially divisive (Adelman and Alexander, 1982). These sleeping dogs are usually left to lie! However, the absence of a need for truces on an off-site course may make it more possible to challenge the views of others and be critical of one's own practice.

Whatever the benefit of off-site experiences, however, it is recognised that implementation of training or of a new curriculum is done within the realities of one's school culture and classroom conditions, and furthermore that these conditions vary. It is for this reason that complementary on-site activity has been provided in this course. The two-phase model of training (integrating off-site and on-site work) that the Diploma exemplifies is becoming increasingly recognised as a highly positive strategy in LTE.

Additional strategies

Some proven course design strategies could not be used in this case, most notably the enrolment of teachers in small teams from the same school, for reasons of mutual support, challenge and 'critical mass' (Vulliamy and Webb, 1991). There is much to be gained from the development of teacher teams in schools: they can provide support and the critical mass which may be needed to overcome constraints presented by school culture. However, it was not possible as participants were highly dispersed.

Connecting up

A constructivist perspective on INSET proposes that each teacher will reconstruct their awareness of themselves and their own beliefs, and will personalise course inputs. It suggests that they should be encouraged to become independent in their practice. The social dimension of personal change lies in awareness of the relationship between practice and context; critical dialogue and supportive relationships; and activities which integrate the private and social dimensions of learning (see sections 1.1.4 and 1.1.5 for a summary of our position). It therefore also suggests a denotation of reflection which would include the dimensions of self awareness and awareness of one's social landscape (see section 1.3).

A summary of key lessons suggested by this programme suggests a consistency with a broadly social constructivist perspective.

- The course design is framed by its particular political, moral and resource conditions.
- Large-scale centrally funded training in order to meet system needs should also take into account the individual learning needs of participating teachers, their personal theories and their individual classroom concerns.
- The central authority's role in such training is to provide the best preconditions for the course (e.g. provision of incentives); and adequate funding for the most effective course structure (e.g. periods of full-time secondment).

- The 'theory of action' of course providers was to work in partnership with teachers to help them organise their own thinking and to develop their own theories and practices, dynamically and progressively over an extended timescale.
- The design of the course enabled an integration of experiential learning, theoretical input, reading, discussion, reflection, formal writing and experimentation.
- The effectiveness of the course may be due to the following design features:
  - powerful larger-scale factors promoting the course objectives;
  - a 'two-stage' (off-site and on-site) design;
  - provision of inputs on theory and classroom management;
  - experiential learning opportunities;
  - opportunities for peer discussion;
  - opportunities for teachers to take stock of their current practice and to reflect on the differences between current and new practices over an extended period;
  - provision of enabling skills (e.g. language development, self-monitoring skills) as well as behaviourial skills (classroom techniques);
  - the preparation from the outset and throughout the programme for the culminating action research project, which required the translation of course inputs into the context of each participant's classroom;
  - a framework of support for the personalised implementation of training;
  - teachers' control over implementation attempts.
- A desirable further strategy would have been to enrol teachers as teams from the same schools.
- A more searching and direct evaluation of course impact than participant self-report is desirable.

The more specific connections between our account and research knowledge on INSET can best be done by cross-referring it with section 2.6, summarised in 2.6.5 and Table 2.1.

Endnote

This section has attempted to illustrate some principles of effective teacher education by means of the portrayal of an effective centrally funded teacher training programme, designed to meet system needs but also to meet the individual learning needs of teachers. Its effectiveness required the political will to commit adequate public funds, and the political orientation that values the autonomy of schools and teachers.

The next case study, in contrast, portrays teacher development in response to a perceived gap in individual practice that was conducted by means of self-direction and collaboration, and that made no funding demands on central authorities (Linder, 1991; Roberts, 1993).

8.3   Self-directed curriculum inquiry in a secondary school[2]

8.3.1   Description

Hof Hacarmel school is a regional secondary school, at the time of writing accountable to the rural division of the Ministry of Education. It was set up in the early 1970s and consists of Junior and Senior High schools.

At the time of the study and since its inception the student population consisted of kibbutz children and groups that came to live in kibbutzim. Hence it was and is strongly affiliated to the kibbutz ethos and educational principles, although since the study the student body has broadened to include children from other communities and villages in the area, with the continued application of a nonselective entry policy.

At the date of our case study (1989–90), the English department consisted of 10 EFL teachers teaching some 800 children from 15 kibbutzim for classes of four or five hours a week.

The school ethos centred on principles of equality of opportunity, and autonomy of teachers and learners, some effects of which are particularly relevant to this description. First, classes in all subjects were unstreamed except for the top three years of senior high which were streamed to meet the requirements of matriculation exams, which were divided into three levels of difficulty. In the case of English, there were small top and bottom sets (for bilinguals and recent arrivals respectively) with a large and heterogeneous middle set taught in mixed-ability groups. For the top three years, classes were separated only a few months before the examinations to prepare for special components. At the time of the case study, as new staff joined the school, there were indications that not all were as committed to the principle of heterogeneous classes as more established staff.

Second, the school was and is run by a Pedagogic Council, consisting of Heads of Department, teachers and student representatives. It is therefore a democratic structure (compared, for example, with a typical UK school in which power and accountability lie with the head teacher). Additionally, curriculum decisions are made at departmental level by collaborating groups of teachers. A further significant aspect of the school climate was the tradition of regular study group sessions, apart from other school INSET activity.

The project arose because English department staff were concerned that they were not managing the mixed–ability classes as well as they wished, given the

[2] My warm thanks to Pnina Linder for her help in preparing this description, which is closely based on Linder (1991).

goal of developing students' communicative ability. Thus the issue explored was: 'how can we best develop the students' communicative ability when they are in mixed-ability classes?' A long-term collaborative project was agreed to explore current practices in mixed-ability teaching, and to attempt improvements. The proposal was taken to the School Council and agreed by it.

Ten teachers with differing experience and backgrounds took part in the project, though for timetable reasons not all could always meet at the same time. Other subject teachers expressed an interest and joined sessions informally. Two senior members of staff acted as process leaders and also offered individual support as needed. The process leaders were established and practising members of staff, and also had considerable experience in teacher support and development work, and a knowledge of action research in theory and in practice.

The aims of the inquiry were:

- to explore approaches to mixed-ability teaching in communicative ELT classes;
- to explore the congruence between participants' beliefs and actions;
- to work within institutional opportunities and constraints;
- to adopt dialogue and reflection as central activities.

The inquiry was divided into in two phases: an introductory period of three weeks and a year of repeated action research cycles (for more on methods see Kemmis and McTaggart, 1982; McNiff, 1988). The purpose of the first three weeks was for participants to arrive at a common understanding of what action research was, and what mixed-ability teaching meant to them. For the inquiry itself, the group agreed a structure to give coherence to the work, the cycle summarised below.

Dialogue	Negotiate, select and describe the issue to be addressed.
Decision	Individual commitment to action in class.
Action	Teachers engaged in a range of activities in class (which included the adaptation of materials to differing levels within one class; carrying out learner training and learning-to-learn activities with students; the use of specified class-management strategies; observation of students in group activities; self-monitoring; peer observation).
Reflect	Write down descriptions; present and discuss descriptions and interpretations with group.
Evaluate	Observe the effects of strategies and materials, use evaluation instruments, draw conclusions.
Dialogue	Review the initial issue, revise the problem if necessary.

The team approach extended to an element of team teaching, and to peer observation by invitation. Encouraged by a process leader, the participants used structured observation and evaluation instruments to help focus their data collection (see also Open University, 1981; Wajnryb, 1993; Weir and Roberts, 1994). These were developed by the participants themselves, and seem to have served as a useful means to focus their thinking. Examples of their monitoring instruments appear in Appendix 8.3. The classroom behaviour checklist derived from the teachers' objectives in communicative teaching, in the context of mixed ability. Next to each point for observation they have left a space for comment, and a prompt to note the evidence on which judgment is based (see also section 1.1.4 on Lewin's view on the need for evidence). In Appendix 8.3 we see a group work observation form, which suggests the benefit for each teacher's thinking of designing such an instrument and then using it to focus their monitoring of learners. Appendix 8.3 also contains a self-evaluation form. The use of a form designed by oneself maintains one's autonomy and independence, whereas the imposition of a proforma from 'outside' inevitably constitutes its denial.

It would have been less consistent with the goals of action research (teacher autonomy and personal/professional development) to have used ready-made instruments, because the categories they contained may not have been appropriate to the teachers' purpose, and because the categories might have been based on assumptions and values that participants did not accept (section 5.3.4). Participants did not produce written reports, but did collect, present and interpret classroom data collaboratively, and pursued issues systematically.

Outcomes

The assessment of the effects of action research can be interpreted in terms of change in students. However, this project aimed to combine professional development and curricular development. Therefore pre- and post-measures were made of teachers' thinking by means of repertory grid technique to reflect the development of the participating teachers' thinking over the year (Linder, 1991; Belleli, 1993; Sendan 1995a).

The results suggested that by the end of the year teachers' thinking showed: less emphasis on language skills; greater emphasis on flexibility of task setting; and more emphasis on and acceptance of divergency of learning styles. Less formal indicators (interviews, observation and minutes of discussions) also suggested considerable changes in teachers' practice and thinking (for example, in coming to 'decouple' the concepts of individualisation and increased teacher workload).

Additionally, enabling 'process' benefits were noted, such as better monitoring skills (e.g. 'Now I am more observant of what is happening as a result of those activities' – Linder, 1991) and increased readiness to learn from colleagues. These outcomes are consistent with other teacher-as-researcher studies (e.g. Vulliamy and Webb, 1991; Roberts, 1993). The generally positive view

of the project is supported by the fact that the action research meetings continued into the following academic year, if less formally.

The above results suggest that the project had contributed to development in
the teachers' thinking. However, the nature and degree of change varied
according to the different starting points and concerns of individuals, for example between novice and experienced teachers.

Also, we should note that the benefits of action research lay in process (in the
form of developing social interactions and relationships) as well as product (in
the form of identifiable changes). As two participants observed:

> we all feel comfortable with the each other and do not feel that an expert,
> judgemental outsider's eye was upon us.

(Linder, 1991)

> The fact that we worked so closely as a team, entered each other's classes
> and learnt to be more specific and careful in our observations was a growing
> experience.

(Linder, 1991)

These insights confirm our adoption of a social constructivist framework in
INSET design, emphasising social process in teacher learning (section 1.1.5).

8.3.2   Discussion

If we accept that action research met the development needs of the school and
of these 10 teachers, it is important to identify some contributing contextual
factors, for two reasons.

First, one should never see action research (or any other teacher development activity) as being an all-purpose solution that can meet all teachers' learning needs. Other forms of INSET will be suitable for other teachers according
to their predispositions, interests, needs and context of work.

Second, should action research seem to be the best form of INSET in a given
setting, it is necessary to assess the balance of 'helping' and 'obstructing' factors
in the teachers' place of work to carry it through. Such an assessment might
indicate it to be necessary to develop the preconditions required to support
action research rather than to try to initiate projects at once.

The recognition of positive and negative conditions might also be very
important when introducing action research as part of an award-bearing course,
in that participants from different schools are likely to attempt the work under
varying conditions, with consequences in terms of stress, teacher support and
guidance needs, and the nature of the projects undertaken.

Ownership and collaboration

The decision to explore mixed-ability teaching in this school arose from a
pressing need felt by the teachers. The decision to adopt action research

procedures, and the structure they took, were discussed and agreed by participating teachers. Observation/feedback was done by peers, on negotiated terms.
The issues to be explored in successive cycles were also negotiated. We can
therefore recognise that these teachers had a high degree of ownership over
their own development, as defined in its strong sense of teacher control and
assumption of responsibility (rather than its occasional weaker interpretation of
teachers being successfully convinced of an idea by a higher authority).

Institutional climate

The school's political organisation was democratic and pluralist, devolving
responsibility for curricular issues to staff and offering them representation in
the making of school policy. Also, there was a long standing tradition among
staff of self-directed collaborative work, in the form of study groups. Both these
features provide a positive climate for collaborative action research. In contrast,
a highly authoritarian and centralised school regime would be unlikely to provide a conducive setting for self-directed teacher inquiry, since it would not be
able to countenance this form of 'power-sharing'. Similarly, in schools where
there is a culture of entrenched 'privatism', attempts to initiate collaborative
action research would have to be preceded by the development of appropriate
structures for staff dialogue. INSET structures are inseparable from the hierarchy and politics of the school (see also sections 7.4.1 and 8.6).

Process leaders

The availability of two process leaders enabled the negotiation of group
processes which led to agreed structures serving to focus and systematise discourse. Also, a 'division of labour' between those in a group focusing on personal and curriculum development, and those focusing on the process itself, can
be highly enabling.

Furthermore, 10 teachers of different backgrounds naturally had differing
needs, concerns and feelings at different points in the year, which were best met
flexibly by individual support. Indeed, the more effective the action research
process in encouraging change in teachers' thinking, the greater need for this type
of flexible individual support: 'if we accept that practitioners' own sense of self is
deeply embedded in their teaching it should not be surprising to us that they find
real change difficult to contemplate and accomplish' (Rudduck, 1988: 208).

Challenge

A significant criticism of action research has been that in their written reports
teachers often describe the application of their plans but fail to analyse the
assumptions underlying their practice and also fail to relate the specifics of
classroom events and outcomes they have described to wider theoretical or

political concerns (Griffiths and Tann, 1992; Elliot and Sarland, 1995). This lack of analysis and criticism tends to be reinforced by teacher 'privatism': a tendency in some school cultures to avoid questioning or challenging others in order to preserve the privacy of one's own practice (Vulliamy and Webb, 1991; Roberts, 1993).

In contrast, in the case described here, it seems that challenge between teachers was available, partly due to the traditions of the school, partly due to the presence of process leaders, and also due to the use of structured observation and evaluation techniques which allowed some objective information to be discussed and interpreted by the group (see Appendix 8.3 and section 1.1.4).

The process of monitoring one's class can be of great value in developing teachers' perspectives, but a critical eye often develops best when description is accompanied by challenge and critical interaction with peers. This appears to have taken place in this project, as reported by one of participating teachers:

> I am stepping aside more often and observing more carefully. As a result I am seeing some things I hadn't noticed before. I found that 'Y' wasn't really reading the assignment. I was able to find time to speak to him. He simply needed some help in overcoming some reading difficulties. The addition of more group assignments has really helped. . . . I am able to see what is going on more of the time.
>
> (Linder, 1991)

Time

The development of personal theories and the adjustment of classroom practices needs time. Change takes place in a gradual, accretive manner. Here, the time-scale and the repetition of systematic, focused action research cycles enabled an evolutionary development in teachers' thinking. As one participant said:

> Our staff has a common purpose and when we renewed our own deliberations our work and progress in our development increased. I have more and more consistently found that continuity of those small changes I attempted has become part of my classroom experience. Though in the past I have always enjoyed trying new techniques they were always sporadic. . . . I still have a problem of reaching the extremes, but more and more of the class seems truly involved in the learning.
>
> (Linder, 1991)

Endnote

There cannot be a separation between teachers' experiences in their own learning, and their approach to the learning of their students. In this case, the experience of democratic communication between teachers enhanced their appreciation of the value of communication between students, both in language and in more general terms. As Linder (1991: 68) puts it: 'collaborative undertakings of such a group can enhance (teachers') insights and understandings, acceptance and appreciation of differences (which contribute) toward enriching the group experience'.

Ultimately, the effectiveness of this project can be explained by the coherence between institutional values, its approach to the curriculum and the mode of INSET used. Collaborative action research was consistent with the implementation of a mixed-ability language curriculum as it derived from common values of autonomy and self-direction. Both were consistent with the ethos and political structure of the school.

The generalisation of teachers' personal learning to that of students, underpinned by a coherent set of values, is implied by a participant, whose voice ends this case study:

> Allowing for choice in assignments has become a regular practice now. At first some pupils (grade 10) resented this. But the class talked it over . . . and the resisters have really accepted this. Believe it or not! The revision of the work is more interesting and as a result they are listening more intently to each other, because they are not all 'chewing' the same sentences and materials again and again. And better listening means better learning, you know. They are really coming through.
>
> (Linder, 1991)

Connecting up

There seems to be a clear match between this case of teacher learning and our accounts of social constructivism (section 1.1.5) and evidence on effective INSET (2.6). Perhaps above all this account highlights the benefit for personal development of self-directed work in a social context of critical dialogue and personal support (Newell, 1996). The account shows the impossibility of abstracting a teacher's development from his or her context. It also shows that the organisation and climate of a school, so significant for its teachers' development, must be affected by its original mission, its ethos and its place within society at large.

8.4   Exploring a new curriculum: 'Teachers' Voices'[3]

8.4.1   Description

The National Centre for English Language Teaching and Research (NCELTR) action research project 'Investigating Course Design in a

[3] The author wishes to thank Anne Burns and Sue Hood for their extremely detailed comments on and improvements to an earlier draft.

Competency-based Curriculum' is fully reported and discussed in Burns and Hood (1994; 1995) and Burns (1995). This brief summary can only allude to the intense professional activity involved, and further reading is advised. Professional and curriculum development by means of action research is also discussed in section 2.6.3.

Context

The Australian Adult Migrant English Program (AMEP) is a nationwide English language programme funded by the Department of Immigration and Ethnic Affairs (DIEA), which has since been retitled DIM (M = Multicultural)A, and implemented by AMEP-funded teaching institutions in each state and territory. Some 1 500 teachers are employed to meet the language and settlement needs of immigrants in their first three years of residence.

In the 1980s, course design and implementation in AMEP was decentralised, with complete autonomy of teaching staff in all aspects of the curriculum. A collaborative action research orientation toward course development had become well established in the AMEP (e.g. Nunan, 1989; Brindley, 1990). The AMEP is a recognised site for innovative, learner-centred ELT curriculum development (e.g. Nunan, 1988).

Consistent with the Australian Government's public spending cuts from the late 1980s, and concomitant demands for accountability and targeted use of public money, the programme has been changed in significant respects: the scope of courses was limited; enrolment was restricted to 510 hours per learner; and attendance fees were introduced in some cases. Furthermore, in order to meet government demands for clear accountability and evidence of programme effectiveness most states adopted competency-based and accredited curriculum frameworks developed at the AMEP, most importantly by means of the introduction of the Certificate in Spoken and Written English in 1993 (Hagen *et al.*, 1993).

This established three target levels of language learning competency defined in terms of performance criteria and performance variables. This represented a fundamental change in the theoretical base and structure of the curriculum, and in the role of teachers in course design and implementation: while learners and teachers can still negotiate specific objectives, this is now done within the framework of competency-based outcomes. Thus, while a process orientation retains its importance, teachers now have to ensure that they negotiate their programmes within the new structure and aim to achieve certain required kinds of learning outcome.

There had been moves toward greater consistency and continuity in the AMEP curriculum from the late 1980s. The limitations of a pluralist and decentralised curriculum had been recognised: the duplication of course design activity; the lack of an explicit basis for teachers to plan, teach and assess learning; and the lack of continuity for learners moving from one centre to another.

In spite of these earlier changes, however, the major structural innovations of the early 1990s confronted many established teachers with complex personal, professional and ethical challenges, at the levels of:

- their immediate implementation concerns (of course design, method, use of class time);
- the potential discrepancy between their personal theories of teaching and those underlying the new curriculum;
- potential value conflict, as regards their own and learners' rights in educational processes. The competing interests as teachers saw them were also present in political, economic rationalist and industrial training influences.

The project

The one-year 'Teachers' Voices' project was initiated in 1993 by NCELTR at Macquarie University, with funding from the Commonwealth Department of Immigration and Multicultural Affairs (DIMA) and parallel to the introduction of the new Certificate.

DIMA provides funds for NCELTR Special Projects, which NCELTR is responsible for managing, conducting (often in collaboration with AMEP providers) and reporting. The selection of projects is determined by a collaborative process in which AMEP programmes across all states submit ideas within certain proposed general areas. A number of states suggested investigation of the implementation of the new Certificate, which led to the adoption of the action research project. Its purpose was to investigate the impact of the curriculum changes, notably the introduction of a competency-based Certificate, on teachers' course design and classroom practices.

The emerging pattern of collaboration is that, while individual researchers at state level still collaborate with NCELTR, there is a trend towards combinations of states being involved, with the role of NCELTR to provide input, management or principal researcher involvement. Hence 'Teachers' Voices' exemplified an external research project integrated with institutionally supported teacher-researcher activity (Hustler et al., 1986).

Such a design is not intended to be merely descriptive or noninterventionist in nature. The action research model required the participation of teachers in identifying key curricular issues; in developing adaptive teaching strategies; in recording their key curricular decisions and values underlying them; and helping to develop principles and guidelines for other teachers. The focus for the researchers lay in a study of how participating teachers interacted with and adapted to a new framework in which they were working towards the predetermined outcomes represented by the Certificate.

The adoption of action research rather than another design indicated the researchers' purpose to identify practical classroom issues at an early stage in the curriculum innovation process; to engage participating teachers in interpreting the curriculum framework in terms of their institutional settings; and to affirm and value the role of teachers in curriculum development through the use of their action research findings as formative evaluation data.

The participants in the project were:

- 30 teacher-researchers (from different centres across four states) given some paid release time for participation;
- four project co-ordinators (state curriculum support staff);
- two project leaders/researchers (Burns and Hood).

The project occurred in two phases. In the first phase (July–December 1993) there were two workshops in New South Wales (NSW). In the first, the 10 teachers from NSW were introduced to action research and its methodology. As it was difficult for them to come up with a research focus, they chose to develop a proforma to record their planning decisions and the course design strategies they tried out. Some then took on more focused studies which were supported further by Burns and Hood.

In the second workshop eight weeks later, teacher-researchers brought the data they had collected to discussions which helped to identify four broad categories of concern (the selection and sequencing of content; the integration of grammar teaching into task-based teaching; competency-based assessment; documenting learner responses to competency-based teaching). The NSW teachers' involvement then ceased. The ad hoc arrangement of these workshops reflected the need of support staff (Burns and Hood) to search out a workable model for open-ended, process-orientated TD, as opposed to more familiar product-orientated projects.

In the second phase (January–June 1994) Burns and Hood decided to take the four areas further and teachers from other states selected a focus to investigate within these areas. Realising the teachers' need for greater support, they supplemented their two workshops at the beginning and end of the project with the recruitment of local-level co-ordinators to provide workshop and other kinds of support. They also gave more direction to writing up. The process was and is at time of writing still evolving, perhaps towards clearer systems and support structures to enable teachers to carry through their research (Burns and Hood, forthcoming).

The core activities of the project were two main workshops for all participants run by Burns and Hood, who also liaised with state personnel. State personnel provided classroom-based support and/or laid on additional meetings for teachers. As each state-based organisation is quite different, different forms of support were organised but the lead researchers were kept informed throughout. Thus a diversity of group and individual interactions between teacher-researchers and support staff took place (Burns and Hood, 1995: 12–15). These are not easily summarised as roles and relationships evolved through the life of the project. We should note that project funds were committed to state-level personnel for their liaison time with teachers and local costs.

The four support staff in each state were in regular one-to-one contact with teacher-researchers to maintain and support their subsequent inquiries. Teacher-researchers further refined the issues to be explored, collected and analysed data obtained by a wide range of methods, and collaborated with learners and other teachers (Burns and Hood, 1995: 8).

Group discussions between researchers, teachers and support staff provided a critical opportunity for the development of teachers' personal theories and for collaborative work toward models for competency-based teaching. Furthermore, the group discussions represented the interface between the professional and curriculum development aspects of the project:

> At these meetings, the teachers offered critical insights on numerous aspects of classroom practice for which new teaching approaches were now required. Because of the systematic data collection they had undertaken, they were in a strong position to suggest practical solutions and recommendations which could be considered at an institutional level and could channel these through the local project coordinators and researchers.
>
> (Burns, 1995: 7)

The project culminated in the teacher-researchers writing up their inquiries on the four themes. Ten of these reports appear in Burns and Hood (1995) dealing with such topics as functional grammar in the classroom; integrated approaches to assessment; selecting and sequencing content; and learners' views of competency-based language learning.

Developments

The model employed in the 1993 project has been modified to provide a series of five workshops for each group, as two proved to be insufficient. The 1995 'Teachers' Voices 2: Teaching Disparate Learner Groups' (TDLG) project is to be reported in Burns and Hood (forthcoming). On the basis of this evolving model, a further project in 1996 – 'Integrating Action Research into Professional Development (PD)' – has involved state PD personnel who are conducting action research on the process of conducting state-level action research projects.

8.4.2 Discussion: some lessons

The project findings are notably rich and multilevel in nature, contrasted with more conventional research designs which tend to have a narrower focus (Burns and Hood, 1994; 1995). They are concerned with curriculum development theory; the characteristics of competency-based curricula; teachers' interaction with and navigation through innovative curricula; the impact upon teachers of participation in action research; and the necessary conditions to support action research. Findings of special relevance to this book relate to action research as a form of professional development and to the development of teachers' personal theories while experiencing the implementation of an innovative curriculum framework (section 2.6.3).

Specific curriculum implementation changes that have been identified in the research include:

- teachers are now far more inclined to record their course planning and develop programmes systematically;
- a greater balance between learner-centredness and teacher-centredness, with more explicit intervention in the learning process when the need is exhibited by learners;
- a greater focus on teaching the four 'macro-skills' in an integrated way (in part a 'backwash' effect of the new Certificate);
- a greater focus on the text-based and functional teaching of grammar;
- a strong focus on assessment, including debate on issues of practical design, validity, reliability and moderation;
- learners are now able to work within better systems of progression, assessments of progress and certification of achievement.

Feedback

Action research will contribute to both curriculum and teacher development only if there are mechanisms for it to influence curricular policy. Teachers' classroom-based research is made meaningful by its contribution to development decisions, which is determined by the original design of curriculum research projects. As Day argued:

projects should lead to . . . an actual change . . .

project teams should be deliberately and clearly linked to the normal . . . processes and bodies which . . . 'manage' curriculum maintenance and review . . .

(Day, 1990: 215)

In the case of 'Teachers' Voices', the project was given strong support by key staff at state level, such as the professional development units. These staff were also consulted on changes needed in the Certificate as it came up for re-accreditation in 1995. In this way project findings could be fed into the major institutional systems at national level from those participating states. Additionally, one researcher was closely involved in the development of the original Certificate – monitoring its implementation – and in changes made in 1995. Hence information provided by the project on how teachers were working with the Certificate was seen as a very important mechanism for its improvement.

Supporting action research

Action research is recognised as presenting teacher-researchers with consider-able practical difficulties. Conditions are proposed by Burns and Hood (1995) in order to enhance teacher participation (section 2.6.5), which in summary are:

- provide input on action research processes and methods;
- data collection methods should be part of usual teaching activities, not an additional burden;
- provide institutional support (time, payment);
- integrate action research with other institutional teacher development activities;
- enable interaction and collaboration with other teachers and researchers;
- make participation voluntary but encourage wider involvement of other teachers;
- give support and guidance at the writing-up stage;
- enable teachers' presentation of their research to wider audiences.

To this we may add a revised action research model currently being explored in the TDLG project. These conditions indicate that the individual efforts of a teacher-researcher should take place within a system of guidance, support and interaction in order to optimise the developmental and curricular effects of action research (see also sections 8.2, 8.3, 8.5 and 8.6).

Teacher thinking

We view classroom behaviour as founded upon individual, systematic and dynamic personal theories which determine teachers' perceptions of learners, of curriculum objectives and of classroom events. A major finding of the AMEP study lay in the personal and evolutionary nature of teachers' interactions with the new curriculum framework:

> despite the introduction of a curriculum approach some have criticised as being behaviourist and reductionist . . . there was much evidence of the con-tinuity of a rich diversity of course design practices, in terms of the teachers' approaches, methods and content. Rather than being compromised the ideal of the 'negotiated, needs-based learner-centred curriculum' adopted in the AMEP in the 1980s appears to have been to different degrees reconcep-tualised within a competency-based model.
>
> (Burns, 1995: 8)

Findings indicated that teachers' reactions to the new curriculum were highly diverse, according to their personal theories. This is consistent with a constructivist model of teacher thinking as relatively stable, evolutionary and dynamic in nature.

Connecting up

The 'Teachers' Voices' action research project provides us with an excellent example of institutionally supported action research which integrates professional and curriculum development. It indicates the need for ongoing and flexible institutional support when involving teachers in curriculum development. It also shows the need for teachers' curriculum inquiry to be a genuine part of their work, and for their insights to be seen to contribute to larger-scale change. It would seem to be highly consistent with our preferred framework for LTE (section 1.1.5) in that it highlights the exchange between individual development and its social context: positive relationships and opportunities for critical dialogue; and a consistent linkage between a person's work and the landscape in which it takes place. There are numerous consistencies with research evidence on effective INSET which the reader can assess for her/himself by reference to sections 2.6, 2.6.5 and Table 2.1.

8.5   Professional development in the Baltic States: the Professional Development Programme (PDP)[4]

The Professional Development Programme (PDP) was a two-year teacher development scheme for secondary-school teachers in the Baltic States, originally running from 1992–94. Its purpose was to set up an INSET network of regionally based support staff, with a team of 10 in each state (Estonia, Latvia and Lithuania). The notion of critical mass in innovation informed the decision to build teams of ten collaborating tutors in each country.

One British Council consultant, a UK national, in each country supported and advised these staff. Each team came together with the consultant once a month to devise materials and plan training sessions. They then returned to their regions to provide sessions (usually from one to four times a month).

The British Council (largely staffed by Baltic nationals) is intended to be a short-term partner whose present role ends once the INSET networks are firmly established.

PDP was complementary to existing structures. In Latvia there was a system of formal school inspection, and a Ministry INSET structure of regional teachers' associations and workshops. There were no subject advisers, however.

In the two years, the programme developed in popularity and importance. In the first year, about 1 000 teachers were involved in the three states, and after the second this rose to about 500 in Latvia alone. After the first phase of the project, which ended in 1994, the programme has evolved and diversified further. Different patterns have developed in each country. In Latvia a two-level scheme has emerged as newcomers to ELT and to PDP have joined it.

[4] The author thanks Karen Giblin and Chris Tribble (British Council, Baltic States) for their generous help and feedback.

At the time of writing we are able to offer a snapshot of a well-received programme undergoing development and diversification, focusing particularly on the Latvian PDP. Further information can be found in the PRODESS News Newsletter (3 November 1993) and also the IATEFL Newsletter (vol. 26, 1994).

From its outset, the programme was based on principles of teacher autonomy and partnership. Its design is also notable for its clear grasp on priorities and on practical needs. Its success can be related to the strengths of local staff and to the development of long-term constructive and collaborative relationships between tutors and the consultant, and tutors and teachers.

8.5.1 Description

The Baltic states (Latvia, Lithuania and Estonia) regained their independence with the collapse of the Soviet Union in spring 1990. Each state has a distinctive language and culture, but experience of independence has been limited to a period from 1918 to 1939.

From annexation by the Soviet Union in 1945 until 1990, the education system was centrally controlled from Moscow, administratively and in curricular matters. Teachers enjoyed secure employment, with good status and a stable future. However, they were isolated from international trends in EFL: the conventional approach to instruction was of English as a dead language, with the study of literature a priority rather than communication skills.

PDP was designed under a historically unique set of circumstances, with the almost overnight disappearance of comprehensive and highly ideological external control, and the equally sudden access of choice, travel opportunities, business contacts and other influences from the free-market West. As in other cases of rapid economic expansion, there has been a severe brain drain of qualified teachers to other employment, as state salaries lag behind those available in the private sector.

In terms of the English curriculum, teachers were confronted by a dramatic change in the goals of instruction, to meet a widespread demand for functional communication skills. New coursebooks were introduced, along with a skills-orientated English school-leaving exam. State-system teachers have thus become leading participants in a process of extraordinary change, which created a climate that was challenging and stimulating professionally and personally.

Design factors

The British Council was funded to provide input to programme design (in collaboration with national Ministries) and to provide one programme consultant per country. Funds were provided for three months' UK-based training for the 30 tutors. There were no funds for more expatriate consultants, for larger-scale training of tutors, nor for extensive physical resources. Hence the most practical option was to maximise the role of local staff.

Salient features among secondary-school teachers seem to have been:

- teachers were allowed a free choice of textbooks and had to write their own examinations;
- the former Soviet system provided well for INSET, based on the principle that all teachers should also be learners; however, attendance became voluntary rather than compulsory;
- most teachers were well trained (five-year degrees), with a self-perception as such;
- there was a tradition of working collectively rather than going it alone;
- tutors had experience of working in associations and groups, with a resulting awareness of what helps groups function, and an orientation to draw on peers rather than the outside expert;
- many teachers experienced a degree of insecurity in the face of the need for skill-based teaching;
- although they were not clear about the nature of the curriculum changes, most teachers were orientated to expect their own expertise to guide them;
- most teachers were experienced and well established in their schools, with a thorough knowledge of the existing curriculum and school conditions;
- most lacked any knowledge of worldwide EFL developments, particularly in teaching for communication, and perceived this in themselves;
- tutors were already well versed in psychological theory and familiar with humanistic principles of collaboration and autonomous development.

A decentralised model was chosen to use the skills and knowledge of local teachers, and to build a network based on the internal strengths of the system. Thus, the design did not pursue centrally determined curricular objectives and so did not opt for such designs as a cascade model, or a full-time 'master trainer' staff. A partnership approach was appropriate because of the professional capabilities of the 10 tutors: any notion of imposition or dependency would have been inappropriate. Above all, the design was a response to the Latvia of 1992.

Design: summary

Latvia	*Lithuania*	*Estonia*
Ministry	Ministry	Ministry
Consultant	Consultant	Consultant
Meet one day per month		
10 tutors	10 tutors	10 tutors
15/20 teachers		
Meeting 3 hours ×		
1–4 groups per month		

At the start of the programme, the prime need was for skills training packages and for teaching materials. The provision of materials enabled teachers to implement the new curricular goals, and provided them with concrete examples of a communicative curriculum.

The project set up a decentralised network of tutors (10 per country), who were secondary-school teachers on paid day release. Their role was to offer three-hour courses and workshops, run in conveniently located schools. The teachers chosen were in the main senior and experienced staff.

The 30 tutors (15 in 1992, 15 in 1993) were selected by open application, and attended a three-month course in England (at the Bell College, Saffron Walden) the content of which was based on their perceived immediate needs. These focused on understanding skills teaching, and the collation of materials packages for teachers at home to complement the existing syllabus. On return, their first task was to set up local workshops based on these materials. Thus the first packages were produced in the UK, with subsequent production by means of monthly meetings in country.

All teaching in Latvian secondary schools was based on morning and afternoon shifts, consisting of 18×45-minute classes per shift. Tutors changed to a four-day-a-week school timetable, with release for the other day. They had a normal salary and received additional payment per group and per workshop day at a rate proportional to their normal salaries.

Head teachers had to give permission for tutors' release, but most were ready to do so to ensure that they retained such experienced and effective staff. Also, the power of head teachers was balanced in the system by other groups (e.g. a Faculty group in school and regional educational groups outside school).

The tutors' team meetings

Tutors met the consultant monthly to review and plan their activities. These discussions also allowed teachers' reactions and concerns to be known centrally, a valuable feedback loop from regions to the centre.

However, it is their function as a means of support and development which is of special importance to this description. The initial purpose of the meetings was to work jointly on the preparation of teacher training packages/resource materials. Draft packages would be brought in, discussed and worked on. Also, a resource library was developed.

Over the three years, as teachers' needs developed, the role of the tutors also changed. They shifted from offering workshops in their regions in lock step to diversifying topics, and also began to prepare for workshops with more open-ended objectives (see also following section on Option 1 and Option 2 workshops).

While the 1994+ Option 1 workshops continued in more or less the same style as before, Option 2 workshops required a different style, characterised by passing the responsibility for workshop content over teachers (within an agreed theme) and working towards process-orientated objectives. Appendix 8.4

contains an example of an Option 2 two-stage workshop: the first stage is more open ended than an Option 1, and the second stage asks teachers to discuss their experience of trying out projects of different kinds.

This shift in role, from tutor-led to something more open ended was not easy for tutors to achieve: it was unfamiliar and potentially more risky. It took confidence and experience of similar working within the tutor support team itself for them to be able to take on a more facilitative and process-focused role.

Diversification and development

Since 1992, there seems to have been an increasingly strong take-up of the programme by teachers so that a typical tutor would (at the time of writing) be involved in monthly contact with between 20 and 80 teachers. The generally positive teacher response is nicely represented in this Estonian teacher's comments:

> I've attended three courses on methods and now feel much more at ease in front of the class, because I know much more about what's happening in the world and the world is coming into even our tiny school and that makes me feel much more comfortable . . . life is changing very rapidly and you must keep up with it. I think that a teacher must study throughout her life to improve.
>
> (Ellis, 1994: 7–8)

The popularity of the programme has led to increasing diversification. For example, the shortage of qualified teachers in Estonia has led to a demand for bilingual teaching materials. In Latvia, novice teachers tend to request survival materials, while experienced teachers have shown more interest in curriculum theory.

After 1994

The project ended in 1994, but it was decided that it should continue as long as it was helpful to teachers. On taking stock of the programme, tutors felt that it should be adapted to meet the needs of two distinct groups of teachers: those who had been attending from the start and were increasingly confident in implementing communicative goals; and teachers who were new to PDP and in some cases new to ELT, and so were unfamiliar with communicative theory and practice. It was decided to offer PDP at two levels, with teachers able to self-select.

In Option 1, for newcomers, a series of materials-based workshops was offered to introduce methodology, and provide supplementary materials. Its purpose was to offer teachers practical help, to provide a practical basis for their own theory-building, and to boost their confidence. Typical workshop topics would include: defining and exemplifying integrated skill teaching; reading skills; teaching grammar through games and songs; developing listening skills; using newspapers.

Option 2 aimed to deal with teaching and learning at a more theoretical level on a series of self-selected themes. The structure adopted for this was to hold two meetings two months apart. In the first meeting a theme would be identified and discussed, issues developed and classroom research tasks considered. In the second, teachers could report back their experience, insights and reflections. Issues explored have included: classroom management; listening skills; project work; and further uses of newspapers. Teachers wanted an informal structure within which they could direct their own activities, self-monitoring and reporting back in ways that suited them. This enabled teachers to explore their practice and personal theories without the requirement to follow an externally structured scheme. Appendix 8.4 illustrates the difference in style of Option 1 and Option 2 workshops. The first provides extensive materials, and direct experience of doing a project to develop teachers' understanding of a technique new to them. The second is based on a 'two–stage' structure, enabling personal trial and error in the interim and 'debriefing in the second session. Content derives from the concerns and inputs of the teachers themselves. The tutor's role therefore shifts from provider/demonstrator to process leader, on an equal footing with participants on pedagogic matters.

Tutors

There are number of indicators which suggest the strengthening of the network in Latvia (information on the other states was not available at time of writing). Four of the ten tutors have now obtained MA qualifications at the University of Latvia, in which their experience on PDP counted as credits towards the award, and in which their dissertations were all based on aspects of classroom research, the first in Latvia to do so. Then, few tutors have left the scheme, in spite of a serious brain drain of English teachers to other employment. It seems that the personal learning through PDP involvement has been a strong incentive to stay. Also, the tutors are now being called on for other professional activities, and have presented papers at international conferences. Finally, they are starting to give workshops/seminars to teachers of other languages such as Latvian and Russian, applying their ELT experience to teachers and learners of other languages.

In particular, the BC objective of 'working itself out of a job' seems to be taking place: local tutor training is taking place as new tutors enter the scheme; there is long-term Ministry support for its own INSET centre; and local tutors are replacing expatriates as presenters on non–PDP workshops.

The scheme

From an initial phase of working in lock step because of their need for peer support and joint preparation, tutors have moved to providing diversified sessions according to their own and teachers' interests.

An indication that the national network is becoming established is that it was chosen as the medium to disseminate information about Latvia's first central school-leaving exam, because its participants would provide quality feedback and it was the best available means of communication.

Teachers

About 70 per cent of participating teachers have attended Option 2 workshops. The numbers are stable and feedback suggests that their response to the two-stage workshops has been highly positive. It provides a framework for them to reflect on what they do in class, to try out small-scale classroom experiments, and exchange insights with peers. Applicants to Option 1 have been numerous and steadily increasing.

8.5.2 Discussion

Connecting up

Issues discussed in this section are closely related to our account of LTE approaches in section 1.1.5. Constructivist models of LTE are brought to bear on our discussion of cascade models, and in noting the programme's 'feet on the ground' recognition of teachers' needs as they evolve and change. The rest of the discussion, which is concerned with issues of social relationships and support, can be seen as reflecting a social constructivist perspective: of change as located within each individual but mediated and validated by others (section 1.1.5).

Feet on the ground

The PDP has been notable for its sense of what was possible and appropriate at different stages in its life. At first it recognised that skills packages and materials were the prime need and so the role of consultant was to support tutors in providing these. As tutors needed the confidence of shared preparation and decision-making, they began with lock step planning and preparation of workshop sessions, which was maintained until they became capable of more independent work.

Similarly, teachers involved in PDP shifted gradually from needs for materials and practical survival to a concern for the principles underlying materials, and a readiness to explore classroom issues. PDP seems to have observed the principle of 'working from where the teachers are' throughout the scheme.

Also, the PDP worked with the existing strengths in the system, such as optimising the role of experienced and knowledgeable tutors.

A jacuzzi not a cascade!

In Karen Giblin's wonderful metaphor, she likened the tutors' meetings to a jacuzzi, in that each person contributed to a group process, rather than a cascade, in which a central training message is passed on to an inner group, who then go out and pass the message on to others, who then pass it on to others. The logic of a cascade model is that it is highly cost-efficient: expertise from the centre can be transferred out to large numbers of teachers very cheaply.

The problem with a cascade model is that it assumes that each receiver/disseminator is a neutral vessel which has no effect on its content. Constructivist theory tells us that, on the contrary, each receiver filters and interprets input according to personal expectations and assumptions. What is called a washing-out process by some (i.e. the gradual loss of the original 'message' as it is transmitted further down the line) is in fact an inevitable process of reconstruction by each participant of the chain of communication.

A cascade model is based on the assumption that knowledge relevant to teaching can be transmitted from a centre to the periphery, that its transmitters will not affect that knowledge, nor will the manner and social processes involved in its transmission affect the meaning of the message. All these assumptions are highly questionable. Therefore, cascade may work if the message is strictly informational (for example about a new exam) but is liable not to work as intended if the message involves new practices based on new assumptions, theory and values.

Experiential learning theory also tells us that it is only through direct personal experience that we can truly personalise general propositions about teaching. The problem with a cascade training programme can be that the nature of the experience offered the training staff in receiving their messages may either a) be very brief or b) be at odds with the message they are trying to disseminate (for example to be given a formal and theoretical introduction to the value of interactive skills-focused language teaching). Furthermore, experiences will only contribute to attitudinal development if they are analysed, reflected upon, and also if relevant personal theories are uncovered, otherwise the experience itself may be interpreted in a manner consistent with the beliefs of the receiver and at odds with the assumptions underlying the message. For example, an experience of a communicative exercise might be interpreted by an authoritarian teacher as a mere game to be tacked on to normal teaching, or even may be perceived as a teacher-led procedure. The collaborative and progressively more issues-based and open-ended work of the team appears to have provided an experiential correlate to another way of working. In other words, their personal knowledge of a 'jacuzzi' collaborative work style enabled them to employ it with teachers in the workshops.

Long-term relationships

The ten tutors and the consultant met every month for several years. This provided a long-term social context for mutual support and development, as well as providing an experiential equivalent to the tutor's own interactions with teachers.

Teacher and tutor learning are not a matter of the sudden conversion, the instant acquisition of new competencies. It is gradual and evolutionary. It is supported by long-term, trusting relationships and talk. It depends on a combination of practice, trial and error, access to public theory, the perspectives of others, private reflection and . . . talk! It is social process and social interaction, allied to exposure to public theories and reflection, which affect practice and personal theory development (Fullan, 1982; Thatcher, 1990; see also section 1.1.5).

The right climate

The PDP's apparent success suggests that a wider social climate of change and development provides a positive impetus to teacher development. Better-resourced systems may experience far less teacher commitment and participation in development activities, because there is no wider climate of change, whether this is at a broad political and social level, or in the development of the curriculum.

A further helping factor, which applies in many other systems, has been the high status of English teaching in schools. In Latvia, English competence is highly valued, and ELT is seen as a trailblazer in its methodology, offering a lead to other subjects. This gives value to the day-to-day work of the person, and enhances their motivation to attend seriously to occupational affairs.

Head teacher support

Salary and accommodation costs have been kept to the minimum in PDP. The main costs, apart from tutor salary replacement and consultant salaries, are for travel. Such a low-cost scheme depends on the release of staff and the use of school buildings. For this to be possible, there has to be proper negotiation with head teachers. As in other INSET schemes drawing on experienced and effective teachers, practical head teacher support is a prerequisite for effectiveness.

Peer relationships

In INSET there are great advantages in deploying part-time tutors drawn from the classroom rather than full-time master trainer staff. They remain in touch with the classroom, whose complexities and compromises can be so quickly forgotten. Also, teacher-tutors are more likely to form collaborative and power-equal relationships with teachers than are full-time staff, who may be perceived as further up in the hierarchy than the teachers themselves.

In Latvia, a system of inspection runs parallel to PDP, so releasing tutors from any inspectorial functions. This is far preferable to the situation in many other systems, where staff roles combine INSET with inspection duties. The dual function of trying to serve the needs of the system on one hand (quality control) and the teachers on the other (development and support) is widely recognised as dysfunctional: it often inhibits teachers from disclosing concerns derived from their own perceived weaknesses and difficulties, inhibits teacher participation, and tends to push participants into fixed sender and receiver roles.

Endnote

We have only been able to present a snapshot of the PDP at one point in its development. It demonstrates a low-cost and contextually appropriate structure, an alternative to centralised and top-down models of INSET. It relies on open and collaborative relationships between consultants and tutors, and between tutors and teachers. It requires an appropriate cyclic structure enabling long-term social contact and adaptation to changing needs. Such decentralised activity, however, needs constant monitoring, maintenance and ongoing support of front-line staff: providers need support as their role evolves and their own learning progresses.

8.6   Preventive approaches to disruption (PAD): a training resource pack

Preventive Approaches to Disruption (PAD) is a training resource pack designed for on-site use by secondary-school teachers. It has also been used by some universities in initial training programmes. The title is rather misleading because the material emphasises positive teacher strategies, not control and punishment. 'Student Involvement by Better Teaching' would be more appropriate. The premise of the material is that much 'off-task' and undisciplined student behaviour can be remedied by changes in the ethos and curriculum of schools and the attitudes and performance of teachers. Its need arose from the failure of many ITE programmes to prepare student-teachers in management and control strategies, and from the priority given control issues by practising teachers in English secondary schools.

A detailed description of PAD is presented for four reasons:

- it illustrates the principle of 'concerted' learning activities, which derives from the social constructivist view we argue in section 1.1.5;
- it shows how adult learning principles can be applied to structured training materials;
- it shows that it is possible to meet both training and development needs by providing input on classroom strategies while offering teachers self-direction, choice and opportunities for reflection;
- it demonstrates the crucial importance of process and collaborative relationships in teacher development.

The pack is for use by a cross-disciplinary, collaborative group of teachers, preferably of about six to eight, led by a tutor-process leader whose role is to organise, facilitate and sustain activity. The tutor would normally be chosen from school staff. PAD is not prescriptive in content or structure. It contains a wide choice of classroom strategies which are presented as a menu of possibilities, from which teachers choose what to try out in their classes. The focus is on teachers managing their own learning. In structure, PAD is designed with maximum flexibility so that tutors can choose from it by negotiating with the group. Significantly, its publishers have produced the pack as a loose-leaf file with copyright waived for handouts.

The materials

Principles

The material is based on some general principles which should be understood by users from the outset. They are:

- disruptive pupils are not disruptive all the time;
- the behaviour of pupils is influenced by the teacher's behaviour;
- 'prevention is better than cure': disruptive behaviour can be anticipated and avoided;
- effective teachers acquire strategies to avoid or de-escalate unacceptable behaviour;
- effective classroom management strategies can be identified;
- these strategies can be practised and acquired by teachers;
- teachers learn best through on-site collaboration with peers, but with support and access to expertise;
- teachers learn through changes in both their attitudes and their performance;
- adult learning principles can be built into training materials.

Organisation of materials

PAD consists of eight sections, in which units 1–4 provide core course input (study material and activities are summarised in Table 8.3). Unit 1 lays the ground for effective teamwork in using units 2–4. This is done by establishing principles of group communication.

The study materials (letter coded) are short handouts using plain non-academic English for the input of ideas and techniques. They are designed to be read in about 15 minutes between sessions, so relieving the tutor from an input or lecturing function. The related activities offer a set of related experiences intended to enable cognitive and behavioural change. Each activity is accompanied by handling notes for the tutor. Activities aim to promote development at

Table 8.3 Structure of PAD (Chisholm *et al.*, 1986)

Section		Content
Introduction		Assumptions, content and uses
Guidelines for tutors		How to plan, run and evaluate the INSET course
Unit 1:	Using PAD in school Study materials A–H 5 related activities	Starting the course: orientation, ground rules, team-building, introduction of activities
Unit 2:	Nonverbal communication Study materials I+J 13 related activities	Strategies to avoid disruption and promote on-task behaviour by students
Unit 3:	Lesson organisation Study material K 9 related activities	Strategies to avoid disruption and promote on-task behaviour by students
Unit 4:	The management of pupils Study material L–O 28 related activities	Strategies to avoid disruption and promote on-task behaviour by students
Unit 5:	The observation guides Study material P 1 related activity	Instruments for use in paired observation when teachers try out strategies from units 2–4
Unit 6:	Developing teaching skills Study material Q+R 3 related activities	For teachers wishing to plan and carry out further, more detailed teaching skill development, using strategies from units 2–4

the levels of *awareness raising* of classroom issues, the *recognition* of ways that strategies can influence students' behaviour, and the facilitation of *behaviour change* by teachers applying skills to their own classes (Table 8.4).

These activity types are consistent with the components of the cycle suggested in Box 4.3, and are also consistent with a broadly social constructivist approach (section 1.1.5). Access to new information is provided by short readings. Personalisation, interpretation and linkage to the teacher's own context of work is promoted by activities K.1 (private reflection) and K.2 (discussion). Behaviour change is supported by observation, role-play and structured classroom experiment (K.4). The element of dialogue is provided in the discussion of readings and the video, and in planning for and then debriefing the classroom experiment.

Readings	access to general theory (readings, lectures).
Awareness	activities to raise the learner-teachers' awareness of her past experiences, and current beliefs, practice and knowledge;

opportunities to discuss the social pressures affecting personal practice;

opportunities to reflect on these inputs and experiences in order to develop one's personal theories (by means of discussion and private reflective writing).

Recognition   observation and analysis of examples of teaching.

Behaviour   teaching: skill practice
experiment in skill application
problem-solving.

Table 8.4   Related activities in PAD (Chisholm *et al.*, 1986)

Level of activity	Types of activity	Sample unit 3
AWARENESS	Reflective exercise (alone, between sessions)	K.1
	Paired/group discussion	K.2
	Questionnaire of pupils' views	K.3
RECOGNITION	Observation (video)	K.5–9
	Role play (rehearsal of strategies)	
	Simulation (rehearsal of strategies)	
	Paired observation (recognition and classification tasks)	Unit 6
BEHAVIOUR	Small-scale behaviour change	K.4
	Long-term skills development	Unit 6

Team-building and ground rules (Unit 1)

In changing their practice, teachers cannot be expected to go it alone, nor can they be expected to disclose their weaknesses, successes or failures to peers who may be uninterested, competitive or even destructive in attitude. A collaborative team provides the trusting and supportive relationships necessary to enable personal change. It is essential to negotiate and maintain certain ground rules for a support group to work effectively. Therefore, study materials in this unit include: ground rules for the group, features of effective listening, acknowledging positives in yourself and others, and giving and receiving feedback constructively.

Ground rules are needed because teachers are accustomed to the control of classroom discourse, and may not necessarily take easily to the responsibilities of collaborative group activity (see Appendix 8.5). Learning to listen constructively and to give and receive feedback are prerequisites to any successful collaborative activity. Ground rules also protect the autonomy of individuals, by the adoption of conventions applying to all, including the right of participants to 'pass' an activity they are unhappy with. The process-leading skills of the tutor are very important in the effectiveness of PAD.

The introduction of a PAD course

PAD could be introduced in a top-down manner, by senior staff deciding the content, timing and participants. However, PAD is far more suited to negotiated or self-directed adoption. This could be through senior staff informing all teachers about the opportunity to participate in a PAD course, inviting some and allowing volunteers to attend, and then consulting with them on the aims and objectives of the course. Alternatively, a group of teachers could run PAD on a self-help basis, with a rotating tutor.

However it is initiated, it should be seen as part of the school's staff-development programme, not as a fringe activity. It should be supported by senior staff, part of whose responsibilities are to ensure that the necessary resources and timetable arrangements are made to enable the course to run effectively. It would also be desirable for them to arrange for tutor induction and training sessions, since the characteristics of the tutor are so crucial to making PAD work as intended.

Before embarking on the course, it is necessary to negotiate with participants on its duration, location and timing to ensure that they can participate without seriously compromising other aspects of their work or private time.

Summary of a sample unit: unit 3 'Lesson Organisation': study material K, activities K.1–K.9

Sequencing

The sequence of activities (see summary in Table 8.4) can be varied according to the needs of the group. For example, the questionnaire activity (K.3) might be dropped or deferred and observation activities (K.5–K.9) might be introduced early on to resolve different interpretations of the study material. The order is decided by group discussion.

The study material

Summary

Research findings on eight general features of a well-organised lesson are summarised in two pages to be read between sessions, for example:

5. Vigilance
a A constant overview of the class was kept during the lesson
b Teachers were aware of what individual pupils were doing in the lesson
c Intervention was prompt when problems arose

The research summary is followed by 12 helpful tips from experienced teachers, for example:

1. Control the pupils' entry to the classroom . . .
6. Start the lesson with a 'bang' and sustain interest and curiosity

Comments

- The material is short enough for a busy teacher to read between sessions.
- Plain English is used.
- Research and craft knowledge are included on an equal footing.
- Readings release the course tutor from the role of lecturer or 'authority figure'.
- Criticism of the study material is not confused with criticism of the tutor.

K.1   Reflective activity

Summary

After the reading, teachers are asked to give about 20 minutes to a private reflective activity which invites them to think critically about the content of the reading, and to reflect on their current practice relevant to the input (Appendix 8.5.).

Comments

- Teachers are encouraged to criticise the input.
- Teachers are asked to reflect on their current classroom strategies. Much teacher classroom behaviour is, necessarily, automated, deriving from a rationale which may be implicit rather than fully articulated. These automated actions and implicit theories should be made explicit as a prerequisite to change (Shulman, 1988; Griffiths and Tann, 1992). However, the material does not challenge teachers to justify these strategies, nor to contrast them with those in the reading, nor to disclose them as problems.
- The content of these reflections remains private to the teacher, to be disclosed if they wish.

K.2   Group discussion

Summary

The tutor takes five minutes to summarise the reading and then chairs the discussion. In larger groups, paired discussion may precede a full group discussion.

The questions in K.2 (Appendix 8.5) focus discussion on participants' views and experiences. They refer to the validity of the study material; its relevance to different kinds of teachers; the strengths and weaknesses of participants' own training; their personal practical tips; constraints which might prevent them from giving well-managed classes; special characteristics of their subject; constraints and opportunities presented by the organisation of their school.

Comments

- Teachers are able to approach the issue from a variety of angles, so optimising personal relevance.
- Teachers can begin to articulate and clarify their current personal theories.
- Ground rules ensure that equal value is given to each teachers' views by constructive listening and structured discussion.
- The contrasting perspectives and experiences of others are available.
- Teachers can consider the relevance and appropriacy of the menu of proposed strategies to their own context.
- The discussion is not expected to have a product, but is structured by the questions and the tutor acting as chair.
- Paired discussion ensures time for self-expression and attention, and may give less outgoing teachers a chance to formulate their ideas in what they may find a safer situation.
- The 'agenda' suggested by the questions in K.2 reflects an exchange between individual perspectives, dialogue and an awareness of links between context and personal practice (see also section 1.1.5).

K.3   Questionnaire of pupil views

Summary

Questionnaires and collation forms are provided to obtain pupils' views on good lesson organisation and effective teaching. Participants can choose whether to elicit their pupils' views or not. The collated results from different classes are compared and their implications for classroom practice discussed (in pairs or groups).

Comments

- The exercise has the potential to upset participants' preconceptions about their pupils' views.
- The activity presents pupils as critical participants in their own learning, a role which the group may not have conceived of before.
- Both activities may face participants with surprises, which can challenge their current personal theories and stimulate some rethinking.

K.5–K.9   Observation

Summary

Each of the five observation activities involves viewing two short video sequences. These are of two teachers in surprisingly convincing simulated teaching episodes, focusing on the strategies covered in the unit. Each teacher displays both some positive and some negative strategies in the episode. Observers use a simple instrument on which to note comments on the teachers' performance of each strategy (see Appendix 8.5). After viewing, comments are collated by the tutor on an OHP acetate and then discussed. Alternatives to negative strategies can also be suggested.

Comments

- Participants are helped to relate study materials to concrete exemplars so as to clarify their understanding of the strategies.
- Concrete cases provide a good basis for discussion since they resolve differing interpretations of what strategies actually are.
- Instead of model 'super-teachers', examples are shown of teachers who are a human mix of strengths and weaknesses. This frees teachers from comparing themselves with perfect models which they could never attain. For many years, ELT teachers have suffered from training in which they are presented with artificially perfect native-speaker teaching models, which set unrealistically high expectations.

K.4   Making changes in lesson organisation

Summary

In this critical phase, teachers are invited to try out a change in classroom management from the menu offered by the input and discussion. K.4 offers them a framework to plan and evaluate experimental lessons with support and feedback from peers (see Appendix 8.5). Teachers choose the content, scope and context of the experiment (side 1). A proforma is also provided for reflections to be noted and used in paired discussion in planning (side 1) and in debriefing (side 2). The purpose of side 2 is to focus the teacher's attention before and during their trial lesson. It provides a common structure for teachers at the 'debriefing' stage. It also supports private reflection, in that considerable preparatory thinking has to go into debriefing colleagues. The opportunity to discuss an experiment with colleagues is a critically important stage in the material. It reflects the need for social exchange as an element in teacher development. At the feedback stage, two important interpretations of the process that the tutor is encouraged to make (suggested in the tutor notes) are:

a) participants should not expect a large immediate change in students' behaviour as a result of a short-term change in their lesson organisation;

b) a more in-depth review of lesson organisation can be enabled by the use of a unit 5 observation guide, either for individual retrospection, or for paired observation.

Comments

- This activity represents the crucial bridge from awareness and skill-recognition activities to the attempt to change teaching strategies. In process, it has a lot in common with 'action learning' structures (McGill and Beaty, 1992) in that the content and process of the change is controlled by each individual, but the group offers structure: support, feedback and an expectation that the agreement to try out strategies will be honoured (Lewin, 1946; Kemmis, 1982).
- The exercise of choice protects the autonomy of each teacher.
- Teachers will only try changes they can cope with. Quite possibly the first trials will be quite small-scale and safe in nature, to avoid discouraging large-scale disasters which could also damage the teacher's confidence and credibility with pupils.
- In some other INSET activities, teachers may be forced to attempt behaviourial changes that they have not chosen, to students they may not wish to try them on, possibly with an audience whose reactions may be quite negative or competitive in nature: altogether a very poor context in which to take risks.
- The activity is modelled on the way teachers naturally introduce changes in their practice: progressively and by trial and error.
- The teacher is committed to monitoring and reporting back to colleagues, a powerful motivation to take the exercise seriously and see it through.
- The need to report back is likely to make monitoring more systematic and reflection more articulated than if there were no audience.
- The debriefing and feedback activity is made as safe and private as possible, as we can assume that in paired discussion teachers will seek out a colleague they trust.
- The activity is designed to boost confidence in attempting changes and discussing them with others, which can lay the ground for further development.
- Learning derives from the teachers' self-monitoring and self-evaluation, enriched by the perspectives of colleagues. Ultimately, self-monitoring is the only possible basis for long-term change because feedback from others, while possibly contributing to a change in perspective, can only be a brief intervention in the teacher's experience of teaching and may not fit the teacher's personal theories.

- Further self-monitoring is enabled by the observation guides, including the introduction of peer observation. Peer observation in this design avoids a quality control form of observation by the teacher's choice of who observes, and by the use of a structured observation guide.
- A similar strategy of collaborative planning, trial and reporting back is reported by Tilinca (1996a), working without the framework of a training package.

Connecting up

PAD integrates the social, cognitive and behavioural faces of teacher development. The implementation of new strategies (derived from research and good practice) is done by teachers who self-direct and self-evaluate the changes, in the context of supportive group relationships.

In Table 8.5 we restate adult learning principles (section 2.6) and suggest how PAD addresses them. Individual variation (Table 8.5: 1, 2) is addressed in the tutor guidelines, which emphasise the need to negotiate key aspects of the course with participants, particularly priorities in content and the timing and location of sessions. Autonomy (3) is maintained by the control participants have over access to the classrooms (K.5) and control over changes (K.4). The evolutionary nature of teacher change (7) is addressed by the teacher's control over the scale and nature of changes they will try out. Social and emotional needs (4–6) are met by the adoption of group ground rules, and extensive opportunities for discussion, much in pairs. The need for private reflection on one's practice, past and beliefs, as relevant to the input of new ideas (8–10), is met by private reflection which is enhanced by discussion (K.1+K.2). The need for challenge or surprise to stimulate rethinking (11) is met in the questionnaire activity, which may uncover unexpected pupil perceptions. The integration of such personal and social dimensions is also consistent with our preferred framework for LTE (section 1.1.5).

Apart from 'content' changes in teachers' knowledge and use of strategies, there can be powerful 'process' outcomes that enable further independent development. These include the acquisition of attitudes and skills developed by the experience of taking part in a support group that can be applied to other contexts; the possible continuation of the group for other purposes; and the use of peer observation for other purposes. Some participants may move on from PAD to more formal action research, by retaining its framework of collaboration and self-directed monitoring while investigating other features of the curriculum.

The process aspects of PAD are, for our purposes here, perhaps more important than its content. Teacher autonomy and self-direction make for comfortable slogans, but to achieve them there is a need for consistent and theoretically coherent intervention by school administration and by tutors, beginning with

Table 8.5 INSET principles and design in PAD

Adult learning principle	Feature of materials
1 Teachers' needs vary	Negotiation and choice in content (tutor guidelines)
2 Teachers' personal theories vary	Negotiation and choice in content (tutor guidelines)
3 Teachers need a sense of autonomy and control in changing their practice	Teacher controls what strategy to try, when and with which group (K.4)
4 Self-disclosure of difficulties, and countenancing change are potentially painful	Tutor training and group guidelines designed to develop the learning group as a support group (unit 1)
5 Teachers need support during change	Tutor training and group guidelines designed to develop the learning group as a support group (unit 1, K.4)
6 The development of trusting and collaborative relations with others supports change	Tutor training and group guidelines designed to develop the learning group as a support group (unit 1, K.4)
7 Teachers introduce change on a trial-and-error basis	Materials focus on small-scale changes open to group discussion (K.4)
8 Opportunities for private reflection needed, on new ideas, on personal experiences, and on their links to one's beliefs and past	Reflection on input (K.1) Reflection on experience and context (K.2)
9 Awareness of one's own current practice and thinking is a prerequisite to change in perspectives and behaviour	Awareness activities include reflection on current thinking and context (K.1, K.2)
10 Dialogue is an essential part of change	Negotiation of ground rules Discussion tasks K.2 Reporting back K.4
11 Challenge or surprise needed to stimulate the rethinking of assumptions	Potentially present in dialogue Potentially present in results of eliciting learner perceptions relevant to input (K.3)

the way in which a PAD course is introduced into a school's INSET programme, and throughout its planning and implementation.

The structure of the PAD package provides a good model for LTE design: cycles of activity which relate the integration of input in accessible form, private critical reflection, discussion, skill recognition, and practical experiment controlled by the teacher.

8.7   How teachers learn: a summary

From skill learning (sections 1.1.1, 2.4.4)

- Teaching skills will be integrated into a personal repertoire under certain conditions: if training is consistent with classroom conditions; if there is a sufficient amount of demonstration, practice, application and feedback; if diverse learning task types are used; and if the principles underpinning methods are understood.
- Practices that are inconsistent with a teachers' assumptions and beliefs will tend either to be modified until they fit or not be taken up at all.

From experiential learning theory (section 1.1.3)

- Each of us personalises public knowledge through our experience, an interaction between private experiences and shared public knowledge.
- Personal knowing is built from complementary sources: direct experience of real-life incidents; watching and talking to others; the written word. There is no inherent priority of one means over any other: all contribute to learning.

From constructivist psychology (section 1.1.3)

- The location of teacher learning is within: it is determined by each person's developing perception of herself as teacher, the teacher she is now and the teacher she wants to be.
- Input (e.g. models of teaching, theories of language learning) is essential in learning to teach, but it is filtered and personalised by each learner-teacher.
- Personal theories (about ourselves as teachers and about the nature of classrooms) develop in a complex, evolutionary manner in response to incidents and experiences in our working life.
- Our personal theories change as they are either confirmed or challenged by the reactions of others. It is for this reason that individual beliefs are orientated by social norms.
- Very often shocks and surprises are needed for us to rethink our personal theories; change in assumptions will arise when we experience a gap between what we hope to achieve and what we are achieving in class; or between what we think is going on and what we find is actually the case: the confrontation of discrepancy is the starting point for change.

- Self-awareness (uncovering personal theories) is a prerequisite to change in established patterns of perception and behaviour.
- Deep change in teachers will be accompanied by strong feelings, not all necessarily negative, but in need of expression and acceptance by others.
- Providers need to understand how teachers and learners perceive their own experiences; the attainment of sociality is a condition for effective provider work.

From theories of expertise in teaching (Chapter 1)

- Teaching requires the orchestration of different types of knowledge.
- The diverse knowledge bases of teaching imply varied activity types in an LTE curriculum.
- Becoming a teacher requires first-hand trial-and-error experience which is interpreted and then generalised by means of deliberation and dialogue with others.
- One aspect of language teachers' expertise is procedural: to develop smooth classroom routines which free us up to monitor learners and think ahead.
- A complementary aspect of expertise is deliberative: to deal with teaching problems by considering the widest range of relevant variables; by drawing on our recall of comparable events; and by monitoring our own performance and assumptions.

From a social perspective (Chapters 2 and 3)

- Teaching is a public, socially constructed role, subject to the perceptions and expectations of learners, colleagues, schools and the community.
- The nature of a teacher's development is influenced by the learning opportunities that are available to her; these consist of a sample of incidents which is bound to be skewed in some way.
- Teachers' learning opportunities are strongly affected by school culture, but not wholly determined by it; school culture structures role expectations and norms of interaction, teacher to teacher, teacher to pupil; it is a reflection of wider social forces.
- While we each construct personal representations of the world, these draw on traditional images of teaching and knowledge available in our culture; and we develop our representations through affirmation or contradiction by other people.
- The English language teacher often fills a particularly sensitive and important role in the curriculum, because her discipline raises issues of cultural identity and political self-determination (e.g. Bisong, 1995; Hyde, 1995).
- The occupational cultures of state and private English language teaching are radically different and offer different contexts for teacher development.

- Effective LTE requires the systematic and concerted *integration* of activities which focus on all these dimensions of teacher learning (Chapters 4 and 7).

Personal note

A reward of the writer's work has been to watch ELT professionals develop. While their growth can be analysed in terms of discrete strands (knowledge, skill, beliefs, values and awareness), it is clear that it takes place within a complete person, not in separate compartments: a change in one dimension affects all the others. It is idiosyncratic: everyone is different. It is evolutionary: each new state grows out of the one preceding it. It is inseparable from each person's cultural and social experience, and the nature of the job they have to do. Changes in knowledge or skill both depend on and contribute to more fundamental personal growth which is revealed in each person's sense of their own value, their self-confidence, and their sense of control over their work and future learning.

This all seems very abstract. But every abstraction has a human face, the people we work with over the years; in my case the Pauls, Marcias, Mamoyos, Fehmis, Johns and Mohammeds. How else do we learn other than through our relationships? What better way to learn than to teach?

Appendix 8.1   A visualisation activity[5]

Section 1.1   Personal theories of teaching and learning

1.1.a.   Is your classroom a courtroom, a garden ... ?

Aim: to help teachers articulate and discuss personal teaching and learning theories

1.   Ts look at class cartoon (see opposite); ask what the teacher in the cartoon is saying. Elicit ideas in whole-group discussion.

2.   Ask about the role of the teacher and learners in the process of teaching and learning. Elicit replies like: '*The teacher's a judge!*' Prompt discussion à la ...

T: '*In that case, what are the pupils? The classroom?*' Answer: '*A courtroom.*'
T: '*So the pupils are on trial.*'

In the remaining steps, the whole group analyses the metaphor and then thinks up other metaphors for the language classroom; groups select one, and then discuss, draw and display it. The process leader then elicits further discussion.

---

[5] Idea for activity provided by Peter James; for a full account of these procedures, see James (forthcoming).

Appendix 8.2   Action research topics

Below is a selection of action research studies by the 1993/94 group.

- Our town and how we can get from Basauri to London.
- Learning English through songs with 8–9-year-olds.
- Games for developing speaking skills with beginners.
- Communicative activities to improve spoken English with 5th graders.

- Developing listening comprehension through songs and chants.
- Complementing the coursebook with communicative activities.
- Role play to improve speaking skill in 4th grade.
- The use of communicative activities with 8-year-olds.
- Reinforcing basic structures with video.
- Building vocabulary with beginners.
- Promoting reading skills through reading about the British Isles with 12-year-olds.
- TPR activities to develop children's understanding skills.
- Performing a play to improve my pupils' speaking and listening skills in 3rd grade of primary.
- In search of a more balanced model of classroom interaction at 6th grade. . . .
- An attempt to increase pupil's motivation and autonomy through learning to learn.
- Different ways of using stories to develop beginners' listening comprehension.

Appendix 8.3

(From Linder, 1991.)

Classroom behaviour checklist

Chart for evaluating classroom behaviour:

Checklist items	Comment	How do I know?
The pupils They listened to each other more readily.		
They employed self-check devices to a greater extent.		
The work they handed in was more carefully executed.		
The talk was in English to a greater extent.		
They managed to divide the work in the group more effectively.		
There was greater evidence of co-operation.		
They learned to select from options.		
They learned to accept variety rather than uniformity in assignments.		
There is more evidence of learning.		
They are participating in classroom management functions.		

Checklist items	Comment	How do I know?
There is evidence that they are working more independently and turning to each other for guidance.		
The teacher: I am able to do less of the work.		
I am able to step aside and observe what is going on.		
I can attend to individual pupils more readily.		
I have been able to relinquish some of the classroom management responsibilities.		
The proportion of teacher/pupil talk has changed.		
Materials are being exploited more effectively.		
My voice is more often at a lower pitch.		
I am ready to have learners prepare materials.		
Language is being used for a greater variety of contents.		

Group work observation instrument

Jan. 4, 1991 –
Prepared after discussion and probings related to group work in our EFL classes.
For our next meeting
Prepare a group work activity for one of your classes and answer the following questions.

1. **Instructions** What were the instructions that you gave to the class?

_____

_____

_____

2. **Learning skills** What preparation did the students have prior to getting into groups which enabled them to carry out the group work task?

_____

_____

_____

3. **Introduction of group work activity** What explanation did you give the students for doing this specific task in groups?

_____

_____

_____

4. The group work task What was the task that made working in groups a necessity?

_____

_____

_____

5. Evaluation How did the group work activity go?

_____

_____

_____

Would you do a similar group work activity like the one you did again? Why? / Why not?

_____

_____

_____

Self-evaluation form

TEACHER'S SELF EVALUATION FORM OF THE LESSON

During and after the lesson, think about some of the following and record your responses.

1. Evidence that the lesson was: successful; unsuccessful; went smoothly; was poorly organised; was interesting; boring.
2. Think of a student who seemed not involved in the lesson. What do you think the reason was?
3. What would you have liked to improve/have done better in the lesson?
4. What have you learnt?
5. How would you like to improve/change/develop your teaching in the future?
6. What subject/issue would you like to discuss in the next staff inservice session?
7. What evidence was there that the pupils were interested/not interested?
8. What will you do next as a follow-up to this lesson?
9. Which of your/your pupils' aims were achieved? Were there other unplanned-for achievements?
10. How do you feel about the lesson?
11. What are your feelings about the class that you were teaching?
12. How suitable was the material?
13. Looking back, what might you have done differently?
14. What areas do you think you should work on, on yourself? with the pupils?
15. What are you going to do when you teach this class again?
16. Were there any smiles/laughter during the lesson?

DURING THE LESSON

Try to observe your class. Are the pupils involved? If not, why not?

Stand aside for a few minutes while they are working and observe them. See what you can learn.

Is the seating arrangement appropriate?

Listen to what some of the pupils are saying. Write down one or two of the things that were said. What can you learn from them?

AFTER THE LESSON

Think carefully about your lesson and respond to the following:

1. Which part/s went well? Why?
2. Which part/s went badly? Why?
3. What changes are you planning for the coming lessons?
4. What aspects of your teaching would you like to work on?
5. Is there any technique/approach/arrangement you would like to try out with your class?
6. If you were disappointed with some attempt at change, would you like to give it another try?
7. Would you like the project leader to observe another lesson? If so, when?
8. Any other thoughts?

Appendix 8.4   Workshop content

Option One

TEACHER TRAINING SEMINAR

PROJECT WORK

AIMS:
- to introduce the participants to project work and the ideas behind it
- to encourage the participants to use projects in the classroom
- to carry out two different projects with the participants.

SESSION PLAN:
Time 180 min.
1. Warmer (5 min.)
2. What is project work? (theory - 30 min.)
3. Carry out Project 1 - 'The Cover' (45 min.)
4. Feedback on Project 1 (10 min.)

5. Carry out Project 2 – 'Fashion Show' (75 min.)
6. Feedback on Project 2 – (10 min.)
7. Conclusion (5 min.)

MATERIALS:
Trainer's notes (pp 1-6)
Handouts:
  2.1. Mind map 'Projects'
  2.2. Examples of lead-in activities
  2.3. Sample project timetable
  3.1. Extracts from four novels
  3.2. Complete the chart
  3.3. Questions about the extracts
  4.1. Feedback sheet
  5.1. Roles and tasks for Project 2
  5.2. How to write invitations
  5.3. Speaker's notes
  6.1. 'The Perfect School' – project plan
  7.1.a.b. More ideas for projects in the class

FURTHER READING:
1. Projects for the EFL Classroom, Simon Haines,
   Nelson and Sons Ltd, 1989
2. Choices, Jean Mills and Les Stringer, Oxford
   University Press, 1987
3. Introduction to Project Work, OUP, 1991
4. Project Work, Diana L Fried-Booth, OUP, 1988
5. Real Language Activities and Projects, C.
   Edelhoff, 1983
6. Process and Experience in the Language
   Classroom, Michael Leguthe and Howard Thomas
7. Project 1 – Teacher's book and Student's book,
   Tom Hutchinson, OUP, 1985
8. Hotline – Starter, Tom Hutchinson, OUP, 1991
9. Hotline – Elementary, Tom Hutchinson, OUP, 1991

Option Two

TEACHER TRAINING SEMINAR
PROJECT WORK
(Two sessions)
AIMS:
I session   1. By the end of the first session the

participants will have defined a
project work, its types,
characteristics, organisation and
some problems which may be
encountered.
2. They will have discussed learner's
strategies that are involved in
language learning in general and in
project work in particular.
3. They will have planned a project,
discussed its timing, final product,
stages, etc.
4. They will have presented their
project to other participants.

II session   5. They will have practised and
discussed different types of
projects, starting with mini-tasks
to full-scale projects.

I Session Plan:
  Time 175 min.

1. Warmer (15 min.)
2. What is project work (30 min.)
3. Learner strategies involved in project work
                              (Theory - 15 min.)
                              (Discussion - 20 min.)
4. Planning a project (Group work - 45 min.)
5. Presenting a project (20 min.)
6. Conclusion (5-10 min.)

Materials:
1. Trainer's notes
2. Handouts:
   1. Questionnaire on teacher's weekend activities
   2. Mind map 'Projects'
   3. Scheme on learner strategies

Further Reading:
1. Projects for the EFL Classroom, Simon Haines
   (Nelson and Sons Ltd, 1989)
2. Project Work, Diana L. Fried-Booth (OUP, 1988)
3. English Project 1,2,3, Tom Hutchinson
   (OUP, 1985)

Appendix 8.5   Extracts from *Preventive Approaches to Disruption*

Study Material C

Ground rules for the group

THE NEED FOR GROUND RULES

Teaching is a somewhat isolated profession; once initial teacher-training is completed, teachers have few, if any, opportunities to teach alongside their colleagues, and to observe how other teachers organise their lessons and deal with difficult pupils. One of the purposes of a PAD course is to erode this isolation. The following ground rules aim to provide a framework within which you, as course members, can share your experiences, ideas and difficulties constructively.

1 Material contributed by course members is confidential.

During the PAD course you may wish to discuss issues or give examples from your own classroom experience. You will not want this information passed on to the staff at large, or indeed to anyone not on the course. This type of confidentiality, in which the group does not pass on information to outsiders, is common. However, to raise the level of trust in the group further, the ground rule on confidentiality should be extended: after a PAD meeting you should not discuss, even among yourselves, any confidential material raised by a group member.

2 Offer alternatives rather than give advice.

It can take a great deal of courage for group members to identify and discuss situations in which they do not feel competent. Others in the group, therefore, should not give advice in the form 'If I were you, I would ...'. This could be irritating and discouraging to the person who shared the problem. Rather the group could brainstorm a range of approaches to a problem, so that the teacher who presented the difficulty retains responsibility for investigating the options available and developing an approach based on his or her understanding of the issues.

3 Speak for yourself and avoid generalisations.

In any discussion there is a danger of talking in broad, general terms without addressing specific problems. Putting a light-hearted ban on 'theorising' will help people contribute from their own experience. The ban can be put aside temporarily if the group arrives at a point where a more general discussion would be helpful. Try to use the pronoun 'I' when speaking about your own experiences or views. Commonly people use 'You' or 'One' when talking about themselves! 'You really have to summon all your energy to keep the lesson going last thing on a Friday' really means '<u>I</u> have to summon all <u>my</u> energy ...'. By using 'You' there is a danger that others in the group may feel that the person is speaking for them. Making an 'I' statement is always valid for a group member, it minimises typecasting, and keeps communication in the group clear.

4 You have the right to opt out of any activity.

Some activities, such as discussion, are not usually threatening. Other activities such as role play, paired observation and video recording can be threatening at times. It should be clear that anyone who wishes to opt out of an activity can do so and will not be asked to give reasons. As a group, avoid putting pressure on each other, even in jest, to take part in an activity.

5 Take responsibility for your own learning.

This ground rule makes it easier for you to say if you are unclear about instructions, points raised in discussion, or arrangements on the course. You are encouraged to give feedback to your tutor so that issues can be brought into the open, discussed and decisions made as necessary.

6 Develop your skill in listening attentively to each other.

In groups it is common for people to compete with one another to have their own 'say'. While one person speaks, others may not be listening with the intention of understanding the person's point of view. Instead they may be thinking of their own replies or searching impatiently for an opportunity to speak. The result is that insight and communication are hampered. Try to give your attention to whoever is speaking in the group and concentrate on understanding their message.

7 Acknowledge the 'positives' in yourself and others.

Many people find it easier to identify and acknowledge their weaknesses rather than their strengths. Probably this is because there are strong social taboos on speaking openly about our own strengths as we may be regarded as big-headed or conceited.

There are two reasons for setting aside these taboos and acknowledging the 'positives' in yourself and others. First, many of the activities in PAD involve helping course members to detect and deal with weaknesses in their teaching skills. Spending some time on strengths helps to counterbalance the potentially negative effects of this process. Second, for individuals to improve their overall teaching skills it is important to be aware of, and develop, existing assets. Therefore, on a PAD course, you are encouraged to put aside this social taboo and state your own strengths openly, as well as those you recognise in other group members.

SUMMARY

Ground rules are guidelines which affect the way group members relate to each other during PAD sessions, and to other colleagues who are not taking part in the course. Respecting confidentiality, refraining from giving patronising advice, avoiding blanket statements or theorising, listening attentively, and being pre-pared to acknowledge the positive qualities of group members are important in facilitating communication and learning during the course. Each individual has the right to opt in or out of any activity. Try to take an active part in the group's learning rather than adopt a passive role which is overdependent on your course tutor.

Handout K.1

Lesson organisation: reflection

The purpose of this activity is to relate the content of the study material to your own classroom experience. When you have read the study material, spend about 20 minutes considering the points in this handout.

You may wish to make brief notes in the spaces provided.

1 Research suggests that good lesson organisation reduces the likelihood of disruptive behaviour occurring in lessons. How true do you think this is?

2 What strategies do you use to ensure lessons start and finish well?

3 What steps do you take to ensure that the transition points in your lessons run smoothly?

4 How do you use questions in your classes?

5 How do you try to ensure that students remain involved in your lessons?

6 How do you decide whether activities and tasks are appropriate for your students?

Handout K.2

Lesson organisation: discussion

Consider and discuss the following questions.

1 What was your reaction to the study material? Did you feel the points raised were valid?

2 Would any of the tips listed in the study material be of less relevance to experienced teachers than to their newly qualified colleagues?

3 How helpful was your own initial teacher training in enabling you to prepare and deliver lessons which are geared to the various backgrounds, interests and abilities of pupils? Can you identify particular strengths and weaknesses in your own training?

4 If you were asked for some advice by a newly qualified colleague, what would be your own personal 'top 5 tips'?

5 In practice, what are the main constraints (if any) that have prevented you, on occasion, from organising or delivering lessons of a consistently high quality? How might these constraints be overcome?

6 Do you feel your subject specialism imposes specific constraints, or presents specific difficulties, which other subjects do not?

7 In what ways do you feel the internal organisation of your school:

a helps
b hinders

your planning and delivering of good-quality lessons?

Handout K.5 (extract only)

Lesson beginnings: observation (1)

Please watch the two video sequences and comment on the performance of the teacher.

1 Arrival time in relation to pupils.
  a) First sequence

  b) Second sequence

2 Organisation of pupils' entry to classroom.
  a) First sequence

  b) Second sequence

3 Clear statement of teaching goals/lesson objectives.
   a) First sequence

   b) Second sequence

Handout K.4

Making changes in lesson organisation (1)

There are no 'hard and fast' instructions in this activity. What may be a useful technique for one teacher may not be so for another, so feel free to experiment with changes according to your knowledge of your teaching style and the classes you take.

If you wish to remind yourself about lesson organisation, re-read Study Material K.

Choose a lesson and a class that you will be teaching over the following week. It may be a lesson that does not run as smoothly as you feel it could, or a class that finds difficulty working together. You may even choose a lesson that is already running smoothly, in order to improve it further or because you wish to make changes in a 'safe' environment.

Choose one of the following areas to focus on:

   lesson beginnings;
   use of questions, instructions and explanations;
   transitions;
   momentum;
   lesson endings.

Consider your chosen area.

1 Briefly describe it and what changes you intend to implement.

2 List any possible problems in using your changed lesson organisation.

3 What will you do if the changes do not have the desired effect?

Discuss your answers with a colleague.

During the trial lesson, try to implement the changes in lesson organisation that you have chosen, then at the end of the lesson, fill in side 2 of this handout and bring it to the next session.

Handout K.4

Making changes in lesson organisation (2)

1 Give a brief description of the trial lesson and the changes in lesson organisation that you managed to implement.

2 List any difficulties experienced as a result of changing aspects of lesson organisation.

3 List any advantages experienced in changing aspects of lesson organisation.

4 Will you continue to use the changes in your lesson organisation that you have just tried out?

5 Will modifications be necessary before the changes in lesson organisation are practical?

6 General comments:

Bibliography

ADELMAN, C. 1989: The practical ethic takes priority over methodology. In Carr, W. (ed.), *Quality in teaching*. London: Falmer Press.

ADELMAN, C. and ALEXANDER, R. 1982: *The self evaluating institution*. New York: Methuen and Co.

ALEXANDER, L. G. 1978: *Mainline beginners*. London: Longman.

ALEXANDER, R. J., CRAFT, M. and LYNCH, J. (eds) 1984: *Change in teacher education: context and provision since Robbins*. London: Holt, Rinehart and Winston.

ALLWRIGHT, D. and BAILEY, K. 1991: *Focus on the language classroom: an introduction to classroom research for language teachers*. Cambridge: Cambridge University Press.

ALLWRIGHT, D. and LENZUEN, R. 1997: Exploratory practice: work at the Cultura Inglesa, Rio de Janeiro, Brazil. *Language Teaching Research* 1 (1): 73–80.

AMERICAN ASSOCIATION OF HUMANISTIC PSYCHOLOGY (AAHP) 1962: *Articles of Association* AAHP.

ANDERSON, L. W. (ed.) 1995: *International encyclopedia of teaching and teacher education*. Oxford: Pergamon.

ANDREWS, I. 1987: Induction programs: staff development opportunities for beginning and experienced teachers. In Wideen and Andrews (1987).

ARGYRIS, C. and SCHÖN, D. 1974: *Theory into practice*. San Francisco: Jossey-Bass.

ARGYRIS, C., PUTNAM, R. and McLAIN SMITH, D. 1985: *Action science*. London: Jossey-Bass.

ASHTON P. M. E., HENDERSON, E. S. and PEACOCK, A. 1989: *Teacher education and classroom evaluation*. London and New York: Routledge.

AVALOS, B. 1985: Training for better teaching in the third world: lessons from research. *Teaching and Teacher Education* 1(4): 289–99.

BAILEY, F. 1996: The role of collaborative dialogue in teacher education. In Freeman and Richards (1996).

BAILEY, K. M. 1990: The use of diary studies in teacher education programs. In Richards and Nunan (1990).

BAILEY, K. M., BERGTHOLD, B., BRAUNSTEIN, B., JAGODZINSKI FLEISCHMAN, N., HOLBROOK, M. P., TUMAN, J., WAISSBLUTH, X. and ZAMBO, L. J. 1996: The language learner's autobiography: examining the apprenticeship of observation. In Freeman and Richards (1996).

BANNISTER, D. (ed.) 1970: *Perspectives in personal construct theory*. London: Academic Press.

BANNISTER, D. and FRANSELLA, F. 1980: *Inquiring man* (2nd edition). Harmondsworth: Penguin.

BARR, P., CLEGG, C. and WALLACE, C. 1981: *Advanced reading skills*. London: Longman.

BARTLETT, L. 1990: Teacher development through reflective teaching. In Richards and Nunan (1990).

BEAIL, N. (ed.) 1985: *Repertory grid technique and personal constructs: applications in clinical and educational settings*. London: Croom Helm.

BELL, B. and GILBERT, J. 1996: *Teacher development: a model from science education*. London: Falmer Press.

BELL, J. 1987: *Doing your own research project*. Milton Keynes: Open University Press.

BELLELI, L. 1993: How we teach and why: the implementation of an action research model for in-service training. In Edge and Richards (1993).

BEN-PERETZ, M. 1984: Kelly's theory of personal constructs as a paradigm for investigating teacher thinking. In Halkes and Olson (1984).

BEN-PERETZ, M., GILADI, M., DOR, B.-Z. and STRAHOVSKY, R. 1990: Teachers' thinking about professional development between plans and actions. In Day *et al.* (1990).

BENTON, P. (ed.) 1990: *The Oxford internship scheme*. London: Calouste Gulbenkian Foundation.

BERLINER, D. C. 1987: Ways of thinking about students and classrooms by more and less experienced teachers. In Calderhead (1987a).

   1988: *The development of expertise in pedagogy*. Washington DC: American Association for Teacher Education.

BINSTEAD, D. 1980: Design for learning in management training and development: a view. *Journal of European Industrial Training* 4(8), 1–32.

BISONG, J. 1995: Language choice and cultural imperialism: a Nigerian perspective. *English Language Teaching Journal* 49(2), 22–32.

BOEHM, A. E. and WEINBERG, R. A. 1977: *The classroom observer: a teacher's guide for developing observation skills*. New York: Teachers College Press.

BOLAM, R. 1986: Conceptualising inservice. In Hopkins (1986).

BOLITHO, R. and TOMLINSON, B. 1995: *Discover English* (new edition). Oxford: Heinemann.

BOOKER, R. 1996: An organisational response to survival. In Jennings and Kennedy (1996).

BORG, W. R., KELLEY, M., LANGER, P. and GALL, M. 1970: *The mini-course: a microteaching approach to teacher education*. Beverley Hills, Cal: Collier Macmillan.

BOSE, M. N. K. 1996: Indian problems and Indian solutions. *The Teacher trainer* 10(2), 12–13.

BOWERS, R. (ed.) 1983: Project planning and performance. In *Language teaching projects for the third world*, ELT Document 116. Oxford: Pergamon Press and the British Council.

BOYDELL, D. 1986: Issues in teaching practice supervision research: review of the literature. *Teaching and teacher education* 2(2), 115–25.

BRAMLEY, W. 1979: *Group tutoring: concepts and case studies*. London: Kogan Page.

BRASKAMP, L. A. 1980: What research says about the components of teaching. In Duckett, W. R. (ed.) *Observation and the evaluation of teaching*. Bloomington IN: Phi Delta Kappa, 62–86.

BREEN, M. 1987a: Contemporary paradigms in syllabus design. Part 1. *Language Teaching* 20(2), 81–92.

   1987b: Contemporary paradigms in syllabus design. Part 2. *Language Teaching* 20(3), 157–74.

BRINDLEY, G. P. 1990: Towards a research agenda for TESOL. *Prospect* 6(1), 7–26.

BRITTEN, D. 1996: How to prepare and give a workshop. *The Romanian Journal for Language Teacher Educators* 2, summer 1996: 61–64. Bucharest: British Council.

BROMME, R. 1987: Teachers' assessments of students' difficulties and progress in understanding in the classroom. In Calderhead (1987).

BROWN, A. L. and PALINSCAR, A. 1989: Guided cooperative learning and individual knowledge acquisition. In Resnick, L. (ed.) *Knowing, learning and instruction: essays in honour of Robert Glaser.* Hillsdale, NJ: Erlbaum, 393–452.

BROWN, G. 1975: *Microteaching: a programme of teaching skills.* London: Methuen.
1978: *Lecturing and explaining.* London: Methuen.

BROWN, G. and YULE, G. 1983: *Teaching the spoken language.* Cambridge: Cambridge University Press.

BROWN, G., ANDERSON, A., SHILLCOCK, R. and YULE, G. 1984: *Teaching talk.* Cambridge: Cambridge University Press.

BROWN, R. W. 1990: The place of beliefs and concept formation in a language teacher training theory. *System* 18(1) 85–96.

BULLOUGH, R. V. Jr 1990: Supervision, mentoring and self-discovery: a case study of a first year teacher. *Journal of Curriculum and Supervision* 5: 338–60.

BURNS, A. 1995: Exploring course design in a changing curriculum. Paper presented at the CIS Conference, Hyderabad.

BURNS, A. and HOOD, S. 1994: The competency-based curriculum in action: investigating course design practices. *Prospect* 9(2), 76–89.
(eds) 1995: *Teachers' Voices: exploring course design in a changing curriculum.* NCELTR: Macquarie University.
forthcoming *Teachers' Voices 2: teaching disparate learners.* NCELTR: Macquarie University.

BURTON, J. and MICKAN, P. 1993: Teachers' classroom research: rhetoric and reality. In Edge and Richards (1993).

CALDERHEAD, J. (ed.) 1987a: *Exploring teachers' thinking.* London: Cassell.
1987b: The quality of reflection in student teachers. *European Journal of Teacher Education* 10(3), 269–78.
(ed.) 1988a: *Teachers' professional learning.* London: Falmer Press.
1988b: The development of knowledge structures in learning to teach. In Calderhead (1988a).
1989: Reflective teaching and teacher education. *Teaching and Teacher Education* 5(1), 43–51.
1990: Conceptualising and evaluating teachers' professional learning. *European Journal of Teacher Education* 13(3), 153–59.

CALDERHEAD, J. and GATES, P. (eds) 1993: *Conceptualizing reflection in teacher development.* London: Falmer Press.

CALDERHEAD, J. and ROBSON, M. 1991: Images of teaching: student teachers' early conceptions of classroom practice. *Teaching and Teacher Education* 7, 1–8.

CAMBRIDGE INTEGRATED TEFL SCHEME 1992: *Report on data collected as feedback on outline proposals October 1992.* Cambridge: RSA/UCLES.

CARR, W. and KEMMIS, S. 1986: *Becoming critical: education, knowledge and action research.* London: Falmer Press.

CARTER, K. and DOYLE, W. 1987: Teachers' knowledge structures and comprehension processes. In Calderhead (1987a).

CARVER, D. and WALLACE, M. J. (eds) 1981: *SCEO microteaching papers.* Edinburgh: Scottish Centre for Education Overseas, Moray House College.

CENTER FOR PERSON-COMPUTER STUDIES 1993: *RepGrid manual version 2*. 3019 Underhill Drive, NW Calgary, Alberta, Canada T29 4E4.

CHISHOLM, B., KEARNEY, D., KNIGHT, G., LITTLE, H., MORRIS, S. and TWEDDLE, D. 1986: *Preventive approaches to disruption: developing teaching skills*. London: MacMillan Education.

CHOMSKY, N. 1957: *Syntactic structures*. The Hague: Mouton.

1959: Review of B. F. Skinner, Verbal Behaviour. *Language* 35, 26–58.

CIEFL 1994: *Teacher as researcher: mini-project reports presented at the First Review Workshop held at CIEFL, Hyderabad, September 1994*. Hyderabad, India: CIEFL.

1995: *CBSE–ELT curriculum implementation study interim report 2*. Hyderabad, India: CIEFL.

CILTS 1995a: *An overview of progress to June 1995*. Cambridge: UCLES.

1995b: *CILTS bulletins 1–35*, February 1992–June 1995. Cambridge: UCLES.

1996: *Bulletin 40: certificate developments*. Cambridge: UCLES.

CLARK, C. M. 1986: Ten years of conceptual development in research on teacher thinking. In Ben-Peretz, M. *et al.* (eds), *Advances of research on teacher thinking*. Lisse: Swets and Zeitlinger.

CLARK, J. L. 1987: *Curriculum renewal in school foreign language learning*. Oxford: Oxford University Press.

CLINE, T., FREDERICKSON, A. and WRIGHT, A. 1990: *Effective in-service training: a learning resource pack*. London: Department of Psychology, University College London.

COGAN, D. 1995: Using a counselling approach in teacher supervision. *The Teacher Trainer* 9(3), 3–6.

COLCLOUGH, E. 1996: *The reflective practitioner: possibilities and problems on pre-service teacher education programmes*. MA dissertation, University of Reading.

COOK, M. A. and RICHARDS, H. C. 1972: Dimensions of principal and supervisor ratings of teacher behaviour. *Journal of Experimental Education* 41(2), 11–14.

COOKE, B. L. and PANG, K. C. 1991: Recent research on beginning teachers: studies of trained and untrained novices. *Teaching and Teacher Education* 7(1), 93–110.

CORTAZZI, M. 1993: *Narrative analysis*. London: Falmer Press.

CROSSLEY, M. 1992: Teacher education in Papua New Guinea: a comment on comparative and international observations. *Journal of Education for Teaching* 23(1), 23–28.

CULLEN, R. 1994: Incorporating a language improvement component in teacher training programmes. *English Language Teaching Journal* 48(2), 162–172.

CURRAN, C. 1976: *Counseling-learning in second languages*. Apple River IL.: Apple River Press.

DAVIES, I. and MACARO, E. 1995: The reactions of teachers, tutors and students to profiling student competences in initial teacher education. *Journal of Further and Higher Education* 19(2), summer 1995, 28–41.

DAY, C. 1990: The development of teachers' personal practical knowledge through school-based curriculum development projects. In Day *et al.* (1990).

DAY, C., CALDERHEAD, J. and DENICOLO, P. 1993: *Research on teacher thinking: understanding professional development*. London: Falmer Press.

DAY, C., POPE, M. and DENICOLO, P. (eds) 1990: *Insight into teachers' thinking and practice*. London: Falmer Press.

DAY, C., WHITAKER, P. and WREN, D. 1987: *Appraisal and professional development in primary schools*. Milton Keynes: Open University Press.

DAY, R. 1990: Teacher observation in second language teacher education. In Richards and Nunan (1990).

DENICOLO, P. and POPE, M. 1990: Adults learning–teachers thinking. In Day *et al.* (1990).

DEPARTMENT FOR EDUCATION 1992: *Initial teacher training: secondary phase circular 9/92.* London: HMSO.

   1993: *The Government's proposals for the reform of initial teacher training.* London: HMSO.

DEPARTMENT OF EDUCATION AND SCIENCE 1982: *The new teacher in school, a report by Her Majesty's Inspectors.* London: HMSO.

   1983: *Teaching quality.* London: HMSO.

   1984: *Initial teacher training: approval of courses (circular 3/84).* London: DES.

   1987: *Quality in schools: the initial training of teachers–an HMI Survey.* London: HMSO.

DEWEY, J. 1904: *The relation of theory and practice in education.* The Third Yearbook of the NSSE, Part 1, Chicago.

   1910: *How we think.* Boston: D.C. Heath and Co.

   1938: *Experience and education.* New York: Collier Books.

   1958: *Experience and nature.* New York: Dover.

DIAMOND, C. T. P. 1985: Becoming a teacher: an altering eye. In Bennet, N. and Carre, C. (eds), *Learning to teach.* London: Routledge.

   1991: *Teacher education as transformation: a psychological perspective.* Milton Keynes: Open University Press.

DOFF, A. 1988: *Teach English: a training course for teachers.* Cambridge: Cambridge University Press.

DOVE, L. 1986: *Teachers and teacher education in developing countries.* London: Croom Helm.

DOYLE, W. 1977: Learning the classroom environment: an ecological analysis. *Journal of Teacher Education* 28, 51–55.

   1986: Classroom Organization and Management. In Wittrock, M. C. (ed.), *Handbook of research on teaching* (3rd edition). New York: Macmillan.

DUFF, T. (ed.) 1988: *Explorations in teacher training: problems and issues.* London: Longman.

DUNKIN, M. J. (ed.) 1987: *The international encyclopedia of teaching and teacher education.* Oxford: Pergamon.

EASEN, P. 1985: *Making school centred INSET work.* London: Croom Helm.

EBBUTT, D. 1985: Educational action research: some general concerns and specific quibbles. In Burgess, R. (ed.), *Issues in educational research.* London: Falmer Press.

EDGE, J. 1992: *Cooperative development.* Harlow: Longman.

EDGE, J. and RICHARDS, K. (eds) 1993: *Teachers develop teacher research – papers on classroom research and teacher development.* London: Heinemann.

ELLIOTT, J. 1981: *Action research: a framework for self-evaluation in schools.* Schools Council Programme 2 Working Paper No.1.

   1991: *Action research for educational change.* Milton Keynes: Open University Press.

ELLIOTT, J. and SARLAND, C. 1995: A study of teachers as researchers in the context of award bearing courses and research degrees. *British Educational Research Journal* 21/3/1995, 371–86.

ELLIS, G. 1996: How culturally appropriate is the communicative approach? *English Language Teaching Journal* 50(3), 213–18.

ELLIS, M. (ed.) 1994: Teacher development: the newsletter of the IATEFL teacher development group, No 26.

ERAUT, M. 1994: *Developing professional knowledge and competence*. London: Falmer Press.

EVERARD, K. B. and MORRIS, G. 1985: *Effective school management*. London: Paul Chapman Publishing.

FANSELOW, J. F. 1987: *Breaking rules: generating and exploring alternatives in language teaching*. New York and London: Longman.
    1990: Let's see: contrasting conversations about teaching. In Richards and Nunan (1990).

FEIMAN-NEMSER, S. and FLODEN, R. E. 1986: The cultures of teaching. In Wittrock (1986).

FISH, D. 1989: *Learning through practice in initial teacher training: a challenge for the partners*. London: Kogan Page.

FITZGIBBON, C. T. and MORRIS, L. L. 1987: *How to design a program evaluation*. Newbury Park, CA: Sage.

FLOWERDEW, J., BROCK, M. and HSIA, S. (eds) 1992: *Perspectives on second language teacher education*. Hong Kong: City Polytechnic of Hong Kong.

FRANSELLA, F. 1995: *George Kelly*. London: Sage.

FRANSELLA, F. and BANNISTER, D. 1977: *A manual for repertory grid technique*. London: Academic Press.

FREEMAN, D. 1990: Intervening in practice teaching. In Richards and Nunan (1990).
    1992: 'Language teacher education, emerging discourse, and change in classroom practice. In Flowerdew *et al.* (1992).

FREEMAN, D. and RICHARDS, J. C. 1993: Conceptions of teaching and the education of second language teachers. *TESOL Quarterly* 27(2), 193–216.
    1996: *Teacher learning in language teaching*. Cambridge: Cambridge University Press.

FROST, D. 1993: Reflective mentoring and the new partnership. In McIntyre *et al.* (1993).

FUKUDA, M. 1996: Developing teachers' awareness and autonomy through action research. *The Japan–Britain Association for English Teaching Journal* 1, 21–32, Hirosaki, Japan: JBAET.

FULLAN, M. 1979: School focussed inservice education. In Hopkins (1986).
    1982: *The meaning of educational change*. New York: Teachers College Press.

FULLER, F. F. and BROWN, O. 1975: Becoming a teacher. In Ryan, K. (ed.), *Teacher education: seventy-fourth yearbook of the National Society for the Study of Education*, Part 2. Chicago IL: University of Chicago Press, 25–52.

FURLONG, J. and MAYNARD, T. 1995: *Mentoring student-teachers*. London: Routledge.

FURLONG, V. J., HIRST, P. H., POCKLINGTON, K. and MILES, S. 1988: *Initial teacher training and the role of the school*. Milton Keynes: Open University Press.

GEBHERD, J. G. 1990: Models of supervision: choices. In Richards and Nunan (1990).

GHANI, A. A., NAIDU, S. and WRIGHT, T. 1997: Teacher support teams in action. In Kenny, B. and Savage, W. (eds), *Language and development: teachers in a changing world*. London and New York: Longman.

GIBBONS, M. and NORMAN, P. 1987: An integrated model for sustained staff development. In Wideen, M. and Andrews, I. (1987).

GIBBS, G. 1981: *Teaching students to learn: a student centred approach*. Milton Keynes: Open University Press.

GIBBS, G., HABERSHAW, S. and HABERSHAW, T. 1987: *53 interesting things to do in your lectures* (2nd edition). Bristol: Technical and Educational Services.

GRABER, K. C. 1996: Influencing student beliefs: the design of a 'high impact' teacher education program. *Teaching and Teacher Education* 12(5), 451–66.

GRELLET, F. 1981: *Developing reading skills*. Cambridge: Cambridge University Press.

GRIFFITHS, M. and TANN, S. 1992: Using reflective practice to link personal and public theories. *Journal of Education for Teaching* 18(1), 69–84.

GRIFFITHS, R. 1977: The emergence of a cognitive perspective in microteaching. *Educational Studies* 3(3), 191–97.

GRIMMET, P. and ERICKSON, G. (eds) 1988: *Reflection in teacher education*. New York: Teachers College Press.

GUILLAUME, A. M. and RUDNEY, G. L. 1993: Student teachers' growth toward independence: an analysis of their changing concerns. *Teaching and Teacher Education* 9(1), 65–80.

HAGEN P., HOOD, S., JACKSON, E., JONES, M., JOYCE, H. and MANIDIS, M. 1993: *The certificate in spoken and written English* (2nd edition). Sydney: AMES NSW and NCELTR.

HAGGERTY, L. 1995a: Identifying the complexities of school based teacher education. *Teacher Development* 4(1), 38–47.

1995b: The use of content analysis to explore conversations between school teacher mentors and student teachers. *British Education Research Journal* 21(2), 183–98.

HALDEN, S. 1995: *Trainees' perceptions of the impact of an inservice training programme: a post course evaluation*. Unpublished MATEFL dissertation, Centre for Applied Language Studies, University of Reading.

HALKES, R. and OLSON, J. K. (eds) 1984: *Teacher thinking: a new perspective on persisting problems in education*. Lisse: Swets and Zeitlinger.

HARINGTON, H. L., QUINN-LEERING, K. and HODSON, L. 1996: Written case analyses and critical reflection. *Teaching and Teacher Education* 12(1), 25–37.

HARRISON, M. 1991: *An investigation of the usefulness of collection and provision of baseline data on education systems prior to beginning ELT aid projects overseas*. MATEFL dissertation CALS, University of Reading.

HENDERSON, E. S. 1979: The concept of school-focused inservice education and training. *British Journal of Teacher Education* 51(1) 17–25.

HENERSON, M. E., MORRIS, L. L. and FITZ-GIBBON, C. T. 1987: How to measure attitudes. London: Sage.

HENRY, C. and KEMMIS, S. 1985: A point by point guide to action research for teachers. *Australian Administrator* 6(4), 1–4. School of Education, Deakin University, Australia.

HENRY, N. B. (ed.) 1957: *In-service education* (56th National Society for the Study of Education Yearbook) Chicago: NSSE.

HER MAJESTY'S INSPECTORS (HMI) 1991: *School-based initial teacher training in England and Wales: a report by HM Inspectorate*. London: HMSO.

HERMAN, J. L., MORRIS, L. L. and FITZ-GIBBON, C. T. 1987: *Evaluator's handbook*. London: Sage.

HERON, J. 1986: *Six category intervention analysis*. University of Surrey Human Potential Research Project.

1993: *Group facilitation: theories and models for practice* London: Kogan Page.

HEYNEMAN, S. P. no date: Table 1: stages of development in school quality. In Harrison 1991.

HILLGATE GROUP 1989: *Learning to teach*. London: Claridge Press.

HOOK, C. 1981: *Studying classrooms*. Australia: Deakin University Press.

HOPKINS, D. 1985: Making perfect? Form and structure in teaching practice. In Hopkins, D. and Reid, K. *Rethinking teacher education.* London: Croom Helm.

(ed.) 1986: *Inservice training and educational development: an international survey.* London: Croom Helm.

1993: *A teacher's guide to classroom research* (2nd edition). Buckingham: Open University Press.

HOPKINS, D. and REID, K. (eds) 1985: *Rethinking teacher education.* London: Croom Helm.

HORE, T. 1971: Assessment of teaching practice: an attractive hypothesis. *British Journal of Educational Psychology* 41, 327.

HOUSTON, W. ROBERT 1987: *Competency-based teacher education.* In Dunkin (1987).

(ed.) 1990: *Handbook of research on teacher education.* Basingstoke: Macmillan.

HOWEY, K. R. and JOYCE, B. 1978: A data base for future direction in inservice education. *Theory into Practice* 17(3), 206–11.

HOYLE, E. and MEGARRY, J. (eds) 1981: *World yearbook of education 1980: professional development of teachers.* London: Kogan Page.

HUBERMAN, M. 1989: The professional life-cycle of teachers. *Teachers College Record* 91(1) 31–58.

HUSTLER, D., CASSIDY, T. and CUFF, T. 1986: *Action research in classrooms and schools.* London: Allen and Unwin.

HYDE, M. 1995: The teaching of English in Morocco: the place of culture. *English Language Teaching Journal* 48(4), 295–305.

JAMES, P. 1996: Collaborative teacher development/action research: a way forward. *APAC News. Bulletin de l'Associacio de Professors d'Angles de Catalunya* No. 27, June.

(forthcoming): *Teachers-in-action.* Cambridge: Cambridge University Press.

JARVIS, J. 1991: Perspectives on the inservice training needs of NNS teachers of English to young learners. *The Teacher Trainer* 5(1), 4–9.

1992: Using diaries for teacher reflection on inservice courses. *English Language Teaching Journal* 46(2), 133–43.

JENNINGS, C. and KENNEDY, E. 1996: *The reflective professional in education.* London and Bristol: Jessica Kingsley Publishers.

JOHNSON, K. E. 1994: The emerging beliefs and instructional practices of preservice English as a second language teachers. *Teaching and Teacher Education* 10(4), 439–52.

JOYCE, B. and SHOWERS, B. 1980: Improving inservice training: the messages of research. *Educational Leadership* 37, 379–85. Also reprinted in Hopkins (1986).

1984: Transfer of training: the contribution of coaching, In Hopkins, D. and Wideen, M. (eds) *Alternative perspectives on school improvement.* London: Falmer Press.

KAGAN, D. M. 1992: Professional growth among preservice and beginning teachers. *Review of Educational Research* 62(2), 129–69.

KARAVAS-DOUKAS, E. 1996: Using attitude scales to investigate teachers' attitudes to the communicative approach. *English Language Teaching Journal* 50(3), 187–98.

KELLY, G. A. 1955: *The psychology of personal constructs: a theory of personality, 2 vols.* New York: W. W. Norton & Co. Inc.

1970: A brief introduction to personal construct theory. In Bannister (1970).

KEMMIS, S. (ed.) 1982: *The action research reader.* Victoria: Deakin University Press.

KEMMIS, S. and McTAGGART, R. 1982: *The action research planner.* Victoria: Deakin University Press.

KENNEDY, J. 1995: Getting to the heart of the matter – the marginal teacher. *The Teacher Trainer* 9(1) 10–14.

KETTLE, B. and SELLARS, N. 1996: The development of student teachers' practical theory of teaching. *Teaching and Teacher Education* 12(1), 1–24.

KING, J. A., MORRIS, L. L. and FITZ-GIBBON, C. T. 1987: *How to assess program implementation*. London: Sage.

KNEZEVIC, A. and SCHOLL, M. Learning to teach together: teaching to learn together. In Freeman and Richards (1996).

KNOWLES, M. S. 1984: *The adult learner: a neglected species* (3rd edition). Houston: Gulf Publishing Co.

KOLB, D. 1984: *Experiential learning*. Englewood Cliffs, NJ: Prentice-Hall.

KRAMSCH, C. and SULLIVAN, P. 1996: Appropriate pedagogy. *English Language Teaching Journal* 50(3), 199–212.

KYRIACOU, C. 1991: *Essential teaching skills*. Oxford: Blackwell Education.

LACEY, C. 1977: *The socialization of teachers*. London: Methuen.

LAKATOS, I. 1970: Falsification and the methodology of research programmes. In Lakatos, I. and Musgrave, A. (eds), *Criticism and growth of knowledge*. Cambridge: Cambridge University Press.

LAMB, M. 1995: The consequences of INSET. *English Language Teaching Journal* 49(1), 72–80.

LANSLEY, C. 1994: Collaborative Development: an alternative to phatic discourse and the art of co-operative development. *English Language Teaching Journal* 48(1), 50–56.

LAWLOR, S. 1990: *Teachers mistaught: training in theories or education in subjects?* London: Centre for Policy Studies.

LENNON, A. and JAMES, P. 1995: *What do successful INSET trainees do to promote their professional development? a case study*. Unpublished paper, IATEFL Teachers Develop Teachers Research Conference, Cambridge.

LENZUEN, R. and BANNELL, R. 1994: Quality and reflective practice. *Views and News 9 July 1*, Cultura Inglesa, Rio de Janeiro, Brazil.

LEWIN, K. 1946: Action research and minority problems. *Journal of Social Issues 2*, 34–46.

LEWIN, K. 1952: Group decisions and social change. Reprinted In Kemmis, S. (ed.), *The action research reader*. Australia: Deakin University Press, 1981, 38–47.

LINDER, P. 1991: *Collaborative action research into mixed ability communicative EFL teaching*. MA dissertation, University of Reading.

LINTER, R. 1989: Improving classroom interaction: an action research study. In Lomax, P. 1989.

LIPPITT, R. and FOX, R. 1971: Development and maintenance of effective classroom learning. In Rubin (1971).

LOMAX, P. (ed.) 1989: *The management of change: increasing school effectiveness and facilitating staff development through action research*. Clevedon: Multilingual Matters Ltd.

(ed.) 1990: *Managing staff development in schools: an action research approach*. Clevedon: Multilingual Matters Ltd.

LONG, M. H. 1980: Inside the 'Black Box': methodological issues in classroom research on language learning. *Language Learning* 30(1), 1–42.

LORTIE, D. 1975: *Schoolteacher: a sociological study*. Chicago IL: University of Chicago Press.

MACE, S. 1996: Microteaching: a developmental activity in ELT pre-service teacher training. *The Romanian Journal for Language Teacher Educators* 2, summer 1996, 33–41. Bucharest: British Council.

MACKAY, A. 1989: *Reliability of assessments of teaching performance.* MATEFL dissertation, University of Reading.

MAINGAY, P. 1988: *Observation for training, development or assessment?* In Duff (1988).

MALVANKAR, A. 1988: Teachers' work: a case study in three secondary schools in Goa. *International Journal of Educational Development* 8(3), 253–63.

MASLOW, A. H. 1968: *Towards a psychology of being.* New York: Van Nostrand Reinhold.

1987: *Motivation and personality* (3rd edition). New York: Harper and Row.

MATHEW, R. no date: *Initiating teachers into curriculum development: an Indian experience.* Hyderabad: CIEFL.

1996: *Evaluation in the classroom 1. evaluating language skills: a handbook for resource persons,* Hyderabad: CIEFL, Introduction.

MATHEW, R. and LALITHA EAPEN, R. (eds) 1996: *The language curriculum dynamics of change, volume 2, teacher as researcher, II report of the International Seminar (August 1995).* Hyderabad: CIEFL.

MATHUR, P. 1986: A process oriented approach to teacher education: overview. In *Process oriented in-service education for English teachers.* Singapore: British Council.

MAYNARD, T. and FURLONG, J. 1993: Learning to teach and models of mentoring. In McIntyre *et al.* (1993).

McDONALD, F. J. 1982: *Study of induction programs for beginning teachers.* Princetown NJ: Educational Testing Service.

McGILL, I. and BEATY, L. 1992: *Action learning: a practitioner's guide.* London: Kogan Page.

McINTYRE, D. 1980: The contribution of research to quality in teacher education. In Hoyle and Megarry (1981).

1988: Designing a teacher education curriculum from research and theory on teacher knowledge. In Calderhead (1988b).

1993: Theory, theorizing and reflection in initial teacher education. In Calderhead and Gates (1993), 39–52.

McINTYRE, D., HAGGER, H. and WILKIN, M. (eds) 1993: *Mentoring: perspectives on school based teacher education.* London: Kogan Page.

McINTYRE, D., MacLEOD, G. and GRIFFITHS, R. (eds) 1977: *Investigations of micro-teaching.* London: Croom Helm.

McLAUGHLIN, D. 1996: Who is to retrain the teacher trainers?: a Papua New Guinea case study. *Teaching and Teacher Education* 12(3), 285–301.

McLAUGHLIN, M. W. and MARSH, D. 1978: Staff development and school change. *Teachers College Record* 80(1), 69–94.

McMAHON, A., BOLAM, R., ABBOTT, R. and HOLLY, P. 1984: *Guidelines for review and internal development in schools: secondary school handbook School Council programme 1.* York: Longman.

McNAMARA, D. and DESFORGES, C. 1978: The social sciences, teacher education and the objectification of craft knowledge. *British Journal of Teacher Education* 4(1), 17–36.

McNIFF, J. 1988: *Action research: principles and practice.* London: Macmillan.

MERCER, N. and EDWARDS, D. 1987: *Common knowledge.* London: Methuen.

MILES, M. B. and PASOW, A. H. 1957: Training in the skills needed for in-service education programmes. In Henry (1957).

MILLER, A. and WATTS, P. 1990: *Planning and managing effective professional development*. Harlow, Essex: Longman.

MITCHELL, R. and MARTIN, C. 1997: Rote learning, creativity and 'understanding' in classroom foreign language teaching. *Language Teaching Research* 1(1), 1–27.

MOON, J. 1994: Teachers as mentors: a route to in-service development. *English Language Teaching Journal* 48(4), October, 347–55.

MORINE-DERSHIMER, G. 1993: Tracing conceptual change in preservice teachers. *Teaching and Teacher Education* 9(1), 15–26.

MOSKOWITZ, G. 1978: *Caring and sharing in the foreign language class: a sourcebook on humanistic techniques*. Rowley, MA.: Newbury House Publishers.

MUNBY, H. and RUSSELL, T. 1993: Reflective teacher education: technique or epistemology? *Teaching and Teacher Education* 9(4), 431–38.

MYERS, M. 1993: To boldly go. . . . In Edge and Richards (1993).

NATIONAL CHILDREN'S BUREAU *Highlight Series*. London: National Children's Bureau.

NEWELL, S. T. 1996: Practical inquiry: collaboration and reflection in teacher education reform. *Teaching and Teacher Education* 12(6), 567–76.

NEWSTROM, J. W. and SCANNELL, E. E. 1980: *Games trainers play: experiential learning exercises*. New York: McGraw Hill Inc.

NIXON, J. 1989: Determining inservice needs within specific contexts. *British Journal of Inset* 15(3), 150–55.

NUNAN, D. 1988: *The learner-centred curriculum: a study in second language teaching*. Cambridge: Cambridge University Press.

1989: *Understanding language classrooms: a guide for teacher-initiated action*. London and New York: Prentice Hall.

1990: Action research in the language classroom. In Richards and Nunan (1990).

O'HEAR, A. 1988: *Who teaches the teachers?* London: Social Affairs Unit.

OLDROYD, D., SMITH, K. and LEE, J. 1984: *School-based staff development activities: a handbook for secondary schools*. York: Longman for Schools Council.

OLSON, J. 1980: Teacher constructs and curriculum change. *Journal of Curriculum Studies* 5, 99–121.

OLSON, J. K. and EATON, S. 1987: Curriculum change and classroom order. In Calderhead (1987).

OMOKHODION, J. O. 1989: Classroom observed: the hidden curriculum in Lagos, Nigeria. *International Journal of Educational Development* 9(2), 99–110.

OPEN UNIVERSITY 1981: *Curriculum in action: an approach to evaluation P234*. Milton Keynes: Open University Press.

OPPENHEIM, A. N. 1992: *Questionnaire design, interviewing and attitude measurement*. London: Pinter.

PARLETT, M. and HAMILTON, D. 1977: Evaluation as illumination: a new approach to innovatory programmes. In Hamilton, D., Jenkins, D., King, C., McDonald, C. and Parlett, M. (eds), *Beyond the numbers game*, Basingstoke: Macmillan.

PARROTT, M. 1993: *Tasks for language teachers*. Cambridge: Cambridge University Press.

PENNINGTON, M. C. 1990: A professional development focus for the language teaching practicum. In Richards, J. C. and Nunan, D. (eds), *Second language teacher education*. Cambridge: Cambridge University Press.

1996: When input becomes intake: tracing the sources of teachers' attitude change. In Freeman and Richards (1996).

PERROTT, E. 1977: *Microteaching*. London: Society for Research into Higher Education Ltd, University of Surrey.

1982: *Effective learning: a practical guide to improving your teaching.* London: Longman.

PETERSON, K. D. 1995: *Teacher evaluation: a comprehensive guide to new directions and practices.* California: Corwin Press Inc.

PHILIPS, S. U. 1972: Participant structures and communicative competence. In Cazden, C., John, V. and Hymes, D. (eds), *Functions of Language in the Classroom.* New York: Teachers College Press.

PHILLIPS, R. D. and OWENS, L. 1986: The transfer of teaching and classroom observation skills across cultures: a case study. International Journal of Educational Development 6(4), 223–31.

PHILLIPSON, R. 1992: *Linguistic imperialism.* Oxford: Oxford University Press.

PHILPOTT, P. 1993: Seating patterns in small language classes: an example of action research. *British Educational Research Journal* 19(2), 191–210.

POPE, M. L. 1991: Researching teacher thinking: a personal construction. In Carretero, M., Pope, M., Simons, R. and Simons, J. I. (eds), *Learning and instruction: European research in an international context, vol. 3.* Oxford: Pergamon Press.

1993: Anticipating teacher thinking. In Day, C., Calderhead, J. and Denicolo, P. (eds), *Research on teacher thinking: understanding professional development.* London: Falmer Press.

POPE, M. L. and DENICOLO, P. 1993: The art and science of constructivist research in teacher thinking. *Teaching and teacher education,* 9(5/6), 529–44.

POPE, M. L. and KEEN, T. 1981: *Personal construct psychology and education.* London: Academic Press.

POPE, M. L. and SCOTT, E. 1984: Teachers' epistemology and practice. In Halkes and Olson (1984).

PORTER, P. A., GOLDSTEIN, L. M., LEATHERMAN, J. and CONRAD, S. 1990: An ongoing dialogue: learning logs for teacher preparation. In Richards and Nunan (1990).

POWNEY, J. and WATTS, M. 1987: *Interviewing in educational research.* London: Routledge and Kegan Paul.

RICHARDS, J. C. and LOCKHART, C. 1994: *Reflective teaching in second language classrooms.* Cambridge: Cambridge University Press.

RICHARDS, J. C. and MAHONEY, D. 1996: Teachers and textbooks: a survey of beliefs and practices in perspectives. *Working papers 8.1* Spring, Hong Kong: City University of Hong Kong.

RICHARDS, J. C. and NUNAN, D. 1990: *Second language teacher education.* Cambridge: Cambridge University Press.

RICHARDS, J. and RODGERS, T. 1982: Method: approach, design, procedure. *TESOL Quarterly* 16(2), 153–68.

RINVOLUCRI, M. 1985: *Grammar games.* Cambridge: Cambridge University Press.

ROBERTS, J. L. and ROBERTS, R. A. 1986: Differentiating in-service through teacher concerns about education for the gifted. *Gifted Child Quarterly* 30(3), 107–109.

ROBERTS, J. R. 1993: Evaluating the impacts of teacher research. *System* 21(1), 1–19.

ROBERTS, J. R., SAKA, R. and SENDAN, F. 1995: Personal construct psychology (PCP) as a framework for inquiry into the perceptions of individual EFL teachers and learners: the experience of 2 PhD candidates. Paper presented to the University of Leicester School of Education Research Conference.

ROGERS, C. 1961: *On becoming a person: a therapist's view of psychotherapy.* Boston: Houghton-Mifflin.

1982: *Freedom to learn for the eighties.* Ohio: Merrill Publishing.

ROSSI, P. H. and FREEMAN, H. E. 1993: *Evaluation: a systematic approach 5.* London: Sage.

ROTH, I. (ed.) 1990: *The Open University's introduction to psychology, vols 1 and 2.* Hove: Lawrence Erlbaum, in association with the Open University.

ROWELL, P. M. and PROPHET, R. 1990: Curriculum in action: The 'practical' dimension in Botswana classrooms. *International Journal of Educational Development* 10(1), 17–26.

RSA/UCLES 1992: *Cambridge Integrated TEFL Scheme: report on data collected as feedback on outline proposals* Cambridge: UCLES.

1995: *Certificate in the Teaching of English as a Foreign Language to Adults: guidelines and regulations for centres, course tutors and assessors 1995/1996.* Cambridge: UCLES.

RUBDY, R. 1989: Maximising intrinsic relevance in teacher education in ELT. *Regional English Language Centre Journal* 20(2), 10–22.

RUBIN, L. (ed) 1971: *Improving inservice education: proposals and procedures for change.* Boston, MA: Allyn and Bacon.

(ed.) 1978: *The inservice education of teachers.* Boston, MA: Allyn and Bacon.

RUDDUCK, J. 1982: *Making the most of the short in-service course.* London: Methuen Educational.

1988: The ownership of change as a basis for teachers' professional learning. In Calderhead (1988a), 205–22.

1991: The landscape of consciousness and the landscape of action: tensions in teacher education. *British Educational Research Journal* 17(4), 319–31.

RUSSELL, T. 1988: From pre-service teacher education to first year of teaching: a study of theory and practice. In Calderhead (1988a).

SAKA, A. R. 1995: *The teaching and learning of English as a foreign language: a constructivist approach.* PhD thesis, University of Reading.

SALMON, P. 1995: *Psychology in the classroom.* London: Cassell.

SANDERS, J. R. 1992: *Evaluating school programs: an educator's guide.* Newbury Park, CA: Corwin Press Inc.

SANO, M. 1996: Action research in writing class: how to develop writing proficiency in Japanese university students. *The Japan–Britain Association for English Teaching Journal* 1, 1–20. Hirosaki, Japan.

SAUNDERS, S., PETTINGER, K. and TOMLINSON, P. 1995: Prospective mentors' views on partnership in secondary teacher training. *British Educational Research Journal* 21(2), 199–218.

SCHMUCK, R. A. 1974: Interventions for strengthening the school's creativity. In Nisbet, J. (ed.), *Creativity of the school.* Organisation for Economic Co-operation and Development (OECD).

SCHÖN, D. A. 1983: *The reflective practitioner: how professionals think in action.* Aldershot: Arena (1995 edition).

1987: Educating the reflective practitioner: towards a new design for teaching and learning in the professions. San Francisco: Jossey-Bass.

SCRIVEN, M. 1981: Summative teacher evaluation. In Millman, J. (ed.), *Handbook of teacher evaluation.* Beverley Hills, CA: Sage, 244–71.

SENDAN, F. 1992: *Learning to teach: a case study of EFL students teachers' pre-active thoughts and decision making.* MA dissertation, University of Reading.

1995a: *A constructivist approach to tracing personal and professional development.* Paper presented at the Second International Teachers Develop Teachers Research Conference, Cambridge.

1995b: *Patterns of development in EFL student teachers' personal theories: a constructivist approach.* PhD thesis, University of Reading.

SENDAN, F. and ROBERTS, J. forthcoming: Orhan: a case study in the development of a student teacher's personal theories. Unpublished paper.

SHARKOVA, K. D. 1996: Connecting theory with practice in an awareness raising context: integrating the ELT methodology course with reflective observation. Paper presented at the 1996 IALS Symposium for Language Teacher Educators.

SHULMAN, L. 1987: Knowledge-base and teaching: foundations of the new reform. *Harvard Educational Review* 57(1), 1–22.

1988: The dangers of dichotomous thinking in education. In Grimmet and Erickson (1988).

SKINNER, B. E. 1957: *Verbal behaviour.* New York: Appleton-Century-Crofts.

1971: *Beyond freedom and dignity.* New York: Knopf.

SLIFE, B. D. and WILLIAMS, R. N. 1995: *What's behind the research? Discovering hidden assumptions in the behavioural sciences.* London: Sage.

SMYTH, J. (ed.) 1987: *Educating teachers: changing the nature of pedagogical knowledge.* London: Falmer Press.

SOMEKH, B. 1993: Quality in educational research – the contribution of classroom teachers. In Edge and Richards (1993).

1995: The contribution of action research to development in social endeavours: a position paper on action research methodology. *British Educational Research Journal* 21(3), 339–56.

STENHOUSE, L. 1975: *An introduction to curriculum research and development.* London: Heinemann Educational Books.

STEVICK, E. W. 1990: *Humanism in language teaching.* Oxford: Oxford University Press.

STODOLSKY, S. S. 1984: Teacher evaluation: the limits of looking. *Educational Researcher* 13(9) 11–18.

STOFFLET, R. T. 1996: Metaphor development by secondary teachers enrolled in graduate teacher education. *Teaching and Teacher Education* 12(6), 577–89.

STONES, E. 1975: *How long is a piece of string?* London: Society for Research into Higher Education.

1987: Student (practice) Teaching. In Dunkin (1987).

STONES, E. and MORRIS, S. (eds) 1972: *Teaching practice: problems and perspectives.* London: Methuen.

STRASSER, B. 1972: A conceptual model of instruction. In Stones and Morris (1972).

TABACHNIK, B. R. and ZEICHNER, K. 1984: The impact of the student teaching experience on the development of teacher perspectives. *Journal of Teacher Education* 35(6) 28–36.

TANN, S. 1993: Eliciting student teachers' personal theories. In Calderhead and Gates (1993).

THATCHER, D. 1990: Experience as learning. *Simulation/Games for Learning* 20(3), 276–302.

THOMAS, L. and HARI-AUGSTEIN, S. 1985: *Self organised learning.* London: Routledge.

THORNBURY, S. 1997: *About language.* Cambridge: Cambridge University Press.

THORNE, C. and WANG QIANG 1996: Action research in language teacher education. *English Language Teacher Education* 50(3), 254–62.

TILINCA, M. 1996a: Micro-planning: a new technique in in-service training. *The Teacher Trainer* 10(1), 17.

1996b: New ways in pre-service training. *The Romanian Journal for Language Teacher Educators* 2, summer 1996, 24–26. Bucharest: British Council.

TILLEMA, H. H. 1994: Training and professional expertise: bridging the gap between new information and pre-existing beliefs. *Teaching and Teacher Education* 10(6), 601–15.

TISHER, R. P. and WIDEEN, M. F. 1990: *Research in teacher education: international perspectives.* London, New York and Philadelphia: Falmer Press.

TURNEY, C. (ed.) 1977: *Innovation in teacher education.* Sydney: Sydney University Press.

TURNEY, C., CAIRNS, L. G., ELTIS, K. J., HATTON, N., THEW, D. M., TOWLER, J. and WRIGHT, R. 1982: *The practicum in teacher education.* Sydney: Sydney University Press.

1982b: *Supervisor development programmes: role handbook.* Sydney: Sydney University Press.

UCLES 1992: *Cambridge Integrated TEFL Scheme: report on data collected as feedback on outline proposals.* Cambridge UCLES.

1995: *CITS Bulletins* 1–35 (February 1992 to June 1995). Cambridge: UCLES.

1996: *Cambridge/RSA Certificate in English Language Teaching to Adults (CELTA): revised pilot assessment and guidelines, August 1996.* Cambridge: UCLES.

UNDERHILL, A. 1992: The role of groups in developing teacher self-awareness. *English Language Teaching Journal* 46(1), 71–80.

UNDERWOOD, M. 1989: *Teaching listening.* London: Longman.

UNIVERSITY OF READING 1995: *Reading University/schools partnership PGCE (secondary) course handbook 1995/6.* Faculty of Education and Community Studies, University of Reading.

UR, P. 1984: *Teaching listening comprehension.* Cambridge: Cambridge University Press.

1996: *A course in language teaching.* Cambridge: Cambridge University Press.

VALLI, L. (ed.) 1992: *Reflective teacher education: cases and critiques.* New York: State University of New York Press.

VAN TULDER, M., VEENMAN, S. and SIEBEN, J. 1988: Features of effective in-service activities: results of a Delphi study. *Educational Studies* 14(2), 209–23.

VULLIAMY, G. and WEBB, R. 1991: Teacher research and educational change: an empirical study. *British Educational Research Journal* 17(3), 219–36.

WADE, R. C. and YARBROUGH, D. B. 1996: Portfolios: a tool for reflective thinking in teacher education? *Teaching and Teacher Education* 12(1), 63–79.

WAJNRYB, R. 1993: *Classroom observation tasks.* Cambridge: Cambridge University Press.

WALLACE, M. 1979: Microteaching. In Holden, S. (ed.), *Teacher training.* London: Modern English Publications.

1991: *Training foreign language teachers: a reflective approach.* Cambridge: Cambridge University Press.

1996: Structured reflection: the role of the professional project in training ESL teachers. In Freeman and Richards (1996).

WEINTROUB, E. 1993: The 'Ghosts' Instrument. *The Teacher Trainer* 7(3), 24–25.

WEIR, C. and ROBERTS, J. 1994: *Evaluation in ELT.* Oxford: Blackwell.

WEST, M. 1960: *Teaching English in difficult circumstances.* London: Longman.

WHITE, R. 1988: *The ELT curriculum: design, innovation and management.* Oxford: Blackwell.

WHITE, R. V., MARTIN, M., STIMSON, M. and HODGE, R. 1991: *Management in English language teaching* Cambridge: Cambridge University Press.

WHITEHEAD, J. and LOMAX, P. 1987: Action research and the politics of educational knowledge. *British Education Research Journal* 13(2), 175–90.

WIDDOWSON, H. 1994: The ownership of English. *TESOL Quarterly* 28(2), 377–88.

WIDEEN, M. and ANDREWS, I. (eds) 1987: *Staff development for school improvement.* London: Falmer Press.

WILKIN, M. 1990: The development of partnership in the UK. In Booth, M., Furlong, J. and Wilkin, M. (eds), *Partnership in initial training.* London: Cassell.

(ed.) 1992: *Mentoring in schools.* London: Kogan Page.

WILLIAMS, E. and MORAN, C. 1989: Reading in a foreign language at intermediate and advanced levels with particular reference to English. *Language Teaching* 22(4), 217–28.

WILLIAMS, M. 1994: Teacher training for English language teachers. In Harvard, G. and Hodkinson, P. (eds), *Action and reflection in teacher education.* Norwood, NJ: Ablex Publishing Corporation.

WILLIAMS, M and BURDEN, R. L. 1997: *Psychology for language teachers: a social constructivist approach.* Cambridge: Cambridge University Press.

WILLIS, J. 1983: *Teaching English through English.* London: Longman.

WILSON, S. M., SHULMAN, L. S. and RICHERT, A. E. 1987: 150 different ways of knowing: representations of knowledge in teaching. In Calderhead (1987a).

WITTROCK, M. C. 1986: *Handbook of research on teaching* (3rd edition). New York: Macmillan.

WOODWARD, T 1991: *Models and metaphors in language teacher training.* Cambridge: Cambridge University Press.

1992: *Ways of training.* London: Longman.

WOOLGER, D. 1989: *The Pasdunrata College of Education internship scheme: an experimental induction programme in Sri Lanka.* MA dissertation, University of Reading.

WRAGG, E. C. 1982: *A review of research in teacher education.* Windsor: NFER Nelson.

1993: *Primary teaching skills.* London: Routledge.

WRAY, D. J. 1989: Negotiating needs in school focussed INSET. *British Journal of In-Service Education* 15(3), 145–49.

WRIGHT, T. 1990: Understanding classroom role relationships. In Richards and Nunan (1990).

YAXLEY, G. 1991: *Developing teachers' theories of teaching: a touchstone approach.* London: Falmer Press.

ZEICHNER, K. M. 1983: Alternative paradigms of teacher education. *Journal of Teacher Education* 34(3), 3–9.

ZEICHNER, K. M. and GRANT, C. 1981: Biography and social structure in the socialization of student teachers. *Journal of Education for Teaching* 1, 198–314.

ZEICHNER, K. M. and TABACHNIK, B. R. 1982: The belief systems of university supervisors in an elementary student teaching program. *Journal of Education for Teaching* 8(1), 34–54.

ZEICHNER, K. M., TABACHNIK, B. R. and DENSMORE, K. 1987: Individual, institutional, and cultural influences on the development of teachers' craft knowledge. In Calderhead (1987a).

Index

Accommodation 23
  see also Personal theories, changes in
Action learning 19
Action research 40–2, 57, 95ff, 224, 230,
    266ff, 278ff, 281ff
  definition 41
  examples of 42, 266–7, 276–8, 283–5,
    311–12
  problems in 59, 95–6, 266–7, 287
  support during 266–7, 271–2, 274, 278–9,
    284–5, 287
Action science 40–2
Adult learning 88–9, 236–7, 297ff, 307
Apprenticeship of observation 66
  implications for ITE 67, 69
  and self-awareness 66
  see also Personal theories
Assessment in ITE 81–2, 161, 189ff, 202–3,
    205, 206, 265–6
  assessor–teacher relations 29, 158, 195,
    208
  bias in 165–6
  competencies 15, 164–5, 189, 191, 213–15
  good practice 17, 159, 169–71, 189–91
  methods 189–92, 202–3, 209
  observation 166 ff
  problems in 74, 162 ff, 209
  profiling 189ff, 206
  and providers 297
  purposes of 117, 161–2
  values in 162
Assimilation 23–4, 26–7
  see also Personal theories, changes in
Australia: Teachers' Voices Case Study
    281ff
  description
    action research project 283–5
    context 282–5
    curriculum change 282–3
    outcomes 286
    summary 257–8

  lessons
    personal theories, change in 285–6
    social constructivism 288
    supporting teachers 286–7
    use of teachers' findings 286
Autonomy of teachers 18, 19–21, 22, 40, 49,
    103, 115, 170, 175–7, 192–3, 231–3,
    241–5, 258, 261, 268, 274, 275, 277, 279,
    281–3, 289, 300, 301, 305, 306–7,
    318–20, 323–4

Basque Country Diploma Case Study 258ff
  description
    action research project 266–7, 309–10
    assessment 265–5
    autonomy 258, 261, 268, 274
    awareness activities 308–9
    changing curriculum 261
    collaboration in design 263
    context 260–1
    course outline 259–60, 262–7
    developments in program 263–4
    evaluation findings 267
    incentives 262
    objectives 262–4
    on-site and off-site 264–7
    philosophy 262
  discussion
    central support 267–8
    dialogue 268
    dissonance 269
    experience 269
    on-site/off-site 272–3
    ownership 269
    preconditions 276ff, 273
    reflection and gradualness 269–70
    relevance 271
    social constructivist view 273
    summary 273–4
    support 271–2
    theory, place of 271

Behaviourism and model based LTE   13–18, 208, 211–12

Cascade training   227, 290, 294–5
Case Studies
    in INSET
        see Australia: Teachers' Voices   281ff
        see Basque Country: Diploma Case Study   258ff
        see Israel: Secondary school   275ff
        see Latvia: the PDP   288ff
        see PAD: a training package   297ff
    in ITE
        see Reading Partnership   181ff
        see UCLES CELTA   198ff
Catflaps   24
Checklists see observation
Coaching   56, 73, 94–5
Coherence in ITE design   74–5, 81, 87, 130, 132–3, 134–8, 180–1, 192–3
Competency based teacher education   15
    see also Assessment
Concerted cycles in LTE   34–5, 44–6, 60, 122, 136–7, 138–9, 173–9, 240, 258, 297–300, 308–10
    and activities
        in INSET   297ff, 306–7
        in ITE   138ff, 152–3, 173–9
Constructive alternativism   29
Constructivism   23–4
    criticisms of   27–8
    and ELT   24–5
    and INSET   287, 294
    and ITE   26, 183–5, 196, 208–11
    and Kelly   28–33
    and Kolb   33–6
    and LTE   25–7
    and microteaching   25
    see also Personal theories, Personalisation, Reflection, Teacher learning, Teacher thinking
Constructs   29
    and Kelly   29–33
    systems   30–3, 76–7
    see also Uncovering
Construing, definition   29
Courses for teachers
    effectiveness of   73–4, 89–91, 92–4
    high/low intensity   129–30, 180, 205, 209–11
    on-site/off-site   229, 264–7, 272–3
    planning checklist   249–52
    'two stage' design   100, 257, 260, 264–7, 269–71, 272–4, 293
Craft model of LTE   16
Cultural variation   3, 36ff, 46–7, 64–5, 84–5, 97, 108, 119–20, 96–7, 128–34, 163–4, 225–30, 309–10

    see also Case studies: context
Curriculum in LTE
    approach, design, procedure   102–3, 148–51
    design checklists   148–51, 237–41, 249–52
    as a system   102
    values in   104, 111–12, 115–16
Curriculum development and teacher learning   59, 89, 95–6, 224, 230, 286
    see also Action research

DELPHI technique   244–5
Design
    of INSET see Inservice education of teachers
    of ITE see Initial teacher education
Development, definition   221–2
    and ITE   189–92, 206–8
    see also INSET, Teacher learning, Teacher thinking
Dewey   47ff, 211–12
Diversity in INSET   223, 224–5
    and context   225–30
    and purpose   223
    and ways of learning   224–5

Effective INSET   89ff, 236–7
Employee, teacher as   110
Established teacher
    research summary   88–100
    see also INSET
Evaluation in INSET   235–6, 246–9
    see also case studies
Experiential Learning   33ff
    critique   35
    cycle   33
    Kolb   33–6
    and LTE   33–5
    and talk   34, 44, 175–7, 269–70, 302, 307, 321
    see also Concerted learning cycles
External dimension of knowing   111
    see also Positivism

Feedback and supervision   154ff
    obstacles   156–7, 193–6
    principles   158ff
Filtering in ITE   69
Fine tuning   236, 237
Fractured ITE curriculum   74, 81, 182

GRIDS   242–4
Group size and INSET activity   239

Humanistic psychology   18–23
    critique of   21–2
    and ELT   20–1
    and LTE   19–21
    and non-directive intervention   19
    and social dimension   22
    see also Kelly; Sociality

Images of teaching   31, 66–7, 69–70
    definition   27
Individualism
    and constructivism   28
    and humanistic psychology   21
    and Kolb   35–6
    and phenomenology   114–15
    see also Privatism
Initial Teacher Education
    assessment   2, 189ff, 202–3
    design   127ff
        activities summary   138–9
        coherence   134 ff, 192–3
        funding   131
        implications of research   77–83
        objectives checklist   139–48
        planning checklist   148–51
        pre-conditions for   128ff
        staff roles   131–4, 152 ff
        staff relationships   82ff
    constructivist view   69ff, 173–7, 183–5,
        196
    diversity of intake   68–9
    'fractured curriculum' problems   74–5
    input and self-awareness   69, 152–4,
        174–5, 177–9
    and model based approaches   206–8
    and non-native speakers   55, 96–7
    and personal theories   69–71, 76–7, 80, 83,
        193–6, 206–8
    preconditioned   128ff
    relations with supervisors   75–6, 193–6
    teaching practice   46, 74, 76–7, 78, 79, 83,
        134–6, 138–9, 188–9, 204–5
    see also Reading University; UCLES
Inservice Teacher Education and Training
    (INSET)
    activities in   239, 308–22
    cascade training   227, 290, 294–5
    coaching   94–5
    context   281–2
    courses   92–4
    curriculum development projects   59, 89,
        95–6, 266–7, 276–8, 283–5, 311–12
        see also action research
    cycles of   230ff
    definition   221
    design   236ff
        and context   282–3, 260–1

    decisions   237ff
    funding   226
    implications of research   77ff, 97ff, 307
    needs assessment   231ff, 241ff
    planning checklist   249–52
    politics   226
diversity
    of needs   223
    of teacher learning   224–5
effective INSET   89ff
evaluation of   235ff, 246–9
and innovation   90–2
marginal teachers   86
models in   184–5, 190, 268, 304
non-native speaker teachers   175, 258ff,
    275ff, 288ff
preconditions   221–9
purposes of   222–3
role types   226–7
school focus   229–30
social dimension   225–6, 227–8, 255–6
teacher learning   236–7, 258, 297ff, 307
see also case studies: Australia, Basque
    country, Israel, Latvia, PAD
Internal dimension of knowing *see also*
    Phenomenology
Israel: Secondary School Case Study   275ff
    description
        autonomy   275, 277, 279
        context   275
        curriculum Project
            characteristics   276–7
            outcomes   277–8
        school: characteristics   275–6
    discussion
        autonomy   281–3, 278–9
        challenge   279–80
        dialogue   275ff
        ownership   278–9
        pre-conditions   279
        process leaders   279
        school climate   279
        time   280

Jacuzzi   46, 294–5

Kelly   29–33
Knowledge centred paradigm   110–15
    see also Paradigms

Language awareness   139, 175, 178, 203, 204
Language teaching, characteristics of   7,
    106–9, 139–48
Latvia: the Professional Development Project
    (PDP)   288ff
    autonomy   290, 295–7
    cascade model, critique   295

Latvia: the Professional Development Project
(PDP) *cont.*
  change in teachers' role   289
  context   289
  diversification of programme   292–4
  external support   289
  jacuzzi   294
  on-site, off-site; Options 1 and 2   292–3,
    313–15
  options 1 and 2   292–3, 313–15
  outcomes   293–4
  pre-conditions   289–90, 296
  relationships, long-term   295
  summary   257–8, 288–9
  support
    from Heads   296
    from peers   296–7
  teachers' needs, change in   292
  team meetings   295
  tutors   291, 293
  tutor role change   291–2
  tutor training   291
Learners' experience
  and action research   312–14
  awareness of in ITE   80, 160
  see also action research
Lewin   40–2
  see also action research
Loop input   174

Marginal teachers   86
Mentors, and problems of communication
  75–6
  see also Reading/School Partnership
Metaphor,   264–5, 310–11
Metaprocessing
  definition   47
Microteaching in ITE   15
  and constructivism   25
Model based learning   13–18
  behaviourist theory   13–14
  and criticisms of   16–18, 206–8
  and INSET   269–70, 291–2, 295, 322–3
  and ITE   152–4, 163–4, 206–8
  and LTE   14–16, 80
Models of the person *see* Views of the person

Needs assessment   231 ff
  methods   234–5, 241–45
  and ownership   231–4
  and planning   233–4
  and professional learning   232
New teacher
  concerns of   85
  implications of research   87
  interaction with school   84–5
  and ITE   86

  and personal theories   84
  subject knowledge   85
Nominal group technique   241–2
Non-native speaker teacher   55, 96–7, 175,
  258ff, 275ff, 288ff

Observation
  and assessment   168ff
  methods   171ff, 312–15, 322–3
  problems in   166–9
Occupational culture   37–40, 64–5, 68–9, 78,
  108, 119–20, 163, 195, 227–9, 229, 309
On-site/off-site, integration of   100, 229,
  257, 260, 264–7, 269–71, 272–4
Operative, teacher as   110
Organisational development (OD)   229–30,
  242–4
Ownership
  in INSET   88, 184, 271, 278–9
  and needs assessment   231ff
  see also participation

PAD (Preventive Approaches to Disruption)
  297ff
  autonomy   300, 301, 305–7, 318–20
  context   297
  design and principles of professional
    learning   297, 307
  dialogue in   302–3
  ground rules   300–1, 318–20
  initiation   301
  making classroom changes   304–6, 323–4
  models in   304
  observation   304
  organisation of materials   298–300
  principles in   298, 307
  pupil questionnaire   303
  reflective activities   302, 303, 320–2
  social constructivism   297
  support   300–3, 304–8
  team building   300–1, 318–20
Paradigms: knowledge and person centred
  109ff
  critique   83, 118–23
  contrasted   110
  and language curriculum   116–18
  of teacher education   118
  of teaching   104, 110
  value of   115–18
  and values   111–12, 115–16
Participation   98, 184, 241–5, 283
  see also Autonomy, Ownership
Partnership schemes   81–2
  summary   181–2
  see also Reading University
PDP *see* Latvia
Pedagogic content knowledge   85, 105

Person centred paradigms   110–15
  see also Paradigms
Personal Construct Psychology   29–33, 76–7
  see also Teacher thinking
Personal theories
  change in   23–4, 25, 30–3, 66–7, 70–1,
      76–7, 80, 206–11, 227–8, 283, 287
  definition of   27
  examples of   31, 60–1, 76–7
  filtering in ITE   69
  interaction with school   39–40, 84–5
  sources of   66, 82
  of supervisors   165ff
  and teacher learning   2, 22, 156–7, 193–6,
      208–9, 228, 287
  uncovering   67, 194–4, 308–9
  see also Teacher thinking, evolutionary
      model
Personalising (of information, theory)   23ff,
      54, 57, 70, 152–3, 173, 207, 210, 273,
      295, 299, 323
Phenomenology   114–15
  see also Paradigms
Pooling knowledge   253–4
Pooling technique   176
Positivism   110–14
  critique of   113–14
  see also Paradigms
Preconditions   128ff, 221–9, 267
  see also ITE and INSET design; case
      studies
Prescriptive ITE, *see* Model based learning
Primary school teachers   258ff
Private and public knowing   35
Privatism   78–9, 227–8
Process leader   2, 100, 222, 279, 308
Professionalism   38–9, 53, 122, 195
  see also Autonomy
Profiling
  see Assessment of teaching
Progressive education and reflection   50
Providers
  and assessment   59, 158, 196, 208, 297
  and cultural awareness   3, 158–9
  expectations   82–3
  role change   1–2
  role types   132–4, 222, 226–7
  self-awareness   3, 158–9, 194–5, 255–6
  sociality   3, 44–5, 108, 255–6
  see also Cultural variation; case studies

Reading University Partnership scheme, case
      study   181ff
  description   184ff
    assessment   189ff
      competencies   191, 213–15
      flexibility of   191

      method   189–92
      profile   189–91
    context   181–2, 196–8
    model of teaching   185–6
    objectives   186
    roles   186–7, 192
    summary   257–8
    year structure   187–9
  issues
    administration of   192, 196–8
    coherence and assessment   192–3
    dialogue with mentors   193–6
    reflection and ITE   194–5
    roles   193
Reflection   47ff
  and action research   41–2, 266
  concepts of   47, 53, 54, 210
  definitions   54, 121
  and Dewey   47ff
  examples of   48, 138–9, 177–9, 253, 265,
      269–70, 310–13, 318–20
  issues   58ff
  and ITE   72–3, 193–6
  and LTE   54ff
  pre-conditions   46, 58ff
  reframing   47–50
  and routines   107–8
  and Schon   50ff
  and teacher development   47ff, 211–12
  types of   54ff, 210
  see also Concerted learning cycles;
      Uncovering
Reflective practitioner model *see* Schon
Reframing   47–50
  and reflection   48–9
Related learning activity cycles *see* concerted
      learning activities
Repertory grid technique   30–1, 277
Rogers   18ff
Routines   106–9, 195, 207, 228, 309

Schon (and reflective practitioner)   50–3,
      113, 121–3
  critique of   51–2
  and expertise   51
  and LTE   52–3
  and professionalism   53
  reflection in action   51
  reflection on action   51
  and schools   53
  technical rationality   113, 121
School culture
  and teacher development   39–40, 53, 64–5,
      229–30, 242–4, 279, 309
  see also context in case studies
Self-agency   18
  see also Humanistic psychology

Self-awareness
    activities   177ff
    and apprenticeship of observation   66
    and input   152
    in ITE   152, 177ff
    see also Reflection, Uncovering
Social view of person *see* Views of the person
Sociality   3, 44–5, 64–5, 108, 154, 255–6
    definition   3
    see also Uncovering
Socialization into teaching   36, 66–9, 88
Social constructivism   42–7
    definition of   44
    examples in case studies   196, 273, 281,
        288, 294–7, 316–22
    implications for LTE   44–7, 109, 152–4,
        175–7, 227–30
    new teachers   39–40
    summary   4, 6–7, 322–4
Stage theory of teacher learning   4–5, 63–4,
    76–7, 272–3, 287
Stenhouse   95
Student teachers
    change in thinking   70–1, 76–7, 80
    concerns   71–2, 79
    deficits   67–8
    and input   69–70, 152–4, 173–9
    learning about learners   80, 160
    and reflection   72–3
    relationship with supervisors/mentors
        74–6, 80, 193–6
    sense of competence   69–70
Supervision
    counselling model of   20, 52, 155–6, 157
    and feedback   154ff
    principles for   158ff
    principles for   158ff
    problems in   75–6, 80, 156–7, 193–6
    role analysis   154–6
    see also Providers
Support
    during innovation   91–2, 240–1, 271–2
    and personal change   175–7, 266–7, 271–2,
        274, 278–9, 284–5, 287, 316–18,
        219–20, 323–4
System, curriculum as   102, 223, 225–6

Teacher development
    and reflection   47–50
    school development   39–40, 229–30, 275
    see also Reflection, teacher learning
Teachers' knowledge
    components of   103–6
    models of and LTE   104, 106ff
    pedagogic content knowledge   85
    tacit nature of   27

Teacher Learning chapters 1 and 2 passim;
    summary   308–10
    and INSET, summary   236–7
    multi-level nature of   6–7, 42–7, 122–3,
        258, 308–10
    and school   229–30, 275
    and social constructivism   44–7, 122–3, 258
    see also Case studies
Teacher thinking
    evolutionary model   4–5, 63–4, 76–7,
        272–3, 280, 287
    stage model   4–5, 63–4, 76–7, 272–3, 287
Teaching
    characteristics of   106–9
    language for   77–8, 178, 270–1, 322–3
    paradigms of   104, 110–12, 185–6
    related to LTE   108–9
Teaching Practice   46, 74–6, 78, 79, 83,
    132–3, 134–6, 186–9, 196–8, 204
    coherence of   134–5, 193
Technical rationality   113, 121
    see also Schon
Trainer *see* Provider
Training
    and cognition   208–11
    definition   73, 221–2
    effective training   73, 88
    related issues in case studies   184–6, 189–92,
        205–12, 216–17, 264–5, 284–5, 291, 297ff
    see also effective INSET

UCLES CELTA, Case study   198ff
    description
        assessment   202–3, 205, 206, 209
        context   199–200
        course   202–3
        example of CTEFLA (Japan)   203–5
        history   199–200
        syllabus   203, 216–17
    issues
        assessment   209
        development of teachers   206–8
        high/low intensity   203–4, 209
        prescription   208
Uncovering tacit knowledge   27, 58–60, 67,
    78, 193–4, 229
    activities   67, 78, 138–9, 177–9, 253, 265,
        269–70, 310–11, 312–15

Views of the person   12–13, 43–4, 110–12
    behavioural   13–18
    cognitive   23–36
    humanistic   18–22
    social   36–42, 59, 64–5, 229–30
    social constructivist   42–7
    summary   4